The Reputation of the Roman Merchant

The Reputation of the Roman Merchant

Jane Sancinito

University of Michigan Press

Ann Arbor

Published in the United States of America by the
University of Michigan Press
Manufactured in the United States of America
Printed on acid-free paper
First published January 2024

A CIP catalog record for this book is available from the British Library.

Library of Congress Cataloging-in-Publication data has been applied for.

ISBN 978-0-472-13348-2 (hardcover : alk. paper)
ISBN 978-0-472-22141-7 (e-book)

for my parents

Contents

Digital materials related to this title can be found on the Fulcrum platform via the following citable URL: https://doi.org/10.3998/mpub.11855639

Illustrations

Acknowledgments

Just as footnotes and bibliographies acknowledge intellectual debts, there are a host of figures who are owed gratitude at the conclusion of any book project. It is a privilege to take a moment to offer my thanks here for the many and varied kindnesses I have been shown over the five years I have been writing this book and over the decade it has taken to transform my first, niggling questions into something concrete and coherent.

My first thanks go to Cam Grey, who supervised the dissertation from which this book originates. No adviser could have better balanced the push and pull required to get my thoughts in line or been more firmly on my side throughout the highs and lows of discovering who I was as a scholar and young adult. Thank you, Cam, for giving me both direction and room to grow.

Thanks are naturally owed to my entire dissertation committee: Cynthia Damon, Ann Kuttner, and Alan Stahl. Each offered me valuable comments, kindness, and support and I hope that their good influence continues to be visible in this finished project. Special thanks are due to Alan, who came down to Philadelphia for my defense and cheered me on, even though monetization did not end up being a major part of that project, and who introduced me to the inimitable and dauntless Ellen Bauerle before this book was even a twinkle in my eye. My debt to her, and the reviewers she enlisted, is visible on every page. Thank you.

My graduate cohort, understood in the broadest possible terms, were a huge and inexhaustible source of support and comfort to me during my time at the University of Pennsylvania and beyond. I offer special thanks to Eyal Meyer, Marcie Persyn, Jordan Rogers, Petra Creamer, Jillian Stinchcomb, Jae Hee Han, and Alexander Ramos. They, and so many others at other institutions, have reaffirmed my belief that no one does anything alone and that our greatest resource, against all odds, is always each other.

I owe a big debt to my colleagues at Oberlin College, Andrew Wilburn, Kirk Ormand, Chris Trinacty, and Ben Lee, who guided me through the earliest stages of pitching this book to editors and gave me, with the financial support of the Thomas F. Cooper Postdoctoral Fellowship, the time to think about how the long-winded, clunky dissertation might be transformed into something readable and clear. Thanks are also due to all my wonderful students there, especially Emily Hudson, Emma Glen, Sarah Passannante, and Justin Godfrey, for their kindness and overwhelming support, especially as I pulled my first, real draft of *Reputation* together.

My current colleagues and friends at the University of Massachusetts Lowell deserve all my gratitude and already have my deepest respect as generous scholars and inspiring educators. Special thanks to the chair of the History Department, Christopher Carlsmith, and to Abby Chandler, whose friendship and mentorship managed to make moving to a new institution, even in the middle of a global pandemic, a joy. To my cohort of pandemic-hires at UML: thank you and keep your heads up!

Though they are (to me) nameless and faceless, I also want to express my gratitude to the brave and determined souls who worked to unionize the faculty of the University of Massachusetts Lowell. Their efforts secured the rights I now enjoy as a worker, including the junior sabbatical I used to finish the last edits on this manuscript, so that I can study workers who lacked those privileges.

Finally, I am unspeakably grateful to all my friends and family. Thanks to Mollie Celnick, who welcomed me to Massachusetts with open arms, to Joanna McCunn, Luke Tatam, Andreas Televantos, Mercedes Broadbent, and Emily Barritt, who have been with me since before I began graduate school and whose continued friendship sustains me, and to Nancy Ameen, Laurie Jensen, and Donna St. Louis, who have known me at every stage of this project and decided, despite everything, that they could still have a fondness for me. I will conclude my thanking with my new goddaughter, Astrid, whose life I hope will be easy and happy and fulfilling, my grandmother, whose love was a constant and whose strength of character inspired me, and my parents, who have been so united in their confidence in me that I have almost started to believe it myself. They know, more than anyone, where I have struggled, where I have stumbled, and what it has taken to get back up and get back to it. May everyone who reads this have people like them in their corner.

Introduction

Early in the third century CE, the sophistic writer Philostratus began a treatise on the nature of heroism, engaging with the Homeric tradition and analyzing the presentation of valor in the *Iliad* and *Odyssey*. The text was designed as a dialogue between a vinedresser and a Phoenician merchant, who meet by chance in Thracian Chersonese and strike up a conversation. Their discussion takes the tomb of the hero Protesilaus as its starting point, but before the discussion begins in earnest, Philostratus first establishes a thin pretense for their meeting: the merchant is waiting for a good omen to sail and the vinedresser is interested in him as a, presumably, rare foreigner. Despite the work's purpose, the two do not immediately fall into pleasant conversation about heroes and gods, first, in fact, the vinedresser effectively insults the merchant:

> Ἀμπελουργός: σοφοί γε, ὦ ξένε, τὰ ναυτικὰ ὄντες· ὑμεῖς γάρ που καὶ τὴν ἑτέραν ἄρκτον ἐνεσημήνασθε τῷ οὐρανῷ καὶ πρὸς αὐτὴν πλεῖτε. ὥσπερ δὲ τὰς ναυτιλίας ἐπαινεῖσθε, οὕτω τὰς ἐμπορίας διαβέβλησθε ὡς φιλοχρήματοί τε καὶ τρῶκται.
>
> Φοῖνιξ: σὺ δὲ οὐ φιλοχρήματος, ἀμπελουργέ, ζῶν ἐν ταύταις ταῖς ἀμπέλοις καὶ ζητῶν ἴσως ὅστις μὲν ὀπωριεῖ καταβαλὼν σοι δραχμὴν τῶν βοτρύων, ὅτῳ δὲ ἀποδώσῃ τὸ γλεῦκος ἢ ὅτῳ τὸν ἀνθοσμίαν; ὅν, οἶμαι, καὶ κατορωρυγμένον φῂς ἔχειν ὥσπερ ὁ Μάρων.
>
> Ἀμπελουργός: ξένε Φοῖνιξ, εἰ μὲν εἰσί που τῆς γῆς Κύκλωπες, οὓς λέγεται ἡ γῆ ἀργοὺς βόσκειν φυτεύοντας οὐδὲν οὐδὲ σπείροντας, ἀφύλακτα μὲν τὰ φυόμενα εἴη ἄν, καίτοι Δήμητρός γε καὶ Διονύσου ὄντα, πωλοῖτο δ᾽ ἂν οὐδὲν ἐκ τῆς γῆς, ἀλλ᾽ ἄτιμά τε καὶ κοινὰ φύοιτ᾽ ἄν, ὥσπερ ἐν συῶν ἀγορᾷ· σπείρειν δὲ ὅπου χρὴ καὶ ἀροῦν καὶ φυτεύειν καὶ ἄλλο ἐπ᾽ ἄλλῳ πονεῖν προσκείμενον τῇ γῇ καὶ ὑποκείμενον ταῖς ὥραις, ἐνταῦθα πωλεῖν τε χρὴ καὶ ὠνεῖσθαι. δεῖ γὰρ καὶ γεωργίᾳ χρημάτων, καὶ ἄνευ τούτων οὔτε ἀρότην θρέψεις οὔτε ἀμπελουργὸν οὔτε βουκόλον οὔτε αἰπόλον, οὐδὲ κρατὴρ ἔσται σοι πιεῖν ἢ σπεῖσαι.

καὶ γὰρ τὸ ἥδιστον τῶν ἐν γεωργίᾳ, τὸ τρυγᾶν ἀμπέλους, μισθοῦ χρὴ πράττειν· εἰ δὲ μή, ἄοινοί τε καὶ ἀργοὶ ἑστήξουσιν, ὥσπερ γεγραμμέναι. ταυτὶ μὲν, ὦ ξένε, ὑπὲρ παντὸς εἴρηκα τοῦ τῶν γεωργῶν κύκλου, τοὐμὸν δὲ πολλῷ ἐπιεικέστερον· οὐ γὰρ ξυμβάλλω ἐμπόροις, οὐδὲ τὴν δραχμὴν ὅ τι ἐστί γιγνώσκω, ἀλλὰ βοῦν σίτου καὶ οἴνου τράγον καὶ τοιαῦτα τοιούτων ἢ ὠνοῦμαι ἢ αὐτὸς ἀποδίδομαι σμικρὰ εἰπών τε καὶ ἀκούσας.

VINEDRESSER: Stranger, you are at least skilled in nautical affairs, for you have even designated Cynosura as a sign in the sky, and you sail by reference to it. Yet just as you are praised for your sailing skill, in the same way you are stereotyped as money-lovers and greedy rascals because of your business dealings.

PHOENICIAN: But aren't you also money-loving, vinedresser, living among these vines and presumably seeking someone who will gather grapes after paying a drachma for them, and looking for someone to whom you will sell sweet or fragrant wine, which, I think, you will say you have hidden, just like Maron?

VINEDRESSER: Phoenician stranger, if somewhere there are Cyclopes, whom it is said the earth nourishes, though they neither plant nor sow, there things would grow unattended, even though they belong to Demeter and to Dionysos, and none of the produce of the earth would be sold. Instead, everything would be produced without price and common to all, just as in the agora of the pigs. But wherever it is necessary for someone to sow, plow, plant, and suffer one toil after another, because they are bound to the land and obedient to the season, there it is necessary to buy and sell. For money is needed for farming, and without money, you will not feed a plowman nor a vinedresser nor a cow or a goatherd, and you will not have a krater for drinking or pouring libations. Additionally, the most pleasant thing in farming, gathering fruit, one must pay to do. Otherwise, the vines will stand idle and yield no wine, as if they had been cursed. Stranger, I have said these things about the whole crowd of farmers, but my way is much more honorable, since I do not associate with merchants, and I do not know what a drachma is. I trade a bull for grain and a goat for wine and other such exchanges, and I allow only a little haggling.[1]

1. Philostr., *Her.* 1.3–1.7.

The exchange reflects on the nature of the work that the two men do, on the interrelation of all economic activity, and on the attitude of Roman society toward merchants and money. The men are a relatively unusual pair of interlocutors in Roman literature, which tends, like the vinedresser, to hold retail and artisanal work at a distance from the agricultural world. The latter sphere is one that was deeply respected by the ancient world at large, while the former, as the vinedresser states, was associated with profit and greed. The merchant pushes back against the accusation relatively gently, by reminding the vinedresser that he, too, must buy and sell to run the vineyard, and makes the case that these vices are shared ones, rather than denying their presence in him and his work.

In response, the vinedresser assures the merchant that he is not "money-loving" at all. He only trades in kind for what he needs, and he does not associate with merchants. To do so, it is implied, would be wrong in some way, even if it seems to be common practice. Perhaps it would take him too far away from the lofty ideas that he is about to discuss or would place greater emphasis on profit than on care for the land, but whatever the reasoning, the vinedresser is quick to draw the line: on one side, he, an agriculturalist, sits, while merchants and tradesmen, like his new Phoenician acquaintance, remain on the other side. Though the two would make for natural allies, the producer and the wholesaler, the vinedresser maintains his distance and will not associate with such people, beyond the present conversation.

This divide is typical in Roman writing and the vinedresser sums up the matter nicely: while merchants were not believed to be totally without skill, they were known to be greedy, and, beyond that, generally dishonest in their pursuit of gain. Some were undoubtedly worse than others, but no merchant could be viewed as a respectable, trustworthy, or reputable member of society. Both elite authors and common people recognized that trade was necessary, but viewed it as a necessary evil, a practice that invited vice, and which upstanding members of society avoided as much as possible. Philostratus represented this attitude in a different case, with the story of a young elite Spartan who was making plans to go into trade to make his fortune. In that case, the philosopher Apollonius told the young man "for a man who is a citizen of Sparta and the child of forebears who have lived in the heart of Sparta, to hide himself 'in the hold of a ship,' forgetting Lycurgus and Iphitus, and thinking about his cargo and nautical skills, is a disgrace."[2] He stressed that trade would destroy the nobility of the family line, bring shame upon the man's good name, and squander the natural benefits that the Spartan enjoyed as a man of high birth.

2. Philostr., *V. A.* 4.32.3.

Of course, people of all ranks took part in trade. Figures like the vinedresser were not divorced from the economy simply because they bartered rather than took money for their goods, and those who did not sell products often sold their labor or services instead. Roman elites publicly despised trade and those who made their fortunes through it, but nevertheless diversified their property to profit from shipping or artisanal production. Most opted to use slaves or freedmen to carry out this work, the better to keep their own hands clean, but they nevertheless directly profited from the business.[3] The major economic difference between the senator and the vendor in the forum was one of scale and stigma, not of practice, and while the former might be known as a leading figure in society, the latter would be shamed for his greed and baseness.

Infamy surrounded trade and worked in tandem with a host of economic challenges to make life for Roman merchants extremely difficult. The Phoenician merchant of the *Heroicus* not only faced the stigma of being seen as greedy by, in this case, a potential source of goods, but he also managed a litany of other concerns, ranging from the weather and state of the sea to the price of goods in numerous ports, as well as the trustworthiness and reliability of his own trading partners. Information in the ancient economy was unevenly available, risks were great, and transaction costs were high.[4] Merchants were at a major disadvantage, with most operating at margins tight enough that a single bad deal might shut down their small businesses for good.[5] We can trace many individuals from Roman Egypt who ran single-donkey operations and whose sudden appearance and disappearance from our records might well reflect

---

3. Elite trade has been expertly analyzed by John H. D'Arms, *Commerce and Social Standing in Ancient Rome* (Cambridge, MA: Harvard University Press, 1981). Elite work done by proxy is examined in Jean-Jacques Aubert, *Business Managers in Ancient Rome: A Social and Economic Study of* Institores, *200 B.C.–A.D. 250* (Leiden: Brill, 1994).

4. Peter F. Bang, *The Roman Bazaar: A Comparative Study of Trade and Markets in a Tributary Empire* (Cambridge: Cambridge University Press, 2011), though it should be noted that Bang is at times overly pessimistic about the viability of the Roman economy.

5. It is difficult to assess the scale of most trade in the Roman world due to the uneven preservation of our material, which is biased in favor of large-scale, long-distance business that interacted with the state, but it is generally understood that most trade happened locally and on the scale of the individual or family's needs. See discussions in Peregrine Horden and Nicholas Purcell, *The Corrupting Sea: A Study of Mediterranean History* (Oxford: Wiley-Blackwell, 2000), 365–67; D'Arms, *Commerce and Social Standing*, 85–87; and Keith Hopkins, "Models, Ships and Staples," in *Trade and Famine in Classical Antiquity*, ed. Peter Garnsey and C. R. Whittaker (Cambridge: Cambridge Philological Society, 1983), 85: "Short-haul transport of the agriculture surplus . . . constituted the greatest proportion of all transport which occurred in the Roman world." Importantly, some Romans seem to have understood how close to subsistence most merchants truly were, e.g., Luc., *Fug.* 12–13, though it did not stop them from disparaging them and their work at every opportunity.

gambles they made on their futures and their ultimate failure to thrive in a competitive and unstable market.[6]

Periodic efforts made by the state to restrict the work of merchants added another layer of complication to operating a business. Though enforcement was uneven and unreliable, the Roman state occasionally passed laws to restrict the social and economic mobility of merchants. New regulations cut both ways, potentially offering helpful structures and increasing transparency, but also posing a risk that might upset the delicate balance of trust and tradition upon which economic activity depended. Rather than offering a neutral judgment, the state often echoed the commonplace stigma against merchants and amplified the pressures put upon traders by society overall.[7] Thus, the words and actions of state agents and market officials often shared the bias against merchants that was found in the gossip on the street. Formal legislative efforts to restrict and direct merchants not only complicated the physical work of trade, but also normalized the social isolation that merchants could face and hindered merchant access to many kinds of public support.[8]

In combination, these difficulties potentially held the power to grind trade itself to a halt. Working as a merchant was highly disincentivized and customers were extremely wary of their trading partners. Commercial exchange requires a baseline of mutual tolerance, and it benefits from a more general culture of trust and acceptance. This seems to have been largely absent from the Roman world. Instead, commerce was viewed as a competitive, if not combative, activity that most tried to avoid. Romans construed trade as a zero-sum game, in which merchants were not only frequent winners, but also frequent cheaters, who made sure that the odds were in their favor.[9] It was difficult, if not impossible, for a Roman to imagine that a customer or producer might "win" in a contest with such immoral figures. Though fictional, the vinedresser's willingness to tell a merchant, to his face, that he and his colleagues were greedy and to be avoided, exemplifies the feelings of this society. The Roman world not only did not understand the challenges of working in trade, but it also lacked sympa-

6. These figures, recorded in toll receipts and the ledgers of customs houses, have been studied by Pieter Johannes Sijpesteijn, *Customs Duties in Graeco-Roman Egypt* (Zutphen: Terra Publishing, 1987).

7. E.g., Ulp., *Dig.* 4.9.1.1.

8. Discussed thoroughly in Sarah E. Bond, *Trade and Taboo: Disreputable Professions in the Roman Mediterranean* (Ann Arbor: University of Michigan Press, 2016), who clarifies that the state's position was variable over time, but also was targeted to keep some people locked in trade, while preventing others from entering it.

9. As stated by the Republican aphorist Publilius Syrus, *Sent.* 337: "Profits in trade can only be made by another's loss."

thy for those who did this labor. Taking these emotions to an extreme, it would be logical for no one to engage with merchants, and if they chose that path, the whole economic system of redistribution, production, and services would cease to exist. Fundamentally, if a vinedresser will not trade with a merchant, who will drink the wine?

Merchants had every reason to try to find other professions, to work hard until they could buy their way into a more respectable field, like agriculture, yet our evidence shows that they not only persisted in the face of this adversity, but they also often proclaimed their work loudly and with pride. In fact, the identification that merchants offer for themselves is often the best and only means to find them in our extant sources.[10] While texts like Philostratus' apply this identity to figures like the Phoenician, in nonfictional contexts it is generally merchants who adopt some version of the label for themselves, naming a specific trade and identifying themselves by their work.[11] Of course, "merchant" included numerous professions, and a range of social and economic positions, including some extremely wealthy and prominent people along with many who continually struggled at the edge of poverty and lived in relative obscurity. Nevertheless, every person within this category experienced some share of the social stigma that Romans attached to their work, and many found reasons to connect their identity and character to their profession.

In English, the term merchant may be utilized as a category to gather these diverse figures, in that they are united by a commonly shared goal of receiving payment for some form of goods, skill, or service. "Merchant" gathers many kinds of work under its domain, including many individuals who only periodically dabbled in merchant-hood, selling goods on the side while primarily being engaged in agriculture, just like, and despite the protestations of, Philostratus' vinedresser. Such a definition perhaps risks being too capacious, but it helps us to see "merchant" as part activity and part identity, thereby clearing the path to an analysis of the consequences of, on the one hand, doing merchant work, and, on the other hand, being recognized as a merchant in Roman soci-

10. Discussed in Sandra R. Joshel, *Work, Identity, and Legal Status at Rome: A Study of the Occupational Inscriptions* (Norman: University of Oklahoma Press, 1992), esp. 16–20, for the phenomenon in funerary inscriptions, though it transcends any specific source base as a challenge for anyone working on nonelite groups.

11. Philostr., *Her.* 1.2–1.3, the Phoenician is somewhat cagey around his profession. He admits only to seeking a favorable wind, not to being a tradesman of some kind. This work is attributed to him by the vinedresser, and he does not deny it. This may be compared with the enthusiastic representation of the baking profession seen in the Tomb of Eurysaces, see Lauren Hackworth Petersen, "The Baker, His Tomb, His Wife, and Her Breadbasket: The Monument of Eurysaces in Rome," *Art Bulletin* 85.2 (2003).

ety. While most merchants exist at the center of that Venn diagram, there was a distinction made in Roman culture between the casual or occasional merchant, someone for whom necessity sometimes compelled this kind of work, and the full-time retailer, artisan, or transporter, who actively and consistently chose this profession and lived with the full force of the stigma attached to it.

There is a real variety of purpose that lingers below the surface of "merchant" as a catch-all term, not only in English, but also in Greek and Latin, which used general terms like *mercator*, *negotiator*, ἔμπορος, or κάπηλος, along with numerous specific words for particular trades. This variety of terminology is both a help and a hindrance, in that it reveals a massive range of lived experiences, each shaped by their own unique set of circumstances, while being united by common anxieties and cultural perceptions. Thus, Philostratus' Phoenician merchant faces similar accusations of greed and deceitfulness as Roman prostitutes, and while Roman barbers might be chastised for their chattiness and tanners for their bad smell, both are part of a common "mob" that were kept at a distance by "polite" Roman society.[12] These commonalities, borne out by Roman stereotypes and prejudices, gave merchants their common purpose: to rise above the low estimation of their communities. In many cases, it drove merchants to embrace their professions, displaying them prominently as the core of their identities and complementing them with forms of self-praise and self-promotion.

Critically, merchants did not attempt to brazen out the stigma. They did not seek to reject societal norms or even to reclaim social and economic power by embracing Roman stereotypes. While either might have been viable options in the right circumstances, merchants instead opted to insist, through quiet, consistent behavior, that they and their work were worthy of respect. This effort did little to dislodge the stigma against trade, which was pervasive and had been entrenched in Mediterranean society since at least the time of Homer, but it was often possible for merchants to convince others, on the small scale, that they themselves were respectable, honest, and reputable.[13]

12. On prostitutes and greed: Anise K. Strong, *Prostitutes and Matrons in the Roman World* (Cambridge: Cambridge University Press, 2016), ch. 1; on chatty barbers: Sian Lewis, "Barbers' Shops and Perfume Shops: Symposia without Wine," in *The Greek World*, ed. Anton Powell (London: Routledge, 1995); Jerry P. Toner, "Barbers, Barbershops and Searching for Roman Popular Culture," *Papers of the British School at Rome* 83 (2015); on tanners: Bond, *Trade and Taboo*, ch. 3.

13. Hom., *Od.* 8.158, Euryalus mocks Odysseus for not looking like an athlete, but rather for resembling a merchant shipper, and explicitly mentions the greed of such people.

Roman Reputation

At the heart of the matter lies reputation. Merchants, artisans, and service providers all believed, at some conscious or unconscious level, that they were good people, and that those around them also knew it. They believed themselves to be virtuous and deserving of support from their friends, neighbors, and customers, who witnessed and understood their efforts to be honest and responsible. Even in the face of generalized prejudice and pervasive negative stereotypes, individual merchants believed that they could be recognized as an exception to the rule on account of their personal goodness, professional standards, and essential roles in the community. Accordingly, it was theoretically, and even practically, possible to be the rare, good merchant among a crowd of cheats and liars. One's claim on that position was not something that could be relied upon to be stable or permanent, but, with sufficient work and luck, a merchant might achieve a good reputation, and once acquired and properly maintained, that reputation could be used to overcome the stigma against merchants, to reduce an individual's transaction costs, and to smooth the way to a successful career.

Merchants understood this and worked hard to build and maintain a reputation. They knew that if they demonstrated their virtues and avoided any public display of their vices, they could harness the goodwill of those around them, securing the personal trust of their communities, thereby rendering stereotypes less harmful. Romans, in general, understood that reputation was a valuable commodity, not just socially, but economically. Perhaps it is most concisely treated in words attributed to the aphorist Publilius Syrus: "a good reputation is better than money."[14] Reputation gave a merchant more economic benefit than an influx of wealth. When properly cared for, a reputation could secure loans or major contracts, could help find apprenticeships for sons, husbands for daughters, could prevent scandal, or offer protection against one's enemies.

Still, reputation required work. In the face of negative stereotypes, no merchant began their career with a perfect reputation, and maintaining a good name throughout a career was a challenge that required sacrifices. At times, the pursuit of a good reputation dissuaded a merchant from taking the most

14. Publilius Syrus, *Sententiae falsae inter publilianas receptae*, 158. Syrus was a mime performer in the late Republic. As his name suggests, he was likely a Syrian who came to Rome as a slave. His *Sententiae* were popular and were quoted and misquoted for centuries after his death. As a collection of aphorisms, some genuine and others attributed to Syrus, they are not only Syrus' personal work, but also a collection of popular sayings and attitudes that grant us access to something approaching "common knowledge." Thus, among genuinely Syrian quotes, we also see *Sent.* 75 and 254: "The good opinion of men is safer than money," and "A good reputation is a second inheritance." The same thought is also captured in Proverbs 22:1: "A good name is better than great riches."

profitable course of action, or the most satisfying one. A figure like the Phoenician merchant might have wished to take offense at the vinedresser's words, yet Philostratus depicts him as conciliatory, trying to soften the opinion of this potential business partner. Though the merchant is not successful in winning over the man's business, he is still careful not to offend him or to present himself as quick-tempered or untrustworthy. Many merchant choices were structured by concern for their reputations, and it was reputation that underpinned the strength of other social and economic norms in Roman society. Fear of losing a good reputation, or developing a bad one, pressured merchants to avoid certain kinds of conduct, and encouraged them to behave in socially acceptable ways. The Phoenician merchant chooses not to give the vinedresser the last piece of his mind, consciously or unconsciously believing that doing so could jeopardize his good name, while being pleasant, even to this rude man, could only reflect well on him. Reputation offered both a carrot and a stick, a potential reward and a real and present threat. In this way, it acted with the force of an economic institution, laying out a path merchants might follow to maximize their chances of occupying a respected place in society and gaining many different social and economic benefits.[15]

Reputation did not have this institutional force for merchants alone. Across Roman society, people were incentivized to care about how they were perceived by others and everyone carried some fear that they would be shamed and fall into disrepute.[16] While reputation was not unique to merchants, this group was among the most despised in Roman society, and this bias made personal

15. New Institutional Economic theory originates in the work of Coase and Williamson, but is best known from the scholarship of Douglass North, esp. Douglass C. North, "The New Institutional Economics," *Journal of Institutional and Theoretical Economics/Zeitschrift für die gesamte Staatswissenschaft* 142.1 (1986); Douglass C. North, *Institutions, Institutional Change and Economic Performance* (Cambridge: Cambridge University Press, 1990); and Douglass C. North, "Institutions," *Journal of Economic Perspectives* 5.1 (1991). Oliver E. Williamson, "The New Institutional Economics: Taking Stock, Looking Ahead," *Journal of Economic Literature* 38.3 (2000), returns to the theory and presents the *status quaestionis* as of that moment. Institutional theory is discussed further below.

16. See Jean G. Peristiany, *Honour and Shame: The Values of Mediterranean Society* (Chicago: University of Chicago Press, 1966), on the pervasive concern with respectability in Mediterranean culture. Beyond honor and shame, the matter is deeply integrated with the value Greek and Roman society placed on reciprocity in all their relationships, including personal friendship. On *amicitia* in this sense, see Aaron Kirschenbaum, *Sons, Slaves, and Freedmen in Roman Commerce* (Washington, DC: Catholic University of America Press, 1987), 160–71; Koenraad Verboven, *The Economy of Friends: Economic Aspects of Amicitia and Patronage in the Late Republic* (Brussels: Latomus, 2002); Koenraad Verboven, "Friendship among the Romans," in *The Oxford Handbook of Social Relations in the Roman World*, ed. Michael Peachin (Oxford: Oxford University Press, 2011); and Zofia H. Archibald, "Making the Most of One's Friends: Western Asia Minor in the Early Hellenistic Age," in *Hellenistic Economies*, ed. Zofia H. Archibald, John Davies, Vincent Gabrielsen, and G. J. Oliver (New York: Routledge, 2001).

reputation and social standing all the more important. They could not rely on having the benefit of the doubt in their society, so they had to invest in strategies that would build up personal networks of trust. It was also reputation that enabled trade, in a general sense, to happen at all. A merchant's good reputation made it possible for trading partners to count on one another, even if other mechanisms that could have increased trust were weak or lacking.[17]

Only recently have historians been able to view reputation in this light. This perspective is the culmination of developments in multiple fields of study that have made it possible to view an individual's choice to self-identify as a merchant as the statement of pride that it was, or to understand that merchant behavior and choices were directed by their concern for their reputation. The intersection of social and economic history, especially with regard to merchants, has been a relatively recent development in the field, and just a handful of works since the 1980s have pioneered the study of merchants as both social and economic figures simultaneously.[18] Earlier debates over the nature and scale of the Roman economy largely left the agency of tradesmen to the side, and even within most modern considerations, which have adopted a form of New Institutional Economics as their basis, merchants and other economic actors are generally held to be constrained by systems larger than themselves, like the state and its coercive powers, rather than viewing them as participants in the social and normative structures to which they both contributed and were obedient.[19]

Within the field of social history, merchants have also largely been considered within the framework of their relationship with the state. The legal status

17. See chapter 1 for a full discussion of the limitations of formal institutions, such as the state and its law, at the local and interpersonal level.

18. E.g., foundationally, D'Arms, *Commerce and Social Standing*; Onno van Nijf, *The Civic World of Professional Associations in the Roman East* (Leiden: Brill, 1997).

19. The literature is, perhaps predictably, vast, but some varied approaches are represented by Moses Finley, *The Ancient Economy* (Berkeley: University of California Press, 1973); Richard P. Duncan-Jones, *The Economy of the Roman Empire: Quantitative Studies* (Cambridge: Cambridge University Press, 1982); Alan K. Bowman and Andrew Wilson, eds., *Quantifying the Roman Economy: Methods and Problems* (Oxford: Oxford University Press, 2013); Peter Temin, *The Roman Market Economy* (Princeton: Princeton University Press, 2013); and recently, and polemically, Kim Bowes, "When Kuznets Went to Rome: Roman Economic Well-Being and the Reframing of Roman History," *Capitalism: A Journal of History and Economics* 2.1 (2021). The relevance of New Institutional Economics was argued most forcefully in Walter Scheidel, Ian Morris, and Richard P. Saller, eds., *The Cambridge Economic History of the Greco-Roman World* (Cambridge: Cambridge University Press, 2007), but there have been some recent shifts that suggest this narrative is no longer as dominant as it once was. Compare Miko Flohr, *The World of the* Fullo: *Work, Economy, and Society in Roman Italy* (Oxford: Oxford University Press, 2013), discussing fullers without much reference to the state, or elements of the 2021 SCS panel on "New Institutionalism and Greek Communities," which, especially the work of Linda Rocchi, stressed that NIE may also be used to assess the force of social norms.

of merchants has been of preeminent concern, and substantial work has been put into understanding two specific issues: the restrictions placed upon elites who wished to take part in economic activity, and the limitations on freedmen and enslaved people as they pursued their trades.[20] Freed people, in particular, have received substantial attention, as the study of nonelite subjects has become more mainstream and the prominence of freed people in trade has been recognized beyond its place as a common trope in Roman literature.[21] It is only recently that ideas of reputation have been considered by this field, most prominently in Sarah Bond's recent examination of the nature of taboos surrounding specific trades. Even in that excellent case, legal stigma, *infamia*, remained a critical element of her analysis, rather than studying reputation as a system for incentivizing good conduct that was enforced as much by peers as by social superiors.[22]

While the Roman state did structure both the economy and Roman society, the force of the state in the lives of merchants has been somewhat overestimated. Evidence of merchant and state interactions is plentiful, but there is also a substantial bias in favor of its preservation, as pronouncements of the state were more likely to be memorialized in stone or other lasting materials, and the merchants who dealt with the state were, themselves, often more affluent than those trading exclusively in the private sector.[23] Furthermore, it is increasingly clear that the enforcement of state regulations was highly irregular, localized, and, critically, embodied by officials who were themselves subject to the same social forces as everyone else.[24] In light of this, the greatest progress in under-

20. On legal status, see Joshel, *Work, Identity, and Legal Status*; Bond, *Trade and Taboo*; D'Arms, *Commerce and Social Standing*. To an extent, this interest goes back to the nineteenth century where the legal status of tradesmen and their organizations were analyzed in works like Theodor Mommsen, *De collegiis et sodaliciis romanorum* (Kiliae: Libraria Schwersiana, 1843); and Jean-Pierre Waltzing, *Étude historique sur les corporations professionelles chez les Romains depuis les origines jusqu'à la chute de l'Empire d'occident* (Louvain: Charles Peeters, 1895).

21. On freed people, e.g., Susan Treggiari, *Roman Freedmen during the Late Republic* (Oxford: Oxford University Press, 1969); Kirschenbaum, *Sons, Slaves, and Freedmen*; Henrik Mouritsen, *The Freedman in the Roman World* (Cambridge: Cambridge University Press, 2011); Pedro López Barja de Quiroga, "Freedmen Social Mobility in Roman Italy," *Historia: Zeitschrift für Alte Geschichte* 44.3 (1995); Joshel, *Work, Identity, and Legal Status*; Sandra R. Joshel and Lauren Hackworth Petersen, eds., *The Material Life of Roman Slaves* (Cambridge: Cambridge University Press, 2014).

22. Bond, *Trade and Taboo*, 10. It is important to note that while *infamia* was a legal category with a specific meaning, the adjective *infamis*, "disreputable" was still used independently of the law. It was possible to be subject to legal *infamia* but not be, within one's community and with one's peers, *infamis*, or to be *infamis* but not constrained by legal *infamia*.

23. Horden and Purcell, *The Corrupting Sea*, 365–67.

24. On the minimal investment of the state in economic activity, see Elio Lo Cascio, "Setting the Rules of the Game: The Market and Its Working in the Roman Empire," in *Roman Law and Economics*, vol. 1, ed. Giuseppe Dari-Mattiacci and Dennis P. Kehoe (Oxford: Oxford University Press, 2020), though he believes the state more committed to market regulation than is plausible when looking at the evidence from merchants. Though he refers to the state

standing Roman merchants in recent years has come not from the study of legal structures, but from analyses of private modes of organization, especially the study of merchant associations and small, internally regulated communities.[25] Recent work by Philip Venticinque, Cam Hawkins, and Taco Terpstra, among others, has shown that merchant lives were shaped by interpersonal connections, networks of mutual obligation, and nonstate institutions that not only built and maintained trust, but also developed extralegal systems of punishment and accountability.[26]

There is some momentum growing behind these ideas in ancient history, though merchant reputation as an institutional force has not yet been studied on its own. Still, "reputation as institution" is a powerful explanatory tool that is very much in line with the conclusions of these most recent works: that ancient merchants monitored each other and structured their business lives and obligations around the ties that bound them to one another, that they depended upon and utilized the information that they gathered and circulated about the relative trustworthiness of those around them, and that behaving in a way that conformed with social norms benefited merchants in the short and long term, as it served as a reflection of their character to the community around them. Reputation forms the core of that morass of concern and effort. It is an institution that is both inward looking, focused on the identity of the actor, and outwardly determined, as it is witnessed, assessed, and spread by an audience of community members of all kinds.

---

as a "player among the other players" (115) his belief in a consistent state "policy" is a problem addressed in chapter 1.

25. Van Nijf, *Civic World of Professional Associations* is foundational, but Koenraad Verboven, "Professional Collegia: Guilds or Social Clubs?" *Ancient Society* 41 (2011); Koenraad Verboven, "Resident Aliens and Translocal Merchant Organisations," in *Frontiers in the Roman World*, ed. Olivier Hekster and Ted Kaizer (Leiden: Brill, 2011); Nicolas Tran, *Les membres des associations romaines: Le rang social des collegiati en Italie et en Gaules, sous le Haut-Empire* (Rome: Publications de l'École française de Rome, 2006); Jinyu Liu, "Group Membership, Trust Networks, and Social Capital: A Critical Analysis," in *Work, Labour, and Professions in the Roman World*, ed. Koenraad Verboven and Christian C. Laes (Leiden: Brill, 2016); and Wim Broekaert, "Partners in Business: Roman Merchants and the Potential Advantages of Being a Collegiatus," *Ancient Society* 41 (2011) are also relevant.

26. Philip Venticinque, *Honor among Thieves: Craftsmen, Merchants, and Associations in Roman and Late Roman Egypt* (Ann Arbor: University of Michigan Press, 2016); Cameron Hawkins, *Roman Artisans and the Urban Economy* (Cambridge: Cambridge University Press, 2016); Taco Terpstra, *Trading Communities in the Roman World: A Micro-Economic and Institutional Prospective* (Leiden: Brill, 2013), each drawing on associations literature, but there is also much to be learned from literature on *amicitia*, e.g., Verboven, "Friendship among the Romans"; Verboven, *The Economy of Friends*; Archibald, "Making the Most of One's Friends"; John T. Fitzgerald, ed., *Greco-Roman Perspectives on Friendship* (Atlanta: Scholars Press, 1997); David Konstan, *Friendship in the Classical World* (Cambridge: Cambridge University Press, 1996); and Kirschenbaum, *Sons, Slaves, and Freedmen*, 160–71. There is also a growing understanding in the field of the social utility of violence, e.g., Ari Z. Bryen, *Violence in Roman Egypt: A Study in Legal Interpretation* (Philadelphia: University of Pennsylvania Press, 2013).

Because reputation operates both internally and externally, it is a concept that can be challenging to define. In English, one "has" a reputation, generally "for" something—whether virtue or vice—that is known to others. Simultaneously, however, it is possible to say that someone's reputation "is" good, bad, or some other descriptor. Recent work on reputation has rightly complicated the matter further by integrating concepts of reputational networks and audience theory into our understanding, explaining that reputation is a flexible, dialectical, and elusive concept that neither the audience nor the reputed ever grasped in full, but rather was continually shaped and refined by new information as it was communicated to a variety of audiences over time.[27]

Historically, theoretical treatments of reputation have straddled several fields of study. The earliest scholarship on the subject may be dated to the late nineteenth century and is epitomized in the work of the psychologist William James. James' work framed reputation as one manifestation of humanity's "social selves," which could be as numerous as the social groups that a person encountered and depended not only on that individual's actions, but, more broadly, on how he or she was perceived and understood by others.[28] Following James, social scientists took up reputation as a useful concept for interpreting relationships and social decision-making. Most modern work on reputation owes some debt to Erving Goffman and his wide-ranging studies of self-representation, social stigma, and communication.[29] In each case, social personae, whether adopted and presented by the actor, or assigned and attributed by others, take a position of prominence in Goffman's interpretation of how humans interact with one another and carefully select and construct who they want to be. Reputation is closely related to Goffman's assessments of identity, though unlike many of Goffman's cases, reputation is critically dependent on external assessment, in that it is essentially the self as it is perceived and understood by others.[30] Building on this work, through the mid-twentieth century, advancements were steadily made to improve our ability to assess and

27. E.g., Gloria Origgi, *Reputation: What It Is and Why It Matters* (Princeton: Princeton University Press, 2018); Kenneth H. Craik, *Reputation: A Network Interpretation* (Oxford: Oxford University Press, 2009); Nicholas Emler, "A Social Psychology of Reputation," *European Review of Social Psychology* 1.1 (1990).

28. William James, *The Principles of Psychology* (London: Macmillan, 1890), discussed in D. B. Bromley, *Reputation, Image and Impression Management* (New York: John Wiley and Sons, 1993), 18–19.

29. Erving Goffman, *The Presentation of the Self in Everyday Life* (New York: Doubleday, 1959); Erving Goffman, *Behavior in Public Places* (Oxford: Blackwell, 1963); Erving Goffman, *Frame Analysis: An Essay on the Organization of Experience* (Cambridge, MA: Harvard University Press, 1974), especially.

30. Origgi, *Reputation*, 4, describes this as a second self, drawing on the work of Charles Horton Cooley, another prominent scholar of reputation, and his "looking glass" metaphor, which elucidates the difference between what we believe others think about us, and what they actually think.

map the extent and spread of reputation, largely through experimentation in the social sciences, rather than via case studies from historical moments.[31]

Recent work, and especially that of Kenneth Craik and Gloria Origgi, has sought to expand the theoretical framing of reputation still further, and they have done so in two ways that are essential to this work. Craik has expanded on the importance of social networks to the formulation of reputation(s), and developed a model that explains the, at times, long delays between information about reputation being received and dispersed.[32] His work highlights how a community may act as "storage" for reputation, only "activating" and working to spread reputation information when circumstances require it. Critically for this work, given the prevalence of funerary evidence for Roman merchants, Craik's argument is one of a few to take on the challenge of posthumous reputation, both as a puzzling phenomenon interconnected with our ability to process our own mortality and as a strategy for mourners and the beneficiaries of reputation in the next generation.[33]

Origgi's approach is more individualistic, and consequently more able to assess the role of reputation in the decision-making process of a particular person, especially in economic contexts.[34] She has stressed that investment in and concern for reputation is, or can be, a rational choice that need not conflict with traditional visions of economic rationality. Nothing in the consideration for or pursuit of reputation inherently hinders the goal of maximizing personal profit, in that energies expended in this direction are not "wasted" in any way. Origgi makes the case that "profit" can be variably defined but is best understood as achieving or acquiring whatever it is that one values. Accordingly, if a person values the appreciation and respect of their peers, then pursuing a good repu-

31. E.g., Jacob Levy Moreno, *Who Shall Survive? Foundations of Sociometry, Group Psychotherapy, and Sociodrama* (Washington, DC: Nervous and Mental Disease Publishing, 1934) on sociometry; or Read D. Tuddenham, "Studies in Reputation. III: Correlates of Popularity among Elementary-School Children," *Journal of Educational Psychology* 42.5 (1951); and Read D. Tuddenham, "Studies in Reputation. I: Sex and Grade Differences in School Children's Evaluations of Their Peers. II: The Diagnosis of Social Adjustment," *Psychological Monographs: General and Applied* 66.1 (1952) on methods of testing personalities and their impact on others. The former is generally more applicable to the study of ancient reputation, given a handful of well-documented social networks, but there are also valuable lessons to be taken from the study of how comfortable people are in publicly stating their opinions of one another. Shyness regarding the frank assessment of one's peers is culturally dependent, but regardless of the context, we should probably expect some distance between private thoughts and public statements about reputation.

32. Craik, *Reputation*.

33. Geoffrey Scarre, "On Caring about One's Posthumous Reputation," *American Philosophical Quarterly* 38.2 (2001); and Steven Luper, "Posthumous Harm," *American Philosophical Quarterly* 41.1 (2004) provide the most thorough studies of posthumous reputation beyond Craik, *Reputation*, ch. 9.

34. Origgi, *Reputation*.

tation can be a rational course of action. Further, economic rationality itself can be better understood when reputation is taken into account, as reputation can be used to explain the decision to forgo short-term gain in favor of larger, long-term profit. The fact that reputation is, to some degree, a collaborative endeavor, merely means that rational choices must consider the input and reaction of society to maximize the actor's chances of making a good decision.

For the purposes of this study, reputation will be understood as the opinion, or collection of opinions, that are held about an individual's character or behavior based on available data, derived from a variety of potential sources. It comes with the understanding that information can change rapidly and that the spread of both information and reputation is dependent upon the relative position of both the actor and the audience.[35] These moving parts account for the possibility of multiple reputations, among different audiences, that traveling merchants often developed across a number of locations, while also allowing for a variety of opinions to coexist within single communities, based on both what was known and by whom. As we will discuss, there is also a form of attraction between the reputation of individual merchants and the broader reputation of their professions, which complicates our study and the intentions behind merchant actions regarding reputation.[36]

In searching for reputation within the Roman world, there is a variety of terminology that reflects elements of the concept. In Latin and Greek, *fama* and δόξα are the most common terms, though a handful of other words, including *existimatio*, which appears with some regularity, are also used in some contexts. They do not, however, represent an exact one-to-one equivalence either to reputation or to each other. Δόξα, for instance, with its roots in judgment and worth, more often holds positive connotations in ancient literary sources, while *fama*, with its root in speech, is often more associated with gossip or rumor. As a result, *fama* seems to have held a greater potential to be inaccurate or even malicious. In ancient sources, these terms are supplemented with words for opinion and rumor, thought or judgment, as well as phrases conveying the fundamentally oral nature of much of reputation, such as hearing or speaking

35. This definition follows J. C. Sharman, "Rationalist and Constructivist Perspectives on Reputation," *Political Studies* 55 (2007); Cam Grey, *Constructing Communities in the Late Roman Countryside* (Cambridge: Cambridge University Press, 2011); and, to different extents, those of Craik, *Reputation* and Bromley, *Reputation*. These may be contrasted with the definition of reputation as a "collective phenomenon" that is not necessarily attached to a single person, proposed by Emler, "Social Psychology of Reputation," 171.

36. Bromley, *Reputation*, 4–5. This will be especially important in considering the intersection of stereotypes and reputation, as the reputation of "a merchant," in particular, may be different from the stereotype of "merchants," in general, though each may inform the other in certain cases and contexts.

something about someone. It is also common to see individuals described, or describing themselves, as being "known" for particular qualities. At its most abstract, reputation can even manifest as mere description, adjectives applied to an individual without the explicit frame of reputation-language, just as they are sometimes used in English.

Whatever its phrasing, reputation is especially prominent in Roman economic contexts. It was understood to be intrinsically valuable, an asset that could be used, transactionally, to advance certain goals or attain specific material gains.[37] In this setting, it is often presented as something akin to social capital, a store of goodwill that could be leveraged to overcome obstacles, but it often operated in a more generalized way. Rather than serving to enable specific, large goals, reputation could also smooth the way through many small day-to-day interactions.[38] It helped merchants to overcome negative stereotypes and facilitated the function of regular business, even, at times, resolving larger issues in the economic system by offering shortcuts for decision-making and reducing the number of disputes.

Reputation and New Institutional Economics

In so far as reputation worked in this way, it operated as an institution, a pattern of behavior that provides structure and predictability to the economic world. Institutions hold power as regulatory constructs. They can incentivize or disincentivize behavior and offer either specific or general guidelines for conduct in a given society. Within an economic setting, the theory of Institutional Economics states that institutions, be they formal or informal, shape economic practices and evolve in parallel with new technologies, changes to the environment, and other shifts in cultural, political, or religious life.[39] In the 1970s, the framework of New Institutional Economics, hereafter NIE, was developed to describe a variation on the original theory, one which married institutional

37. As in Publilius Syrus, *Sent.* 75 and 254.

38. As social capital, see Pierre Bourdieu, "Le capital social," *Actes de la recherche en sciences sociales* 31 (1980); Pierre Bourdieu, "The Forms of Capital," in *Handbook of Theory and Research for the Sociology of Education*, ed. J. G. Richardson (New York: Greenwood Press, 1986); Robert D. Putnam, *Bowling Alone: The Collapse and Revival of American Community* (London: Simon and Schuster, 2000), and discussion in chapter 4. We must also consider the impact of the culture of reciprocity in the Mediterranean (e.g., Verboven, *The Economy of Friends*), which also contributed to lowering transaction costs.

39. The papers collected in Warren J. Samuels, ed., *The Founding of Institutional Economics* (New York: Routledge, 1998) reflect on the foundations of this field, going back to the work of Thorstein Veblen and John Rogers Commons.

economics with some elements of neoclassical economic thought, primarily the notion that economic actors are rational and seek to increase their profits by lowering their transaction costs, in part by obeying, and in part by utilizing, institutions.[40] These institutions, generally, restrict tradesmen's choices by making some actions too "costly," in that the negative consequences, or even the risk of negative consequences, outweighs the potential gain. Understanding this, a rational individual will generally avoid costly actions and accept the constraints of the institution, understanding that the limitations are the price of receiving access to the predictability and lowered transaction costs that the institution offers in return.[41]

NIE has recently found a central place in discourse on the ancient economy, and has been touted as both a solution to previously insolvable irrationalities in ancient market behavior and a fad theory that has raised as many issues as it resolves.[42] The theory's recent application among ancient historians, who have been interested, nearly exclusively, in state institutions, such as the law, has warranted both the praise and critique that NIE has lately engendered.[43] While this work has rightly examined the legal institutions that established basic parameters for the Roman economy, including weights and measures, market days,

40. On Institutional Economics as compared to New Institutional Economics, see Jairo Parada, "Original Institutional Economics and New Institutional Economics: Revisiting the Bridges (or the Divide)," *Revista de Economia Institucional* 5 (2005).

41. The name "New Institutional Economics" originated in the work of Oliver Williamson but was popularized by Douglass North. Rudolf Richter, "The New Institutional Economics: Its Start, Its Meaning, Its Prospects," *European Business Organization Law Review* 6.2 (2005) offers a history of the theoretical framework, which was established in North, "The New Institutional Economics"; North, "Institutions"; and Williamson "The New Institutional Economics." Another important early player is Ronald H. Coase, "The New Institutional Economics," *Zeitschrift für die gesamte Staatswissenschaft* 140.1 (1984), whose earlier work laid essential groundwork for NIE.

42. Koenraad Verboven, "The Knights Who Say NIE: Can Neo-Institutional Economics Live Up to Its Expectation in Ancient History Research?" in *Structure and Performance in the Roman Economy: Models, Methods and Case Studies*, ed. Paul Erdkamp and Koenraad Verboven (Brussels: Latomus, 2015) addresses the drawbacks in terms of the adoption of a specifically 1970s version of NIE, which remained quite close to neoclassical economic theory, and presents a pair of visions of a more productive model, including one that embraces behavioral economics, as in this work. More recently, David B. Hollander, Thomas R. Blanton IV, and John T. Fitzgerald, eds., *The Extramercantile Economies of Greek and Roman Cities: New Perspectives on the Economic History of Classical Antiquity* (New York: Routledge, 2019) offered *régulation* theory as another viable alternative. Both behavioral economic theory and *régulation* theory place further emphasis on the impact of social connections on the economy.

43. NIE was presented as central to the field of ancient economics throughout Scheidel, Morris, and Saller, *Cambridge Economic History*, which has been succeeded by work like Alain Bresson, *The Making of the Ancient Greek Economy: Institutions, Markets, and Growth in the City-States* (Princeton: Princeton University Press, 2015); Dennis P. Kehoe, David M. Ratzan, and Uri Yiftach, eds., *Law and Transaction Costs in the Ancient Economy* (Ann Arbor: University of Michigan Press, 2015); Giuseppe Dari-Mattiacci and Dennis P. Kehoe, eds., *Roman law and Economics*, 2 vols. (Oxford: Oxford University Press, 2020).

and opportunities for recourse via magistrates and the courts, it has been selective, at best, in its consideration of merchant agency. It has been made clear that merchant choices were curtailed by legal institutions, that the punishments meted out by officials offered a real incentive for compliance, and that transaction costs were lowered by having the weight of the state behind contracts, but the issue of the different "rationalities" that may have motivated economic decision-making in the ancient world has never been resolved.[44]

Several works on the state and Roman law have recently demonstrated that state institutions were not divorced from the society around them.[45] Governmental and legal structures were inextricably tied to Roman social norms, and they needed to reassert their legitimacy and authority regularly by appealing to the standards of society as a whole. Furthermore, the power of the state and its laws was not applied evenly across Mediterranean communities nor across merchant groups, which must mean that its institutions also lacked uniformity. Corruption and noncompliance were possible, in some cases commonplace, and the system itself survived, in part, because it picked and chose the battles it fought over enforcement, especially over which merchants it would attempt to regulate closely.[46] The strength of state institutions depended, in part, upon the willingness of the community to insist upon widespread compliance with the law and to report misdemeanors to its representatives.

The law was a powerful institution, but it was hardly alone among the institutional pressures that directed merchant decision-making. Fortunately, NIE as it was developed, especially by Douglass North, does not, by definition, limit itself to state institutions.[47] Rather, NIE considers a wide range of possible determinants on market activity, including the powerful structures created by

44. E.g., Lo Cascio, "Setting the Rules of the Game"; and Bruce W. Frier and Dennis P. Kehoe, "Law and Economic Institutions," in *The Cambridge Economic History of the Greco-Roman World*, ed. Walter Scheidel, Ian Morris, Richard P. Saller (Cambridge: Cambridge University Press, 2007). It is worth noting that much of this work remains, in a sense, a response to Finley, *The Ancient Economy*, whose strength was his sensitivity to the differing logics of exchange practices. Dominic W. Rathbone, *Economic Rationalism and Rural Society in Third-Century A.D. Egypt: The Heroninos Archive and the Appianus Estate* (Cambridge: Cambridge University Press, 2012) offers an example of the rationalism that can be found in our sources.

45. Clifford Ando, "Legal Pluralism in Practice," in *The Oxford Handbook of Roman Law and Society*, ed. Paul du Plessis, Clifford Ando, and Kaius Tuori (Oxford: Oxford University Press, 2016); Caroline Humfress, "Thinking through Legal Pluralism: 'Forum Shopping' in the Later Roman Empire," in *Law and Empire: Ideas, Practices, Actors*, ed. Jeroen Duindam, Jill Harries, Caroline Humfress, and Nimrod Hurvitz (Leiden: Brill, 2013); Ari Z. Bryen, "Law in Many Pieces," *Classical Philology* 109.4 (2014); but even earlier Kirschenbaum, *Sons, Slaves, and Freedmen*, was arguing for the power of social norms in economic settings.

46. Bang, *The Roman Bazaar*, ch. 3 and 4.

47. North, "The New Institutional Economics," 231, swiftly turns to state and institutions, but he first acknowledges that some institutions are "self-enforcing," dependent upon social and cultural norms and policed by the community, rather than a political entity.

social norms. Just like the law, informal, social institutions rewarded conformity and discouraged deviance, and, in the market, social norms did much of the same work of dissuading the same bad behavior that the law was created to punish. Norms are culturally, and at times even locally, specific and are at their strongest in communities that are small, invested in replicating themselves, and aware of the dangers of allowing group members to benefit from the consistency that norms provided without adhering to the system's restrictions.

Such figures, known as "free riders," can threaten the integrity of informal or social institutional systems.[48] While a few free riders are often inevitable, too many will weaken the force of an institution by reducing the overall predictability that the institution can provide.[49] If it cannot be relied upon that a merchant will use honest weights and measures, because too many have begun taking advantage of the honesty of others and have started to cheat, then the costs of transactions will rise as trading partners feel the need to double-check, reweigh, or reevaluate their goods. To avoid these rising costs, free riders, once uncovered, must be outed as such, and either brought back into the fold or exposed and subsequently punished or avoided. Often in our sources, it is free riders, those who have sought to take advantage of low transaction costs without accepting restrictions, who have earned a bad reputation. They are known to be untrustworthy, selfish, or greedy and to be the kind of person who would take advantage of the good behavior of others without obeying norms themselves. Their bad reputation is the natural result of the institutions that they have outraged, and a bad reputation acts as an externally enforced institutional limit: the free rider will be involuntarily constrained by the community and his choices will remain limited until he can improve his reputation by demonstrating that he has atoned or otherwise changed his ways.

The language surrounding this behavior—"bad" and "good" reputation—is consistently moralizing. This is the natural consequence of the formation and maintenance of informal, social institutions, which hold their power because they are firmly integrated into the moral landscape of society. The outrage of

---

48. The "Free Rider Problem" has been present from the inception of NIE theory. See Douglass C. North, "Transaction Costs, Institutions, and Economic History," *Zeitschrift für die gesamte Staatswissenschaft* 140.1 (1984): 16; North, "The New Institutional Economics," 234; and North, *Institutions*, ch. 2 and 3. More recently, discussions have branched out to consider a wide range of challenges that free riding could pose to (formal) institutional frameworks, e.g., Michael E. Sykuta and Michael L. Cook, "A New Institutional Economics Approach to Contracts and Cooperatives," *American Journal of Agricultural Economics* 83.5 (2001): 1275; Neil S. Siegel, "Free Riding on Benevolence: Collective Action Federalism and the Minimum Coverage Provision," *Law and Contemporary Problems* 75.3 (2012); Özgür Gürerk, Bernd Irlenbuschand, and Bettina Rockenbach, "The Competitive Advantage of Sanctioning Institutions," *Science* 312.5770 (2006).

49. Explored productively in Carlisle Ford Runge, "Institutions and the Free Rider: The Assurance Problem in Collective Action," *Journal of Politics* 46.1 (1984).

free riding is not objectionable merely because it is an unfair advantage that causes imbalances in the market, but because it is emblematic of unethical behavior: cheating, lying, or another flaw in a person's very nature. These failings are closely aligned with the values of the community, its bedrock beliefs and vision of itself, so any violation is seen as an assault on the integrity of traditions and standards that everyone is, or should be, invested in preserving. In order to protect these *mores*, bad conduct must be immediately elided with bad character, which requires far more effort than a simple apology to emend in the mind of the community, and which brands the malefactor, at times, for life.

Thus, good or bad, a reputation acted as an institution in its own right. The pursuit of a good reputation incentivized certain behaviors, while the hassle of a bad reputation disincentivized others. At the same time, a reputation could also be the consequence of conformity with, or rebellion against, other institutions, of both formal and informal varieties, and functioned as part of the interconnected structures that directed Roman economic activity. Viewing reputation through this lens explains the effort that merchants put into their public conduct, as well as the specific ways they utilized their good name, which is central to the purpose of this work. Investing in a good reputation led to benefits because it communicated a merchant's commitment to social and economic standards, which the community then rewarded as a way to support the continuation of the system as whole.

Like other, informal institutions that were determined and enforced by Roman *mores*, reputation was often more or differently reliable than its formal, state counterparts. While the opinions of some figures might hold more moral weight than others, general community disapproval, social stigma, and both public and private forms of shaming were predictable and commonplace parts of daily life that everyone, including merchants, participated in as a means of regulating their community. While normative behavior could evolve over time, the values of Roman society were largely stable, and frequently aligned with state institutions.[50] Thus legal prohibitions against theft, for example, were well matched with Roman moral standards, and state efforts to regulate the status of merchants, through the use of *infamia*, matched the distaste of the commu-

50. These align with the concepts of "honor" and "shame," explored in John Kennedy Campbell, *Honour, Family and Patronage: A Study of Institutions and Moral Values in a Greek Mountain Community* (Oxford: Oxford University Press, 1964); Peristiany, *Honour and Shame*; David G. Gilmore, ed., *Honor and Shame and the Unity of the Mediterranean* (Washington, DC: American Anthropological Association, 1987); Frank Henderson Stewart, *Honor* (Chicago: University of Chicago Press, 1994); and J. E. Lendon, *Empire of Honour: The Art of Government in the Roman World* (Oxford: Clarendon Press, 1997).

nity for members of certain professions.[51] Moreover, even if a matter could not be brought before Roman justice because of a lack of evidence, corruption, or inadequate access to magistrates, it could still be shamed and punished in the context of Roman society.

The enforcement of norms happened, both publicly and privately, in a variety of ways. Values were instilled in young people to set the tone for proper behavior, while adults were judged according to their adherence to those standards. Malefactors, at an extreme, could be ostracized or publicly shamed, while those who bent the rules might be quietly taken aside by friends or gossiped about behind their backs by their more general acquaintance. These efforts all had an impact on the reputation of the actor, whose standing in society, and access to its benefits, was tied to the expectations that the community held, not only of that person, but of members of their social group, profession, or community members, more generally.

Community self-policing is commonly known as a form of private ordering or private enforcement, the systems by which nonstate actors bring about compliance with nonstate institutions.[52] Private ordering comes in numerous forms but is most visible among merchants in the Roman world through the contracts and charters developed by groups of allied merchants.[53] These documents have been well studied in recent years, and the evidence shows that merchants held specific, clearly articulated ideas about what constituted acceptable behavior, in a context where the behavior of the individual would not only affect their personal reputation, but also the reputation of the group.[54] These standards were made publicly available in order to broadcast the good reputation and good intentions of the association as well as to make the shame and punishment of any who would disregard these rules all the more apparent. Those who violated the regulations could expect to be met with sanctions, which could come in a variety of forms ranging from minor fines to exclusion and expulsion from the group.

Such documents record a semiformal arrangement that played out among peers who had consented to follow the rules of the collective, but it is also possible to trace the institutional force of reputation in the daily lives of merchants

51. Bond, *Trade and Taboo*, esp. 7–16.

52. Discussed fully in chapter 5.

53. These were often preserved, interestingly, because they were filed with government offices or inscribed in public places. Michaela Langellotti, "A World Full of Associations: Rules and Community Values in Early Roman Egypt," in *Private Associations in the Ancient Greek World: Regulations and the Creation of Group Identity*, ed. Vincent Gabrielsen and Mario C. D. Paganini (Cambridge: Cambridge University Press, 2021) discusses this hybrid of public and private authority in early Roman Egypt.

54. Venticinque, *Honor among Thieves*; and Hawkins, *Roman Artisans*.

who were not affiliated with an association. In those cases, the expectations of family, friends, colleagues, and neighbors established parameters for the behavior of merchants, and we can see that merchants expressed, in many ways, their dedication to meeting or exceeding those expectations. Their efforts to build a good reputation are apparent both in the way they speak about themselves and the way they are spoken about by others, and it is equally clear that Roman society had several ways to punish merchants who failed to meet the standards set by the community at large.

The language surrounding merchant reputation reflects the notion of collective standards by leaning heavily upon morality. Not only is it a merchant's reputation that is "bad" when he or she fails to meet the expectations of the community, but the merchant him- or herself is understood to be morally corrupted, as well. Merchants, in the abstract, were thought of as immoral figures, and when evidence was available to corroborate this stereotype, it was understood that the general principle was correct, and the thinker or speaker was justified in their beliefs and statements.[55] "Goodness" was difficult to achieve as a merchant, but our evidence shows that this was indisputably their goal. Their written and visual media is filled with indications that they shared the *mores* of their communities and sought to demonstrate their commitment to virtue.

Nevertheless, whether the perspective is that of the elite person, looking at merchants from the outside, or comes from merchant peers or customers, our evidence is clear that trade was a potential source of moral degradation. Even when addressing each other, merchants evidently believed that their fellow businessmen were not necessarily trustworthy, and that it was, in general, a good idea to trust, but verify, by seeking out as much external information as possible. While we inevitably see merchants mostly represented from external perspectives, there are many instances where merchants speak for themselves, and it is telling that they regularly stress their own exceptional personal virtue, rather than try to make a case for the morality of their professions in a broader sense. Like Philostratus' Phoenician, they understood that their own reputation was something they could influence, while societal perceptions of trade were far too large and complex to be readily shifted by the actions of an individual.

---

55. This tendency is generally known as "confirmation bias" and has been studied extensively. Some useful framing was done by John J. Skowronski and Donal E. Carlston, "Negativity and Extremity Biases in Impression Formation: A Review of Explanations," *Psychology Bulletin* 105 (1989); John J. Skowronski and Donal E. Carlston, "Caught in the Act: When Impressions Based on Highly Diagnostic Behaviours Are Resistant to Contradiction," *European Journal of Social Psychology* 22.5 (1992); and Michael B. Lupfer, Matthew Weeks, and Susan Dupuis, "How Pervasive Is the Negativity Bias in Judgments Based upon Character Appraisals?" *Personality and Social Psychology Bulletin* 26.11 (2000).

Sources

In what follows, a wide range of sources will be used to assess how merchants worked to build, maintain, and utilize their reputations. Beginning from the outside, looking in, elite sources quickly make themselves apparent. Most obvious are narrative sources like Philostratus, whose fictional depictions of merchants often mingle generic traits and tropes with situations that may well have occurred in reality. Novels, parables, and fables all occasionally use merchants as characters, and, as has been argued persuasively by Fergus Millar and Koenraad Verboven, it is often possible to find in such stories elements of daily life, used by the authors to help the audience suspend their disbelief.[56] While none of these sources may be taken at face value, there are professionals in these texts who are not simply intended to be comic or serve to advance the plot, but rather populate the world with figures who would be recognizable to a Roman reader. While it is right for us to doubt the historicity of a character like Petronius' Trimalchio, there remains value in the casual way in which his world is populated by tradesmen socializing with, gossiping about, and assessing one another.[57]

Similarly, satirical writing occasionally selects merchants, and often specifically merchant freedmen, as a target for derision. Such references signal that there were instances where social and economic boundaries might be threatened by those in trade, especially when they grew too wealthy or powerful to be ignored.[58] Historical texts also occasionally report cases where a merchant interacts with a famous political figure or where it is revealed that a noble Roman family had merchant-skeletons in its closet.[59] For the purposes of understanding merchant reputation, these sources offer the essentialized view of Roman merchants—the stereotype—presented through the lens of elite distaste. It is often impossible to assess the original actions or intentions of such merchants, but their interactions with elites, and distinctions drawn between their work and forms of trade undertaken by others, are nevertheless enlightening.

56. Fergus Millar, "The World of the Golden Ass," *Journal of Roman Studies* 71 (1981) and Koenraad Verboven, "A Funny Thing Happened on My Way to the Market: Reading Petronius to Write Economic History," in *Petronius: A Handbook*, ed. Jonathan Prag and Ian Repath (Oxford: Wiley-Blackwell, 2009) both present models for drawing historical realities out of fictional, and even hyperbolic, narratives. In such efforts, sensitivity to genre is essential and it is rarely main characters who will furnish the best evidence.

57. Petron., *Sat.* 28–71, the *Cena Trimalchionis*, introduces at least five merchants (not counting those among the entertainers or enslaved workers), casually discusses a number of commercial professions through Trimalchio's digression on astrology, and regularly uses metaphors relating to trade and artisanal work.

58. Trimalchio remains the archetypal figure here, though Roman satire and epigram contain many similar upstart freedmen, e.g., Mart. *Epigr.* 2.58.

59. E.g., Suet., *Aug.* 4.2; Plut., *Cic.* 1; Gell., *N. A.* 15.4.

Beyond fictional or historical narratives, there is substantial evidence of merchants in Roman legal sources. These offer us the mechanics of at least some kinds of Roman trade, as well as insight into the efforts of the state to regulate and police market activity. While this material privileges the view of the state and those merchants who worked directly with it, the state's attempts to claim (or reclaim) authority over the economy offer us a sense of the extent of state intervention. In these sources, we see merchant agency and can even occasionally find points where merchants dodged state regulations.[60] Naturally, any deviation from the law is presented as a reflection of the true, bad character of merchants, but the existence of free-agent merchants provides an interesting window into how merchants dealt with authority. While direct statements about the reputation of merchants are rare in these sources, they are fairly consistent in their negative portrayal.[61] More common are neutral statements of what the law is and how it should be obeyed, along with records, especially in papyrological documents, showing merchant compliance with the state's regulation.

Merchant responses to the state are quite rare, but the few examples we have show how the Roman government was viewed from the outside. As we will discuss, and despite their negative press, merchants with state contracts seem to have felt empowered to negotiate with Roman officials, to defend their rights and privileges, and to bring cases to higher powers when they felt themselves abused or mistreated. Generally, they appeal to the state by providing evidence of their good service and utility to Rome, rather than by arguing for their good character, which is a tactic they reserve for working with each other and the general public.

The reputation strategies of merchants are most visible in those latter, outward-facing efforts, where merchants invested time, energy, and funds into crafting and displaying a public persona. Much of this work is only now extant via funerary markers, which offer a complicated perspective on merchant reputation. Not only is the epigraphic record biased, including a heavy preponderance of data from the Italian peninsula and North Africa in the imperial period, but these sources were often created either by the merchant in anticipation of their death, or were posthumously commissioned by family, friends, or freedmen, whose own authorial voice and intentions complicate the meaning of the words themselves. The impact of grief in such commemorative objects is unclear, though the corpus reveals that, in many cases, *formulae* were employed

60. A good case is *Cod. Theod.* 13.5.16.1–2 (Trier, February 6, 380 CE), where merchants have not only demanded the state offer them support, but where merchants outside of a corpus are shown attempting to masquerade as members to enjoy their privileges.

61. E.g., Edict on Maximum Prices, lines 122, 145–53; Ulp., *Dig.* 4.9.1.1.

to capture more general aspects of a merchant's life and achievements. These sources can also offer visual evidence in the form of reliefs of merchants, who use imagery in several ways. While many merchants emphasize their professions in these settings, showing themselves in their workshops or traveling with their goods, others prefer to show themselves in more traditional portrait styles, and it is impossible to know what motivations lay behind these choices, or how many merchants may lurk behind images that lack specific references to economic activity.

We often have more insight into decisions that were made by living merchants in pursuit of their good reputations. Wall paintings, monuments, participation in festivals, and public dedications, as well as more private acts like household decoration, apprenticeship contracts, and acts of generosity, all provide evidence of concerted efforts made by merchants to demonstrate their goodwill, trustworthiness, and community mindedness through references to their professions. As we will discuss, no single act, nor even many acts in concert, could generate a good reputation without the support of daily, casual reliability, quality, and honesty, but these efforts leave us with substantial proof that a good reputation was deemed a worthwhile investment and that merchants believed it could be built up through concrete means.

Among and between merchants, we also have the evidence of contracts and associations. Archives of charters and legally binding documents, especially from Egypt, offer us insight into when and how reputation was useful to merchants. It is apparent that deals were struck on the strength of a merchant's good name, and admission into societies helped merchants to make new ties and discover new avenues for displaying their character. These groups were not always explicitly economic in their focus, but even groups that were primarily religious or social in nature could be useful as tools for networking and spreading a good reputation. Additionally, the evidence of religious texts should not be underestimated, as these works offer a variety of different kinds of evidence, ranging from letters of introduction to narratives and parables. These often offer insight into the situation of merchants, especially in the eastern Mediterranean, and lend weight to the case that reputation was understood as a representation of one's moral worth.

Generally, the funerary and nonfunerary sources produced by merchants are concerned with displaying the best characteristics of the professions they describe. The positive bias of these sources offers insight into what strategies merchants thought would be effective means of spreading their good character, as well as evidence for the anxieties that plagued the population of professional retailers, artisans, and transporters. It is from these sources that we may assess the extent to which stereotypes and negative bias against tradesmen was felt, since it is in these settings that we see merchants stress generosity, honesty, and quality, in the face of accusations of greed, deceit, and cheating. Merchant emphasis on these traits demonstrates that they felt an impulse to push back against specific portions of the stereotype, while allowing other negative claims to slip away without comment.[62]

Finally, merchant reputation is depicted from the outside in a variety of forms of evidence produced by customers and nonelite individuals. Ranging from graffiti to jokes, fables, and idioms, merchants are common figures in popular statements, and these can be found offering both praise and condemnation. Quality, or lack thereof, is often stressed in these contexts, with merchants at times called upon by name to answer for their bad service, dishonest measures, or personal peccadilloes. While it is evident in these sources that stereotypes about merchants were believed at all rungs of the social ladder, popular culture seems to have been interested in the mockery of merchants in the abstract, and specific praise, or censure, at the level of the individual. This is not necessarily surprising, given that nonelite people would be more greatly harmed by a cheating merchant than a wealthy person, but the general bias is perhaps less intuitive, as these are the people who also would have lived and worked among merchants, and would have known them first as neighbors and acquaintances, if not as friends and family.

Roman Perceptions of Trade

The source of this distaste originates more clearly in the general perception of trade in Roman society than from any universal experience. As mentioned above, trade was considered a competitive undertaking, where the terms of a deal did not reflect a mutual agreement between the parties so much as the uneasy truce between combatants who anticipated further hostilities. Customers did not so much experience buyer's remorse, as the conviction that they might have just managed to pull off an unlikely victory over an enemy. The language of haggling in the Roman world reflects this perspective, often using metaphors of wrestling, fighting, or combat.[63] While this battle-narrative might

62. Negative traits are emphasized in texts like Cic., *Off.* 1.150–51 (42). Interestingly, cleanliness is not generally addressed in merchant sources but is a common accusation in sources about them, see Jack J. Lennon, *Dirt and Denigration: Stigma and Marginalisation in Ancient Rome* (Tübingen: Mohr Siebeck, 2022); Bond, *Trade and Taboo*, ch. 2–3.

63. Apul., *Met.* 1.24 uses *vix . . . extorsimus* to describe the process of haggling; Philostratus' vinedresser (Philostr., *Her.* 1.7) describes what he feels is the unnecessary step of haggling as

have cast the merchant as a "worthy opponent," under different circumstances, instead, it often represented them as the party to blame for the unnecessary labor exerted by customers trying to get a fair deal.[64] Not only were merchants hindrances, but there was also no public conception that merchants performed any valuable labor in the economy.[65] In fact, the term *labor* was not considered a concept that applied to the work of most wholesalers and retailers, who were seen as middlemen who raised prices on goods without providing any added value to the products themselves.[66]

To the Roman mind, there were producers, who had some skill, and therefore some utility to society, and then there were associated hangers-on, whose work was an unnecessary intervention between consumers and the sources of goods themselves.[67] The ideal scenario was the elimination of these parasitical figures, especially if it was possible to replace them, in some way, with one's own personal production. This was considered the ideal state for humans in Roman society, and the dream of self-sufficiency was commonplace not only among the general public, but also among merchants themselves.[68] While, as we will discuss, reputation and the successful operation of any business required contact with and dependence on others, many merchants still strove to demonstrate that they were not a burden on others or society, that they made their own way, and that they rendered more services than they required. This creates a tension in our sources by and about merchants, as we see those in trade trying to show that their only impact on the community was in the positive, while those around them argue for the superfluity of merchants as drains on society, creating unnecessary steps in the supply chain of the ancient world.[69]

"speaking and listening," εἰπών τε καὶ ἀκούσας. These kinds of negotiation are an understudied corner of Roman trading practice, but the language choices offer critical insight into Roman attitudes toward trade. They reveal a preference, as noted by Andrea Giardina, "The Merchant," in *The Romans*, ed. Andrea Giardina (Chicago: University of Chicago Press, 1993), 248–49, for "silent barter" which was believed to prevent lying and fraud.

64. There was an ongoing concern about getting a "just" price for goods, see discussions: Paul Veyne and Osywn Murray, *Bread and Circuses: Historical Sociology and Political Pluralism* (London: Penguin, 1992), 52–53; Lo Cascio, "Setting the Rules of the Game"; Marta Giacchero, "L'illusoria imposizione del giusto prezzo nell'editto-calmiere di Diocleziano," *Rendiconti* 19 (1964).

65. Giardina, "The Merchant," 246–47.

66. The case of Hadrian's law on middlemen in the fishing trade is instructive, IG II-III 1103 (sometimes written as IG 2^3.1103), see discussions of Morris Silver, "In Dubious Battle: An Economic Analysis of Emperor Hadrian's Fish and Olive Oil Laws," *Roman Legal Tradition* 7 (2011); and Luuk de Ligt, "The Nunidinae of L. Bellicius Sollers," in *De agricultura: In Memoriam Pieter-Willem de Neeve*, ed. Heleen Sancisi-Weerdenburg (Amsterdam: J. C. Gieben, 1993), 250–51.

67. Cic., *Off.* 1.150–51 (42) offers the most extensive ranking of merchants, as well as a basis for their classification into further subtypologies.

68. E.g., Trimalchio's claims at Petron., *Sat.* 48, or Paul's urgings in 1 Thessalonians 4:10b–12.

69. *Pace* Finley, *The Ancient Economy*, who would dispute the awareness that ancient economic actors could have had of such a concept.

There is an obvious tension present in how merchants wished to be viewed and in the reputations that they ultimately developed. In what follows, we will consider the varying tactics that merchants used to promulgate their vision of themselves, as well as their successes and failures within the context of Roman society. Navigating the challenges of the social and economic landscape of the Roman world was a heavy burden on merchants, but our evidence demonstrates that they were creative in their problem-solving, judicious in their decision-making, and ultimately committed to building and utilizing social institutional power to advance themselves economically. Reputation was their tool of choice, as it was flexible and effective in a range of circumstances. Furthermore, it could be built and maintained by anyone in Roman society, making it universally recognized, even as an antidote to other forms of prejudice. Fundamentally, reputation could lead a merchant to "success," regardless of what that looked like at the level of the individual.

Chapters

It will be the purpose of this book to offer an analysis of reputation as an institution among Roman merchants across the whole of the geographic and temporal extent of the Roman world, but with emphasis on the imperial period. While our evidence does not suggest that merchant strategies for or uses of reputation change greatly over the period, the empire provides a density of evidence that enables us, at times, to spot practices that were more or less common in different regions, while also setting these merchants within a similar legal and political landscape. If state institutions form a substantial and important backdrop to Roman merchant activities, then the imperial period should offer something approaching the most even playing field they could have experienced. However effective they were, state institutions are likely to have been at their most efficacious in the first three centuries CE, and any variations that persist in merchant behavior are therefore more likely to be the consequence of other factors than of state influence.

The first chapter of this work examines these formal economic institutions, the Roman state and its laws, in relation to Roman merchants, aiming to assess the scale and circumstances of their impact. By examining the law, and by considering its intentions, promulgation, and enforcement, we will determine the extent to which we may attribute a concerted "policy" to Roman economic law. We will analyze the circumstances in which merchants engaged with the state directly and the options that were available to merchants within and beyond state structures. While it will be apparent that the state held a vested interest in seeing the economy operate smoothly and that it held substantial political, cultural, and economic power to implement its institutions, it will also be argued that the state's was one power among numerous others, and that the state's efforts display not so much a desire to shape and structure the daily work of the economy, as an effort to maintain the status quo, and especially its revenues from, and limited investments in, the provinces. Corruption and irregularities in local practices are common in our sources, and evidently caused merchants and local officials alike to depend on informal institutions. These helped compensate for the unpredictable economic landscape that resulted from the state's, at times, sporadic and uneven enforcement. The interrelation of state and social institutions will be explored in the context of tolls and customs, where personalities and relationships directed the course of merchant business as much as the law itself, and particular attention will be paid to instances where private-ordering supplemented state regulations and punishments.

In the second chapter, we will turn to reputation and analyze its nature. Throughout this effort, we will examine different aspects of reputation, including major factors in developing a good name, the relationship between one reputation and another, and the processes by which neutral information was converted into evidence for reputation. In particular, this chapter looks at how the consistency of a merchant's character and behavior was a major factor in both building a good reputation and preventing a bad one. Because merchants were likely, due to the prevalent bias against them in Roman culture, to have a bad reputation, it was essential to amass as much evidence of good behavior as possible, the better to offset the confirmation bias that accompanied any accidental or incidental misconduct. Though merchants at times invested in larger displays of virtue, a choice that redirected merchant wealth, time, and energy away from their businesses, this chapter emphasizes the power of small, daily acts of reliable quality and good character. These were the primary means through which the community judged merchants and the best hope of merchants who sought a good name. Reputation, in that setting, developed dialectically, through the constant involvement and witnessing of the community, which attributed meaning to merchant behaviors, big and small, and constantly compared merchants to one another, assessing not only who was good and who was bad, but also who was better and who was worse.

Chapter 3 considers reputation as it was developed and maintained by merchants over their lifetime. Beginning with apprenticeships and other instances of merchants starting a career, the chapter analyzes how junior merchants relied on the reputations of others to support them and to secure the funds and goodwill needed to begin a new venture. In providing clarity for how reputation shaped the interpersonal relationships of merchants from the very start of their careers, it is possible to see that the playing field was by no means level, as merchants with better connections had a substantial advantage over their peers. They would move swiftly through the obstacles of getting a start in their profession and would swiftly become respected fixtures in their communities. These well-reputed midcareer merchants had a range of means for supporting and expanding on their good reputations, including options for engaging in collaborative reputation strategies with other merchants, making public displays of generosity, or advertising their businesses. The chapter concludes with an examination of the posthumous reputation strategies used by merchants in their attempts to have the "last word" about their characterization. As much of our evidence from merchants comes from funerary contexts, it is essential to understand the impulses that drove merchants to care for their reputations even after death. In this, theoretical approaches to posthumous reputation offer us insight for why both merchants and their survivors might invest in these ways, in this moment: to control the posthumous conversation, to offer protection to a surviving family business, or to offer a final demonstration of the virtues that had supported a career from its start to beyond its finish.

Since it took more than a lifetime to develop, expand, and protect a good reputation, chapter 4 turns to the reasons for making such efforts: the uses of a good reputation, especially in the face of negative stereotypes. The chapter focuses on the return on the investment merchants received—the positive side of the institutional balance—where merchants were rewarded for conforming to social norms and performing Roman *mores*. The chapter begins by analyzing the impact of stereotypes, and especially on the tropes of greedy and deceitful merchants, to understand how merchants responded when faced with the tacit or explicit assumption that they would conform to stereotypes. Especially vital in this setting is merchant *fides* and the role of trust in business, both as a form of social capital and as the literal framework that determined who would receive loans and who would not. Beyond lending, the chapter also looks at disputes and how the relative power of reputation, more than logic or evidence, often settled such matters. Merchants leveraged their reputation in such scenarios, and often held, through their reputations, substantial power within their local contexts, at times even beyond more elite outsiders.

Finally, in chapter 5, we turn to the mechanisms that spread information about reputation and the negative institutional power that reputation held to prevent and punish behavior that contravened social norms. After merchants did their best to project their self-image to the world around them, the next step was for their audiences to communicate their interpretations of that image to others. In the Roman world, this generally occurred in one of two ways: through letters and other written means, on the one hand, or through oral communication, especially gossip, on the other. While written sources tend to preserve examples of the spread of good reputation, as in the case of letters of recommendation, the oral culture around reputation more often spread negative information, the sort of thing one might hesitate to put in writing, but which needed to be told, both as exciting news and as a warning to those who might consider involving themselves with a new, or old, trading partner. Though, as we will discuss, gossip need not be idle, vicious, or (in)accurate, it functioned as a regular outlet for communities to spread news, with or without hyperbole, about merchants and their actions. Merchants were nervous about what unrestrained talk of this kind might do to their reputations and recognized that much of their work to preserve their good name was actually about shaping the form that the community's gossip would take. Since gossip occurs, by definition, behind the back of the person it is about, merchants generally operated without full knowledge of what was being said about them, having to imagine it and make choices in light of that imagining. Above all, merchants knew that the gossiping communities around them might choose to punish a bad actor in their midst, and that they could do so with a few well-chosen words or elevate the matter to action. Private-order enforcement of this kind structured merchant choices and manifested in a range of different levels of punishment, from a quiet word of warning to a public display of shaming. Fear of these rebukes kept merchants in line, lest public ridicule exacerbate the stigma that already existed. The rules of the institution were unwritten, but powerful, and kept merchants on the straight and narrow of Roman societal expectations.

Collectively, this work argues that merchants were cognizant of these pressures, and that they recognized the institutional power that their reputations held, even if they lacked the terminology to define it as such. Merchants knew that they needed to develop and protect their good name and their investment in it shaped every element of their personal and economic lives. Social norms shaped all the daily workings of the Roman world, but, for merchants, navigating these constraints and building a good reputation was the key to a successful business and made the difference between getting lost or getting by in the unpredictable world of the Roman economy.

CHAPTER 1

Merchants and the Roman Empire

Semina ferendi leges fragilitas humani generis subministrat, repetitio vero legum nostrae est humantitatis indicum, si quidem, cum priorum aculei adversus temeratores earum sufficerent corrigendos, admoneri tamen per legis repetitionem delinquentes volumus quam poenas exigi delictorum. Ideo calcatam legem . . . olim fuerat promulgata, suggestione tuae sublimitatis edocti humanis sensibus saluberrima repetere scita conpellimur.

The frailty of the human race provides the opportunities for producing laws, but the repetition of laws is a sign of our humanity. Accordingly, although the stings of earlier acts against violators of the law were sufficient for correcting them, nevertheless we want people who are committing a crime to be warned by the repetition of the law, rather than for penalties to be exacted for crimes committed. Therefore, informed by the suggestion of your splendor that the law, which had once been promulgated, has been trampled upon . . . we are compelled by our human feelings to repeat our most beneficial ordinances.

—Novels of Theodosius 8 (Constantinople, April 7, 439 CE)[1]

Economic activity can never be fully divorced from the society in which it takes place. Inevitably, social and cultural norms intrude upon economic decision-making and determine where, when, and how commerce will occur. No matter how rationally the path to economic success is laid out, "human frailty" has a way of necessitating that we reexamine its course in light of the world that exists around it. This concept, generally referred to as "economic embeddedness," was introduced to the study of the ancient economy through the work of Moses Finley, and it has continued to shape the debates of the field even as arguments have been marshaled for and against Finley's other positions.[2] Since Finley

1. *De navibus ultra duorum milium modiorum capacitatem non excusandis*, based on the text of Theodor Mommsen and Paul M. Meyer, eds., *Codex Theodosianus* (Berlin: Weidmann, 1905).

2. Finley, *The Ancient Economy*, with responses coming early and often. For a recent retrospective, see Alessandro Launaro, "Finley and the Ancient Economy," in *M. I. Finley: An Ancient Historian and His Impact*, ed. Daniel Jew, Robin Osborne, and Michael Scott (Cambridge: Cam-

strongly believed that "economics" was an anachronistic category that could not be productively applied to ancient forms of exchange, many scholars have sought to defend the complexity of ancient commerce and demonstrate that intricate economic systems existed in antiquity, even if they were not supported by explicit economic theory. Nevertheless, few have found substantial reason to question Finley's instinct that it is vital to contextualize our discussions within ancient social and cultural practices.[3] Most are satisfied with this much: economic behavior, however sophisticated or rudimentary it may be, occurs within a social and cultural setting, and this backdrop influences how, and under what conditions, production, distribution, and exchange will happen.

In recent years, the study of ancient economics has devoted substantial attention to how the economy was embedded in the political world, and how political circumstances shaped economic activity by offering, or withholding, the structures that economic actors required to trade with confidence. In fact, this is the main theoretical advancement that has been derived from North's presentation of NIE.[4] North held that institutions, structures of various types that placed limits upon economic actors, existed in the world and their strength or weakness had a direct correlation to the level of confidence that buyers and sellers had that their contracted agreements could be enforced. In the years since North, NIE has been rightly critiqued for its belief that a market economy will rationally police itself and that "bad" institutions will naturally give way to "good" ones through a process akin to natural selection, but the basic conception of institutions has remained relevant due to its utility—as a tool to discuss abstractions and their impact on market confidence and interpersonal trust.[5]

Within the study of the ancient economy, NIE grew in popularity as an explanatory tool in the 1990s and early 2000s. It came fully to the fore in the

bridge University Press, 2016), who emphasizes the correctness of Finley's "embedded" approach. Finley was heavily influenced by both Karl Polanyi and Max Weber, from whom he drew essential conclusions; see the foreword to Finley: Ian Morris, foreword to *The Ancient Economy* (Berkeley: University of California Press, 1999).

3. Though the question of a "modern" versus "primitive" ancient economy has largely been sidelined as unfruitful, it was a debate that occupied a large portion of the nineteenth and early twentieth centuries. For a summary of the debate, see Richard P. Saller, "Framing the Debate over Growth in the Ancient Economy," in *The Ancient Economy: Evidence and Models*, ed. J. G. Manning and Ian Morris (Stanford: Stanford University Press, 2005).

4. Presented, in different ways, in North, "Transaction Costs"; "The New Institutional Economics"; "Institutions"; and Douglass C. North, *Understanding the Process of Economic Change* (Oxford: Oxford University Press, 2005). North has become the most famous proponent of NIE, but his work owes much to the scholarship of Oliver Williamson and Ronald Coase.

5. A useful analysis, including critiques, is Verboven, "The Knights Who Say NIE." Some scholars have also asserted that society and culture are not useful in a NIE framework, though this was never part of North's original formulation and, as we will argue, is patently false in the case of the ancient economy.

Cambridge Economic History of the Greco-Roman World in 2007, where it was heralded as the path forward and a means of moving away from previous, stagnated (and stagnating) debates about modernity, scale, and growth.[6] NIE was proposed as a way to discuss changes in the economy that did not require hard, quantitative data, a problem that had led to a series of dead ends in years previous, and aligned with the general consensus that the economy could not, and should not, be divorced from the Roman world at large. The *Cambridge Economic History* presented NIE as the tool that would explain the relationship between changes in the economy and changes in the apparatus of the state by taking law, especially, as the institution par excellence of the ancient world. In recent years, this perspective has taken off, even as NIE itself has been criticized, defended, and reasserted.[7] "Law and the economy" is now one of the dominant forms of analysis in ancient economic history, uniting even scholars who once held opposing opinions.[8] Within the study of ancient merchants, the principles of NIE have lately become axiomatic, with the pervasive assumption that legal status and institutional limitations were the dominant structuring mechanisms in merchant lives.[9]

In order to discuss the reputation of Roman merchants, and to establish reputation as an institution in its own right, it is necessary to address this perspective and, to an extent, to dislodge both "law" and "the state" from positions of absolutely centrality in our considerations. Government and legal structures

6. Scheidel, Morris, and Saller, *Cambridge Economic History*, especially Frier and Kehoe, "Law and Economic Institutions."

7. Criticisms have come from numerous scholars: e.g., Claude Menard, "Methodological Issues in New Institutional Economics," *Journal of Economic Methodology* 8.1 (2001); Giorgos Meramveliotakis, "New Institutional Economics: A Critique of Fundamentals and Broad Strokes towards an Alternative Theoretical Framework for the Analysis of Institutions," *Asian Journal of Social Science Studies* 3.2 (2018); Verboven, "The Knights Who Say NIE."

8. Recently in Dari-Mattiacci and Kehoe, *Roman Law and Economics*, especially volume 1, which brings together a wide range of topics under an explicitly institutional umbrella, but also Kehoe, Ratzan, and Yiftach, *Law and Transaction Costs*.

9. Though the field was focused on the impositions of law as a structure in merchant life well before use of NIE became widespread, especially with regard to slavery, e.g., D'Arms, *Commerce and Social Standing*; Joshel, *Work, Identity, and Legal Status*; Robert Knapp, *Invisible Romans* (Cambridge, MA: Harvard University Press, 2011); and Sarah E. Bond, "Altering Infamy: Status, Violence, and Civic Exclusion in Late Antiquity," *Classical Antiquity* 33.1 (2014). NIE, in conjunction with legal institutions is now well-rooted in ancient economic scholarship, e.g., Elio Lo Cascio, "The Role of the State in the Roman Economy: Making Use of the New Institutional Economics," in *Ancient Economies, Modern Methodologies: Archaeology, Comparative History, Models and Institutions*, ed. Peter F. Bang, Mamoru Ikeguchi, and Harmut Ziche (Bari: Edipuglia, 2006); Alain Bresson, "Économie et Institution: Bilan critique des thèses polanyiennes et propositions nouvelles," in *Autour de Polanyi: Vocabulaires, théories et modalités des échange: Nanterre, 12–14 juin 2004*, ed. Philippe Clancier, Francis Joannes, Pierre Rouillard, and Aline Tenu (Paris: De Boccard, 2005); Bresson, *Making of the Ancient Greek Economy*; Terpstra, *Trading Communities*; Taco Terpstra, *Trade in the Ancient Mediterranean: Private Order and Public Institutions* (Princeton: Princeton University Press, 2019); Kehoe, Ratzan, and Yiftach, *Law and Transaction Costs*; Dari-Mattiacci and Kehoe, *Roman Law and Economics*.

undoubtedly shaped the lives of Roman merchants and provided limitations that constrained merchant choices, but the evidence of the Roman world amply demonstrates that the power of these institutions was not absolute, nor were their effects always evenly distributed. As the Novel of Theodosius quoted above indicates, it was often necessary to repeat laws, refine them, and try again, as laws were "trampled upon" over time and regularly fell into disuse. The law was always a work in progress, and one that affected some residents of the Empire differently than others, and at different times. In fact, the very unevenness of Roman law, on the one hand, and the distribution and (in)efficacy of enforcement, on the other hand, lies at the heart of reputation's power in the lives of Roman merchants. Because the state and its legal judgment was, at times, unreliable, unavailable, or even unfair, social institutions were necessary to supplement legal institutions—to smooth the way for trade and to prevent behaviors that would erode consumer and trader confidence, weakening the bonds of trust that were essential for the market to operate.

Roman law, itself a complicated category, as we will discuss, was not always available or considered inherently trustworthy. Had there not been informal systems that bridged the gap between the law and the practical operation of daily commerce, hesitancy about the law, like the pervasive distrust of merchants, could have led to a collapse of the economy. Without some trust, however it was generated, contracts, and even simple promises, could not have been enforced. If contracts failed, a domino-like sequence could kick in, culminating in an end to the distribution of goods, services, and capital as producers and distributors lost faith in the system and, through their growing distrust, lost faith in one another.

Ultimately, it was a medley of different institutions that collectively generated enough trust to keep the system working. The Roman state was one, important means of seeking redress when a dispute became otherwise insoluble, and social institutions, like reputation, provided additional structures to support economic activity—before, as, and after a deal was made. Each institution was generated by and relied upon different kinds of input and stimulus to be maximally effective. Reputation depended, as we will discuss in the following chapters, on the strength of interpersonal relationships and private systems of enforcement, while the state-issued local, regional, and imperial pronouncements developed in response to specific complaints. As others have argued, Roman law was primarily a reactive system, which, even when it could have utilized the precedent of earlier judgments or legal pronouncements, tended to deal with each case individually.[10] Emperors addressed issues as they were

10. Fergus Millar, *The Emperor in the Roman World, 31 BC–AD 337* (Ithaca: Cornell University

brought to their, or their staff's, attention, and magistrates, who served as the primary arbiters of Roman justice in the cities and provinces of the Empire, tended to use their own judgment, or appealed up the ladder to the governor or to Rome, when they lacked the requisite knowledge themselves.

Consequently, Roman law was only as accessible or as fair as the magistrates themselves chose to, or could, be, and there was a wide range of intentions and abilities among them, not always corresponding to their level of responsibility. As a result, receiving justice from the state could be an uncertain undertaking.[11] Magistrates could be difficult to access and similar disputes could be resolved very differently in different parts of the Empire. Though both customers and merchants made use of the law, our evidence suggests that everyone involved understood that, in all likelihood, justice would only be received through a mixture of knowledge of legal processes and precedents, access to and familiarity with relevant magistrates, and a combination of good fortune and being in the right to begin with. Reputation and interpersonal connections were ever present considerations, even, and perhaps especially, when dealing with state representatives. Those who were disconnected or noncitizens at times had difficulty getting their matter heard speedily and fairly before Roman justice, while well-established locals and prominent citizens had many advantages, including social capital that they could leverage to their own benefit.

Magistrates generally did not reach out to address even obvious problems within their provinces, towns, or neighborhoods. Roman magistrates had limited staff and resources, and they were, at times, unfamiliar with the regions where they held jurisdiction. They largely depended on local customs and local figures to maintain economic activity. Thus, even when we see the state attempting to use the law to control merchants, those efforts are overwhelmingly targeted at the professionals who supplied the state, not the everyman retailer or artisan in a local marketplace. The former, as we will discuss, were the most "visible" to state agents, while the latter might escape the notice of authorities if they regulated themselves, did not openly oppose or undermine Roman rule, and had the good fortune of not needing legal assistance.

In the following, we will consider these interrelated issues: the shape and accessibility of Roman law, the methods of enforcement that were available to the Roman state, and the efforts that were made to control merchant activity.

Press, 1977); and Serena Connolly, *Lives behind the Laws: The World of the Codex Hermogenianus* (Bloomington: Indiana University Press, 2010). See also the discussion of laws regarding immunity below.

11. Connolly, *Lives behind the Laws*, ch. 1, discusses many of the challenges as well as the procedures and some of their alternatives.

We will see that Roman law was hardly a monolith, but rather was derived from a combination of formal regulations and informal, often local, practices that created, even at the time of the great codifications of Roman law in the fifth and sixth centuries CE, a variety of sources of legal authority and extralegal avenues for redress. Next, it will become apparent that the state often lacked the resources, especially in the provinces, to adequately enforce the law and bring about punishment when warranted. Moreover, it was not cost-effective for the Roman state to invest in the kind of on-the-ground representatives necessary to enforce the law. It was cheaper, and, for the state's purposes, nearly as effective, to leave peacekeeping in the hands of local magistrates and authority figures, and to deal primarily with matters that were brought directly to their attention. It will be argued that this was not a failure of the system, but rather a widely understood reality that merchants were well prepared to accommodate. Finally, when the state did pass laws designed to manage, direct, and control merchant activity, it will be argued that these were mostly targeted, in enforcement if not always in letter, at those merchants whose work directly served the state. The state had a vested interest in monitoring the actions of these figures, if not in absolutely controlling their businesses, and was content to allow other, small-scale, and private merchants to regulate themselves, which they mostly did by relying on other, informal institutions that shaped their decisions and helped to prevent or resolve their disputes.

The Pluralism of Roman Law

As Roman political power grew and its control expanded over the course of the mid- and late Republic, Rome did not encroach upon a legal tabula rasa. Civilizations, ancient and complex by Rome's own standards, had controlled southern Italy, the Greek mainland and islands, the coasts of the eastern Mediterranean, and North Africa for centuries. In each case, legal frameworks had already been established, providing structures for commercial activity and maintaining mechanisms for settling disputes. Strictly Roman law was also prepared to deal with these concerns and had provided some structure from at least the time of the Twelve Tables. These rules were emended throughout the Republic by further legislation—itself supplied by magistrates who were increasingly aware of these earlier, non-Roman systems as they served as governors and generals abroad.

In part because the residents of the provinces remained, until the promulgation of the *Constitutio Antoniniana*, noncitizens, and in part because the bureaucratic machinery did not exist to enforce such a step, Rome generally did not bring Roman law to its newly acquired territories. Instead, they lay a veneer of Roman practice over and alongside the legal traditions of these areas. Roman law was well known and, as the supreme political power, Roman judgment and arbitration was frequently sought by noncitizens and foreigners, but cities across the Mediterranean nevertheless retained their own systems of law and order. Often, they maintained these at their own expense and drew authorities from their own population, saving Rome the hassle of supplying the provinces with legal resources beyond the governor and his staff.[12]

The imperial period largely followed this tradition. Direct rule of some provinces came into the hands of the emperor, primarily for military purposes, but little changed in terms of administration on the ground. Some emperors chose to impose laws on the provinces, with mixed success and a spotty record of enforcement, but, on the whole, provinces, or rather individual cities and towns, especially in the eastern Mediterranean, remained independent in so far as their legal systems were concerned. Thus, cities like Athens continued to elect archons and other officials, while Egyptian papyri record a complex system of local laws and magistrates that persisted into the late Empire. Even in territories that were viewed as having been "lawless" prior to Roman conquest, such as Gaul, local potentates retained significant influence and Roman magistrates continued to hold relatively lax attitudes toward legal control and enforcement.[13]

Until recently, scholarship on Roman law has stressed the systematic nature of Roman legal thinking and practice.[14] This line of thinking is encouraged by

12. Millar, *The Emperor in the Roman World*, remains the essential text on the position of the emperor and the essentially reactive rule of Rome. Governors, of course, were subject only to Roman law, which caused serious trouble. Locals often responded with rioting rather than with appeals to higher justice, as is evident in the case of Pontius Pilate, discussed in Paul L. Maier, "The Fate of Pontius Pilate," *Hermes* 99.3 (1971). Compare with the response to Verres, which Cicero, at least, characterizes as an untypical success of Roman justice.

13. Charles Ebel, "Southern Gaul in the Triumviral Period: A Critical Stage of Romanization," *American Journal of Philology* 109.4 (1988): esp. 584–87, argues that tribal organization persisted until the Augustan era, with little intervention before that point and rapid transformation after, largely driven by the foundation of colonies that operated without respect for earlier systems of governance. Roman law, however, remained reserved for settled veterans and Roman citizens, not for local peoples. Change only came as local magistrates chose to be more liberal with citizenship enrollment, and this accounts for the rapid Romanization of the region and the swift transition to Roman law. On the agency of provincials in legal contexts, generally, and on the essentially legally pluralistic landscape of the Roman Empire, see Kimberley Czajkowski and Benedikt Eckhardt, "Law, Status and Agency in the Roman Provinces," *Past and Present* 241.1 (2018); and Ando "Legal Pluralism in Practice."

14. Within ancient studies, this has been an essential part of the debate regarding the compilation of the Theodosian and Justinianic Codes. Sirks, especially, has argued forcefully for a truly systematic process of compilation, as well as for a strong centralized intention behind Roman law in general. See A. J. Boudewijn Sirks, "The Sources of the Code," in *The Theodosian Code: Studies in the Imperial Law of Late Antiquity*, ed. Jill Harries and Ian Wood (London: Bristol Classical

the legal compilations of the fifth and sixth centuries CE, and the rhetoric of Roman law itself. These stress that law in the Roman world was derived from and based upon a coherent and consistent policy that was subsequently curated by generations of lawyers and legal theorists. The evidence of the provinces, however, demonstrates that the legal landscape of the Roman world was far more complex than what may be inferred from the law-as-codified. Accordingly, scholars have recently turned to the idea of legal pluralism, a theory that posits that law is defined, not by the political entity that promulgates and (sometimes) enforces it, but by the experience of the users and the culture that they create as they select which law to use in a particular context.[15]

Using the framework of legal pluralism, it is possible to speak of a Roman legal system that did not emanate from the state alone, but which grew from a variety of sources and functioned differently depending on the time, place, and parties involved. Legal pluralism as a theory elevates the local, placing it on par with the imperial, and recognizes that legal legitimacy can be drawn from social and normative authorities just as easily as it may be derived from written texts. Rather than granting priority to one form of legal thinking, legal pluralism stresses that the law is embodied in legal practice, and consequently it is an approach that opens new avenues for research in ancient legal studies.

This approach has gained traction in recent years because of its flexibility. Legal pluralism does not mean that it is necessary to discard the achievements of years of study on the Roman legal canon, nor to doubt the sincerity of the rhetorical claims made in documents about the change that laws could, would, or should enact. Rather, these traditional sources of law are placed in conversation with new sources of legal authority, which are, in turn, taken more seriously than they had been in previous approaches.

For the purposes of this study, this is essential. The decision to view Roman

---

Press, 1993); A. J. Boudewijn Sirks, "The Colonate in Justinian's Reign," *Journal of Roman Studies* 98 (2008); A. J. Boudewijn Sirks, "Where Did the Theodosian Compilers Take Their Texts From?" in *Société, économie, administration dans le Code Théodosien*, ed. Sylvie Crogiez-Pétrequin and Pierre Jaillette (Villeneuve d'Ascq: Presses Universitaires du Septentrion, 2012). The tendency to treat, especially the Justinianic Code, as the final, evolved form of Roman law and to be relatively uncritical about the complications of Rome legal practice and "policy" is relatively commonplace in scholarship on legal history. For a discussion of the use and influence of Roman law in contemporary English practice, see, e.g., James Lee, "*Confusio*: Reference to Roman Law in the House of Lords and the Development of English Private Law," *Roman Legal Tradition* 5.1 (2009), which also does not thoroughly define the category of "Roman law" or reflect any sense of the complications inherent in that concept.

15. Bryen, "Law in Many Pieces"; and Humfress, "Thinking through Legal Pluralism"; make the case most clearly for what legal pluralism means in the Roman context. Martha-Marie Kleinhans and Roderick A. Macdonald, "What Is a *Critical* Legal Pluralism?" *Canadian Journal of Law and Society* 12.2 (1997) offer an essential explication of the distinction between legal pluralism and critical legal pluralism.

law as a "system" that was developed from a uniform "policy" has consistently served to emphasize the kind of commercial activity that warranted imperial attention: primarily large-scale and long-distance trade in goods that were directly useful to the state, such as grain or military equipment. Peregrine Horden and Nicholas Purcell have termed this kind of trade "high commerce," and noted that its prevalence in our sources, and consequently in our scholarship, is the result of its being the easiest to track in legal documents drawn up by the state itself.[16] These were important industries in the ancient world, but production and transportation for the *annona*, for example, was hardly typical of trade in foodstuffs, let alone of commercial activity on the whole. The businesses that supplied the state necessarily operated at a large scale and developed impressive logistical systems to move goods over long distances to meet the demand of their wealthy, imperial client.

For Roman economic historians, the work of these merchants has been of central importance for arguing for a "modern" and well-developed market economy, yet, as early as 1980, it was becoming apparent that "low commerce," and not its "high" counterpart, likely represented the majority of commercial activity.[17] The challenge, however, was its relative invisibility. "Low commerce" occurred at local and regional levels, where practices could be idiosyncratic and pluralistic. Trade in these settings was comparatively casual, habitual, and in many cases occurred without either written record or recourse to the state systems that would have generated a paper trail. Our best evidence for this trade comes from a few, exceptionally well-documented places, and even in those cases it is likely that we are still only seeing a fraction of the total picture.[18]

Of course, the Roman legal system claimed just as much authority over small, local trade as it did over its large-scale, long-distance counterpart, and the government reserved the right to intervene in the day-to-day practice of trade wherever it might be and however petty its scale. As we will discuss, whether the rhetoric employed by the law was, or could be, backed by real

16. Horden and Purcell, *The Corrupting Sea*, 144–52 and 365–77.

17. On the "modern" market economy of the Roman world, see, e.g., Mikhail Ivanovich Rostovtzeff, *The Social and Economic History of the Roman Empire* (Oxford: Clarendon Press, 1957); and Temin, *The Roman Market Economy*. On the dominance, and challenging invisibility of "low commerce," see Hopkins, "Models, Ships and Staples," esp. 84–85; and Horden and Purcell, *The Corrupting Sea*, 150–52.

18. Thus, the Egyptian toll records, discussed below, exist only because of the coincidence of fortunate conditions for preservation and the record keeping necessary for a (possibly) unusually mobile region. The typicality of Egypt is always a pressing concern, and the lack of direct comparanda for these documents exacerbates the problem. Alan K. Bowman, "Documentary Papyrology and Ancient History," in *Atti del XXII Congresso internazionale di papirologia, Firenze, 23–29 agosto 1998*, ed. Isabella Andorlini, Guido Bastianini, Manfredo Manfredi, and Giovanna Menci (Florence: Istituto Papirologico G. Vitelli, 2001), 139, discusses, for the papyri, that "typicality" is unlikely to be a profitable line of inquiry, though it must still be acknowledged.

enforcement was another matter, but the empire maintained that it could and did control all aspects of the economy. From time to time, the state even interfered in cases of local trade, as when Hadrian passed a law controlling the sale of fish in Attica, but such actions were relatively rare.[19] Instead, as numerous scholars have noted, most legal action on the part of the state, even into the late antique period, was fundamentally reactionary and driven by citizens (and other inhabitants of the Roman Empire) who sought out legal advice, arbitration, and adjudication.[20]

That the state's advice was sought demonstrates that there was a belief among the general public that the state could resolve disputes and held the power and authority not only to pass judgment, but also to bring about some measure of redress.[21] Still, even the great collections of imperial legal determinations, the *Codices Theodosianus* and *Justinianus*, show that the state generally waited to be invoked, either by magistrates or by individuals. These collections preserve large numbers of rescripts, replies from the emperor or his staff to governors, magistrates, or even private individuals, who came seeking answers or opinions. Comparatively little legal activity was proactively undertaken by the state, and this reticence to impose its will encouraged the continuation of local legal practices as well as the extralegal settlement of disputes. Of course, the state did not have the resources to address every case that might require arbitration, but the state also never instituted a system for discovering matters that were not brought to its notice. Furthermore, there is evidence to suggest that, at least in Egypt, recourse to Roman magistrates and legal systems was viewed by the public as a final means of escalating a dispute after other avenues of settlement had failed to bring about a satisfactory conclusion.[22]

As we shall discuss, the reputation of merchants was a tool for preventing such conflicts from arising in the first place, but in considering the impact of law on commercial activity, it is necessary to assess the many kinds of legal authority that coexisted, and to say something about how merchants and their

19. IG II-III (2^3) 1103, James H. Oliver, *Greek Constitutions of Early Roman Emperors from Inscriptions and Papyri* (Philadelphia: American Philosophical Society, 1989), #77. See discussion by Yves Lassard, "Epistula Hadriani ad Athenienses (IG II-III, 1103)," *The Roman Law Library*, 2013. Hadrian was an unusually hands-on emperor when it came to both law and provincial administration. The involvement of an emperor in the Roman legal system was actually relatively rare, to the point that dedication to (or disinterest in) one's legal obligations was a notable rubric for discussion within Suetonius' lives.

20. Connolly, *Lives behind the Laws*, esp. ch. 1, covers the mechanics of this process. Below, a more ambitious effort, the Edict on Maximum Prices, is discussed in the context of its enforcement and intention. There, the rhetoric is clearly more forceful than its contemporary implementation.

21. Clifford Ando, *Imperial Ideology and Provincial Loyalty in the Roman Empire* (Berkeley: University of California Press, 2013) presents the notion of consensus as a tool in Roman administration, discussed further below.

22. Venticinque, *Honor among Thieves*; Bryen, *Violence*, ch. 6; Bang, *The Roman Bazaar*, ch. 4.

customers navigated their competing options. In order to do so, it will be best to consider a form of legal activity that affected most, if not all, merchants, regardless of their "level" of commerce: the assessment of tolls and customs fees. Whether tradesmen were bringing goods long distances or merely coming to a regional market, imperial and local governments alike sought to extract fees on their cargo. On the surface, these *vectigalia*, or *portoria* if the goods were transported by sea, would seem the perfect case by which to measure state involvement in merchant lives. In theory, the state mandated that a tax would be levied on goods at predetermined crossing points. Within the Empire, internal rates were meant to be between 2 and 5 percent and to have been substantially larger, perhaps between 12.5 and 25 percent, at external borders.[23] These, among other taxes, were to be collected by contracted workers, often called *publicani* or τελῶναι, who assessed the value of goods and collected money from transporters and sellers.[24]

Though inexact, this system seemingly represents a rule to which we should subsequently find some exceptions. However, upon closer inspection, neither these rates nor the processes of collection are in any way stable. Our evidence shows that a variety of magistrates, and at times even military divisions, were responsible for toll collection, and even imperial rulings on the subject demonstrate that the law surrounding tolls was regularly in flux.[25] A concrete case may be taken from two laws preserved in both the Theodosian and Justinianic Codes, issued in 365 and 366 CE, respectively, by the emperors Valentinian and Valens. The texts deal with a potential exemption to customs duties for military personnel. This was a valuable prize in return for service to the state, and, if granted, would mean that a soldier could move himself and his possessions with relative freedom, and make a profit on the side as a merchant.

That there should be a formal law regarding this issue is not surprising;

23. Neil Middleton, "Early Medieval Port Customs, Tolls and Controls on Foreign Trade," *Early Medieval Europe* 13.4 (2005): 316, based on Siegfried J. de Laet, *Portorium: Étude sur l'organisation douanière chez les Romains, surtout à l'époque du Haut-Empire* (New York: Arno Press, 1975), 297–310. Though these rates are commonly accepted, there is still significant debate about whether these tariffs were imposed on goods for import, export, or both. As we will discuss, there is also substantial reason to doubt whether this relatively neat system was ever put into practice, or, if it was, precisely where and when. Bang, *The Roman Bazaar*, 213–15, strongly disputes the external rates, especially, as being based on only one border in the eastern Empire, rather than as a universal standard.

24. Other titles are also used, depending on location and time. Useful surveys may be found in Sijpesteijn, *Customs Duties*, ch. 11, and the later chapters of De Laet, *Portorium*. On *publicani*, specifically, see Ernst Badian, *Publicans and Sinners: Private Enterprise in the Service of the Roman Republic* (Ithaca: Cornell University Press, 1972). This was a system that was, if not controversial, at least known to be open to abuse, as discussed by Bang, *The Roman Bazaar*, ch. 4.

25. On these tolls: De Laet, *Portorium*. On the many subtle differences in the law, see, e.g., *Cod. Theod.* 4.13.

in fact a similar law had been in effect since at least the early third century, but these two laws demonstrate that the legal system was continually being assessed and reassessed based on individual circumstances.[26] In the Justinianic Code, the texts appear sequentially under the heading of "Duties on Merchandise," clarifying their interrelation and applicability to the same subject.[27] These headings, and the organizing principles behind them, have been the subject of intense debate among scholars of the Codes, but it is evident, in both the recycling of older texts and the categorization that has been preserved, that texts were being systematized, perhaps for the first time.[28]

The first law, issued in 365 CE and sent to the *comes sacrarum largitionem* in Milan, grants immunity from tolls to those who were in service to the state, but the language remains ambiguous as to whether the exception was available to all those in civilian and military service or to some more restricted subgroup.[29] The term used is *militaria*, a category of imperial service that, by the fourth century CE, could refer to both soldiers and civil servants. This matter had evidently been unclear for some time, as Ingenuus, a soldier of unknown rank,

---

26. *Cod. Just.* 4.61.3 (unprovenanced, Septimius Severus and Caracalla). The repetition of the same or very similar laws in the codes is an issue that also supports the theory, promoted, among others, by Tony Honoré, "The Making of the Theodosian Code," *Zeitschrift der Savigny-Stiftung für Rechtsgeschichte* 10 (1986): 160–61, that the codifications sought to gather all possibly relevant laws under headings, with a later task being editing to remove inconsistent, contradictory, repetitive, and obsolete laws.

27. *Cod. Just.* 4.61, *De vectigalibus et commissis*. Concerning duties on merchandise, and their offenses. In the Theodosian code, the texts are not even preserved in the same book, and therefore cannot be interpreted as being inherently related, despite their subject matter.

28. No consensus has yet been reached regarding the compilation or enforcement of the Theodosian and Justinianic Codes. The key text for understanding the former is *Cod. Theod.* 1.1.5 (March 26, 429), see Benet Salway, "The Publication and Application of the Theodosian Code: NTh1, the *Gesta Senatus*, and the *Constitutionarii*," *Mélanges de l'École française de Rome: Codifications et réformes dans l'Empire tardif et les royaumes barbares*, 125.2 (2013); and especially Honoré, "The Making of the Theodosian Code," for the debate over this text and its implications. As Honoré persuasively argues, the proposed "editing" process for the Code, which would eliminate redundancies and identify gaps, was never completed, which makes it impossible to argue that what was created ever functioned as a completed "system" of Roman law. The organizational principles of the two Codes are also related, but clearly different, which suggests that new or different considerations shaped the creation of the Justinianic Code—and, explicitly in that case, a desire to simplify and streamline litigation, see Simon Corcoran, "The Codex of Justinian: The Life of a Text through 1,500 Years," in *The Codex of Justinian: A New Annotated Translation, with Parallel Latin and Greek Text*, ed. Bruce Frier (Cambridge: Cambridge University Press, 2016). The lack of stability between the two texts (i.e., that the Justinianic Code was not merely an updated version of the Theodosian) is only problematic if we insist on reading Roman law as a stable, systematic entity, rather than as an evolving category that was flexible in both its compilation and execution.

29. *Cod. Theod.* 11.12.3 (February 20, 365 CE, Milan). The relevant section reads: *hoc si quando militibus nostris hisve, qui in palatio nostro degunt, praestamus adprobantibus se sacramentis militaribus adtineri, quod concessimus firmum sit adque robustum.* If ever we should grant to those people in our service or who serve in our palace, after they have proved that they are bound by their oaths, what we grant will be firm and effective.

had received a rescript regarding the status of his own immunity, and especially about his obligation to make a full customs declaration, in the reign of Septimius Severus and Caracalla.[30]

Since the first law evidently did not resolve the matter, the second law of 366 CE appears to clarify its intention by eliminating the immunity of soldiers entirely.[31] In fact, in this case, no one at all was to be granted immunity or be allowed to pay less than "the customary eighth," *octavas solite*. The answer is unequivocal, and the turnaround of a year would seem to be a relatively swift response, signaling a desire for clarity and the uninterrupted flow of customs duties. Yet the matter is complicated by the fact that this law was sent, not to Milan, as the previous law had been, but to Beirut, where the Count of the East had apparently requested information about the same issue. It is therefore not a law of clarification, but either an about-face of imperial position or a distinction being drawn between legislation intended for two different parts of the Empire.

It is difficult, really, to argue that these laws had anything to do with one another prior to the codification of the Justinianic Code, the only place where they appear to be "naturally" related. Both laws also appear in the Theodosian Code, but in different books and under different headings, and when the Justinianic Code puts them side-by-side, it edits the texts heavily to avoid the appearance of direct contradiction.[32] Even though the laws originate in the same reign, a mere year apart, and have been organized in such a way as to suggest order and intent, it is impossible to claim that texts such as these reflect some coherent imperial policy toward customs and tolls before their compilation by Justinian.[33] Instead, they indicate that tolls and habits around their

30. *Cod. Just.* 4.61.3, *Omnibus militibus nostris prospeximus, ne ob omissas professiones poena commissi tenerentur. Proinde deposito hoc metu, si qua portoria debere te apparuerit, exsolve.* We have provided for all our soldiers that they are not held liable for the penalties for defrauding the customs by not making declarations. Therefore, having set aside this fear, if it is apparent that you owe any tolls, pay them.

31. *Cod. Theod.* 4.13.6=*Cod. Just.* 4.61.7 (January 29, 366 CE, Berytus) *ex praestatione vectigalium, nullius omnino nomine quicquam minuatur, quin octavas more solite constitutas omne hominum genus, quod commerciis voluerit interesse, dependat, nulla super hoc militarium exceptione facienda.* Regarding the payment of tolls, no reduction whatsoever is to be made under any pretext at all, but every type of person who wishes to engage in commerce will pay the customary one-eighth fee, and no exception will be made for military persons in this regard.

32. The editorial process of the Code is a matter of debate, one well covered in Jill Harries and Ian Wood, eds., *The Theodosian Code* (Ithaca: Cornell University Press, 1993), especially Sirks' and Matthews' contributions to that volume. See also Honoré, "The Making of the Theodosian Code."

33. Cam Grey, "Contextualizing *Colonatus*: The *Origo* of the Late Roman Empire," *Journal of Roman Studies* 97 (2007); and A. J. Boudewijn Sirks, "The Colonate in Justinian's Reign," *Journal of Roman Studies* 98 (2008) discussed this issue, in the specific case of *coloni*, and it became apparent that the most generous interpretation of the Codes would be a moment of coherent policy in the reign of Justinian, rather than any kind of systematic approach prior to that point.

collection were still essentially local in character, dependent upon where one lived, and that the emperors, or at least the legal staff of the emperors, saw no contradiction in sending different laws to different parts of the Empire.

Though the Codices would seem to indicate a desire on the part of the state for a more universalizing Roman law, the extant evidence, both of the years before and after these great codifications, makes it clear that local habits and individual actors were given, or had claimed for themselves, a substantial degree of personal freedom over daily operations in the realm of tolls and customs. Preserved customs laws from across the Mediterranean clearly show that the "customary eighth" named in 366 CE was by no means a universal standard with an ancient and respected pedigree. Instead, they indicate that local habits were generally the driving force behind the law, whether or not that law carried a veneer of *Romanitas.*

This balance of Roman and local needs is apparent in the city of Zarai in North Africa, which publicly inscribed a law regarding customs tariffs in the early third century CE. Its testimony indicates that even laws that clearly only applied to local circumstances could still be enforced by Roman military officials, mingling a variety of "nonstandard" practices in toll collection, while nevertheless utilizing Roman authority.[34] The law, which primarily takes the form of a long list of goods arranged by categories including animals, garments, and hides, determines the tolls owed as flat fees assigned to units. These do not align to any standard rate of internal or external tax and seem to prioritize quick assessments over maximal profits or evaluation of the worth of cargo. As a result, animals are taxed per head, while palms are assessed by their weight in pounds.[35] By itself, this deviation from what is assumed by the state to be "customary" might seem insignificant, especially given the fact that the law explicitly states that it is promulgated and enforced by the local cohort, but the law is clearly local in its character and imagined scope.[36] In fact, it is likely

34. CIL 8.4508 (202 CE), Zarai.

35. Andrew M. Riggsby, *Mosaics of Knowledge: Representing Information in the Roman World* (Oxford: Oxford University Press, 2019) addresses these systems of measurement as a reflection of Roman thought and information processing. Though this law uses Roman units, many others do not, and *Digest* 18.1.71 preserves a description of Antoninus and Verus that says local measures were perfectly acceptable in cases of sale, provided both parties had agreed to their use.

36. The law is titled *lex portus post discessum coh(ortis) instituta.* David Cherry, *Frontier and Society in Roman North Africa* (Oxford: Clarendon Press, 1998), 55, notes that cohorts are not typical in this kind of toll enforcement. There is some evidence for a similar practice in Judaea, where the cohort was connected to the road system, but not to customs duties, specifically. It is unclear why Zarai should have needed military involvement, but it may have reflected relatively underdeveloped local magistracies. It is also uncertain whether this was a legionary or auxiliary cohort. CIL 8.4524, also from Zarai, records the death of a veteran of the legion III Augusta, but this is the only known evidence that could resolve the matter, either way.

that this law constituted the formalization of older, possibly even pre-Roman practices, as it makes explicit reference to granting *immunitas* to those traveling with herds on market days.[37] Wouter Vanacker has persuasively argued that this clause was intended to clarify the tolls for nomadic or seminomadic pastoralists in the region, who came into Zarai to trade the hides that are so prominently displayed in the inscription, and are, uniquely in the extant law, described by grades of quality.[38] Pastoral nomads were not uncommon in this region, and it seems likely that the law was meant to accommodate them, while also establishing clear guidelines for the customs that would be levied on the types of goods they traded. The herds would be immune, as raw materials unready for sale, while prepared hides would be subject to tolls.

On the surface, the cohort, as the armed power in this region, had little need to make any exception for this population, just as the state, with its substantial capability to employ force to compel obedience, had little obvious reason to permit, let alone support, such a diversity of legal pronouncements. The pastoralists of Zarai deserved no special treatment as they were likely not citizens and had done no special service to the state. The cohort could have forced them to pay for their animals as well as their hides, revoking this historical *immunitas*. Doing so, however, would likely have upset the economic balance of the region. As we will discuss, merchants were not without options, and, had the law been changed to their economic detriment, they may well have begun to trade in other towns, where their herds were more welcome and economic conditions were more favorable.

Thus, this concession from the city and the cohort maintained economic equilibrium and allowed the state to profit from the trade in hides. This kind of balancing act was not unique to this city nor to North Africa. Considerations for local needs and the history of economic activity are found in customs laws from all over the Empire. Legal pluralism is apparent throughout laws regarding customs, and local practices of protecting (or persecuting) merchants are equally apparent. A law from Oxyrhynchus, for example, states that merchants must be reimbursed by inspectors if they are wrongfully forced to unload their cargo, recognizing that merchant time lost to unnecessary inspections had value.[39] The provision is unique in our available evidence, and may reflect a

37. Line 15, *pecora in nundinium immunia*.

38. Wouter Vanacker, "Differentiated Integration Trajectories of the Nomadic Population in Roman North Africa," in *Integration in Rome and in the Roman World*, ed. Gerda de Kleijn and Stéphane Benoist (Leiden: Brill, 2014), 203. See also Wim Broekaert and Wouter Vanacker, "Raiders to Traders? Economics of Integration among Nomadic Communities in North Africa," in *Rome and the Worlds beyond Its Frontiers*, ed. D. Slootjes and M. Peachin (Leiden: Brill, 2016).

39. P.Oxy. 1.36, Column 2 and 3 (100–225 CE).

specifically Egyptian problem, but it certainly demonstrates that different customs houses placed varied emphasis on the rights of the taxed in the process of collection.[40]

Merchants did not have universal access to this kind of protection, and thus had to know where they could expect both fair and unfair treatment. This was a factor as they selected what routes to use as they transported their wares and as they determined the level of risk involved in each of their economic decisions.[41] Institutionally, then, the law had an impact upon merchant choices, but not in the regular, predictable way that traditional interpretations of "economy and the law" have made out.[42] The unevenness merchants experienced when interacting with the law and its officials led merchants to foster other kinds of institutional protections, including personal friendships and financial relationships with local toll collectors as a means of increasing predictability and security. These connections appear as irregularities in our sources, which adopt a rhetorical stance of perfect equality and justice (except when they decry the evils of corruption). Through these moments, we can see not only the predatory behavior of toll collectors, but also the flexibility of merchant responses.[43] Enforcement of the law, whether fairly or unfairly, required, as we will see, both the attention of the governing and the cooperation of the governed, though both could potentially be unreliable.

Legal Enforcement and Corruption

The Roman legal system was fundamentally pluralistic in practice and design, especially with regard to commercial activity. Local ordinances governed marketplaces, as, simultaneously, imperial laws claimed that they were universal regulations obeyed across the Roman world. On top of these legal efforts were conventional practices and social norms that put other pressures on merchant actors. These structures, these institutions, were frequently complementary, if not identical. Both legal edicts and social *mores* cautioned merchants against cheating and other wrongdoing. What was often less than obvious was who was

40. We know of several instances of corruption in and around Egyptian customs houses, e.g., in the report of Pabous (P.Amh. 2.77). Concerns about fairness are also hinted at in the widespread use of customs receipts and ledgers, which suggest a desire for a record in case of disputes.

41. Bang, *The Roman Bazaar*, ch. 3, covers the uncertainty and risk that was associated with decision-making in the Roman world.

42. This is also evident in the customs house papyri, discussed in Sijpesteijn, *Customs Duties*.

43. Bang, *The Roman Bazaar*, ch. 4, covers the extent of predation by officials, though his interpretation precludes any collusion or acceptance on the part of merchants, which we will discuss shortly.

meant to enforce norms and laws and how state officials were expected to bring about a peaceful and law-abiding society.

Like the law itself, enforcement in the Roman world was unsystematic and pluralistic. It varied greatly depending on where and when one was, as well as on what kind of offense had occurred. In theory, there were many avenues to justice and sources of judgment, nearly as many as there were sources of law. At the highest level, the emperor and his governors were available to give judgment, at least nominally, since most work was outsourced to their staff and they themselves were often mobile and inaccessible to those without influence.[44] Magistrates existed at regional and local levels, with the most relevant for merchants usually being *agoranomoi* and their western equivalent, local *aediles*. These figures regulated marketplaces, monitored weights and standards, and kept an eye on both tolls and tax collectors.[45] As the following chapters will explore, there were also many unofficial sources of authority who might pass judgment or offer arbitration. Elders, people of wealth or status, and even friends and family members might be called in to help resolve disputes, with methods ranging from semiformal hearings, to violent retribution, to a quiet word of warning.

Any combination of these sources of authority might exercise regulatory power or resolve disputes, depending on the type, severity, or duration of the issue at hand. As we will discuss in subsequent chapters, merchants sometimes sought arbitration, sometimes utilized social pressure, and even periodically resorted to violence to achieve their ends. What is clear is that many of the paths to conflict resolution did not rely upon the state to bring matters to a reasonable conclusion. Records from Egypt, which are the most complete of those available from the Roman world, demonstrate that even in cases where the law was eventually brought in, it was often only after matters had escalated to a point that required the involvement of some kind of external authority.[46] As Christopher Fuhrmann's work has demonstrated, policing the Roman world was no easy task, and with relatively few official sources of protection and con-

---

44. *Pace* Connolly, *Lives behind the Laws*, who is much more optimistic about access, even if she acknowledges the challenges.

45. On *agoranomoi*, see Susan Rahyab, "The Rise and Development of the Office of *Agoranomos* in Greco-Roman Egypt," *New England Classical Journal* 46.1 (2019) on the role in Egypt. See also Riggsby, *Mosaics of Knowledge*, 100–101, on the "personal" quality of many weight standards.

46. There is some complementary evidence from Puteoli archive, see Elizabeth A. Meyer, *Legitimacy and Law in the Roman World* (Cambridge: Cambridge University Press, 2004), esp. ch. 4. Bryen, *Violence*, ch. 6, deals with the issue of escalation of Egyptian conflicts from private, interpersonal feuding to more publicly accessible venues over time. Grey, *Constructing Communities*, 116, notes that conflicts once reported to the state also could be elevated from local official to regional or imperial counterparts if a matter was not resolved.

flict resolution available, the first impulse of many ancient people would have been to try to resolve matters themselves, using the tools that were immediately at their disposal: themselves and their community.[47]

In fact, there is reason to believe that many people, merchants and otherwise, were somewhat hesitant to involve or trust the enforcement of Roman law, even if it was readily available. Though numerous sources attest to the ability of Roman officials to bring about a resolution when their opinion was sought and show that they were recognized to have both power and authority, it does not seem that Roman law was believed to be a reliable source of *justice*. Petronius could, without obvious irony, place complaints that corrupt market officials were in league with merchants to scam innocent customers into the mouth of Trimalchio's guest, Ganymede, and Ulpian speaks axiomatically of the audacity, if not actual criminality, of *publicani*.[48] Complaints to Roman officials from customers and merchants alike record instances of corruption at both local and regional levels, and Roman literature is fairly casual in its record of official incompetence, violence, and blatant disregard for justice.[49]

Peter Bang has made an extensive case for the corruption and predatory nature of the Roman state.[50] His position is that corruption made the economic system of the Roman world unpredictable and unstable, but that corruption was not of any great concern to the state, who continued to take a cut, regardless of how well or poorly commerce was administered and monitored.[51] Though his analysis is right to emphasize that the Roman system tolerated, and indeed fostered, circumstances where imperial law could be abused, Bang's position still implicitly views officials taking bribes or harassing and hindering merchants as a flaw or failing in the system as a whole. He accepts that merchants had some bargaining power, especially through their mobility and range of poten-

47. Christopher J. Fuhrmann, *Policing the Roman Empire: Soldiers, Administration, and Public Order* (Oxford: Oxford University Press, 2012). See also Bryen, *Violence*, esp. ch. 6.

48. Petron., *Sat.* 44 charges that magistrates were in league with bakers in a quid pro quo scheme to keep prices high, though the passage is also a lament for a lost golden age of justice when the magistrates protected poor men. Ulp., *Dig.* 39.4.12, states that the *audacia* and *temeritas* of *publicani* are known to all.

49. Eva Matthews Sanford, "Political Campaigns in Roman Municipalities," *Classical Journal* 25.6 (1930), notes that, rarely, epigraphy records accusations against magistrates that masquerade as campaign slogans (Marcus Cerrinius Vatia's campaign for aedile was reportedly supported by thieves and cutthroats, CIL 4.576, 581). Apuleius' approach to *agoranomoi* echoes that of Petronius, but it is in the Rabbinic literature that the corruption of aediles and *agoranomoi* becomes truly axiomatic, see Daniel Sperber, "On Pubs and Policemen in Roman Palestine," *Zeitschrift der Deutschen morgenländischen Gesellschaft* 120.2 (1970). Complaints by customers and merchants appear primarily via legal texts, where appeals to higher powers reveal the incompetence or malice of market officials.

50. Bang, *The Roman Bazaar*, ch. 4.

51. Bang, *The Roman Bazaar*, 218–25, esp. 223.

tial choices, but he presents this as an unevolved form of both commerce and imperial management.[52]

His interpretation is understandable, given the majority of our evidence, which records bribes and other deviations from a rhetorically monolithic "imperial law" in cases where citizens have complained of officials going too far. These texts are plentiful, as Bang notes, and we are in agreement that these cases likely mask hundreds of thousands of others where misconduct or extra-legal preferential treatment fell within limits that were deemed "acceptable."[53] However, his judgment of this behavior as "predatory" is founded upon the notion that there was a fair and evenly applied framework of legal institutions from which these actions were a terrible deviation, or that later systems of law and empire eventually achieved a more ideal state of justice. This is not necessarily the case. The legal landscape of the Roman world was varied and idiosyncratic, and, in fact, it was so dependent upon the practices of specific people and the traditions of specific places that few could have known, let alone have expected to receive, anything that could really be considered "just treatment under the law." More than this, the system was surprisingly successful and, in its own way, efficient, at least from the perspective of the state. Uneven administration was cost-effective and made resistance and reporting more difficult than it might have been under a more orderly form of government. Roman citizens and residents of the Empire understood this to an extent, and most seem to have anticipated that legal matters would require substantial influence and leverage, drawn from social norms and interpersonal connections, as well as true legal evidence and precedent.

This is apparent in numerous cases, including a law issued by Gratian, Valentinian, and Theodosius, dated to 380 CE, in response to the *Corpora Naviculariorum* of Trier.[54] The law was made in response to a letter from these ship captains, and the internal evidence shows that they had provided not only records of previous legislation and judgments concerning their case, but that they had also made an extended argument for why judgment in their favor would benefit the state. The matter at hand was the protection of the captains, through their status as *honestiores*, from physical violence, likely from state officials, as well as concerning which *munera* they were expected to fulfill.[55]

52. Bang, *The Roman Bazaar*, 225–29, on the balancing act between the greedy *publicani* and merchant bargaining power. Bang consistently presents a (negative) comparison between the tributary empire of the Romans and later mercantilist empires.

53. Bang, *The Roman Bazaar*, 204–7, offers a series of examples.

54. *Cod. Theod.* 13.5.16 (Trier, February 6, 380 CE).

55. The law identifies the staff of the magistrate, perhaps to deflect blame from the person of higher status, perhaps as a genuine reflection of the situation. Corporal punishment was illegal against those of the equestrian class, who were by default considered *honestiores*.

The law records that the *corpora* had sent copies of "ancient constitutions" in support of their case, presumably precedents that they had collected in anticipation of their rights eventually being disputed.[56] Under a more-perfect legal system, these documents likely would have been sufficient to receive redress, but the *corpora* also felt that they should further incentivize state intervention. The law calls the abuse of *navicularii* a "monstrous crime," *inmanis admissi*, and explicitly mentions the "advantages of business," phrases that are likely to have been drawn from the original letter.[57] These "advantages," are a clever way of approaching this situation. They were not advantages to the transporters, though that was likely the central reason for writing to the emperors, but the advantages that these captains offered to the state: their *portoria* payments, their *munera*, the steady and safe delivery of goods to Rome and other imperial centers, and their loyalty to the emperors. These, more than their complaints, were good reasons for the state to offer judgment and assurance that these merchants would receive protection. Justice was legally owed to these merchants, but, tellingly, they felt it behooved them to embellish their request and lean into the issues that truly motivated the state: taxes, supplies, and, in some cases, flattery. Many others adopted similar techniques in the pursuit of their rights and conflict resolution, suggesting that law alone was often not enough to see justice done.[58]

When justice was unavailable or difficult to access, corruption was often the result. For merchants, trying to make a living and without the time or resources to pursue their legal rights fully, offering payment, figuratively and literally, to receive preferential treatment could be seen as at least one logical course of action. Indeed, just because the means were extralegal did not prevent them from potentially bringing about the desired ends for both parties. Our evidence suggests that merchants leaned into social relationships that might lead to special favors, and that they were willing to pay, within limits, to get what they needed from the state. We can see, even in the most banal of documents, a register of tolls collected at the station of Bacchias in the Fayyum, that some merchants enjoyed greater familiarity with magistrates than others.[59] This familiarity may have been the result of day-to-day contact or of pay-to-play arrangements, but the latter is only reported, it seems, when someone was per-

56. *Cod. Theod.* 13.5.16.1, *priscis constitutionibus*.

57. *Cod. Theod.* 13.5.16.2, *Negotiationis commodum advehendasque merces*.

58. Bryen, *Violence*, esp. 199–207, covers the theoretical approach that explicated these moves. Approaching the state in these ways was not only efficacious, but also served as an act of self-presentation and definition.

59. P.Wisc. 2.80 employs a system of notation where some, but not all, who paid tolls at the customs house are recorded by abbreviated names, as in line 80 where ἀπολλ is used as shorthand for Apollonius.

sonally slighted, kept out of the action, or when demands crossed the line from reasonable to extortionate.[60]

Corruption, when it appears in our sources, appears as a "bug," a deviant and criminal enterprise marring the face of Roman justice, but it may well have operated on the ground as something like a "feature." It is the rhetoric around these matters in Roman sources that makes the distinction difficult to see. Both imperial and local laws provide instances where the mistreatment of economic actors is explicitly condemned, but outside of a few localized cases, it is described as a personal failing, attributed to a single malefactor's greed or violence, not a symptom of the kind of systemic problem Bang has described. Nevertheless, it does not seem that much was done to put a permanent end to these practices, or that punishment for individual corrupt actors was even frequently meted out. Indeed, the state could not have marshaled a force adequate to such a task.[61] The expense of fielding agents on the scale required to end or even limit corruption was beyond the financial capability of the Roman state, and the evidence of the state's reactive structure for dealing with local concerns strongly suggests that there was no real motivation to undertake such a Herculean, but ultimately thankless, task.

Motivation for change was unlikely to come from the top down. The emperor had sufficient bureaucratic obligations that taking on corruption was unlikely to rate high among his priorities. Indeed, it seems that when Aurelian attempted to undertake just a small portion of the matter in dealing with the mint workers of Rome, whose corruption affected his own personal finances, his efforts were met with armed resistance and rebellion.[62] Governors, similarly, were not typically invested in stopping corruption at the scale of the tradesman and the toll collector. They anticipated that they would profit from their time in office, and the record of *de repetundis* cases in the late Republic strongly indicates that they were willing to make their own opportunities for both licit and illicit gain if opportunities did not immediately make themselves apparent.[63]

An unusual case is that of Pabous, an Egyptian official who attempted to report the corruption of his immediate superiors:

60. The key example being, P.Amh. 2.77, the report of the Arab archer Pabous, to whom we will return shortly.

61. Bang, *The Roman Bazaar*, 69, "The Empire simply lacked the bureaucratic capacity for [organizing and controlling the economy]." This is also apparent in Fuhrmann, *Policing the Roman Empire* and the discussion of policing or enforcement measures.

62. Historia Augusta, *Vita Aureliani* 38.2; Aurelius Victor, *De Caesaribus* 35.6; and Eutropius, *Breviarium historiae Romanae* 9.14.

63. A. H. Reents, *Prosecutions* de repetundis *under the Roman Republic* (Lincoln: University of Nebraska, 1936); M. I. Henderson, "The Process '*De repetundis*,'" *Journal of Roman Studies* 41.1/2 (1951).

Ἰουλίωι Πετρωνιανῷ τῶι κρατ[ί]στῳ
ἐπιστρατήγῳ
παρὰ Παβοῦτ[ο]ς τοῦ Στοτοήτεως Πανομιέως
ἱερέως ἀπὸ κώμης [Σ]οκνοπαίου Νήσου τῆς
Ἡρακλείδου μερίδος [τοῦ Ἀ]ρσ[ι]νοίτου νομοῦ
Ἀραβο-
τοξότου πύλη[ς] τῆς αὐτῆς Σοκνοπαίου
Νήσου.

To the most powerful epistrategos Julius Petronianus, from Pabous, son of Stotoetis, son of Panomieus, priest from the village of Soknopaiou Nesos in the Heraclides division of the Arsinoite nome, Arab archer of the customs house of that same Soknopaiou Nesos.

[. . . . .]ν̣ κατηγορ ̣[̣ ̣ ̣ ἀ]λλὰ ὁρῶν τὸν
φίσκον
περιγραφόμενον ὑπὸ Πολυδεύκους τετραετεῖ
ἤδη χρόνωι παρὰ τὰ ἀπειρημένα ἐπιτηροῦν-
τὸς τὴν προκειμένην πύλην καὶ ὑπὸ
[Ἀρπαγ]άθ[ου το]ῦ̣ Ερο̣[̣ ̣]τ̣α̣κος ἐπέδωκα
τ[ο]ῖ̣ς τῆς [νομαρχίας ἐπι]τηρητα[ῖ]ς
ἀντί[γρα-]
φον ὧν εἶχ[ο]ν τοῦ Ἀρπαγάθου ἰδι[ογ]ραφιων
ἀναγραφίων τῶν διὰ τῆς πύλης εἰσαχθέντων
[κ]αὶ ἐξαχθ[έντων, ἀ]ξ̣ι̣ῶ̣ν̣ τὴν ἐξέτασιν αὐ̣[τ]
ῶν
γ[ε]ν̣έσ̣[θαι εἰς] τὸ ἐ̣π̣[ιγ]ν̣ῶναι εἰ
προσετ̣έ̣[θησαν][64]
αὐτῶν τὰ τέλη τῷ̣. καὶ

. . . (not) speaking against but because I saw the fiscus being defrauded by Polydeuces, who, against the prohibition, has now for four years been in charge of the aforementioned customs house, and by Harpagathes, son of Ero . . . , I gave the overseers of the nomarchy a copy of Harpagathes' signed records which I had of goods entering and exiting the customs house, requesting their close examination of them to determine whether the taxes on them had been handed over to the treasury account.

ἐπιγνοὺς ὁ Πολυδε[ύκ]ης ἐπελθών μοι
μεθ' ἑτέρων ὧν τὰ ὀνόματα ἀγνοῶι πλείσ̣[τ]
α̣[ι]ς
πληγαῖς με ᾐκίσατο, καὶ μὴ ἀρκεσθε[ὶ]ς
ἐπή[ν]εγκέ μοι Ἡρα[κλ]ᾶν τινα μαχαιρο-
φόρων οὐσιακῶν καὶ ἀμφότεροι βίᾳ̣
βασ[τ]άξαντές με εἰσήνεγκαν εἰς τὸ λογ[ι]
στήριον
τοῦ ἐπιτρόπου τῶν οὐσιῶν καὶ ἐποίησάν με
̣[̣]κ[̣] ̣α̣ι̣ον ὄντα μαστιγοῦσθαι εἰς τὸ ἀναδῶ-
[ναί] μ̣ε α[ὐτοῖς] τὸ τοῦ [Ἀρπ]αγάθου
ἀναγράφιον, ὅπερ
φανερὸν τοῦτο ἐγένετ[ο] τοῖς τε τῆς
νομαρχίας ἐπιτηρη-
τ[αῖς] καὶ τῷ ἐ[πὶ] τῶν τόπων τότε ὄντι
βεφιν[ι]κιαρίωι

Polydeuces, having discovered this, attacked me with other people, whose names I do not know, and tormented me with many blows, and, not satisfied with me, set Heracles on me, a guard of the domains, and both, lifting me by force, took me to the counting house of the overseer of the domains and made me . . . being whipped to give up the record of Harpagathes, which became known to the overseers of the nomarchy and then to the *beneficarii* of the district.

64. While typically emended as προσετ̣έ̣[θη], the text requires a plural to agree with the subject, τὰ τέλη.

vacat 2 lines
[. . . . . . ὅθεν] κ̣ατὰ τὸ ἀνα[γ]καῖ[ον ἐπιδίδ]ω̣μ̣ι
κ̣α̣ὶ̣ ἀ̣ξ̣ι̣[ῶ ἐὰ]ν̣ δ[ό]ξ̣η σοι [πέ]μψαι [πρὸς σ]
ὲ καὶ
τὸν Πολυδεύκην καὶ τὸν Ἁρπα[γάθην τὸ]ν̣
κ̣ρ̣ά̣τ̣ι̣σ̣τον τοῦ κακοῦ καὶ προσεπίτροπο[ν(?)]
ἵνα
δυνηθῶ τὴν ἀπόδιξιν ἐπ᾽ αὐτοὺς π̣[ο]ιησ̣[ά]
μενο(ς)
τυχεῖν καὶ τῆς ἀ̣πὸ σοῦ εὐεργεσίας. διευτύχει.
ἔστι δὲ τ[ὸ] ἀντίγραφον τῶν ἰδιογράφων
τ[οῦ] Ἁρπαγάθο[υ] ἀναγρ[αφ]ίων·
β (ἔτους) Ἀντω[νί]νου Κ[αίσαρος τ]οῦ
κ[υρίου] Ἐπεὶφ
ζ.

. . . [vacat] . . .
Therefore, I am compelled to hand over this and if it seems fitting to you to send for Polydeuces and Harpagathes, the principal source and administrator of evil, so that I can produce the proof against them and may obtain your favor. Be well.
The copy of the record of Harpagathes is the following:
Second year of Antoninus Caesar, the emperor Epiph. 7.[65]

He reports that two senior officials at the customs house of Soknopaiou Nesos had been falsifying documents and enriching themselves through unreported collections. It is unclear from his report whether this action cheated merchants, since, holding to common practice, Pabous describes the matter only in relation to the state's loss of revenue, rather than as merely illegal activity.[66] This kind of report is extremely rare, and potentially dangerous, as Pabous is explicitly targeting officers whom he believes to be violent people.[67] It is likely that Pabous' rationale for reporting was actually more personal than a matter of professional ethics, since he frames his complaint in terms of wrongs done to himself and to the state. He explicitly claims that he is not trying to "tattle" on his peers, which could be read as a telling denial, but whatever the exact rationale behind Pabous' actions, it was likely his own interests that motivated him, rather than an altruistic desire to defend the rule of law and prevent corruption in the customs house.[68]

Of course, it was not only parties on the take who had reasons to resist anti-corruption measures. Provided there was some restraint on the part of officials' extralegal demands, it was not necessarily against a merchant's interest to accept a system that functioned through some exchange of money or

65. P.Amh. 2.77, see also discussion in Fritz Mitthof, "Betrügerische Zollbeamte und der Procurator Usiacus: Bemerkungen zu P.Amh. II 77," *Zeitschrift für Papyrologie und Epigraphik* 159 (2007). The text continues for a further forty-six lines, but covers other material and becomes very fragmentary.

66. He also stresses his own suffering, a theme addressed in Bryen, *Violence*, ch. 4.

67. See Mitthof, "Betrügerische Zollbeamte," on jurisdiction issues in this text.

68. Literally "[not] speaking against (them)" [. . .]ν̣ κατηγορ, P.Amh. 2.77, line 7. There is also the possibility that Pabous had something to gain from the removal of these officials. His own position in the customs house is relatively senior, and a promotion might have been one of the possible outcomes Pabous had in mind.

favors. The Tanhuma suggests that personal bribes were commonplace, and even to be expected, almost as a business cost. In one portion of the text, a seller using false measures tells a market official, "I have already sent a present to your house."[69] The text imagines this as an integrated community in which officials and merchants knew each other, not only by sight, as this passage and others imply, but also well enough to deliver the expected "presents" to a home address. In this case, the merchant wants to bend the rules for his own gain, and the magistrate is content to permit it, provided their relationship continues to be profitable for them both.

These systems were necessarily idiosyncratic and dependent on local customs, which provided locals and regulars with a concrete advantage over outsiders and would-be competitors. Those who were familiar with the "cost of doing business" in a given neighborhood had a greater ability to predict how much an exchange might cost them, how likely they were to get away with rule-bending, and what impact their personal connections might have on their next encounter. Details and exact figures are beyond the scope of our knowledge, but it follows that reputation and interpersonal ties influenced the amounts taken under the table, and that any leniency was likely reserved for the familiar and withheld from the stranger, the outsider, or the marginalized. While the absence of such fees would have been preferable for all traders as a leveling of the playing field, it does not necessarily follow that a crackdown on such corruption would have benefited most merchants. Predictable unfairness could be preferable to its unpredictable counterpart.

Taking corruption as a "feature," it can almost be viewed as another type of law, or rather as an institution in the sense of NIE. As an institution, corruption was regulated, in part by interpersonal ties and in part by the existence of local and imperial law, but it also served to regulate by constraining economic choices and directing merchant behavior. Just as the enforcement and availability of local or imperial law provided institutional checks, the presence of corruption and the absence of enforcement also structured merchant choices, determining what could be done or what paths would be the most profitable. Merchants were subservient to both the action and inaction of state agents and were forced to adapt their lives to meet or avoid those expectations.

Even if merchants found some benefit in the predictability of corruption,

---

69. Tanhuma Tzav, Siman Aleph, Leviticus; the date of the text is difficult, as is its exact meaning. Daniel Sperber, *The City in Roman Palestine* (Oxford: Oxford University Press, 1998); and Fuhrmann, *Policing the Roman Empire*, estimate the fourth century CE, though it is generally Amoraic (200–500 CE). The passage is a parable, attached to the story of Balaam, the false prophet, but is paralleled by other examples of bribery and cheating in Jewish and Roman sources.

the relative laxness of enforcement also made the avoidance of local and imperial law a potentially viable option. Merchants might choose one customs house over another, relying on prior knowledge and word of mouth to select the best or least expensive route, or might seek to dodge imperial power entirely through smuggling or black-market activity. Our evidence suggests that the latter was adopted as a common course of action when attempts at regulation by the state grew too severe or corruption reached unsustainable levels.[70]

The legal sources provide evidence for a handful of times when such behavior was noted and condemned, but it is in the literary record that merchant criminality, if such a phrase is appropriate, becomes a central point of many plots.[71] The line between merchant, smuggler, and pirate was treated as especially blurry in Greek and Latin novels, where buying and selling frequently crosses and recrosses the line between legal and illegal without much change in a merchant's actual behavior. We will discuss the implications of this easy slippage regarding merchant reputation in the following chapters, but in this case, it is critical to note that there was relatively little that the Roman state did or could do about merchant choices to withdraw from legal markets and pursue illegal trade if it was more profitable. Enforcing any part of the Roman legal system required that citizens and those living within the bounds of the Empire accepted, recognized, and continuously supported Roman authority—with merchants accepting institutional limits imposed by the government as the most efficient way to run their businesses.

Controlling Roman Merchants

That governments draw their authority at least in part from the consensual participation of the governed is not a revolutionary claim, though the truth of this statement has, perhaps, been less readily accepted when discussing the Roman Empire. Nearly universally, the power, and especially the military power, of the Roman state has been recognized as a substantial component of the success of the Roman imperial project, and of the maintenance of Roman power, once it was in place.[72] Few would dispute that Roman imperialism

70. The black market itself has been understudied by ancient historians, even though, especially in late antiquity, it seems to have thrived. Numerous sources record instances of black-market trade, including Julian, *Misopogon* 369C and *Cod. Theod.* Novels of Valentinian 24, though most often illicit trade appears as the casual sale of stolen goods.

71. An illuminating example is Philostr., *V. A.* 3.23–24, but other merchant-pirates are less ambiguous, such as Theron in Chariton, *Callirhoe*, 1.11–12.

72. As in Lendon, *Empire of Honour*, esp. 201–6, who emphasized the monopoly the state

required physical force to subdue new territory, and that the state's proprietary claim to licit violence was an indisputable motivation for provincial obedience. Rome used its power to instill enough fear of retribution to make rebellion relatively uncommon and to secure a reasonable standard of obedience to its commands and laws.

Yet scholars have also recognized that there was a strong rhetorical bent to Roman claims to dominance and power.[73] Emperors held their *auctoritas* because they continuously asserted its existence and their rule survived, in part, because that authority received relatively few true challenges. The rhetoric of Roman law, as varied and diffuse as that category was, is similarly framed around declarations of power. While Roman law does not shy away from open discussion of the consequences of disobedience, most legislation places its emphasis on the right of the state to dictate the correct course of action (and to prohibit acts that contravened its standards). Often, the central contention is the reasoning through which the law may be viewed as not only necessary, but just. Appeals are regularly made to Roman tradition and *mores*, rather than to punishment and force, and often citizens are asked to obey the foresight of the emperors and the inherent goodness of the state.[74]

We have already discussed how enforcing the law was a challenge for the Roman Empire, and the justification behind the state's decision to delegate many day-to-day operations to local officials. These agents were not only an effective means of cutting costs, they also served as an interpretive lens for the state's will, often determining for themselves which laws, or what aspects of those laws, would be useful and beneficial in their own, local context. The flex-

held on legitimate violence and the power of fear and coercion. Though, in line with this chapter's argument, absolute control over legal violence does not preclude the regular, illegal use of violence as a solution to various kinds of disputes. See, variously, Bryen, *Violence*; Werner Riess and Garrett G. Fagan, *The Topography of Violence in the Greco-Roman World* (Ann Arbor: University of Michigan Press, 2016); Grey, *Constructing Communities*; and James C. Scott, *Weapons of the Weak: Everyday Forms of Peasant Resistance* (New Haven: Yale University Press, 1987), on how this kind of violence might play out between common people and in the background of state power and efforts to control.

73. E.g., Joy Connolly, *The State of Speech: Rhetoric and Political Thought in Ancient Rome* (Princeton: Princeton University Press, 2007); Robert M. Frakes, Elizabeth DePalma Digeser, and Justin Stephens, eds., *The Rhetoric of Power in Late Antiquity: Religion and Politics in Byzantium, Europe and the Early Islamic World* (London: I.B. Tauris, 2010); and Agnieszka Kacprzak, "Rhetoric and Roman Law," in *The Oxford Handbook of Roman Law and Society*, ed. Paul J. du Plessis, Clifford Ando, and Kaius Tuori (Oxford: Oxford University Press, 2016).

74. Thus, many economic laws emphasize that they are intended to return the Roman world to traditional practice, rather than to introduce novelties (e.g., *Cod. Theod.* 13.5.16.1). On the imperial virtue of *providentia*, see Martin P. Charlesworth, "Providentia and Aeternitas," *Harvard Theological Review* 29.2 (1936); and Simon Corcoran, *The Empire of the Tetrarchs: Imperial Pronouncements and Government AD 284–324* (Oxford: Clarendon Press, 2000), esp. 209–10. The latter specifically treats the Tetrarchic emphasis on foresight.

ible plurality of Roman law permitted them to exercise their own judgment and consequently adopt a form of Roman rule that would be more palatable, and enforceable, in their areas of jurisdiction. Local officials were an efficient solution for the Roman Empire. Their labor cut state expenses, their insight mitigated the effects of any disconnect between the state's will and local praxis, and magistrates drawn from local communities also served an ideological purpose for the state: their cooperation with Rome was a sign to their communities that they, too, should accept Roman governance.

Clifford Ando has argued persuasively that this ideology was essential to the success of the Roman imperial project; ruling the vast and diverse provinces of the Empire required provincials to offer their loyalty to the state voluntarily.[75] His framework determines that consensus was the principle that led to smooth governance and the prolonged peace that the Roman Empire enjoyed.[76] The state accepted that its rules would be obeyed in so far as they were beneficial and just, and, in return, found that they were generally ignored, rather than treated as a justification for unrest, when they were not. Thus, provincials did not go into open rebellion when a new regulation upset their way of life, but rather undertook more passive (or passive-aggressive) forms of resistance to put pressure on officials or negotiate their obligations.[77] In relation to the law, this often meant allowing legislation to fall quietly out of use.

A famous example from an economic context is that of the Edict on Maximum Prices, promulgated by the Tetrarchs in 301 CE.[78] The Edict decreed a cap on prices throughout the Empire and is extant today as a massive, fragmentary inscription recovered from dozens of sites across the Eastern Mediterranean. The wide publication of the Edict suggests the Tetrarchs' intent to see the law widely obeyed, but its provisions were inflexible, impractical, and ultimately led to the law quickly falling from use. Merchants found that price-fixing could not account for differing costs of transportation, variable rates in the value of currency, or for economic change over time.[79] Though the Edict ordered capital punishment for any who charged more than the maximum or who attempted to dodge the Edict through black-market trade, provincial practice, among both merchants and officials, seems to have been to ignore the law and continue as before.

75. Ando, *Imperial Ideology and Provincial Loyalty.*

76. Ando, *Imperial Ideology and Provincial Loyalty*, chs. 5 and 6.

77. This is in line with the arguments of Scott, *Weapons of the Weak*, who found that the greatest "weapons" were intentional ignorance, obstruction, and dilatory behaviors.

78. Marta Giacchero, *Edictum Diocletiani et collegarum de pretiis rerum venalium in integrum fere restitutum e latinis graecisque fragmentis* (Genoa: Istituto di storia antica e scienze ausilirie, 1974) remains the authoritative text for this massive, fragmentary inscription.

79. It is worth noting that the limitations of price-fixing in this form were well known in antiquity, see, e.g., Ammianus Marcellinus, *Res Gestae*, 22.14.1.

Two external witnesses to the Edict, one sympathetic and one hostile, provide us with further insight into the failure and intent of the law. The first is the addendum to the Edict published by Fulvius Asticus, the governor of Phrygia-Caria. Though a regional, rather than local magistrate, Asticus nevertheless offers an example of the kind of mediation that officials could undertake on behalf of the imperial project. He says:

Φούλβιος Ἄστικος ὁ διασημότατος ἡγεμών *vac.* λέ̣γ[ει]
καὶ τοῦτο τῆς θείας προμηθείας λέγοντῶν <τῶν> ἀηττήτων
καὶ πάντα ν̣εικώ̣ν̣τ̣ω̣ν̣ δε̣σ̣π̣ό̣τω̣ν̣ ἡμῶν βα̣σ̣ι̣λ̣έ̣ω̣ν̣ τ̣ε̣
καὶ Καισάρων εὐχ̣ε̣ρ̣είαν β̣ίου, ἵνα τῶν ὠνίων̣ [ca. 5–6]ι̣ας κ̣α̣-
ταστάσης ἐν τειμαῖς δ̣ι̣[κ]αίαις̣ κ̣α̣[ὶ] Ρ̣ΗΤΗΣ[ca. 7]α̣ι̣ς̣ τ̣ὸ̣ αὐτ̣ο̣ ἦ ἀν-
θρώποις ἅ̣πασιν, καὶ δι' ὑπερβάλλουσ*αν ὁ̣ρ̣μην καὶ φιλαργυρίαν
τινῶν ἀπορεῖν τῶν πρὸς τὴν χρείαν ἀνανκαίων μηδένα, ἁ-
πάσ̣ης περικοπείσης ἐνθυμήσεως πανούργου, ἴσην καὶ ὡ-
ρισμ *vac.* ένην τὴν ἐφ' ἑκάστοις τετάχθαι τειμήν· ὅπερ ἵνα πα-
ραφυλ *vac.* {λ}άττηται καὶ δι' ἅπαντος α<ἰ>ῶν{ν}ος μένῃ τῇ θειότητι
αὐτῶν προνενοε̣ῖται, ἀλλ' ἵνα και ὑμαῖ{ι}ν δῆλον καταστῇ σὺν
{σ̣υ̣ν̣} ἐπιμελεία̣{ς} πάσῃ τοῦ θείου δια̣τάγμα̣τος τοῦ ἐ̣πὶ τῆι τειμῇ
τῶν τε ὠνίων καὶ συναλλαγμάτων δοθέντος νόμου τὸ ἀντί-
γραθον μετὰ τοῦ προσήκοντος σεβάσματος τοῦδέ μου τοῦ δια-
τάγματος προτεταγμένον φαίνεται. Proponatur.

Fulvius Asticus, the most eminent governor, declares:

This, too, is said to be the divine foresight of our invincible and all-conquering lords, the Emperors and Caesars for the necessities of life: In order that, with [an abundance] of goods for sale established at fair, fixed prices, (the cost) may be the same for all men and no one lack necessities because of the excessive aggressiveness and greed of some, since all villainy will be foiled, a fair and limited price has been set for every kind of thing. In order that this is preserved and remain through all time, has been provided for by their divinity, but in order that it become clear also to you with all care, a copy of the divine edict of the law on the price of goods for sale and contracts appears, displayed with the proper reverence above this edict of mine. [In Latin] Let it be published.[80]

80. SEG 26.1353. Translation based on James H. Oliver, "The Governor's Edict at Aezani after the Edict of Prices," *American Journal of Philology* 97.2 (1976); and Naphtali Lewis, "The Governor's Edict at Aizanoi," *Hellenika* 42 (1991). The issues with the text, especially its ambiguity of meaning regarding "fixed" or "limited" prices has been noted by all previous scholars on the inscription:

This inscription was published with the list of prices at Aezani and contains several points that deviate from the preface that the Tetrarchs had published with the Edict. Two are especially important here: the first is the framing of the intentions of the Tetrarchs. While the emperors, led, as we conventionally understand, by Diocletian, emphasize that the Edict was intended to put a check on the rampant greed of merchants, Asticus states that the Edict is a reflection of the divine foresight of the emperors and a response to the behavior of an abstract category, "some people."[81] *Providentia* was an essential virtue of late Roman emperors, and raising the specter of heavenly intervention at this moment dovetails with both the self-identification of Diocletian and Maximian with the deities Jupiter and Hercules, respectively, and a major ideological support to the legitimacy of imperial power—divine favor.[82] It is as effective a defense of the Edict as any that might have been mustered. The distribution of Edict fragments strongly suggests that Asticus was eager to display his support for the emperors and that he intended to do so by promoting the Edict throughout his jurisdiction.[83]

But the inscription also deviates from the Edict on a second, critical point: it does not describe the law as a regulation on maximum prices, but rather on *fair, fixed* prices. The distinction is an important one as Asticus' ruling takes the prices listed in the Edict not as the uppermost limit, sharing the assumption of the emperors that prosperity would lead to lower prices, but as the set costs that would now be in force everywhere. The goal was probably to lessen the pressure on traders by accepting the upper limit as the new standard, but it may have exacerbated inflation in cases where goods were plentiful and where there had been no pressure to raise prices in the past.[84] Whatever the intent or the outcome, Asticus was clearly imposing his own reading onto the law. He chose to promulgate an emended version that reflected his own

---

Michael H. Crawford and Joyce Reynolds, "The Publication of the Prices Edict: A New Inscription from Aezani," *Journal of Roman Studies* 65 (1975): 160; Oliver, "The Governor's Edict," 175; Burkhard Meißner, "Über Zweck und Anlaß von Diokletians Preisedikt," *Historia: Zeitschrift für Alte Geschichte* 49.1 (2000): 91; Michael A. Speidel, "Wirtschaft und Moral im Urteil Diokletians. Zu Den Kaiserlichen Argumenten Für Höchstpreise." *Historia: Zeitschrift für alte Geschichte* 58.4 (2009): 495; Lewis, "The Governor's Edict," 19; Corcoran, *The Empire of the Tetrarchs*, 214 and 245.

81. Attribution to Diocletian comes from the work of Lactantius, discussed below. *Avaritia*, greed, especially in connection with merchants, appears eight times in the Edict's Preface: lines 27, 38, 84, 88, 113, 121, 140, 151.

82. Corcoran, *The Empire of the Tetrarchs*, 209–10 and 246, esp. n. 75. On the divine association of the emperors, see Harold Mattingly, "Jovius and Herculius," *Harvard Theological Review* 45.2 (1952).

83. Corcoran, *The Empire of the Tetrarchs*, 245. The greatest concentration of fragments of the Edict have been found in territory controlled by Asticus, suggesting that the governor was possibly a greater supporter of the Edict than most.

84. Corcoran, *The Empire of the Tetrarchs*, 245.

understanding or purpose, rather than offering a direct transmission of the word of the emperors.

Asticus' approach was two-fold, combining ideological promotion with legal mediation. Ultimately, he presented the Edict as a reflection of the emperors' desire for the Empire's well-being. His position has its equal-but-opposite extreme in the work of Lactantius, whose *De mortibus persecutorum* was dedicated to presenting a history of the era from the perspective of the subsequent Christian triumph. The presentation of the Tetrarchs in the work is understandably negative in both general tone and specific accusation, but Lactantius takes the time to focus on the Edict on Maximum Prices as a central example of the cruelty and greed of Diocletian. Of the Edict itself, Lactantius says:

> *Idem insatiabili avaritia thesauros numquam minui volebat, sed semper extraordinarias opes ac largitiones congerebat, ut ea quae recondebat, integra atque inviolata servaret. Idem cum variis iniquitatibus immensam faceret caritatem, legem pretiis rerum venalium statuere conatus est. Tunc ob exigua et vilia multus sanguis effusus, nec venale quicquam metu apparebat et caritas multo deterius exarsit, donec lex necessitate ipsa post multorum exitium solveretur.*

> This same (Diocletian), because of his insatiable greed, never wanted his treasuries to be diminished, but he was constantly amassing extraordinary riches and largess so that he could keep those stores he was hoarding whole and inviolate. The same man, when by various imbalances he caused an immense rise in prices, tried to promulgate a law to set the prices of goods for sale. Then much blood was shed over small and cheap goods, and nothing appeared for sale because of fear, and the prices flared much more harmfully, until the law, after many had been killed, was repealed from necessity itself.[85]

There is no evidence available to corroborate the extreme violence and chaos that Lactantius attributes to the historical moment.[86] It is not inconceivable that there were some localized instances of vocal, perhaps even violent, resistance to the provisions of the Edict, as protest, unrest, and even rioting are known to have occurred in late antiquity, especially when market-prices were

85. Lactantius, *De mortibus persecutorum* 7.5–7, text of J. L. Creed, ed. *Lactantius: De mortibus persecutorum* (Oxford: Clarendon Press, 1984).

86. Corcoran, *The Empire of the Tetrarchs*, 232–33, records the variable length of enforcement of the Edict and the lack of violent response.

involved, but the absence of evidence and Lactantius' exaggerated and biased reporting of Diocletian's actions more generally, should encourage us to view his report with skepticism.[87] It is more likely that, in most cases, initial expressions of displeasure with the Edict faded into disinterest as magistrates and market officials realized that the cost of enforcement greatly outweighed the benefits of compliance.

In fact, the survival of so many fragments of the Edict belies Lactantius' claim that the Edict was quickly repealed. Rather than make such a public statement of failure, one that could potentially harm the credibility of both the emperors and their regional and local agents, the law could fall into disuse, remaining on display but being generally ignored. Other legal sources allude to this practice, especially when emperors wished to repeat earlier laws. Since Roman practice preferred to view laws as returns to tradition, rather than novel interventions, it was common to note that earlier laws that had previously been allowed to lapse would now be revived, whether or not it was true.[88]

This is not to say that all, or even most, efforts to intervene in economic matters or merchant affairs were met with either resistance or indifference. Other Roman laws regarding the economy were proposed, promulgated, and put into use, including a series of economic reforms undertaken by the Tetrarchs. These took other, longer-lasting, forms and were implemented without evidence of similar praise or resistance.[89]

Merchants, in general, accepted or tolerated state efforts to control commercial activity—in part because such interventions were relatively few and in part because many laws were useful to merchants. Retailers, artisans, and transporters all found that some elements of the Roman system like the payment of tolls and the acceptance of weights and standards, the use of Roman money and general, widespread obedience to Roman rule, had value to them. While each, on a personal level, might pose an annoyance or cost, those who study economic institutions are right to emphasize that most economic laws benefited merchants, in that they lowered transaction costs and made contracts

87. Paul Erdkamp, "'A Starving Mob Has No Respect': Urban Markets and Food Riots in the Roman World, 100 BC–AD 400," in *The Transformation of Economic Life under the Roman Empire: Proceedings of the Second Workshop of the International Network Impact of Empire (Roman Empire, c. 200 B.C.–A.D. 476), Nottingham, July 4–7, 2001*, ed. Lukas de Blois and John Rich (Leiden: Brill, 2002); and Peter Garnsey, *Famine and Food Supply in the Graeco-Roman World: Responses to Risk and Crisis* (Cambridge: Cambridge University Press, 1989) cover the unrest that was sparked by famine and food shortages.

88. E.g., Novels of Theodosius 8 (Constantinople, April 7, 439 CE).

89. Corcoran, *The Empire of the Tetrarchs*, offers both solid coverage of the reforms and a persuasive argument for the unique purpose and scope of the Edict on Maximum Prices. See also, more generally, James W. Ermatinger, *The Economic Reforms of Diocletian* (St. Katharinen: Scripta Mercaturae, 1996).

more easily enforceable. Merchants used the state and accepted many of its restrictions as yet another way of making their lives more predictable. Even though they might have seen larger, short-term gains by abandoning the law and taking everything that they could get, they accepted that obedience would minimize risk and bring about more reliable, long-term profits.[90]

As a result, and as we will discuss in subsequent chapters, merchants policed themselves and, critically, each other, often acting as the state's truest, best enforcers. Merchants understood that if everyone accepted and adhered to the limits set by the state, it would be easier to anticipate what a peer might do, as it would likely be the same as their own response. This was desirable for everyone involved, as it lowered transaction costs and maintained the regular process of business. Merchants therefore named and shamed those who disregarded the rules too flagrantly.[91] While obedience to the law was always a process of negotiation between individual needs and the collective good, there were pressures within the merchant community, especially within merchant associations, that kept tradesmen, transporters, and artisans in line.

In this light, the relatively lax enforcement powers of the state make even greater sense. Not only did these reduce the cost of the bureaucratic system, in turn potentially lowering the tax burden on merchants, but they also were not required for the state to see compliance with its will. Merchants accepted the Roman state and its laws to the extent that a great deal of intervention into the realm of economic activity was unnecessary. The consensus of the governed was sufficient to maintain the status quo. When the state did attempt to control commerce, it often upset the equilibrium of the system, which discouraged many emperors from attempting anything more than small, local changes to the law.[92]

The idea that the Roman Empire did not need, and, moreover, did not wish to exercise substantial, active control over merchants runs contrary to the general narrative of Roman economic history, which posits that the state not only wished to demonstrate its power over trade, but that it also grew increasingly controlling of merchants over the course of the imperial period. The evidence for this generally comes from the growing regulation of *corpora* in the late

90. This is central to the framework of NIE and is discussed more fully in chapters 4 and 5.

91. Chapter 5 addresses the methods of sanctioning that were at merchants' disposal.

92. As Hadrian did with his fish law, IG II-III (2^3) 1103. Price-fixing legislation, especially, was generally limited to foodstuffs, and then typically only within a limited geographic scope. They were passed periodically and usually are recorded as having failed, as in the case of Commodus, Historia Augusta, *Vita Commodi* 14.3. Based on context, cereal crops are presumably the target of this reduction, and the measure was almost certainly limited to the city of Rome. It would have been in the interest of the sensationalizing Historia Augusta to embellish the account if the measure had been more ambitious or unusual.

Empire, which, it has been argued, shows that the state steadily laid claim to more and more kinds of labor and products in an effort to reduce its costs in supplying its armies and major cities.[93] The corpus of legislation on this subject is large, and demonstrates particular efforts to control bakers, ship captains, and some kinds of metal workers. While some scholars have attempted to extrapolate, to see in these laws a novel, systemic change that eventually regulated all merchants, the evidence we have suggests that, as in the case of tolls, the state was mostly undertaking an irregular, piecemeal effort to shore up weak points in its tax and supply lines. Moreover, our evidence also shows that, despite the intent or claims of this legislation, merchants continued to have agency in their relationship with the state, and that, rather than control and domination, these laws were merely part of larger negotiations over economic activity.[94]

We have already seen a version of this agency with the *navicularii* of Trier, but a more explicit case is that of the *corpora naviculariorum* of Arles, who not only advocated for their rights as ship captains, but also recognized that they held real power in their relationship with the state.

[I]ULIANVS NAVICVLARIIS
[Mar]INIS ARELA[T]ENSIBVS QVINQVE
[C]ORPORVM SALVTEM.
[Qui]D LECTO DECRETO VESTRO SCRIPSERIM
PROC(uratori) AVG(ugstorum duorum) E(gregio) V(iro) SVBI-

93. The study of this material begins with Mommsen, *De collegiis*, but finds its first, and most influential, full treatment in Waltzing, *Corporations professionelles*. Waltzing posited that the state gradually brought private associations of merchants, *collegia*, under its control and established new *corpora* of tradesmen and artisans who performed services that were necessary for the state. There has been substantial debate about the timeline of this process, and over which professions, in what parts of the Empire, were incorporated into the system. Waltzing's theory has had its fair share of defenders, e.g., A. H. M. Jones, "The Caste System in the Later Roman Empire," *Eirene* 8 (1970); and Lietta de Salvo, *Economia privata e pubblici servizi nell'impero romano: I corpora naviculariorum* (Messina: Samperi, 1992); but also detractors, e.g., A. J. Boudewijn Sirks, "Did the Late Roman Government Try to Tie People to Their Profession or Status?" *Tyche: Beitrage zur alten Geschichte, Papyrologie und Epigraphik* 8 (1993); Wim Broekaert, "Tied Down, Wings Cut? The Relation between the State and the Navicularii during the Later Roman Empire," in *Transforming Historical Landscapes in the Ancient Empires*, ed. Borja Antela Bernárdez and Toni Ñaco del Hoyo (Oxford: B.A.R., 1986). The major issue with the theory is, once again, enforcement and the notion of organized, systematic intent on the part of Roman lawmakers. Sirks, "Did the Late Roman Government," argues persuasively that this legislation was just a means of codifying nonmonetary tax payments and ensuring a stable supply of labor over time.

94. The regular repetition of these kinds of laws in the Theodosian and Justinianic Codes (justified, somewhat thinly, in the Novels of Theodosius 8, Constantinople 439 CE) suggests either that the state could not enforce its will or that we are seeing the results of a geographically and temporally diffuse effort to exercise control. In the latter case, it is not so much repetition as a failure of editing, as argued by Honoré, "The Making of the Theodosian Code," and the consequence of an Empire that lacked a centralized form of information dispersal.

CI IUSSI. OPTO FELICISSIMI BENE VALEATIS.
E(xemplum) E(pistulae)
EXEMPLVM DECRETI NAVICVLARIORVM MA-
RINORVM ARELATENSIVM QVINQVE COR-
PORVM ITEM EORVM QVAE APVT ME ACTA
SVNT SUBIECI ET CVM EADEM QVERELLA LA-
TIVS PROCEDAT CETERIS ETIAM IMPLORANTI-
BVS AVXILIVM AEQVITATIS CVM QVADAM DE-
NVNTIATIONE CESSATVRI PROPEDIEM OBSEQVI
SI PERMANEAT INIVRIA, PETO VT TAM INDEMNI-
TATI RATIONIS QVAM SECURITATI HOMINVM
QVI ANNONAE DESERVIVNT CONSULATVR,
IMPRIMI CHARACTERE REGVLAS FERREAS ET
ADPLICARI PROSECVTORES EX OFFICIO TUO IV-
BEAS QVI IN VRBE PONDVS QUOD SVSCE-
PERINT TRADANT.

(Claudius J)ulianus to the *navicularii marini* of the five *corpora* of Arles, greetings! What I wrote, after reading your decree, to . . . , the egregious, procurator of the *Augusti*, I have commanded, and to be added below. Fortunate people, may you prosper.

Copy of the letter.

I have added a copy of the decree of the *navicularii marini* of Arles belonging to the five *corpora* and likewise (a copy) of the documents from the court case conducted before me. And should the same dispute continue further, and the other (*navicularii*) appeal to justice with what amounts to a formal complaint that they will soon cease to comply with their obligations, if the injustice continues, I request that provision be made for both a guarantee against financial loss in the books and for relief of the people providing services for the *annona*, and that you order the marking of an indelible scale on the (inner sides of the) ship, and that escorts from your staff be provided, who will hand over (details of) the cargo weight that they loaded.[95]

95. CIL 3.14185, text of Jean-Paul Rey-Coquais, "Sur l'inscription des naviculaires d'Arles à Beyrouth," *Syria* 70 (1993).

This inscription was made upon a bronze tablet, discovered at Deir el Qatar, south of Beirut in the late nineteenth century.[96] The tablet has been cut into a circle, leading to some losses in the text, but it records a statement by a certain [J]ulianus, believed to be Claudius Julianus, the prefect of the *annona* under Septimius Severus and Caracalla, in response to a statement, a *decretum*, of the *navicularii* of Arles.

The issue at stake was a matter of cargo weight and the recording practices of state offficials. *Navicularii* were responsible for transporting grain in fulfillment of their *munera*, service to the state, and it seems that disputes had arisen between the recorded weight at the time of loading and the weight measured upon delivery. The final lines of the inscription propose a remedy in the form of an indelible mark to be made on the ship itself. Presumably to prevent the weight being incorrectly recorded or changed during transit. Sirks has plausibly reconstructed the issue by positing that the staff of the procurator, or the procurator himself, had been in the habit of recording higher weights at loading as a means of enriching themselves on the tolls, with the consequence that ship captains were unwittingly transporting less and were facing irate recipients upon arrival.[97] A mark on the ship would provide a visible record that all the officials and captains could verify, and prevent anyone utilizing private ledgers to conceal corruption.

Within the inscription, we can see traces of the original letter that was sent to the procurator. That document not only made a clear case for the need to redress the illegal treatment of the *navicularii*, but also threatened to withhold shipping labor entirely, if the matter was not swiftly addressed.[98] It is a rare example of collective action being proposed as a form of problem-solving in antiquity, and it is evident from the swift and public response of [J]ulianus that this ultimatum was taken very seriously.[99] The grain supply could have been seriously compromised by the loss of the labor of the five *corpora* mentioned in the letter, and, beyond the legal arguments that supported their case, avoiding a labor strike was evidently a major incentive to settling the matter in favor of the *navicularii*.

96. Rey-Coquais, "Sur l'inscription des naviculaires," provides the best overview of the major issues surrounding the text and the complex historiography of the document.

97. A. J. Boudewijn Sirks, *Food for Rome: The Legal Structure of the Transportation and Processing of Supplies for the Imperial Distributions in Rome and Constantinople* (Amsterdam: J.C. Gieben, 1991), 100.

98. CIL 3.14185, line 14.

99. The linguistic choice of *decretum* to describe the letter is also telling. The word indicates a level of legitimacy and suggests that the *corpora* were recognized as partners in negotiations, not as subordinates.

Though we proceed from an absence of evidence, it does not seem that a strike was ultimately necessary to bring about a satisfactory resolution.[100] The inscription of the new rule, it has been hypothesized, delivered to the offices where the *navicularii* of the *corpora* commonly arrived in the eastern Mediterranean, provided an archive of law to which captains accused of lightening their loads could appeal.[101] Through its attachment to the *corpora*, it was also a law that had a specific and exclusive function: it was not available to all and could only be applied to members of these organizations.

This is a critical distinction for our understanding of state control of merchants. Both the Arles-Beirut inscription and the law of Gratian, Valentinian, and Theodosius from Trier, discussed above, refer to other merchants who either shared the concerns of the *corpora* or sought to usurp their rights.[102] The Arles law refers to *ceteris*, others, who were also affected by the corruption and misbehavior of state offices.[103] It is clear from this terminology that these were also ship captains, who paid *portoria* fees to the state, but were not members of a formally recognized organization. The vagueness, in general, suggests that they were not responsible for the same *munera* assessed to the *corpora*, but that they were undertaking similar economic activities.

In the Trier law, we have a still clearer reference to shippers who operated outside state control and who, it seems, actually were eager to join the system.[104] Among their other complaints, the *navicularii* seem to have reported that other shippers were seeking to co-opt the rights and privileges that they enjoyed because of their service to the state, but without performing the required work. There are four essential lessons to be derived from this claim. First, that state control was never comprehensive. Some merchants, even in professions that were valuable to the state, were not contracted to perform specific *munera*.[105]

100. The parallel with the Trier law suggests that the *navicularii* of the western Empire may have been more inclined to petition the state than their eastern counterparts, though this supposition is mostly dependent on an absence of similar evidence from elsewhere. Two cases may be a coincidence, though it is a tantalizing one.

101. Rey-Coquais, "Sur l'inscription des naviculaires," 77–80, discusses the theory of an Arlesian shipping office in or around Beirut. Another option might have been a legal archive kept on some of the ships of the *corpora*, a sort of floating reference library that could have been consulted at need.

102. *Cod. Theod.* 3.5.16.1–2.

103. CIL 3.14185, line 12.

104. *Cod. Theod.* 13.5.16.1–2.

105. This corresponds to the arguments of Sirks, "Did the Late Roman Government"; Ramón Teja, "Las corporaciones romanas municipales en el Bajo Imperio: Alcance y naturaleza," *Hispania Antiqua* 3 (1973); and Geoffrey E. Rickman, "The Grain Trade under the Roman Empire," *Memoirs of the American Academy in Rome* 36 (1980).

Second, the actions of these other captains demonstrates that state service was not undesirable. There were benefits and privileges, as well as responsibilities, associated with *munera* that the *corpora* wished to hold exclusively, excluding those who were not members of their association. The narrative of increasing state control over merchants often depicts *munera* as unambiguously burdensome, rather than as a contract that came with both obligations and valuable benefits. Third, the captains complain that their competitors were regularly successful in passing themselves off as members of the *corpora*, meaning that there was no sign or signal that distinguished a member of the association from a private actor. Neither scale nor self-representation immediately identified these workers, and state officials lacked any means of telling one group from another, revealing to us yet another point of weakness in the state's systems of enforcement.

Fourth and finally, that the *corpora* chose to report these would-be usurpers proves what we have thus far argued about merchant consensus and recognition of Roman power: not only do the *corpora* turn to the state to see their legal rights protected, but they can also identify a gap in enforcement that had not yet been noticed or corrected by the state. While, as we will see, merchants more often turned to various forms of social pressure to coerce their peers into compliance with laws or norms, the state provided merchants with one potential avenue to stop and publicly shame behavior that harmed the balance of institutional benefits and costs.

State control hinged on this kind of merchant self-policing and the willingness of individuals and groups to comply with its will. It did not need to apply much force to get its way, because its own goals were limited, and primarily focused on securing a steady supply of goods and revenue. These aims mostly complemented those of merchants and did not require the kind of widespread social control that was at one time posited by scholars of late antique economic and legal history.[106] Because the state worked alongside preexisting practices and norms, it found that the general population, and merchants in particular, were inclined not only to do as the state required, but also to encourage their peers to do the same. Given what we know of the state's enforcement capabilities, and the evidence of the laws themselves, it is best to see state involvement in the economy primarily as a series of reactions to local issues and specific problems, along with a desire to preserve the status quo, more generally.

---

106. Jones, "The Caste System," especially.

Conclusion

As we will see in the subsequent chapters, the Roman state was merely one source of structure in the lives of merchants, tradesmen, and artisans. Other institutions existed that placed similar limitations on merchant choice, and their enforcement came not from law and licit force, but from social pressure, the threat of ostracism, and potential damage to one's public persona. Often, the incentives (and disincentives) that existed to promote adherence to social norms coincided with and reinforced the expectations of the state. This chapter has argued that the state certainly shaped merchant decision-making, but that it also operated as one influence among many. State regulation and laws could limit merchant choices, and merchants might voluntarily go along with state institutions, but they were not the only, and not necessarily the most powerful, factor for a merchant's decision-making in a given set of circumstances. Other motivations and concerns might cause a merchant to go against the state's directives, to push back gently or openly, or, even more commonly, to circumvent the state through various forms of passive resistance.

That merchants at times succeeded in avoiding laws or even pushing them into obsolescence demonstrates that they were not without their own agency—agency that was permitted, if not encouraged, by the state's lack of substantial enforcement systems. Enforcement was an expensive undertaking across a broad and diverse Empire, and local practices were often deeply engrained even before Roman conquest. Rather than fight against, or invest in practices that would homogenize, these differences, Rome ceded control to local magistrates and accepted that this choice would lead to uneven enforcement. Their decision maintained necessary continuities with the past and supported local systems of power and authority. The state kept its focus on maintaining its tax and supply chains, while it responded to requests for aid as needed. This was a cost-effective solution that prevented the necessity of keeping tabs on local matters in a more systematic way.

Importantly, merchants adapted to the state's pluralistic, and at times lax, approach to the law and its enforcement. While corruption was a fairly natural consequence of imperial distance, merchants found ways to maintain their businesses, resolve their disputes, and even take advantage of their personal connections to corrupt officials—a small gift might go a long way to smoothing the road ahead. Rather than view these as disruptive aberrations that marred the system of Roman law, it is productive to see that local variation and even extralegal practices could be beneficial to local merchants who had a "home-field advantage" over outside competition. Local variety helped both merchants and the state, settling into an equilibrium that was self-sustaining and resistant to large-scale change.

This was reflective of the Roman approach to law overall, not merely in legislation around commerce. Though rhetorically the state laid claim to absolute power and systematic policies of law, the state functioned for most of its history with an ad hoc approach to legislation that flexibly responded to needs as they arose. This was supplemented by a variety of different kinds of legal power, which are best understood through a pluralistic approach. Sometimes it was the law-as-written that determined an individual's course of action, but at other times it was law-as-practiced or dozens of other nonlegal influences that promoted a particular approach or disincentivized certain actions.

In the following chapters, we will look at one of the extralegal pressures that shaped merchant behavior. We will see that reputation, an institution that encompasses both self-representation and social norms, was a central concern of merchant social and economic life, and that concern about how one would be viewed, interpreted, and discussed in society could direct merchant behavior in a way that is comparable to merchant obedience to the law. The pursuit of a good reputation, which was the goal of many merchants in the Roman world, limited and directed merchant decision-making. In doing so, reputation, like the law, forced merchant activity to become more predictable, and activated similar systems of private enforcement. Unlike obedience to the law, however, reputation was subject to a lifecycle, and the work of developing, maintaining, and preserving a good reputation took different forms over the course of a merchant's career, which meant that institutional pressure changed over time in ways that require careful and thorough analysis.

CHAPTER 2

The Nature of Reputation

D • M
IS • CVIVS • PER • CAPITA • VERSORVM • NOMEN • DECLARATVR
FECIT • SE • VIBVS • SIBI • ET • SVIS • OMNIBVS
LIBERTIS • LIBERTABVSQVE • POSTERISQVE • EORVM
LIBER NVNC CVRIS FVERIM QVI RESPICE LECTOR
NOTVS IN VRBE SACRA VENDENDA PELLE CAPRINA
EXHIBVI MERCES POPVLARIBVS VSIBVS APTAS
RARA FIDES CVIVS LAVDATA EST SEMPER VBIQVE
VITA VEATA FVIT STRVXI MIHI MARMORA [F]ECI
SECVRE SOLVI SEMPER FISCALIA MANCEPS
IN CVNCTIS SIMPLEX CONTRACTIBVS OMNIBVS AEQVVS
VT POTVI NEC NON SVBVENI SAEPE PETENTI
SEMPER HONORIFICVS SEMPER COMMVNIS AMICIS
MAIOR AD[huc] HIC LAVDIS HONOR POTIOR QVOQVE CVNCTIS
IPSE MEIS QVOD CONSTITVI TVTAMINA MEMBRIS
TALIAQU[e] FECI NON TAM MIHI PROVIDVS VNI
HEREDVM QVOQVE CVRA FVIT TENET OMNIA SECVM
RE PROPRIA QVICVMQUE IACET ME FAMA LOQVETUR
EXEMPLVM LAVDIS VIXI DVM VITA MANEBAT
SOLLICITVS MULTIS REQUIEM FECI QVOQUE MVLTIS
L • NERVSIVS • MITHRES

For the spirits. He whose name is declared by the first letter of the verses made this for himself during his lifetime and all his freedmen and freedwomen and their descendants.

Reader, consider who I, who am now free from cares, was. Known in the city for selling sacred goat skins, I, whose rare trustworthiness was always praised everywhere, displayed goods suitable for popular uses.

> My life was blessed, I built a marble tomb for myself. I was untroubled, as a contractor I always paid my taxes, I was straightforward in all my dealings, was fair to everyone as much as I was able, and often helped those seeking my aid. I was always honorable, always courteous with my friends. This honor of praise is still greater, even preferable to all (others), that I, myself, put up a tomb for my limbs and I made it in this way not so much looking after myself alone, it was also out of concern for my heirs. He holds everything with him who lies in his own property. Fame will speak of me: I lived as an example of praise while life remained, looking after many, I, Lucius Nerusius Mithres, also made a resting place for many.
>
> —CIL 9.4796[1]

Lucius Nerusius Mithres, a seller of goatskins in the Tiber Valley, composed a long verse inscription describing the achievements of his life and making a record of his character. Mithres' self-representation, at least at the end of his life, was that of a perfectly good man who had done everything right and had lived to see the fulfillment of his hopes. He was a success by every metric that mattered to him and he boasted that he was *notus*, known, in the city of Rome where he traveled to buy and sell his wares. He states, with absolute certainty, that *fama* would speak of him in the time to come.[2] In Latin, *fama*, literally fame but also rumor, fortune, and, critically, reputation, was a personified entity, the goddess of the *Aeneid*'s Book 4, but also a force that might greatly affect the life and livelihood of all men.[3] Related to φήμη, the Greek word for speech, *fama* was also driven by conversation, by the exchange of information, judgments, and ideas that allowed a man like Mithres to be known both during his life and after his death via the discussions that took place about him and his business.

What concerns Mithres is his reputation, the institution that shaped many of the decisions that Mithres and other merchants made during their lifetimes. In his funerary inscription, Mithres attempts to lock in his reputation, to have

1. Though it was not possible to see an image of the stone, there appears to be a gap in the inscription between the first four lines and the rest of the inscription, at the point where the acrostic poem begins.

2. CIL 9.4796/ILS 7542. The inscription is dated to the second half of the second century, or the early third century, CE based on lexical evidence by Martin R. P. McGuire, "Epigraphical Evidence for Social Charity in the Roman West C.I.L., I2, 1212; VIII, 7858; IX, 4796," *American Journal of Philology* 67.2 (1946): 131–36, discussed more fully below.

3. *Fama* TLL, vol. 6.1, p. 206. Jean-Pierre Néraudau, "La 'fama' dans la Rome antique," *Médiévales* 24 (1993); Philip Hardie, *Rumour and Renown: Representations of* Fama *in Western Literature* (Cambridge: Cambridge University Press, 2012); and Gianni Guastella, *Word of Mouth:* Fama *and Its Personifications in Art and Literature from Ancient Rome to the Middle Ages* (Oxford: Oxford University Press, 2017) have done excellent work on this complicated but essential term.

the final word on who he was as a person. As we will discuss, the choices he makes are telling, revealing not only his good qualities but also his anxieties and concern that the work he had invested in his reputation might be lost or change over time. This worry is not necessarily unfounded. Reputation was not a stable concept and its greatest impact on Roman lives was in its very ability to change. Anxiety over the loss of a good reputation, and eagerness to be well thought of, motivated many to change their behavior, to undertake, at times, massive projects to promote their good name, and to fortify themselves against potential reputational assault. Numerous factors might change an individual's reputation, from personal choice, accident, or intentional sabotage by others. Reputation was dependent on these factors. It could be changed, built up, torn down, and remade by them.

To understand the choices merchants made, the strategies they adopted, and the impact that reputation had on the position of merchants in Roman society, it will first be necessary to investigate the nature of reputation, and, even more fundamentally, how the words and actions of merchants became contributing factors to their reputation. Mithres offers a useful case, because many of the claims in his inscription are general and workaday—the kinds of "achievements" that could apply to anyone who went about their life with good intentions. Reputation was often founded upon such commonplace acts of decency, especially when they happened with enough regularity that they could be counted upon. As reputation was an institution, its strength came from the predictability that it generated in business dealings, and Mithres, like many other merchants, is clear that he could always be relied upon.

Another factor in how reputation was formed and used was comparison. Merchants were not only judged on their behavior and its consistency, but also on how they measured up to their peers. At one level, this comparison was against standards that were held at the level of the entire society, to norms of social interaction that structured all of Roman life, but comparison also functioned at the level of the individual. A good reputation was built on, among other things, the appearance of success in direct competition with one's peers. Having a better reputation than others was desirable and drove merchants to make comparative or superlative claims about their conduct. While these declarations are not necessarily trustworthy, nor likely to be perfectly reflective of how a merchant was viewed by others, the desire to outshine one's peers in some way directed reputation strategies and the shape that merchant reputation often took.

Finally, reputation was dependent upon its audience, which did the interpretative work of deciding what information "counted" toward reputation and what was beneath the notice of the community. Reputation, as we will discuss, was developed in conversation between the actor and the audience, who each adapted and revised their beliefs and strategies as new circumstances arose. Audiences could differ widely in terms of their scale and access to information and could view that information very differently. It was also among audiences that unreliable evidence, rumor, and misinformation entered into the system, and merchants could use these private and informal channels in an attempt to influence their reputations on the small scale, even as they made public declarations of their personal goodness in grand fashion.

All together, reputation could be a flexible and unstable commodity for merchants, who might not be able to grasp fully how they were perceived by others or who might win or lose ground over time. While reputation was not a zero-sum game, merchants were still aware they were being judged by an audience that was aware not only of their own behaviors, but also the conduct of their peers. Despite the challenges, merchants understood that a good reputation might benefit their business and social endeavors and, as we will see in the following chapters, they utilized whatever strategies they could to develop a good name.

Regularity, Consistency, and Predictability: The Foundations of Reputation

Mithres' inscription was set up in the small town of Forum Novum, modern Magliano Sabina, about thirty kilometers north of Rome.[4] From that location, it is probable that Mithres traveled into the city to sell his wares, or to purchase the stock that he then sold in Forum Novum. He claims in his inscription that he was known in Rome, *notus*, before he launches into a description of his character and the accomplishments of his life. The long inscription often seems hyperbolic, if not tastelessly proud, and reflective of an individual who did not have a sense of how his words would be received. In fact, his words have been read over the years as indicative of a "smugness and complacency,"[5] that has been seen as characteristic of many freedmen merchants of the period. Comparisons with Petronius' Trimalchio come readily to mind, as he, too, prepared his funerary monument during his lifetime and intended to use it as a platform

4. Though now a settled matter, there was some historical confusion over the exact find spot of this inscription. Though some have attributed the find to Magliano in Tuscany, Franz Buecheler, Alexander Riese, and Ernst Lommatzsch, *Anthologia latina sive poesis latinae supplementum.* Edited by Franciscus Buecheler and Alexander Riese (Leipzig: Teubner, 1895), specifies the more reasonable Magliano Sabina, also known as Forum Novum.

5. Lillian B. Lawler, "Some Lesser Lights," *Classical Journal* 30.2 (1934): 70.

to boast of his accomplishments after death.[6] Both the fictional Trimalchio and the real Mithres created lists of their achievements and descriptions of their character. They used their funerary inscriptions as tools to support their reputations, even if they seem to have acted without understanding how others might judge their words.[7]

The real and potential distance between a merchant's intentions and the perception of his efforts are evident in such cases. Yet Mithres' words were undoubtedly chosen with care, and it would be unjust to assume that his intention had been to appear boastful, "smug," or unaware of the possible effects of his words on his self-representation. A funerary inscription of this type, prepared in advance and costly in its scale and quality, was crafted to project the kind of person that Mithres had honestly believed, or wished to believe, himself to be: a good one. There was no benefit to advertising a poor reputation, so evidence of this kind was designed to project, protect, and preserve the memory of Mithres' good name and the details of the text must all point to the values and characteristics in which he took real pride.

Mithres' life and reputation is exclusively known from this document, but as a testament to what he valued and how he hoped to be remembered, it is an invaluable resource. His choices greatly augment our understanding of how merchants conceived of reputation, what its component parts were, and how it might be projected into a community of family, friends, peers, and customers. Mithres' emphasis on the day-to-day affairs of his life and the consistency of his good conduct, rather than exceptional moments of goodness, is particularly noteworthy. He is neither coy nor subtle about this matter and places his reliability front and center. The word *semper*, always, occurs four times in the inscription, along with a single occurrence of the frequentative *saepe*, often. Mithres claims that he was *semper honorificus*, *semper communis amicis*, as

---

6. Petron., *Sat.* 71. The two texts are largely comparable, though it is important to recognize that Trimalchio's narrative is satirical in nature. It forms an interesting midpoint on a spectrum between the real Mithres and the fanciful *Testamentum Porci* from Jerome, *Against Rufinus* 1.17. On this latter text, see Edward Champlin, "The Testament of the Piglet," *Phoenix* 41.2 (1987).

7. The audience of funerary monuments, and especially funerary inscriptions, hinges on a number of factors. While tombs were, visually, more firmly integrated into daily life in antiquity than modern cemeteries through their location along major roads, it is unclear the extent to which displays in this context were, or became, visual "white noise" for passersby. Time was likely a major factor, as new monuments would attract more attention than older, familiar structures. Literacy is also a major issue. Even though modern scholars on the subject have grown more optimistic about baseline literacy, inscriptions, even or perhaps especially those that "call out" to would-be readers, lose much of their power if their meaning was obscure to an illiterate audience. Maureen Carroll, "Vox tua nempe mea est: Dialogues with the Dead in Roman Funerary Commemoration," *Accordia Research Papers* 11 (2007/2008), provides an excellent analysis of all these issues and concludes that there is also a ritual or symbolic efficacy to inscriptions in cases where literacy or attention may have been lacking.

well as *laudata semper*, and *solvi semper fiscalia*, along with *subveni saepe*. The emphasis is marked and draws our attention to the consistency of Mithres' good traits. He never failed to be honorable, never wronged the people around him, never failed in his obligations, and was always, *always* praised for his efforts. Though he calls the provision of a burial place for himself and his freedmen and women an "honor preferable to all others," his own words demonstrate that the regularity and reliability of his good conduct was his most important trait.

Though reputation required numerous kinds of input to build, consistency generally lies at the heart of reputation, both bad and good, and was, in some respects, the foundation upon which every other element was built. Certainly, consistency was the greatest factor in the institutional use of reputation: it was more valuable for helping others determine the nature of a person than a single, splashy display of good or bad qualities. A consistently bad merchant, for instance, one with a well-founded reputation for unsavory behavior, could be at least be relied upon to be bad, difficult to work with, dishonest, or greedy. If a customer or peer were forced to do business with such a person, they could prepare themselves for the encounter, be watchful, or approach the deal with an appropriate amount of distrust. An irregularly good person, on the other hand, was less predictable, and could not be relied upon to respond in any particular way. A customer would need to be just as wary with them as with a bad merchant, thus eliminating the utility of reputation in smoothing social and economic decision-making. NIE explicates the value of this predictability as the primary force that lowered transaction costs, making deals less expensive by allowing everyone involved to have greater trust in one another and a better chance of guessing what a trading partner would do next.

Consistency also helped to ensure that a similar reputation would spread throughout an individual's reputational network. The people who interacted with Mithres formed their opinions about him based upon his actions, his words, and his disposition. His consistency enabled them to judge him based on a collection of similar data, not a random assortment of dissimilar experiences. Further, as most of his audience would have shared a largely similar cultural framework, his behavior would likely be interpreted, judged, and valued in similar ways throughout that audience, leading to a pervasive and, hopefully, strong belief that he was (or was not) the man he presented himself to be.

Small, steady, and similar actions were the building blocks of reputation, the cumulative opinion about a person based on their actions and character, taken as a whole. Reputation was constructed over a lifetime, with many actions coming together to create a single, comprehensive vision. While a good reputation could be fostered through flashy acts of self-promotion, an act of public generosity or a statement of intent, such strategies could only be verified through constant displays of good character. Thus, while Mithres professed that he was generously providing a burial place for his freedmen and women, this beneficence was a single act, and one that definitionally could not be repeated, since his own death was implicated in the gift. Though it was admirable to provide for others in this way, it could be considered of secondary importance to his constant kindness toward his friends and honor in business.

Though the provision of a burial was certainly a good and generous action, and would not have been ignored, it is easy, when trying to assess someone's character, to set aside large acts as self-serving. Despite the work that it could take to monitor such matters, it was believed that the only way to accurately assess a merchant's reputation was through the conduct of his day-to-day life. It was hardly accidental, then, that many merchants chose to focus on small, regular habits in their self-presentation. Mithres reports that he always did little things, like helping his friends and paying his taxes, while the Italian wool worker Evangelus (Fig. 1) showed himself hard at work in his shop rather than engaged in some, one-time, public act of generosity or kindness in his funerary relief.[8] Evangelus appears as he would have been seen every day, undertaking a task, cleaning wool, that required concentration and skill, but which would have been a regular occurrence in his day-to-day activities. He is shown in profile, and the setting suggests that the viewer has just wandered into his shop and found Evangelus as he would have regularly been: hard at work, doing what he did best.

This scene not only demonstrates Evangelus' dedication to making quality goods, but also depicts his workshop complete with scales, a symbol found on many merchant grave markers and a sign of a merchant's commitment to probity and fair measures.[9] These kinds of signals contributed to a merchant's repu-

---

8. The image comes from a *loculusplatte* (Medelhavsmuseet: MM1997:001), a covering for a niche in a mausoleum, and is not the only funerary object preserved for Evangelus. There is also the front of a sarcophagus, Getty: 88.AA.70, that is apparently the earlier of the two objects. This sarcophagus was, for an unknown reason, unused by Evangelus, who seems to have been interred with his second wife and her family in a mausoleum. On the sarcophagus, see Peter J. Holliday, "The Sarcophagus of Titus Aelius Evangelus and Gaudenia Nicene," *J. Paul Getty Museum Journal* 21 (1993); and Alfredo Buonopane and Carla Corti, "T. Aelius Evangelus: Due inscrizioni, una compagna, una figlia naturale, una moglie e un *lanificium*," *Sylloge Epigraphica Barcinonensis* 16 (2018). Both objects lack archaeological provenance, but are linked, on stylistic grounds, with Italy in the late second century CE. Holliday believes that the sarcophagus is potentially Ostian in origin.

9. For other images of scales in merchant contexts, see e.g., Funerary Relief of a Butcher and His Wife, Skulpturensammlung, Dresden, Inv. no. ZV 44; Metal workshop relief, Museo Archeologico Nazionale di Napoli, Inv. no. 6575. See Carla Corti, "Pesi e misure nei commerci, arti, mestieri e professioni," in *Pondera: Pesi e Misure nell'antichita*, ed. Carla Corti and Nicoletta Giordani (Campogalliano: Museo della Bilancia, 2001) for discussion of these representations.

Figure 1. Loculusplatte of Titus Aelius Evangelus, Medelhavsmuseet: MM1997:001. Ove Kaneberg (CC BY 4.0).

tation in the moment of their display, but the claims they made were only credible if they were supported by day-to-day practice. If Evangelus had produced poor quality wool, or Mithres cheated the state of its share of his profits, someone would have recognized the disconnect between their self-representation and reality. Reputation was formed through the triangulation of how a merchant wished to appear, what he or she actually did, and what the audience knew to be true themselves.

This, to an extent, is why it is potentially easy to lose or dramatically damage a good reputation. Not only are audiences, in general, more likely to lend credence to a negative report, but there was a general belief that merchants, especially, were apt to be boastful about their accomplishments, whether their pride was warranted or not.[10] The whole narrative surrounding Petronius' Trimalchio relies on this cultural stereotype for its humor.[11] The hyperbole of Trimalchio's claims of self-sufficiency and wealth are only comical because of the existence, real or culturally imagined, of many such figures, rather than from

10. Michael H. Birnbaum, "Morality Judgment: Test of an Averaging Model with Differential Weights," *Journal of Experimental Psychology* 99.3 (1973) suggests that a person is commonly "judged by his worst bad deed." See also, Craik, *Reputation*, 50, on "negativity bias." Philostr., *V. A.* 4.22–23, includes a lengthy discussion of the behavior of ship captains, including a claim that even the modestly successful were unduly boastful about their achievements. Chapter 4 addresses the stereotypes on which many of these judgments are based.

11. Harry C. Schnur, "The Economic Background of the *Satyricon*," *Latomus* 18 (1959): 791, recognizes the relationship between satire and the satirist's immediate contemporary circumstances. More generally, the potential use of Trimalchio for historical or economic purposes has been explored by a number of scholars, e.g., Verboven, "A Funny Thing Happened"; Hans Kloft, "Trimalchio als Ökonom: Bermerkungen zur Rolle der Wirtshaft in Petrons *Satyricon*," in *E fontibus haurire: Beiträge zur römischen Geschichte und zu ihren Hilfswissenschaften (Festschrift H. Chantraine)*, ed. Rosmarie Gunther and Stefan Rebenich (Paderborn: Ferdinand Schöningh, 1994); Paul Veyne, "Vie de Trimalcion," *Annales: Histoire, Sciences Sociales* 16.2 (1961).

one randomly boastful individual. Witnessing or learning that a person was not as good as they claimed was satisfying, and also made for powerful gossip that would spread quickly and easily among a wide range of audiences.[12]

In line with this, the destruction of a good reputation typically came suddenly, from a particular catalyst, though it could also be eroded over time through a decline in quality or service. It was difficult to restore a reputation once it had entered this downward spiral, and often merchants were only gradually made aware that their reputation was not what they would like it to be.[13] Milo, a moneylender in Apuleius' *Metamorphoses*, holds a reputation as a greedy miser in his home town of Hypata, and is forced to confront this reputation when welcoming Lucius, the protagonist, into his home.[14] He tells Lucius not to look down on him and begs him to accept that the poverty of his home is not the result of cheapness or avarice, but rather of fear of robbery. Milo even goes so far as to suggest that Lucius' agreement to be a guest in Milo's home would help to improve both their reputations, as acting as a host would improve Milo's reputation for generosity and Lucius' acceptance would demonstrate that he did not hold his pride and physical comfort more important than friendship. To an extent, Milo was even right about this, as Lucius fell victim to a prank as part of a local festival during his visit that seems to have helped Milo reintegrate into his community.[15]

Community, as we will discuss, was critical to reputation, both as the audience that received and assessed it, and as the pool from which the institutional power of reputation was drawn. Reputation was inextricably connected to specific locations and to certain populations, which merchants often realized to their detriment when they arrived in a new, unfamiliar place where they had little history and few connections, and consequently no reputation. Another fictional merchant, this time a merchant-cum-pirate, Theron, of Chariton's *Callirhoe*, used the ignorance of others to his advantage when he arrived in the port of Miletus, masking his villainous intentions under the guise of being new in town.[16] Those with whom he dealt were, perhaps, untypical in their accommo-

12. Craik, *Reputation*, 50; Lupfer, Weeks, and Dupuis, "How Pervasive Is the Negativity Bias"; and Skowronski and Carlston, "Negativity and Extremity Biases in Impression Formation." Chapter 5 addresses gossip and its impact on merchant reputation.

13. Publilius Syrus, *Sententiae*, 572 *quem fama semel oppressit vix restitutur*. It is barely possible to restore someone whom reputation (or gossip) has once put down.

14. Apul., *Met.* 1.23, a local innkeeper provides Lucius with a summation of Milo's reputation at 1.21.

15. Apul., *Met.* 3.7, 9–11.

16. Chariton, *Callirhoe*, 1.11–12, Theron is also described as granting Callirhoe a certain amount of comfort on his ship, ὡς ἔμπορος "as a businessman," who acts ἐκ φιλοκερδίας, out of greed rather than humanitarian motivation. When he approaches locals in Miletus, he states: "Ἔμπορός εἰμι."

dation of a stranger, as other sources suggest that merchants traveling in unfamiliar regions did everything in their power to utilize their friendship network to avoid being completely unknown.[17]

Even with the help of friends, and friends of friends, new merchants were still, at times, met with suspicion. Lucius carries a letter for Milo when he arrives in Hypata, and the document serves as a proof of his identity. With the letter, Lucius secures both a place to stay and a local person to vouch for his character.[18] Though Milo is welcoming, he still grills Lucius for details about their mutual friend and his entire household, including the *vernaculi*, the slaves, in order to confirm Lucius' identity and ensure the safety of his home.[19]

Reputation was founded upon identity as it was presented and received. Much relied on the disposition of both parties, their willingness to trust one another and offer the benefit of the doubt, as well as on the specific characteristics or practices that the merchant displayed. We have already seen Mithres' emphasis on consistency, and Evangelus' on hard work and fairness, but there were many traits that merchants believed contributed to their good name. Generally, these come in two varieties: traits related to their personality and those related to their business practices. Often, as we will discuss, merchants established their good qualities in both these arenas by laying out the inverse, the bad behaviors and traits—especially those consistent with the negative stereotypes surrounding merchants—that they consistently avoided.

Interestingly, these denials could also be made on behalf of others. Philostratus, in his *Lives of the Sophists*, defends the reputation of Proclus of Naucratis, a teacher of rhetoric and businessman trading in Egyptian goods in Athens, by claiming that, οὐδαμοῦ φιλοχρήματος ἔδοξεν οὐδὲ ἀνελεύθερος, οὐδὲ ἐραστὴς τοῦ πλείονος, οὐδὲ ἐπικέρδεια μαστεύων ἢ τόκους, ἀλλ' αὐτὸ ἀγαπῶν τὸ ἀρχαῖον, "he never seemed to be greedy or treacherous or a lover of gain; for he did not seek after profit or usury, but was content with his actual principal."[20] This description places Proclus' trading in a different category from the general merchant population, and helps to define him as a gentleman-sophist rather than as a merchant for Philostratus. Philostratus claims to have been a student

17. As in the case of Encolpius and Ascyltos in Petron., *Sat.* 12–15, where, as strangers, they hesitate even to insist that a thief return a stolen tunic. The Persian messenger in the *Acta Archelai* is similarly lost without a common acquaintance and nearly dies of exposure as he is refused housing by a number of innkeepers along the Syrian-Persian frontier; see Jane Sancinito, "Cross-Cultural Confusion: The Messenger Turbo and the Innkeepers of the *Acta Archelai*," *Journal of Late Antiquity* 12.2 (2019), for a discussion.

18. Apul., *Met.* 1.22. He also relies on a family member in the area, an aunt who also offers him hospitality and support in his business, 2.2–3.

19. Apul., *Met.* 1.26.

20. Philostr., *V. S.* 2.21.603.

of Proclus, and thus in a position to know details about his business, but he also had a vested interest in presenting Proclus in the best possible light. Once again, consistency is a fundamental part of the characterization, as Proclus *never* acted the way that other, nasty merchants did, but was driven by a desire to help others. To Philostratus, Proclus' personality was not "merchant-like" because he was not driven by greed and the deceitfulness that greed inspired. Philostratus even suggests that Proclus made no money at all on his ventures but was content with merely making back what he invested.

While this is certainly unbelievable as a business strategy, Philostratus' impulse to distance his mentor from the stereotype of the "greedy or treacherous" merchant was not an uncommon practice.[21] His goal was to present Proclus' reputation, in this case introduced by ἔδοξεν, as both a good man and an honest wholesaler. To do so, he needed to make the case that Proclus' interest was in supplying the world with good things, not in making a profit. Mithres' inscription shares this impulse. His emphasis is on his provision of useful objects and his fairness in business, rather than on his income. This is implied by the existence of the inscription and in the promised burial plot but are never directly stated. Instead, Mithres' character traits of generosity and helpfulness are foregrounded. Friendship, too, holds a prominent place in these representations, as Mithres says that he was always courteous to his friends, while Proclus is said to have understood the nature of friendship and its responsibilities.[22] Maintaining these connections was a lifelong undertaking, one that required constant effort and consistent messaging—to neglect or damage one of these friendships was to do real harm to one's reputation.

Sociability and social responsibility formed an essential bedrock for merchant reputation, and, as we will discuss in later chapters, efforts to cultivate and support friends, and to receive support from them in turn, were essential elements in the creation and use of reputation. In this context, however, what is most interesting is that reputation depended so much upon others. More than that, reputation was comparative, and merchants who were kinder to their friends, more successful, or more helpful to others gained a better reputation than those who did less, even if they did no wrong. Mithres, as ever, seems to be aware of this. He hedges his own claim to fairness, presumably in business, with the proviso that he "was fair to everyone as much as [he] was able."[23] There were fundamental limits on what a merchant could reasonably do for others,

21. Not even within the corpus of Philostratus' works. The same dynamic is at play in the opening lines of the *Heroicus*, discussed in the Introduction.

22. Philostr., *V. S.* 2.21 (603), ἱκανῶς καὶ τὰ φιλικὰ ἀκριβοῦντος.

23. CIL 9.4796, lines 11–12.

based on their personal wealth and their expenses, but reputation was always based on the distance between their own actions and those of the most able person in the community. Reputation was not necessarily fair in this regard, but comparison was an inextricable component in reputation and its assessment.

A Comparative Endeavor

While an individual merchant might eventually accumulate a reputation for certain qualities based on his or her personality, behavior, and business model, these choices were not enough, by themselves, to shape the entirety of a reputation. Reputation did not exist in a vacuum, and often the efforts of merchants were thwarted, not through their own actions, but by the opinions, actions, and personalities of others. Above all, reputation was a dialectical process that fed into and was fed by a merchant's community and its dynamics. This chapter will conclude with a discussion of the role of an audience in the development of reputation, but how society perceived merchants was both supported and undermined by comparisons between people in similar circumstances.

This meant that reputation was intimately connected with the appearance of success, especially in relation to peers and, in the case of merchants, their direct competitors. The appearance of wealth, the continued survival of a business, and the ability to support not only oneself, but also others, fed into a good reputation as a kind of self-fulfilling prophecy: the merchant who seemed successful, and had gained a reputation for being so, was more likely to become more so in the future. Faking it did, in some cases at least, make it easier to make it.

Yet merchants had to tread with caution. Projecting success was useful; it suggested to the general population that there were personal and professional virtues that lay behind such prosperity, but bragging was not an admirable trait, and if a merchant was discovered to be less well-off than he had claimed, he risked serious damage to his reputation.[24] The appearance of success raised expectations, as audiences assumed that success was the result of quality goods or services. Just as today's consumers want to purchase the best, or even just the most popular, version of a product, so too did Roman customers wish to patronize merchants who seemed to be the best in their field. If, however, those

24. Anthony Fitzsimmons and Derek Atkins, *Rethinking Reputational Risk: How to Manage the Risks That Can Ruin Your Business, Your Reputation and You* (London: Kogan Page, 2017), 39, define "reputational risk" in two, interrelated ways: "The risk that your stakeholders come to believe that you are not as good as they thought you were" and "the risk of failure to fulfil the expectations of your stakeholders in terms of performance and behaviour." Risk of this kind was heightened if a merchant raised expectations through unwarranted displays of success.

expectations were left unmet, the reputation of the merchant might easily shift from merely "unsuccessful" to "fraudulent" or "deceitful."

The appearance of success was nevertheless cultivated by merchants, who understood that their reputation was based, at least in part, on comparison with their immediate peers.[25] While rankings are difficult to see in antiquity, and comparisons between merchants in the same trade are not always directly possible, reputation was nevertheless dependent upon a system by which some were known to be better or worse than others. Merchants always hoped to come off positively and to situate themselves favorably in anticipation of such comparisons, so they laid claim to positive personality traits and displayed their business acumen in as many ways as they could.

Metrics of success and prosperity were vital to merchant reputation and contemporaries had access to many possible sources for this information. In one unusually well-documented case, we can trace the experiences of transporters in and around Lake Moeris in the Fayyum. These figures moved produce around the region and their loads were recorded as they passed through customs houses. Several of these ledgers, and dozens, if not hundreds, of receipts have been recovered, and their content enables us, as it once did ancient merchants and officials, to make direct comparisons among these workers.[26] Through those records we can see, as would have been visibly apparent on the ground, the differences in scale between traders and the physical manifestations of the economic choices that they had made. Degrees of success would have been evident as multiple merchants approached the same customs house with their wares. As some approached with large herds of pack animals and others with single donkeys, it would have been clear who had been making good economic decisions.[27]

The customs house records recreate these scenes down to the experience of the individual trader and how he navigated this world of comparison. One figure, Sotas, traded with a group of peers, traveling along similar routes around

25. Bromley, *Reputation*, 27–28. Though this is an instinctive rationale, and one adopted by many scholarly studies of reputation, comparison and its effect on reputation is an understudied corner of reputational theory, in general.

26. Presented in Sijpesteijn, *Customs Duties*. Strong examples are the ledger of Bacchias, preserved in two pieces: P.Merton 1.15 and P.Wisc. 2.80, and that of Soknopaiou Nesos, P.Lond. 3.929.

27. Though this kind of visual assessment was, as we will discuss, a "cheap" reputational signal, and did not account for a merchant's honesty, hard work, or other virtues. A merchant who inherited wealth, or one who worked as a middleman for a more important merchant, might well look more successful than a peer who transported less but was in fact improving their circumstances more rapidly. Also, in the context of these traders, the evidence suggests that some preferred to operate a business using many smaller trips, rather than one large journey, the better to mitigate risks.

the Fayyum and transporting similar goods.[28] In our evidence, Sotas' business, like those of his fellow traders, was seasonal in nature, dictated by the harvest and the availability of goods, but we can also see that there were elements of choice in Sotas' business model. At times, Sotas sticks with the pack, while at other points he deviates, either because he had access to different suppliers or because he had followed his professional instincts in a different direction.[29] Yet whenever he returned to Soknopaiou Nesos, it is possible to see how his balance of conformity and experimentation was paying off, or not, relative to others.

The customs house documents demonstrate that most traders experienced highs and lows relative to the scale of their business, based on the number of animals each could muster to transport their products, but that few rocketed to previously unknown heights. Some owned or could borrow no more than a single animal at a time, while others could gather a substantial herd, but few moved greatly along this spectrum, except to drop out of our records entirely.[30] It is possible to see moments when Sotas' business thrived, and others when he was outstripped by his peers.[31] In the form of livestock, these highs and lows would have been visible, and would have had a significant impact on Sotas' reputation as a trader. In our records, Sotas reaches a peak of success in March of what is probably 180/81 CE, but then diminishes before dropping out of our records entirely. It is unclear if he was forced out of business or changed his route to no longer include Soknopaiou Nesos, but in looking at his comparable peers in the region, there seem to have been some transporters who were forced to travel with a slower, less successful set after they had faced an economic setback.

28. Sotas trades mainly with Melas, or his agents (P.Lond. 3.929, lines 4–5, 10–11, 17 and 19, etc.); similar evidence comes from the Bacchias record (P.Wisc. 2.80) and the case of Apollonius. Sotas' identity has already been the subject of debate; see Pieter Johannes Sijpesteijn, "Eine weitere Torzollquittung aus der Amsterdamer Papyrussammlung," *Zeitschrift für Papyrologie und Epigraphik* 7 (1971). It is doubtful that all the known attestations can refer to one person, since the whole collection dates from between 163 and 219 CE or even a little later. By contrast, Ludwig Koenen, "Datierung einer Berliner Torzollquittung," *Zeitschrift für Papyrologie und Epigraphik* 8 (1971), believes they are all the work of one man. If he was one person, he worked around fifty-six years and he would have been around seventy at the time of his death or retirement. A further possibility is that a first Sotas had a son of the same name. None of the documents record a patronymic to bar such a hypothesis. The actions of Sotas under consideration here come from one text, P.Lond. 3.929, and therefore are likely to represent a single figure.

29. Thus, Sotas shifted from transporting grain to olive oil, but does so on a slightly different schedule than his peers, and also, more unusually, he transports dates.

30. For Soknopaiou Nesos, Lalion and Artemas hold the record for the largest collection of animals, with a combined seventeen camels in their party (P.Lond. 3.929.68–71). The scale of transport at Bacchias was notably smaller and single donkeys are commonly seen in the customs house records there (P.Wisc. 2.80).

31. Sijpesteijn, "Eine weitere Torzollquittung," knew of twelve examples, to which we can add at least four more: P.Customs 408, P.Customs 441, Sb6 9233, Sb16 12611 (aka, P.Mich. 6182e, 6177c, 6152, 6161a).

The case of the transporter Apollonius offers a strong example. Passing through the customs house of nearby Bacchias, he first carries loads of black beans on a quartet of donkeys. At the peak of his prosperity, the records show that he traveled regularly with a trader named Elis, but he evidently experienced some kind of economic hardship in mid-September 114 CE, and scaled back his business in the subsequent weeks. He changed his schedule to include a greater number of smaller trips and ended up traveling in the company of a new set of traders who shared this business model, using a single donkey to come and go every few days.[32] Beside Elis, Apollonius would have looked like a smaller, less successful trader, but next to his new companions, he seems to have been firmly in the middle of the pack. Arriving at Bacchias with Elis, Apollonius could have expected to be compared unfavorably, but, when he traveled with other small-scale transporters, the diminution of his business may have been more or less invisible except to those with a keen eye and healthy memory.

Thus, a reputation for successful transporting, at least, was something that could be visibly measured and, in general, appearances held great significance for reputation.[33] Apollonius' moneylender, Milo, is judged on these same terms. A local innkeeper reports that Milo always went about town dressed like a beggar and adds this to the long list of his supposed faults.[34] His choice not to dress in a way that matched his social and economic status was viewed by this neighbor as an indication of Milo's greed and untrustworthiness. At the other end of the spectrum, a merchant might easily overdress and seem to be putting on airs above his or her station. This accusation is most often leveled against freedmen, who suffered not only from the stigma of their previous status, but also by an assumed ignorance of good taste and a desire to flaunt their new wealth. Trimalchio is the example par excellence, but similar features are found in Zoilus, the stock tacky freedman of Martial's *Epigrams*. Zoilus flaunts his wealth in lavish home goods and in fancy clothes that, as Martial implies, he has bought on credit.[35] Martial does not identify the source of the wealth against which Zoilus has borrowed, but associates both his taste and social class with the perfumer Cosmus, whose profession not only made him incredibly wealthy but also masked smelly realities with pleasant fictions, a kind of deception that was fitting for freedmen-merchants.[36] Both men are imagined to have moved in

32. P.Wisc. 2.80 (Sept. 18, 114 CE), lines 80–150.

33. This is true for all levels of Roman society, see Andrew R. Dyck, "Dressing to Kill: Attire as a Proof and Means of Characterization in Cicero's Speeches," *Arethusa* 34.1 (2001).

34. Apul., *Met.* 1.21.

35. Mart., *Epigr.* 2.58.

36. Zoilus is *Cosmianus . . . fuscus ampullis* at Martial, *Epigrams*, 3.82.26. On Zoilus (and Cosmus), Rosario Moreno Soldevila, Alberto Marino Castillo, and Juan Fernández Valverde, *A*

social circles far above their own rightful station and Zoilus, at least, is recognized as a shallow parvenu—a perfect target for Martial's invective.

Appearance as a metric for success was, accordingly, a tightrope that merchants struggled to navigate. Visible success was desirable, just as visible poverty was a sign of imminent failure, but flaunting wealth was a sign of an avaricious character and a lack of humility. Elites and peers alike were quick to view fine clothing and expensive possessions as a sign of having unsuitable aspirations, while everyone denigrated indications of poverty as representative of not only bad luck, but also personal failure.[37] The balance was difficult to strike but straying from the path could seriously inhibit merchants in their pursuit of a good name.

Beyond appearances, reputation, more generally, was represented as comparative and dependent upon being better than some, at times ill-defined, other. A retailer from Rome was described in his funerary inscription as *homo super omnes fidelissimus*, a man more honest than all others.[38] The value of *fides* was high in merchant reputations, as its absence was among the most common accusations leveled against those in retail. The claim of superlative honesty, trustworthiness, or fidelity was a powerful one. In their own words, merchants tended to prefer the superlative, either literally, as here, or more figuratively, as in the case of Mithres. Their intent was to convey a positive version of their self-representation, a subject to which we will return in chapter 3, but it was also a comparative strategy. Their superlatives strove to claim success either in terms of their character, or, more mundanely, in terms of economic profit.

The latter is, perhaps unsurprisingly, the most visible in our sources. Merchants projected their financial success in numerous ways precisely because it was so firmly attached to their reputation. While they often missed the mark in their personal appearance, merchants were skilled in visually representing their successful businesses. The streets of Pompeii are filled with visual media being used to its fullest extent to advertise not only the presence of commerce and industry, but also the success of the merchants and artisans associated with those same workshops, stores, and *tabernae*.[39]

Prosopography to Martial's Epigrams (Berlin: De Gruyter, 2019). On freedmen and their position in Roman society more generally: Mouritsen, *The Freedman*; López Barja de Quiroga, "Freedmen Social Mobility"; and Treggiari, *Roman Freedmen*.

37. As in CIL 4.9839b: "I hate poor people. If anyone wants something for nothing, he is a fool. He should pay for it." Among modern analyses, this tendency to blame the poor for their status is discussed in C. R. Whittaker, "The Poor," in *The Romans*, ed. Andrea Giardina (Chicago: Chicago University Press, 1993), 273; Jerry P. Toner, *Leisure and Ancient Rome* (Hoboken, NJ: Wiley Press, 1995), 69–71; Neville Morley, "The Poor in the City of Rome," in *Poverty in the Roman World*, ed. Margaret Atkins and Robin Osborne (Cambridge: Cambridge University Press, 2006), 25.

38. Funerary marker of Lucius Statius Onesimus, CIL 6.9663, line 6.

39. On *tabernae*, see Steven J. R. Ellis, *The Roman Retail Revolution: The Socio-Economic World of the* Taberna (Oxford: Oxford University Press, 2018); on workshops, Miko Flohr, "*Nec quicquam*

The walls of the workshop of Verecundus on the Via dell'Abbondanza, the *decumanus maximus*, of the city, offer a prime example.[40] The shopfront was lavishly decorated in wall paintings to either side of the entrance. To the right (Fig. 2), workers are shown engaged in their profession in a shop overseen by a man plausibly identified as the owner, Verecundus, while on the left (Fig. 3), a woman commonly identified as Verecundus' wife attends to a shop counter.[41] The entirety of the exterior wall is decorated, even beyond these scenes of work, with arresting visuals, including a representation of Venus Pompeiana in a chariot drawn by elephants and a large image of Mercury emerging from a temple.

The iconography of this shop was eye-catching and prominent along a street that would have been busy with foot and cart traffic in antiquity. The scenes are visually interesting, mingling large, impressive visuals with small details that would have been best examined up close. Moreover, the two scenes of work, the workshop to the right and the store to the left, would have been at eye-level for the passerby. Trade is therefore at the forefront of this display, and Verecundus' selections make claims to high quality products and good service. In the workshop, Verecundus himself displays a finished piece of cloth, demonstrating that the work of the employees, or slaves, beside him had led, and would lead, to visibly excellent results. His wife in the shop minds the counter and, presumably,

---

ingenuum habere potest officina? Spatial Contexts of Urban Production at Pompeii, AD 79," *Babesch* 82.1 (2007); on the Pompeian economy more generally, Miko Flohr and Andrew Wilson, eds., *The Economy of Pompeii* (Oxford: Oxford University Press, 2017).

40. Regio IX.7.6–7, known as the House of Verecundus. The interior of the shop has not been excavated, leaving many unanswered questions, most pressing of which would seem to be: is this a house at all? The identification of Verecundus is based on the numerous instances of this name graffitied on the right-hand wall painting. It is a plausible identification, but nevertheless somewhat tenuous. While John R. Clarke, *Art in the Lives of Ordinary Romans: Visual Representation and Non-Elite Viewers in Italy, 100 B.C.–A.D. 315* (Berkeley: University of California Press, 2003), 107; Jens-Arne Dickmann, "A 'Private' Felter's Workshop in the Casa dei Postumii at Pompeii," in *Making Textiles in Pre-Roman and Roman Times: People, Places, Identities*, ed. Margaria Gleba and Judit Pásztókai-Szeöke (Oxford: Oxbow Books, 2013); and Flohr, *The World of the Fullo* believe Verecundus to be a wool worker, a felter, who turned spun wool into fabric. Verecundus is more traditionally identified as a fuller, or a cleaner of wool. Much depends on what one believes that the workers are doing in the wall-painting, whether it be fulling, the process whereby cleaned fabrics were fluffed and returned to their normal shape and texture, or felting, making cloth from woven wool. These processes required similar actions and would have been iconographically similar. Clarke, *Art in the Lives of Ordinary Romans*, 109, refers to an inscription that identifies a Verecundus as a *vestarius*, a clothes merchant. This is strong evidence, since Verecundus is not a terribly common name, but the Via dell' Abbondanza was a street full of fulleries, see Walter O. Moeller, "The Felt Shops of Pompeii," *American Journal of Archaeology* 75 (1971); and Walter O. Moeller, *The Wool Trade of Ancient Pompeii* (Leiden: Brill, 1976), which attempted to tip the scales back in favor of fulling. For our purposes, little rides on the outcome of this debate as both are merchant professions, though fullers were further down the social scale than cloth makers.

41. Clarke, *Art in the Lives of Ordinary Romans*, 109, admits that she is possibly an employee or slave but argues that her prominence in the scene is indicative of her relatively high status and increases the likelihood that she is Verecundus' wife.

Figure 2. Right pilaster of the workshop of Verecundus, Venus Pompeiana, above, with workshop scene, below, Regio IX.7.6–7. Alamy Stock Photo.

engages in pleasant conversation with the customer who sits on a bench to the right. The space she occupies is both a social and an economic one that offered customers comfort and community, as well as their commissioned fabric.

Both scenes show a thriving business. This was critically important information for customers shopping in an area filled with other choices. The immediate region of Verecundus' shop was home to several other wool-working

Figure 3. Left pilaster of the workshop of Verecundus, Mercury exiting a temple, above, shop interior scene, below, Regio IX.7.6–7. Postcard c. 1910. Public Domain (CC-PD).

and wool-cleaning businesses.[42] This arrangement, with neighborhoods often densely packed with members of the same profession, was relatively common in the urban centers of the Roman world. Close proximity facilitated cooperation among members of the same profession and helped guide customers who were searching for a particular type of good or service to a merchant or artisan who could help them.[43] Comparison was therefore often possible over eas-

42. Moeller, "The Felt Shops of Pompeii"; and Moeller, *Wool Trade.*

43. Augustine, *Confessiones*, 6.9, describes silversmiths having their own neighborhood, *vicus*; in *De civitate dei* 7.4, he describes the smiths dividing up the stages of production and working together to complete a commission. Also found in the Via Sacra, as discussed in Nicolas Monteix, "'Caius Lucretius . . . , marchand de coleurs de la rue des fabricants de courroies': Réflexions critiques sur les concentrations de métiers à Rome," in *"Quartiers" artisanaux en Grèce ancienne:*

ily walkable distances, and a streetscape that made one shopkeeper or artisan more prominent than the others was consequently a substantial advantage.[44]

Success, communicated as visual prominence, told the pedestrian that this was the best place to choose, and, as a semipermanent adaption of and investment in the building, it told any potential competition that Verecundus' business was here to stay. As mentioned above, this kind of assertion could be a potentially self-fulfilling prophecy, as these proclamations of success also contributed to bringing it about. Prominent shops held the potential to become local landmarks and could become gathering places in their own right.[45] Verecundus' wife tends to one such gatherer, who is shown to linger at her counter and seems to conceive of the shop as a place of both social and economic importance.

Verecundus and his wife were right to encourage such visitors through their iconographic choices. Loitering locals and regular customers made shops appear busy and prosperous, supplementing the impression aspired to in the decorative program. Even if they were not spending huge sums of money, the presence of customers in a shop advertised to the general population that the business was worthy of patronage. A busy shop encouraged others to approach, see what the fuss was about, and patronize a business they might have otherwise ignored.

Reputation was greatly benefited by the appearance of success, but only in so far as it helped audiences to determine the appropriate ranking among merchants of the same field. Yet such actions and protestations of prosperity could also be a front to disguise a merchant's true struggles. Displays of this nature were expensive but could be an investment designed to turn a failing business around, as much as they could reflect a successful merchant courting new custom. Among the more modestly successful, a display of this kind might mean making a small investment such as paying membership into a *collegium* or other voluntary association. Though membership might be costly for a poor trader, access to a network of peers might help a merchant out of a tough economic position, and, if nothing else, membership often came with a provision of an honorable burial, which could be valuable for a merchant who

Une perspective méditerranéenne, ed. Arianna Esposito and Giorgos M. Sanidas (Villeneuve d'Ascq: Presses Universitaires du Septentrion, 2012).

44. As seen in modern studies such as A. E. Kirby and A. M. Kent, "Architecture as Brand: Store Design and Brand Identity," *Journal of Product & Brand Management* 19.6 (2010).

45. On landmarks, wayfinding, and social occupation of space, see Yi-Fu Tuan, *Space and Place: The Perspective of Experience* (Minneapolis: University of Minnesota Press, 1977); Christopher Tilley, *A Phenomenology of Landscape: Places, Paths, and Monuments* (Oxford: Berg, 1994); Michel de Certeau, *The Practice of Everyday Life* (Berkeley: University of California Press, 2011).

otherwise teetered on the edge of bankruptcy.[46] Poor and wealthy alike joined such groups, which helped to mask the struggle of the poor merchant among a collective of their middling or wealthy peers. Only those who had attempted to rise high in the ranks of an association were forced to lose face in times of personal or financial struggle, while more junior members were able to mask their poverty by remaining in the middle of the pack.[47] By late antiquity, many associations, inspired by Christian calls to charity, had even added provisions to their charters to support poor members of their group.[48]

Yet not all merchants wholly shied away from admitting to failure, as long as that failure was far in their past and could be contrasted with their present prosperity. Merchants often expressed their success in funerary inscriptions by describing how far they had come. An idiom, *ab asse quaesitum*, meaning something akin to, "coming up from nothing,"[49] and literally meaning acquiring wealth from a single *as*, is found in these settings to lay claim to the lifelong achievements of merchants.[50] It is particularly common in the case of freedmen and women whose successes were social as well as financial. This same dynamic is visible in the imagined funerary relief of Petronius' Trimalchio, who boasted, *ex parvo crevit*, that he grew (his fortune) from a tiny amount.[51] He contrasts this with the millions he expected to leave behind. Wealth, in itself, was a good thing, but the process of having earned, especially when it could be explic-

46. Van Nijf, *Civic World of Professional Associations*, 28.

47. Thus, P.Mich. 9.575, in which a member requests to leave a guild because he is too ἀσθενής, literally weak, but here almost certainly poor, to continue acting as the guild's patron, νέμειν τὴν κοινήν, but we lack similar documents expelling group members because of their poverty. Records of gifts to guilds, as P.Mich. 5.246, show that some were only expected to contribute food to communal meals, while others offered several dozen denarii.

48. Richard S. Ascough, Philip A. Harland, and John S. Kloppenborg, *Associations in the Greco-Roman World: A Sourcebook* (Waco: Baylor University Press, 2012), Blueprint (in Syriac) of Regulations for Craft Guilds (VI CE) (Online, #20398), Regulation 25, "If poverty or destitution should befall any of us and that man does not have sufficient to provide his upkeep, then we shall all support him in love." Harland's translation.

49. The translation of this phrase has generated a small amount of debate. Three interpretations predominate: first, "having achieved results with low expenses," second, "not having taken even a penny from anyone," with the implication of self-sufficiency and independence, and finally, something like what is described here. The difficulty is discussed in Ettore de Ruggiero, *Dizionario epigrafico di antichità romane* (Rome: Istituto Italiano per la Storia antica, 1895). I agree with G. Nenci, "Ab asse quaesitum," *Rivista di Filologia e di Istruzione Classica* 11.9 (1964) that the idiom refers to a slow accumulation of wealth over time from meager beginnings, with the implication of hard work and savings. The middle interpretation is the view of the TLL article on *as*, but is based on only three examples, including this inscription. While I do not find this translation convincing, there is a strong theme of ideal self-sufficiency among Roman merchants, which will be discussed more fully in the next chapter.

50. The phrase appears in CIL 9.2029, the funerary inscription of Vibia Chresta, and CIL 5.7647, the funerary relief of Quintus Minicius Faber, a cartwright. A similar formula, *ab asse positum*, appears in CIL 5.6623, though the individual is not explicitly identified as a merchant.

51. Petronius, *Satyricon*, 71.12.

itly stated that it had been earned honestly or, framed in the negative, without deceit or fraud, was even more beneficial to a merchant's reputation.

Claims such as these are relatively common in merchant funerary texts, where, as with Philostratus' instructor-philosopher, Proclus, it was helpful to illuminate a merchant's virtues through the inverse behaviors that they had spurned. Especially common is the formula of *sine* plus some shameful, reputation-tarnishing trait. Thus, we see *sine fraude*, without deceit, appearing in a series of inscriptions across the western Empire, and especially in North Africa, where it appears in at least three instances.[52] These merchants occupied a range of professions, but shared a desire to define their reputation in terms of the success they achieved without resorting to various forms of cheating.

It is generally impossible to judge the truth of such claims today, but it would have been equally difficult to judge the sincerity of merchants in antiquity based solely on inscriptions. It was in such cases that supplementary information was vital. One could not rely exclusively on what a merchant said in his or her own defense or in a public display of reputation. One of the guests at Trimalchio's dinner offers a case in point. While dining and asking about his dinner companions, Encolpius is told the story of a freedman undertaker at the table, who strove, even as his business was failing, to put the best face on a bad situation. Encolpius' dinner companion says, "When his business was in decline, and he was afraid that his creditors would think that he was about to default, he announced an auction of his goods on this pretext: 'Gaius Julius Proculus will have an auction for some superfluous knickknacks.'"[53] Without further context, such careful spin would make it impossible to tell when a tradesman was merely cleaning out his closet and when he was going out of business. Information drawn from peers, neighbors, and customers was essential to finding out what a given action meant and what a merchant might be trying to hide. Reputation was a composite of as much information as the audience could muster, and it was drawn from as many sources as inquiring minds could access.

Critically, just as reputation was built up slowly and steadily over time, and depended upon comparison between peers, reputation grew whether a merchant was actively working on it or not. Trimalchio's dinner guests jovially gossiped about Proculus the undertaker, without his ever realizing it had

52. CIL 9.2029; CIL 8.11824 = CLE 1238 = ILS 07457 = ILTun 528; *L'Année Épigraphique* 1960: 116.

53. Petronius, *Satyricon*, 38. *Inclinatis quoque rebus suis, cum timeret ne creditores illum conturbare existimarent, hoc titulo auctionem proscripsit: 'C. Iulius Proculus auctionem faciet rerum supervacuarum.'*

happened, just as Lucius spoke to an innkeeper about Milo the moneylender, before he had even met the man. Conversations in the real world must have echoed these fictional cases of casual information gathering, and reputation developed behind merchants' backs as much as it is did in their presence, or in their stores and workshops. Thus, day-to-day events and the successes and failures of others added to and detracted from a merchant's reputation whether or not he or she was aware. The process of how these isolated goings on became reputation was dependent upon the network that surrounded a merchant, on his or her audience and what that group believed constituted "good" or "bad" behavior.

Audience

Thus far we have identified qualities that contributed to a good reputation and have discussed how, like Mithres, one might become known for particular traits. Reputation was developed from patterns in merchant behavior, and we have stressed that, to an extent at least, reputation was comparative and dependent upon how successful one looked next to one's peers. What remains is to consider the relationship between those that, as we say in English, *had* a reputation, and those who *gave* them a bad (or good) name.

As the English idiomatic use suggests, reputation was a kind of possession. In antiquity, it was understood to belong to a person, but it could be bestowed on others as well. Modern reputational studies have noted that reputation commonly has, metaphorically speaking, a semiphysical form that can move around. Importantly, however, reputation was not "stored" with the person it "belonged" to, but "resided in" the wider network of people around the subject.[54] While the languages of the ancient world do not exactly mimic this conception, in that reputation is not commonly "held" in Latin or Greek, there are commonalities between ancient and modern understandings of reputation in this regard.[55] For example, merchants commonly describe their reputations with possessives. *Mea fama* appears in both literary and epigraphic contexts, and we see, among merchants, a willingness to attribute a reputation to someone else, recognizing it as their possession.[56] *Fama* as a Latin concept, paired

54. Craik, *Reputation*, ch. 3.

55. δόξαν ἔχειν is a formulation occasionally found in Greek, e.g., Dem. 2.17, but the equivalent is not found for *fama* except in very rare, late instances.

56. *Mea fama*: e.g., Propertius 1.7.9, Livy 1.3, AE 1968, 0074. CIL 6.9663, Rome, funerary inscription of Lucius Statius Onesimus, *cuius fama*.

with the Greek δόξα, did belong to someone, but there is no equivalent theoretical understanding of reputation from antiquity. When reputation is discussed as an abstract in ancient literature, it is thought of as a valuable commodity, and as something that may be gained and lost, but without consideration of where it resided or how exactly it changed location, shape, or quality. The closest our evidence approaches to modern understandings is in its suggestion that it was often difficult to know, precisely, what one's reputation was at any given time and place. Modern and ancient sources agree that it required substantial effort to keep abreast of the current state of one's reputation, and that it was possible, as we saw in the case of Mithres, to have the best intentions and still be perfectly ignorant of how your actions, words, and efforts were evaluated by others.

This is fundamentally because reputation is dialectical in nature. It develops not only based on what an actor does or projects, but also on how those acts and messages are received. Reputation requires an audience, and much depends on the number and disposition of those witnesses: to have no reputation at all was to be a loner without either a friend or an enemy, while a robust reputation was an indicator of either fame or infamy.

Audience opinions differed based on the quality of their information, which was often derived from their social or physical proximity to the individual reputed, and on the cultural frameworks in which they operated. Thus family, close friends, and business partners who lived and worked in the same social and cultural communities were in a position to create detailed and nuanced versions of a merchant's reputation, while more casual acquaintances, irregular customers, or travelers from other places often had incomplete knowledge. They based their judgment on a smaller pool of interactions or interpreted what they witnessed in different ways, based on their differing, previous experiences. Yet getting from the day-to-day behaviors of a merchant, which we have seen are so pivotal, to a good or bad reputation is challenging. How did audiences determine what actions or behaviors were significant for reputation?

Theoretical treatments of reputation have already covered this vital ground. Going back to at least Frederick Bailey in his *Gifts and Poison*, the role of reception in reputation has been an established feature of the field. In his understanding, the interpretation of actions, words, texts, and events and their translation into evidence of reputation is a matter of "signaling." These signals may be consciously projected or may be the unconscious result of everyday actions, but they are built into the things that individuals do or do not do in ways that are culturally encoded and specific.[57] In fact, Bailey has posited that the mes-

57. F. G. Bailey, *Gifts and Poison: The Politics of Reputation* (New York: Schocken Books, 1971),

sages that signals send "may well remain invisible to someone not familiar with the culture concerned."[58] Thus, they are difficult to assess from the outside, and situations that may appear to be neutral moments to an outsider may in fact be highly significant within the community under observation. Within a culture, signals are related to categories, which, in turn, are related to other categories, with the result that positive and negative associations can develop from actions that, on their own, appear to have little to do with reputation.[59] These associations are made quickly, and often with reliance on previous social or cultural knowledge.

The closer the receiver was to the merchant, the more points of social contact they had, the better information he or she would receive. Proximity made it possible for categories to become increasingly specific and the associations with those categories to become ever more detailed, allowing for the eventual assessment of reputation at a high level of nuance.[60]

One may generally say, for example, that a merchant had a reputation for being successful. It might be possible to assess this from his dress, the appearance of his home, or a crowd of customers at his shop. For the merchant, these signals would be relatively "cheap" in that they require little effort, though perhaps some monetary cost, to acquire. They could also be sent easily and be received by those who held little context about the merchant's actual social or economic status.[61] These kinds of signals do not require personal knowledge or private access to the merchant and his affairs but may be "read" by a stranger on the street and interpreted without further context.

Consequently, these signals hold the potential to be misleading. More personal knowledge might reveal that these signals were a crafted mask, like that broadcast by Proculus the undertaker, but not a true reflection of the merchant's financial or social reality. Alternately, they might be the byproduct of acciden-

10. See also Eric Alden Smith and Rebecca Bliege Bird, "Costly Signaling and Cooperative Behavior," in *Moral Sentiments and Material Interests: The Foundations of Cooperation in Economic Life*, ed. Herbert Gintis, Samuel Bowles, Robert Boyd, and Ernst Fehr (Cambridge, MA: MIT Press, 2005); Alex Pentland and Tracy Heibeck, *Honest Signals* (Cambridge, MA: MIT Press, 2008); Emler, "Social Psychology of Reputation"; Bromley, *Reputation*. The latter two use different vocabulary but address the same concept, interpreted according to social norms and cultural reference points.

58. Bailey, *Gifts and Poison*, 10.

59. Bailey, *Gifts and Poison*, 12.

60. Bromley, *Reputation*, 42–44, describes the issue as one of "primary" and "secondary" reputations, those known first-hand, or "primary," being the better informed, while the "secondary" relies on hearsay.

61. John Whitfield, *People Will Talk: The Surprising Science of Reputation* (Hoboken, NJ: Wiley Press, 2012), 30. This signaling, in many respects, runs parallel to the theory of NIE, where institutions helped to reduce transaction costs, the cost of information, and unpredictability in general. Some institutions are more "expensive" than others, but some also produced a more legible economic landscape than others.

tal circumstances, rather than intentional deception or projection. Nuanced, insider knowledge is more "costly," because it takes more time and energy to collect, and it requires more effort from the merchant to broadcast.[62] At some point, and for certain people under particular circumstances, such information might not be considered worth the effort to obtain or to project. For the receiver, most information could be gathered along a spectrum of effort, simply by being an observer within one's community and participating in simple methods of information gathering. In some cases, it would be worth digging deeper, asking around and finding out more from those closer to the merchant, while in other cases a cursory inspection might be sufficient. Thus a customer intending to purchase something cheap would be less circumspect, and engage less effort into learning about the merchant's reputation, than one intending to invest a large amount of money.

While specific circumstances generally dictated the amount of effort an individual put into learning about a merchant's reputation, seeking out the conscious and unconscious signals sent by merchants could be beneficial to one's own reputation, as well as to one's social and economic success. Knowledge about one's peers and competitors, for example, could be vital for determining whom to trust, whose business was thriving, and how best to adapt one's own behavior. Therefore, there were incentives for using various reputation sharing techniques and for exerting some effort to avoid relying exclusively on personal observation or those signals that merchants intentionally projected.

Essential to this is the understanding that both the creation and dissemination of reputation information often happened highly informally, through the regular activity of daily life. While, as we will discuss in the next chapter, merchants often made concerted efforts to shape their reputations with concrete strategies, most reputations, positive and negative, were not built through these large displays, as we have discussed, but rather were founded upon the slow, steady accretion of information that was the result of day-to-day life. Particularly in small communities, predictable face-to-face contact allowed receivers to witness both conscious and unconscious displays of character, business practices, and social status, and to assess how much of that was consciously performed and how much was a reflection of the actor's true character. Often, this data accumulated itself into something like "common knowledge," about

62. Smith and Bird, "Costly Signaling." The audience may also have needed time to consider before passing this information on. Learning in-depth information about a merchant necessitates a type of closeness that may encourage the learner to choose whom they inform with care.

the subject, which closely resembled, or was perhaps even coterminous with, that person's reputation.[63]

As a result, there are relatively few moments that are truly "forgettable," or "passing" when it comes to reputation. Even if a given situation was unworthy of comment in the moment, significance might be read into a seemingly innocuous interaction, particularly in light of information that the receiver might later acquire. It is an easy step to turn a simple, typical moment into a signal, laden with meaning. Again, continuity was essential to ensuring that actions were not misinterpreted. Merchants strove to send positive signals consistently, thereby building up a steady body of evidence for their receivers. This consistency was intended to build a reputation over time, but also to prevent the sudden reinterpretation of their behavior, so that a single off-day did not reinflect a moment from days, months, or years before with new meaning, but preserved it as an anomaly in the mind of the viewer, who knew that the merchant was not "like that," and did not assume that the positive signals of the past were a performance covering some more sinister "truth" about the merchant's character.

Convincing the audience that an action was genuine, and not an elaborate ploy to lure the unwitting into a false sense of trust, was challenging, and it interwove personal behaviors and business practices even more closely together. In truth, signals sent in almost any circumstance could affect one's reputation across the board. The social and the economic, in terms of reputation, were inextricably connected for Roman merchants, so any issue that arose in one part of a merchant's life necessarily influenced all others. Thus, an argument between friends over a private matter could become inextricably connected to the trustworthiness of a merchant in business.

A striking case comes from the Midrash on Psalms 12:1, where a hypothetical band of merchants planned to buy salt to supply their town:

> It once happened that a certain town had no salt, and there was a band (=guild) of caravaneers (literally: donkey-drivers) who said: We will go to such and such a place and buy salt, and sell it before others come. Now, they had a leader, [and] they said to him: Let us go to this place.... He answered them: I have to plough tomorrow, so wait until I have done my ploughing, and afterwards we will go. They said to him: All right.... What did he do? He loaded a sack on his ass and went off alone, while

63. Chris Wickham, "Gossip and Resistance among the Medieval Peasantry," *Past and Present* 160 (1998): 5–6. Gossip is discussed fully in chapter 5.

> his friends slept till morning, [till] they called (her) [him] (i.e., to join them). The neighbours asked: Whom do you want? So and so (i.e., their leader) already went off last night. So they set off in the morning and found him on his way back. They said to him: Why did you act so? He replied to them: Do you not know why? Had we all gone together, the [price] would immediately have fallen to a low level. Now I have brought [salt, and] until you get there mine will have been sold out, so that when you get [there] you can sell yours at a good price.[64]

The text is a common rabbinical form, known as a *ma'aseh*, a fictional, parable-like story created to illustrate a lesson, often with an eye to distinguishing the good, the rabbis and pious Jews, from the bad, the goyim and impious. The characters, as a result, are caricatures or stereotypes, as well as allegories, and their circumstances are only roughly sketched out. Nevertheless, they are founded upon an inherently plausible reality: one in which there are good men and bad whose actions display *exempla* to be emulated or avoided. In this case, the group, a chabora (חבורה) is a fairly well-organized entity of caravaneers, or, more literally, donkey-drivers, with an established leader, whose business model seems to encompass both personal agricultural work and the transportation and sale of goods with a group of peers. These figures are imagined as opportunistic in their mercantile work, seeking out goods depending on the state of their local market, and the lead merchant is shown, pejoratively, to be balancing both his personal advancement with his role in the group.

His *exemplum* is a fundamentally bad one, as he acts the part of the liar and cheat who wrongs his peers and seeks profit above all else. Yet it is not the peers, in this case, whose reaction is most interesting, largely because the *ma'aseh* does not offer it to us. Rather, it is the neighbors whose behavior offers us insight into the role of audience in matters of reputation. The lead merchant apparently lives close to others, in a town or other densely populated area. These neighbors are witnesses to the lead merchant's comings and goings, and from their perspective this scene looks rather different than it would have to the merchant and his associates.

According to the Midrash, the first involvement of the neighbors comes

64. Sperber, *The City in Roman Palestine*, 17. Sperber's translation, based on the text of Buber. Following Leon Nemoy, Saul Lieberman, and Harry A. Wolfson, eds., *The Midrash on Psalms* (New Haven: Yale University Press, 1959), the text is to be dated, at the earliest, to the third century CE, and contains many later additions. The first reference to this particular portion of the Midrash is from the eleventh century CE. Nevertheless, salt merchants have a long tradition of group activity in the eastern Roman world, see, e.g., the famous case of P.Mich. 5.245.

in the evening, when they saw the lead merchant leave his home, presumably with at least one donkey to carry back the salt he meant to buy. This journey does not seem to have surprised them, and probably appeared to be unworthy of comment at the time. Like so much of the evidence for reputation, the merchant going to buy goods was probably a common, if not daily, occurrence that was beneath the conscious notice of the community. The matter only became noteworthy on the following morning, when a group of merchants, again presumably with their animals, turned up and began trying to wake, and then find, the lead merchant. We can imagine that this was a noisy process, which, if it did not wake, at least disturbed the neighbors, whose response was to ask what these merchants wanted. It was at this point that the unintentional and unassuming act of leaving the house became a signal for reputation, and the neighbors went from mere members of the community to an audience for the merchant's reputation.

The Midrash cuts off the rest of the neighbor's experience at this point to follow the merchant and the rationalization he offers for his behavior, yet even this brief comment demonstrates that the actions of both this group as a whole and the lead merchant as an individual, were witnessed and interpreted by others. The neighbors, as bystanders, were able to judge the reputation of all these people, and, whether or not the other merchants forgave the leader for his perfidy, the neighbors could be expected to form their own opinions about the event. They would not have access to the "explanation" that the lead merchant offered to his peers, and they might tell the story to as many or as few others as they wished with their own inflection and emphasis. Their ability to spread and interpret this signal made them effective as enforcers of reputation as an institution. While the fellow group members might choose to drive the merchant from the group or impose a fine, their sanctions would be minimal next to a community that had adjusted his reputation to reflect his behavior and character more accurately.

The lead merchant likely did not consider his neighbors as he set off to buy salt. His concern was for speed and escaping the notice of his peers. Though he could not have hoped to disguise his behavior forever, he hoped that he would be able to secure his profit and deal with his fellow traders later. They would have been his focus, and his explanation for his behavior is targeted to quell their anger and encourage their forgiveness. We cannot know if the lead merchant was violating some official group regulation in lying to his peers, but after the fact, he is genuinely concerned that their censure and distrust will harm his reputation. The irony is that this damage is already done, witnessed by an audience that, unlike his peers, had no reason to cover up the lead merchant's behavior and every reason to share this interesting and dramatic bit of information around the town.

By contrast, groups of merchants, as an audience for reputation, alternated between policing merchant bad behavior and covering it up. While almost all associations maintained some formal or informal mechanism for ousting members who violated group norms, our preserved charters also demonstrate that they often desired to police disputes internally and prevent the airing of the group's dirty laundry in a public forum. Charters account not only for potential conflicts among merchants over business, like the case of the Midrash merchants, but also social conflicts ranging from petty disagreements to cases of adultery among members.[65] These groups generally attempted to keep information about disputes under wraps, as they understood that information of this kind could be damaging to the reputations of the individuals involved, as well as to the reputation of the group.

A useful case from the first century CE is the charter of what is believed to be an association of sheep and cattle herders, who, along with their pastoral duties, presumably leveraged their collective power in the eventual sale of their fleeces and livestock. However, rather than focusing on the economic advantages that the group could provide to its members, or even discussing the structure of the group and its leadership, the extant document lists a number of potential crimes against the group that a member might commit, along with the punishments deemed appropriate:

> ἐὰν δέ τις ἐκπαροινήσῃ ζημιούσθωι ὃ ἐὰν τῶι κοινῶι δόξηι.
> ἐ̣ὰν δέ τιν̣ι̣ ⟦ζ⟧ σύλλο̣[γ]ο̣ς παραγγελῆι καὶ μὴ παραγένηται, ζημιούσθωι
> ἐπὶ μὲν τῆς κώμης δραχ(μὴν) μίαν, ἐπὶ δὲ τῆς πόλεω(ς) δραχ(μὰς)
> τέσσαρας.
> . . .
> ἐάν τις παρίδῃ τινὰ ἐν ἀηδίᾳ καὶ μὴ συνεπισχύσῃ ἐπὶ τωὶ συλλῦσαι
> αὐτὸν τῆς ἀηδίας, δ[ό]τ̣ω̣ι̣ (δραχμὰς) η. ὁ δ' ἐν ταῖς εὐωχίας
> κατὰ κλισίαν προαναπείπτων τοῦ ἑτέρου δότωι περισσότερον
> τριώβολον τοῦ ἰδίου τόπου ἕκασ̣τ̣ο̣ς. ἐάν τις τοῦ ἑτέρου κατη-
> γορήσῃ ἢι διαβολὴν ποιήσηται, ζημι(ούσθω δραχμὰς) η. ἐάν τις τὸν
> ἕτερον ὑπονομεύσῃ ἢι οἰκοφθορήσῃ, ζημιο(ύσθω δραχμὰς) ξ.

And if anyone is drunk and disorderly, let him be fined whatever the group judges to be appropriate. And if anyone is notified of a meeting

65. Venticinque, *Honor among Thieves*, 55–62.

> and does not attend, let him be fined one drachma in the country, but four drachmai in the city. . . . If anyone notices someone in distress and does not assist him to get out of his distress, let him pay eight drachmai. Each one who sits himself down on the couch before another member, let him pay an extra three obols for his own place. If anyone prosecutes another member or slanders him, let him be fined eight drachmai. If anyone plots against another member or corrupts his home, let him pay sixty drachmai.[66]

The charges are an understandable collection of issues that might reasonably arise among a loosely assembled group of competitors. It is easy enough to imagine that pushing and shoving or drunken antics might be issues arising in any number of associations, but all would have carried more weight when such disputes became intertwined with the professional reputations of the members. Specifically, many of the issues proscribed in this charter also seem to have been chosen to prevent private grievances becoming matters of public record. The ruling against prosecuting or slandering another member, with the latter being an offense under Roman law, seems to be aimed at keeping disputes in-house, thereby protecting the group from the appearance of internal conflict. The initial prohibition against misconduct, with the proviso that the group must determine the appropriate fine, may also have been intended to give the group the right to arbitrate its own conflicts, something which is apparent in other group charters.[67]

Merchant groups needed to ensure that the reputation of the group and its individual members was carefully presented and made available to their audience. Groups might seek to define themselves in positive ways, naming themselves "brothers," "feasters," "drinkers," and even "friends,"[68] but their true

66. P.Mich. 5.243, lines 3–4, 6–8. Tebtynis, 13–37 CE.

67. Langellotti, "A World Full of Associations," on the Tebtynis examples; Nicolas Tran, "*Ordo corporatorum*: The Rules of Roman Associations and the *collegia* at Ostia in the Second and Third Centuries AD," in *Private Associations in the Ancient Greek World: Regulations and the Creation of Group Identity*, ed. Vincent Gabrielsen and Mario C. D. Paganini (Cambridge: Cambridge University Press, 2021) on Ostia in the second and third centuries CE; Traianos Gagos and Peter van Minnen, *Settling a Dispute: Toward a Legal Anthropology of Late Antique Egypt* (Ann Arbor: University of Michigan Press, 1994) offers a fifth/sixth-century Egyptian example. For more general treatments: Venticinque, *Honor among Thieves*, 58–59, esp. n. 90; Derek Roebuck, *Ancient Greek Arbitration* (Oxford: Holo Books, 2001); Derek Roebuck and Bruno de Loynes de Fumichon, *Roman Arbitration* (Oxford: Holo Books, 2004).

68. John F. Donahue, *The Roman Community at Table during the Principate* (Ann Arbor: University of Michigan Press, 2004), 126-130; Philip A. Harland, "Familial Dimensions of Group Identity: 'Brothers' (ΑΔΕΛΦΟΙ) in Associations of the Greek East," *Journal of Biblical Literature* 124.3 (2005). See also: *amici subaediani*, CIL 10.6699.

reputation was based on what the community thought about them, and their success in convincing their neighbors, customers, and general acquaintance that they were good people and honest tradesmen. This was not necessarily an easy feat when the simple act of leaving your house might at some point be transformed into an anecdote that could sum up one's professional reputation, and when, intentionally or not, the community was always ready to witness merchant signals. Audiences of all kinds might see or hear some piece of information about a merchant and infer or deduce far more, or far less, than the artisan or trader intended. Thus, some things that merchants hoped would serve as signals failed to hit their mark, while accidents of chance might develop into a reputation that a merchant or merchant group had not expected.

Reputation in the hands of Roman audiences was, in some respects, an unpredictable thing, despite the best efforts of merchants to present and build up a steady and long-lasting vision of themselves. The work that merchants put into their reputations will be the subject of the next chapter, but, in this context, reputation was always in flux as audiences adjusted their perception to fit the information they had, the values they held, and how convinced they were that what they witnessed was genuine. In part, this was influenced by general Roman prejudices against merchants, while in part it was a highly localized process that was inflected by networks of friendship, kinship, and neighborliness that stretched, at times, across generations in small communities.[69] With so many factors at play, Roman merchants needed, at all times, to be considerate of their many different audiences, just as Mithres was when he attempted to ensure that the reputation he held in Rome was equally known in Forum Novum. Both audiences were important to Mithres, and both had the potential to know a different version of the man after a lifetime of trading and reputational signaling. His efforts were targeted to assure everyone that he was always the good man he had seemed to be in life.

Conclusion

Reputation in the Roman world was a hugely useful asset to have and a difficult one to acquire. Merchants needed a reputation to smooth over the rough edges of their trading world, to make commerce more predictable, and help them to choose their business partners. For customers, too, reputation was a vital aid to avoid being cheated or otherwise wronged by unscrupulous and deceitful

69. Grey, *Constructing Communities*, esp. 63–74.

purveyors of goods and services. Institutionally, concern for reputation limited the number of possible actions a merchant might reasonably take. Violence, anger, and cheating were all institutionally disincentivized. A merchant whose character or business was thought to lean in those directions might soon find themselves out of business entirely. The limited number of good options made trading more predictable and easier to undertake. A good reputation fostered trust and dispelled doubts between both familiar trading partners and complete strangers, allowing the market to operate and businesses to continue. As theorists of NIE would say, reputation lowered transaction costs, making valuable information more readily available because it was in the interest of all parties to let reputations be known.

Yet the nature of reputation, beyond what it did in Roman society, is complicated. Its relatively simple definition belies its flexibility, tendency to change, and dependence upon both the actions of the reputation's subject and the reactions of that subject's audience. Reputation could not exist without a community to attribute meaning to actions, words, and appearances, any more than it could exist without the subject itself. Variability in audience led to a collection of reputations that could be similar to each other or directly conflict, presenting different versions of the same person. Audiences kept an eye on reputation and continually adjusted their opinions and beliefs to fit with their information and judgments over time. Those who were close to the subject might frequently add new information to their mental picture, while those who operated at a distance might only see flashes of behavior or dramatic moments of change. Such people would therefore only periodically update their conceptions. As a result, reputation might change slowly or quickly, depending not just upon the behavior of the merchant, but also upon the level of attention paid by the community and the actions of other merchants as well.

The influence of peers and competitors on merchant reputation is critical to our understanding not only of the position of merchants in society but also of how merchants structured their relationships with each other. Reputation, at a fundamental level, involved comparison: the judgment of which individuals were doing well, not just in the abstract, but in direct contrast to others. Being known to be better at something than another person was a means of securing both social and monetary advancement and this kind of excellence helped to insulate merchants from damage to their reputation. If they were known to be the best, they had at least one layer of buffer between themselves and failure. Yet the appearance of excellence also came with risks, as damage to reputation was exacerbated by situations in which merchants had raised themselves up in the mind of their audiences but failed to meet those elevated expectations. Merchants walked a fine line with such claims and struggled to secure the goodwill of their audience, which was predisposed by culturally pervasive stereotypes to think ill of those engaged in commerce, a topic to which we will return.

Despite the many features of reputation that lay outside a merchant's control, reputation nevertheless began and ended with its subject. In the following chapter, we will look at how merchants attempted to develop and shape a reputation, at the strategies they adopted and the values they held. Yet, in looking at the nature of reputation we have seen that the bedrock of a good name lay on a merchant's day-to-day actions, and that it was their consistency that was the most valuable contributor to the ways they would be perceived. The details of their daily life formed the evidence that could most easily prove or disprove the persona they strove to create and disseminate. While this did not negate the effect of the hard work merchants put into their reputations, good reputation depended upon many small positive acts more heavily than it did on large displays of goodness. The tendency of Roman audiences to doubt merchants meant that the more effort and care they put in, the more likely it seemed that they were only feigning goodness and concealing their inner nature. To do nothing to shape a reputation was not an option, but, as in the case of their appearance, merchants had to strike a balance as they tried to shape and project their good name far and wide.

CHAPTER 3

Developing a Reputation, Managing a Good Name

Heu, quam difficilis gloriae custodia est!

Alas, how difficult is the maintenance of reputation!
—Publilius Syrus, *Sententiae*, 240

Reputation, the collection of opinions and beliefs about a person that shaped how they were perceived by society, did not exist in a fully formed, permanent state at any point in the life of a Roman merchant. Reputation was always shifting and changing, depending on what a merchant said, or did, or wore, who they met with, where they were seen, or lived, or a myriad of other potential factors. It was dependent not only on the merchant's actions and behavior, but also on the beliefs, prejudices, and suspicions of those around them, who formed an audience and broad social network that could lift a merchant up or tear him down, if not on a whim, then at least on a thin pretext.

Maintaining a good reputation was a challenge—though worse still was the task of rehabilitating a bad one. Publilius Syrus, ever ready with a pithy quote, summed it up: "He whom reputation has once crushed may scarcely be restored."[1] A merchant who had acquired a bad name would spend long weeks, months, or even years trying to rid himself of the damage and rebuild his position in society, even though it might take only a few choice words to bring him down again. A good reputation took time to build, even without setbacks, and a merchant's reputation was always fragile, more so, in some ways, than the reputation of the farmer or even the senator. Roman merchants sat at a precarious position in Roman society, one in which they were continually doubted, held in suspicion, and at times, as Dio Chrysostom put it, "hate[d] and revile[d]."[2]

1. Publilius Syrus, *Sent.* 572, *quem fama semel oppressit vix restituitur*. The translation of *fama* in this quote is open to interpretation as either reputation, gossip, or rumor. Chapter 5 discusses and explains the relationships between these concepts.

2. Dio, *Or.* 31.37, ἀλλὰ τοὺς μὲν καπήλους τοὺς ἐν τοῖς μέτροις κακουργοῦντας, οἷς ὁ βίος ἐστὶν αὐτόθεν ἀπὸ αἰσχροκερδείας, μισεῖτε καὶ κολάζετε.

Still, Roman merchants did not abandon their hope of a good reputation and rarely leaned into the negative stereotypes that circulated about them. They understood that conforming to stereotypes would deny them the benefits of a good reputation and forever exclude them from the social and economic networks they needed to run their businesses. A good name functioned as social capital and was, as Syrus also said, "a second inheritance."[3] Unlike an inheritance, however, a merchant could not simply wait around to receive a good name, even if he or she was fortunate enough to have a relation in the same trade.

A good reputation required substantial effort to develop, and the ongoing care to maintain it was the work of a lifetime and beyond. Building up and caring for one's reputation were tasks that called for a series of concerted efforts, supported by countless small acts of consistent goodwill, honesty, fairness, kindness, and a dozen other virtues.[4] The passive evidence of a merchant's day-to-day life was always central to their reputation, but the active work of merchants to build a good name offers the best evidence we have for what merchants believed reputation was and how they conceived of their ability to shape their social and economic landscape. By making, for example, a show of their generosity, merchants demonstrated their belief that this was a virtue, and made plain their hope that others would recognize their success and philanthropic nature. At the same time, this action revealed their anxieties about accusations of greed and their earnest belief that they could defy the stereotypes that marked out those in trade as being motivated by profit over honor.

Each merchant determined for him- or herself where, when, and how it was profitable to exert their efforts and what strategies it would be prudent to adopt. Merchants made these choices based on past experiences, both their own and those of others. They watched their peers and worked to maintain parity with the figures they viewed as their primary competition. Lessons were learned from those who succeeded and those who failed, and merchants everywhere operated with their best guess about how they could improve their reputation.[5] They balanced the cost of strategies against their own means, and used those that they believed would advertise their, and their businesses', best features.

Even so, merchants, from time to time, misjudged their reputation strategies, and discovered that their reputation was worse than they believed it to be. Failure on the field of reputation was rarely a small setback, and often snowballed

3. Publilius Syrus, *Sent.* 96, *bene audire alterum patrimonium est*; 254 *Honestus rumor alterum est patrimonium*; and 546, *probo bona fama maxima est hereditas.*

4. Bromley, *Reputation*, 51, notes that consistency is frequently sought by actors, but regularly missed, either in practice or interpretation.

5. This model of watching and learning is seen in Publilius Syrus, *Sent.* 177, *ex vitio alterius sapiens emendat suum*, a wise man betters himself from the vice of another.

into a situation in which former friends and peers would distance themselves from a disgraced merchant for fear of being associated with someone going out of business. Merchants up and down the socioeconomic spectrum lamented the falseness of such friends, who abandoned a person in need and forgot the web of interconnecting obligations that merchants held to one another.[6]

Nearly as challenging as a bad, or even a middling reputation, was having no reputation at all. Young or new merchants struggled to find a foothold on the Roman economic ladder, as did merchants who sought to ply their trade in new and unfamiliar places. It was in these circumstances that a true friend was essential, as such a person could mobilize their own good name to support someone just getting started.[7] Vouching for a friend or colleague, and utilizing one's reputation on another's behalf, was an act of kindness that was expected to be reciprocal, a favor to be called in at some later point. In Heliodorus' *Aethiopica*, a man describes how his son, a merchant, opened his house to strangers from all over the world, specifically because he traveled so much himself and relied on the kindness of others when abroad.[8] Similarly, letters of recommendation attest to the importance of a wide friendship network to help merchants make their way in new markets and among new people, who were unfamiliar with the merchant's reputation.

From the beginning of a merchant's career, to and through its very end, reputation required upkeep. Merchants in the middle of their careers invested in their reputations as best they could, while merchants attempted to get in the last word about their reputation with their dying breath. Funerary evidence, set up by merchants or their family and friends, offers some of the most explicit examples of how vital reputation had been to a living merchant, and how important it remained to preserve it after death. These sources reveal a lifetime of effort, and also hint that merchants feared that they would be misjudged and socially excluded because of their professions.[9]

Developing and managing a good name was no easy task. At times, an effort

6. E.g., Petron., *Sat.* 38.

7. As in Publilius Syrus, *Sent.* 53, *amico firmo nihil emi melius potest.* Nothing can be better to have than a steadfast friend.

8. Heliod., *Aeth.* 2.22, this generosity is also explained as his pious obedience to Zeus. As we will discuss, piety was a virtue that many merchants strove to demonstrate with their reputation strategies.

9. *Pace* Emanuel Mayer, "Money Making, 'Avarice,' and Elite Strategies of Distinction in the Roman World," in *Skilled Labour and Professionalism in Ancient Greece and Rome*, ed. Edmund Stewart, Edward Harris, and David Lewis (Cambridge: Cambridge University Press, 2020), who has argued that elite stereotypes were largely unknown to Roman merchants. See Jane Sancinito, "Rapacious and Chatty, Deceitful and Memorable: Finding Non-Elite Stereotypes of Roman Merchants," in *Working Lives in Ancient Rome*, ed. Jordan Rogers and Del A. Maticic (London: Palgrave Macmillan, forthcoming), on the evidence for and character of nonelite stereotypes.

to improve one element of reputation set a merchant back in other ways. Making bold claims about quality goods or successful business practices, for example, could easily cross the line into tasteless bragging. More conservative strategies risked the appearance of miserliness or even of a lack of success. In other cases, investments in reputation only paid off in the long term, or unexpectedly brought their benefits to a later generation, rather than helping the merchant in the moment. Despite these challenges, merchants were active participants in the creation of their reputations. Though only an audience could say how it would be received, merchants still consciously contributed to those perceptions and strove to build a lasting good name against heavy odds.

Making a Name for Yourself

A merchant at the beginning of his career often found himself in a reputational catch-22: he needed a successful business and a good reputation to secure the credit that would allow him to invest in his business and his reputation, but could not get a successful business and a good reputation without the credit to invest in his business and reputation. As we discussed in the previous chapter, success supported and fed a good reputation, but a good reputation was also fed by success. Even if a merchant did not immediately require credit to set up his business, he needed to appear successful as quickly as possible and, as he was just beginning, he had little ability to fill his shop with customers or his workshop with orders.

Starting out, merchants in the Roman world had to lean heavily on whatever little reputation they had or whatever they could "borrow" from family and friends who were willing to vouch for their honesty, trustworthiness, and future success. Thus, it was the work of family and friends who most often set a young person on the path to prosperity in trade. They lent young merchants funds, talked to likely customers, made introductions, and, in some cases, arranged apprenticeships. The latter practice is sporadically attested in the Roman world, but the evidence suggests that apprenticeships were most often the result of one of two situations: parents setting their children up in a trade or masters choosing to train enslaved people in a skill.[10] In both these cases, apprentice-

10. Though dated, W. L. Westermann, "Apprentice Contracts and the Apprentice System in Roman Egypt," *Classical Philology* 9.3 (1914) still collects many of the primary sources. The best recent examinations are Liu, "Group Membership"; Christel Freu, "*Disciplina, patrocinium, nomen*: The Benefits of Apprenticeship in the Roman World," in *Urban Craftsmen and Tradesmen in the Roman World*, ed. Andrew Wilson and Miko Flohr (Oxford: Oxford University Press, 2016); and Philip Venticinque, "Family Affairs: Guild Regulations and Family Relationships in Roman Egypt,"

ships required some funds to arrange and an investment of time, ranging from a few months to a couple of years, depending on the profession. This required dedication on the part of the student, as well as the continued support from the parent or master who often covered not only apprenticeship costs but also, at times, a share of room and board.

The motivation of the student was by no means guaranteed. While some willingly trained for a profession, others, enslaved and freeborn alike, were sent into a field for which they lacked enthusiasm or natural talent.[11] Lucian, in his semiautobiographical oration, *Somnium*, describes how his father, a man of unknown profession, determined that Lucian would be apprenticed to his uncle, a sculptor.[12] While Lucian's account should not be accepted at face value, his description of his father's rationale seems to reflect a plausible set of reasons for apprenticing a son.[13] According to Lucian, his father's main concern was cost, and the amount of time it would take for Lucian to earn enough to repay the investment apprenticeship required. While Lucian's father entertained the idea of many possible professions, the final decision seems to have been made based on convenience: Lucian's uncle was already a master craftsman, and he was visiting with his sister and brother-in-law at the time.

Lucian's initial disposition toward his apprenticeship was positive, because, as he said, "it seemed agreeable to be able to show off to my peers."[14] Even before a chisel was put into his hands, Lucian already was imagining himself as leader in his field, something echoed later in his dreams, when the figure of Sculpture encourages him with promises that he will be the next Phidias or Praxiteles.[15] Gaining a reputation as the next great master was at the forefront of Lucian's mind, and it was an ambition that was likely shared by many oth-

Greek, Roman, and Byzantine Studies 50.2 (2010). Worth noting also are Bert de Munck, Steven L. Kaplan, and Hugo Soly, eds., *Learning on the Shop Floor: Historical Perspectives on Apprenticeship* (New York: Berghahn Books, 2007); and Eleni Hasaki, "Craft Apprenticeship in Ancient Greece: Reaching beyond the Masters," in *Archaeology and Apprenticeship: Acquiring Body Knowledge in the Ancient World*, ed. Willeke Wendrich (Tucson: University of Arizona Press, 2013).

11. The idea that sons were increasingly expected to follow their fathers into their professions in late antiquity, known alternately as "hereditary professions" or "tied professions," is discussed in chapter 1, and as argued there, was primarily intended as a means of securing tax income, rather than as a principle of social or economic organization. See Broekaert, "Tied Down, Wings Cut?"; and Sirks, "Did the Late Roman Government."

12. Luc., *Somn.* 1–2.

13. See Daniel S. Richter, "Lucian of Samosata," in *The Oxford Handbook of the Second Sophistic*, ed. Daniel S. Richter and William A. Johnson (Oxford: Oxford University Press, 2017), esp. 334–36 on *Somnium*; on apprenticeship and its motivation, we also have *Disticha Catonis* 28: *Cum tibi sint nati nec opes, tunc artibus illos/ instrue, quo possint inopem defendere vitam*. Since you have children, not wealth, teach them those arts through which they can maintain their life without resources.

14. Luc., *Somn.* 3, οὐκ ἀτερπῆ ἐδόκει ἔχειν καὶ πρὸς τοὺς ἡλικιώτας ἐπίδειξιν.

15. Luc., *Somn.* 8.

ers as they started out. Though Lucian would ultimately abandon sculpting as a profession, his focus on his future reputation at this early stage was wise. It was in apprenticeship that young artisans began to build up their name, as they gradually developed skills and built relationships with their masters and fellow apprentices.

In Lucian's case, his career ends almost as soon as it begins, as he claims to have been lured away by the promises of Education, who appeared to him in a dream and assured him that many great thinkers and speakers rose from origins in trade.[16] Many more apprentices persisted in their training and used those months or years to great effect in their future professions. Recently, Jinyu Liu has looked at a collection of master and apprentice weavers in first-century CE Egypt, whose contracts attest to a carefully constructed set of social and economic ties that supported young artisans and helped to build their reputations.[17] In that case, master craftsmen Tryphon and Pausiris apprenticed their sons to other masters in the same trade, many of whom lived in the same quarter of Oxyrhynchus, and likely were members of the same professional association, as well.

The choice made by these master weavers to apprentice their children and to accept apprentices in this way was a carefully calculated strategy that made the most of these overlapping relationships and the reputational networks that existed alongside them. By apprenticing a child to a member of the same profession, merchants could expose their children to reputation strategies that their household had not tried and business practices that might be more or less successful than their own.[18] While master weavers could train their own children, or send them to family members, as in the case of Lucian, apprenticing a child to one's neighbors avoided the appearance of nepotism and built a wider social and professional network for the artisan in training.[19] For the master who took on the apprentice, these contracts offered public recognition of their qualifications and fostered trust between them and the parent-peer. They also

16. Luc., *Somn.* 12.

17. Liu, "Group Membership," 217–26.

18. Apprentices were usually in their early teens, though there has been substantial research on child labor in the Roman world, see, e.g. Keith R. Bradley, "Child Labour in the Roman World," *Historical Reflections* 12.2 (1985); and Christian C. Laes, "Child Slaves at Work in Roman Antiquity," *Ancient Society* 38 (2008). The latter seems to have been more likely to be intrahousehold, the former interhousehold.

19. There is relatively little evidence of direct training of children by their own parents. The best instance is reported in Diod. Sic., *Bibl.* 2.29.4, on the training of Chaldaean soothsayers. διὸ καὶ γονεῖς ἔχοντες διδασκάλους ἅμα μὲν ἀφθόνως ἅπαντα μανθάνουσιν, ἅμα δὲ τοῖς παραγγελλομένοις προσέχουσι πιστεύοντες βεβαιότερον. And since they have their parents as their teachers, they learn everything without reserve and at the same time they devote themselves to what is being transmitted, trusting this with more certainty.

gained the labor of the apprentice for the duration of the contract, and, if they trained the young person well, they could potentially take on more work and increase their profits.

The trainee's reputation was benefited from association with both their family and their contracted teacher. Lucian's perceived affinity for sculpture was mostly based on his tendency to mold wax into figurines as a child, but the Oxyrhynchus weavers were part of a multigenerational network that may have suggested that the child of such a family would have the trade "in his blood." Successful training with a master would only cement this belief in the minds of the general population and prepare a young professional to claim a place of prominence in his community and among other members of his trade.

These apprenticeships formed yet another connection within the group that was already likely bound by a shared professional association and neighborly obligations. Liu's analysis has suggested that the overlapping points of contact among these families may have intensified the hold that the well-connected had over the profession locally, and that the system of apprenticeship may have also been a tool of exclusion that kept some out of positions of prestige in the community.[20] Certainly, young merchants who came out of this system held material advantages over their competitors in the form of a large number of people prepared to vouch for them, as well as the mastery conferred upon them by their instructor. Those without such a background would be left to fend for themselves and would start far behind their better-connected peers.

Once they were trained and independent, young artisans leaned on the connections they had formed during their apprenticeship and fit themselves into a community in which they had many ties, including not only their family and their master, but also their family's apprentices, those with whom they had been training, and the neighbors and friends accumulated over the course of a normal life.[21] Accordingly, a generation of merchants in a community such as Oxyrhynchus could come of age and into their trade with detailed knowledge about a large number of their peers and could have a sense of the reputations of those with whom they would be in competition for the rest of their lives.

For those who trained while enslaved, apprenticeship did not offer these

20. Liu, "Group Membership," 215.

21. It is worth noting that the later, medieval status of "journeymen" for young apprentices did not exist in the Roman period in any formal sense. Apprenticeships in Egypt among weavers lasted one to two years, and generally trained young men in their early teens. These boys were still quite young after their training was complete. Some may have stayed on to work for pay under their masters (as in P.Oxy. 4.725), while others may have returned to their father's shops for a time before striking out on their own. Our records do not leave any indication of a clear "system" in place. See Liu, "Group Membership," 222.

same advantages, nor did it help them to develop a professional network. Further, completing their training did not put them in a position of equality with the craftsman from whom they had learned. A trained slave was a more valuable slave in the eyes of their master, and, while training might improve an individual's quality of life, enabling them to take up work as a scribe or accountant rather than a laborer, apprenticeship was not, in itself, a path to freedom or an independent business.[22] While specialized skills might help an enslaved person to earn the *peculium* from which he or she might buy freedom, their training may have also made them too valuable to free and, in some cases, it seems to have kept them out of situations where they might have received tips.[23] Others were granted, or claimed, opportunities to run businesses without direct oversight, as in the case of Arretine potters or *institores* in a range of occupations.[24]

Many enslaved people with special skills could only expect to be liberated at the death of their enslaver. This is particularly evident among the freedmen at Trimalchio's dinner. Trimalchio himself was freed in his master's will and gained the initial wealth with which he entered the shipping trade through the property left to him.[25] Trimalchio claims that he will imitate this behavior by liberating his own slaves in this way and that he will grant them property as well. Some of the slaves he names are clearly trained—at least one is an inventive cook—and they may have expected to go into business once liberated. Still, as freedmen, they would be older entering into their profession, and would lack a substantial network of connections outside their former master's household. Some could also expect to find hindrances to their reputation in that setting, as in the case of Philargyrus, "silver-lover," whose name, perhaps given to him by Trimalchio, inherently suggests a greedy nature.[26]

Even if an enslaved person with skills were granted his or her freedom, *liberti* often lacked a social network that could support them to the same extent as freeborn people. Sandra Joshel's landmark study of funerary markers involving work demonstrates that a majority of *liberti* in trade continued to live and work with individuals with whom they had been enslaved, and argues that there was little obvious mingling between freed and freeborn tradesmen.[27] *Colliberti*

22. Clarence A. Forbes, "The Education and Training of Slaves in Antiquity," *Transactions and Proceedings of the American Philological Association* 86 (1955).

23. Joshel, *Work, Identity, and Legal Status*, 59.

24. Gunnar Fülle, "The Internal Organization of the Arretine *Terra Sigillata* Industry: Problems of Evidence and Interpretation," *Journal of Roman Studies* 87 (1997): 128–33.

25. Petron., *Sat.* 76.

26. Petron., *Sat.* 70–71. Interestingly, the name is attested in the funerary marker of a gladiator trainer, Gaius Futius Philargyrus: Harry Langford Wilson, "Latin Inscriptions at the Johns Hopkins University III," *American Journal of Philology* 30 (1909): #20.

27. Joshel, *Work, Identity, and Legal Status*, ch. 4. She notes the different spheres of labor

relied on one another, as a kind of "found family" to support each other in their businesses.[28] These groups often involved one or more married couples who were joined by a selection of family members and others freed from the same household. Evangelus, whom we encountered in the previous chapter, offers a prime example of these kinds of ties in the inscription on his *loculusplatte*:

> T(itus) AELIUS EVANGELUS CONPARAVIT SIBI ET ULPIAE FORTUNATAE CONIUCI CARISSIMAE SU(a)E CONCESSUS IBIDEM ULPIO TELESPHORO ITEM GAUDENIAE MARCELLINAE FILIAE NATURALI CONCESSIT T(itus) AELIUS EVANGELUS LIIBERTIS QUII LUBIIRTABU.[29]

> Titus Aelius Evangelus prepared [this tomb] for himself and for Ulpia Fortunata, his dearest wife. The same place is granted to Ulpius Telesphorus. Also, Titus Aelius Evangelus grants [this] to Gaudenia Marcellina, his natural daughter [and] to his freedmen and freedwomen.[30]

Evangelus, a freedman and wool worker, was the head of a somewhat complicated household, and the inscription of the *loculusplatte* records a group that was evidently his second family.[31] This latter group was assembled after

---

recorded in funerary inscriptions, mostly differentiated between those clearly working in domestic spheres and those working outside it. Among freedpeople, she offers a quantitative analysis of how many seem to have continued to work with individuals they had known from their enslavement.

28. Literally known as the *familia*, which consisted of both slave and freed peoples who were connected by a common slave holder, see Joshel, *Work, Identity, and Legal Status*, 100–101.

29. This inscription fills two panels to either side of the image, as well as spilling over into the lower border. The text spans across the image, with words beginning on one side of the image continuing on the other. No effort has been made here to recreate this unusual and difficult-to-read arrangement. In all, the text spans thirteen lines, with some lines containing as few as four letters and others containing as many as eighteen. There is some limited and irregular use of the interpunct visible on the stone, but it is not possible to determine it exactly from photographs.

30. See Figure 1. The final words of the inscription are a garbled version of *libertis libertabusque*, granting burial rights to Evangelus' freedmen and women. Holliday, "The Sarcophagus of Titus Aelius Evangelus," 96, believes that it is a purely formulaic addition, which may have had the benefit of adding to the illusion of Evangelus' wealth and standing. There is no reason to suppose that Evangelus could not have raised himself to such a position of wealth and prominence that he might have owned slaves, though the small *loculusplatte*, compared with the earlier sarcophagus, does somewhat suggest a diminishment of wealth, rather than growth. The text is the only misspelled part of the phrase and raises a question about when and why it was added. Regardless, it is worth noting that the differences in the spelling conventions between his two funerary objects indicate that two different people were responsible for the texts.

31. On the family dynamics, see Buonopane and Corti, "T. Aelius Evangelus." The daughter, Gaudenia Marcellina, seems to have occupied a challenging position in this family unit. She shares her mother's name, rather than her father's, a sign that she was born outside the legal structure of the Roman family. It is unclear whether her parents ever married. Evangelus is adamant about his daughter's legitimacy, which increases the likelihood that there was something irregular about his

Evangelus had a relationship with a woman named Gaudenia, with whom he had the daughter named in this inscription. His wife, Ulpia Fortunata, was a freedwoman from a different household than Evangelus. The inscription relates that she came to this relationship with another man, Ulpius Telesphorus, who is certainly a *collibertus*, though he may have also been her brother. The marriage of Evangelus and Ulpia formed familial ties that were almost certainly also business connections, as Ulpia, Telesphorus, and Gaudenia Marcellina are likely to have been involved in Evangelus' wool working.[32]

Family labor would have been essential for keeping many small-scale businesses up and running, just as the support of fellow freedmen was necessary to help establish the reputation of newly freed merchants. Trimalchio's account of his business suggests that, in times of crisis, he was accustomed to seek help from his fellow freedmen, and he credits his wife, another Fortunata, with the loan that saved his business, as she sold her clothes and jewelry to set Trimalchio up in his trade after a major setback.[33] Relying on *colliberti* or family members for help carried less stigma than seeking aid from more distantly connected acquaintances, or, worse, borrowing from predatory lenders.

Another guest at Trimalchio's dinner boasted that he owed no one money

first relationship. The elder Gaudenia may have had her daughter before she married Evangelus, the pair may never have married, or their relationship may have been complicated by the legal status of one or the other. Gaudenia may have been a slave and that status may have made it impossible for them to marry, though the evidence is inconclusive.

32. Holliday, "The Sarcophagus of Titus Aelius Evangelus," 88, believed this to be true of Evangelus' first wife, and, in general, the wives of wool workers seem to have been commonly involved in their husband's work, as that trade was particularly open to female workers, with or without a husband. See Lena Larsson Lovén, "*Lanam fecit*: Woolworking and Female Virtue," in *Aspects of Women in Antiquity*, ed. Lena Larsson Lovén and Agneta Strömberg (Jonsend: Paul Astroms Verlag, 1998); Lena Larsson Lovén, "Wool Work as a Gender Symbol in Ancient Rome: Roman Textiles and Ancient Sources," in *Ancient Textiles: Production, Craft, and Society*, ed. Carole Gillis and Marie-Louise Nosch (Oxford: Oxbow Books, 2007); Lena Larsson Lovén, "Female Work and Identity in Roman Textile Production and Trade: A Methodological Discussion," in *Making Textiles in Pre-Roman and Roman Times: People, Places, Identities*, ed. Margarita Gleba and Judit Pásztókai-Szeoke (Oxford: Oxbow Books, 2013). For women at work more generally, see Joshel, *Work, Identity, and Legal Status*, 141–42; Natalie Boymel Kampen, *Image and Status: Roman Working Women in Ostia* (Berlin: Gebrüder Mann Verlag, 1981); Teresa J. Calpino, *Women, Work and Leadership in Acts* (Tübingen: Mohr Siebeck, 2014); Susan Treggiari, "Lower Class Women in the Roman Economy," *Florilegium* 1 (1979): 76ff.; Ramsay MacMullen, "Women in Public in the Roman Empire," *Historia: Zeitschrift für Alte Geschichte* 29 (1980); Jane F. Gardner, "Women in Business Life: Some Evidence from Puteoli," in *Female Networks and the Public Sphere in Roman Society*, ed. Päivi Setälä and Liisa Savunen (Rome: Institutum Romanum Finlandiae, 1999); Peter van Minnen, "Did Ancient Women Learn a Trade outside the Home? A Note on SB XVIII 13305," *Zeitschrift für Papyrologie und Epigraphik* 123 (1998); Miriam J. Groen-Vallinga, "Desperate Housewives? The Adaptive Family Economy and Female Participation in the Roman Urban Labour Market," in *Women and the Roman City in the Latin West*, ed. Emily Hemelrijk and Greg Woolf (Leiden: Brill, 2013).

33. Petron., *Sat.* 76.

and had never had a lender publicly shame him.[34] Borrowing, in general, was a behavior that could reflect badly on a merchant and his reputation. It appears among the great failings that Philostratus' Apollonius lists of those in trade, as borrowing at interest put merchants under the power of moneylenders, whom Cicero names as among the greediest merchants and whose authority over others made them equivalent, in some respects, to masters controlling their slaves.[35] Generally, borrowing money undercut merchant claims to self-sufficiency, which, as we will see, were often interconnected with their attempts to appear successful.

This unnamed guest also makes another, interesting claim: that in his forty years in servitude, no one ever knew whether he was free or a slave.[36] Recently, looking at the fulleries of Pompeii, Miko Flohr has argued for the plausibility of this kind of situation, stating that it was likely difficult to tell the legal status of many in trade, where enslaved, free, and freed peoples often worked side by side. Already, this had been viewed as a possibility by Joshel, whose findings demonstrated that, especially in artisanal and banking contexts, an enslaved person might be commonly found working on behalf of a master, but, in the context of a street of shops, such slaves might be virtually indistinguishable from a freed or freeborn person working for him- or herself.[37] Though those in artisanal fields often seem to have owned up to their status in funerary contexts, to being a slave or freed person, Joshel notes that retailers often neglected to include these details, presenting themselves, not necessarily accurately, as freer than their peers in other professions.[38] Those who lived and even worked beside such people might have had little or no idea of the legal status of their peers and neighbors, and a lifetime could have passed with no one ever knowing the difference.

Understanding the impact of slavery on reputation, and its power in the lives of recently freed people, is challenging. Freed merchants rarely reflected on their early reputation, and our evidence is heavily weighted toward funerary inscriptions and reliefs, rather than toward the strategies used by recent *liberti*

34. Petron., *Sat.* 57 *Et nunc spero me sic vivere, ut nemini iocus sim. Homo inter homines sum, capite aperto ambulo; assem aerarium nemini debeo; constitutum habui nunquam; nemo mihi in foro dixit redde quod debes.* "Now I hope to live in such a way that no one may laugh at me. I am a man among men; I walk with my head uncovered. I owe no one a bronze *as*. I have never made a compact. No one has said to me in the forum, 'pay me what you owe.'" It is unclear if this is intended to mean that he had never borrowed money, or that he currently had no debts and had paid all previous borrowings back in a timely fashion.

35. Philostr., *V. A.* 4.32.2; Cic., *Off.* 150.

36. Petron., *Sat.* 57.

37. Flohr, *The World of the Fullo*, 308–9. Joshel, *Work, Identity, and Legal Status*, 110–11.

38. Ibid.

to establish their reputations and their businesses. This bias in our evidence is hardly surprising. Merchants, busily considering the steps they needed to take to support themselves and their dependents, did not have time or the resources to linger over how to preserve their reputation-in-progress, but that is not to say that they weren't highly aware of it and considering how to improve it at all times.

Our best evidence for how they acted comes not from newly trained or newly freed merchants, but from those who were only new to a specific location. Traveling merchants arriving in an unfamiliar place offer the best analog for how a merchant, freed or freeborn, might set himself up in a new business, in a new location, and without much of a reputation to support himelf.[39] Two sources provide the most insight: letters of recommendation and the testimony of the Acts of the Apostles. It is the latter that most concerns us here, as we see in its account how early Christians, and especially early Christian merchants, managed the challenge of continual relocation brought about by a combination of persecution and evangelical aims.

The case of the apostle Paul is especially telling. In Acts of the Apostles, it is recorded that he worked as a maker of tents as well as a preacher of the faith.[40] The passage that conveys this information also relates how Paul adjusted to his many relocations and how he kept both his business and reputation in good shape:

> Μετὰ τραῦτα χωρισθεὶς ἐκ τῶν Ἀθηνῶν ἦλθεν εἰς Κόρινθον. καὶ εὑρών τινα Ἰουδαῖον ὀνόματι Ἀκύλαν, Ποντικὸν τῷ γένει, προσφάτως ἐληλυθότα ἀπὸ τῆς Ἰταλίας καὶ Πρίσκιλλαν γυναῖκα αὐτοῦ, διὰ τὸ διατεταχέναι Κλαύδιον χωρίζεσθαι πάντας τοὺς Ἰουδαίους ἀπὸ τῆς Ῥώμης, προσῆλθεν αὐτοῖς, καὶ διὰ τὸ ὁμότεχνον εἶναι ἔμενεν παρ' αὐτοῖς καὶ ἠργάζοντο, ἦσαν γὰρ σκηνοποιοὶ τῇ τέχνῃ.
>
> After this, Paul left Athens and went to Corinth. There he met a Jew named Aquila, a native of Pontus, who had recently come from Italy with his wife Priscilla, because Claudius had ordered all the Jews to leave

39. Broekaert, "Partners in Business," 231–42.

40. On Paul as tentmaker, see Ronald F. Hock, "Paul's Tentmaking and the Problem of His Social Class," *Journal of Biblical Literature* 97.4 (1978); Ronald F. Hock, *The Social Context of Paul's Ministry: Tentmaking and Apostleship* (Minneapolis: Fortress Press, 1980); and the revaluation of Hock by Todd D. Still, "Did Paul Loathe Manual Labor? Revisiting the Work of Ronald F. Hock on the Apostle's Tentmaking and Social Class," *Journal of Biblical Literature* 125.4 (2006). It is unclear whether Paul would have worked in leather or some kind of canvas, as σκηνοποιός does not specify beyond "tent."

Rome. Paul went to see them and he stayed and worked with them, because they were (also) tentmakers by trade.[41]

Paul's arrival in Corinth is especially interesting. He lands there after preaching, with mixed success, to the council of the Areopagus in Athens.[42] As a major urban and commercial center, Corinth was an important place for both kinds of work that Paul intended to undertake. In Corinth, he could expect to find a range of different faiths, as well as opportunities to practice his trade and earn his living. His first instinct, as recorded here, was to travel to the synagogue, and it is apparent that he used that community to find not only a place to stay, but also colleagues with whom to work, suggesting that synagogues and other associations served as resources for newly arriving merchants.[43] Paul was fortunate to find members of the same profession in the synagogue but Acts hints that this may not have been simple luck. Aquila and Priscilla were also recently arrived in Corinth and were likely in a similar position to Paul: new in town, unknown to most, and hoping to get reestablished with a professional reputation.

By working together, even as new arrivals, Paul, Aquila, and Priscilla were able to utilize the widest possible network of social ties and to vouch for each other. Trust between partners was often a strong indicator that merchants were trustworthy and reputable; thus, it was often better for customers to patronize merchants who worked with others, or who were known members of an association. It was for this reason that merchants joined and then advertised their position in such groups: membership signaled respectability and bolstered reputations, alongside the many other concrete benefits that might come from allying oneself with one's peers. Groups facilitated information sharing, built networks, and provided a forum for monitoring the behavior of one's competition and allies.

Associations, at times, even established moral standards that all members were expected to adhere to. A religious association from Attica required that new members be "pure, pious, and good," ἁ[γν]ὸς καὶ εὐσεβὴς καὶ ἀγ|α[θ]ός.[44] Prospective members were, presumably, vetted to ensure that they met these

41. Acts 18:1–3. This passage is the sole reference to Paul's tent-making, though he mentions other forms of labor elsewhere in his letters. If accurate, the implication of this short passage is that Paul is the single most prolific merchant author from the Roman world, with more words attributed to him than any other tradesman from antiquity.

42. Acts 17:32.

43. Richard S. Ascough, "The Thessalonian Christian Community as a Professional Voluntary Association," *Journal of Biblical Literature* 119.2 (2000) discusses the Christian community described in Thessalonians in this light.

44. IG 2^2.1369 lines 33–34, Liopesi, Attica, second century CE.

criteria, meaning that any customer dealing with a member of such an association could rely upon the group to have admitted individuals of the best reputation and highest principles. For members, and especially for outsiders in the community, these guidelines could be very helpful, as they clarified local norms and the expectations for their conduct.

Regardless of status, many new merchants chose to join an association as a bolster to their reputation. Freed and freeborn alike formed formal and informal groups to support one another, and associations had internal positions of prestige and responsibility that merchants could use to demonstrate and advertise their commitment to a community of peers. Like the synagogue in Corinth, these associations did not need to have an explicit economic purpose to be useful to merchants.[45] Their very existence created a network of interconnected individuals who could offer introductions, partnerships, or access to systems of credit.[46] If a group was not explicitly economic, merchants within the group might also become the de facto providers of goods or services, as members would not wish to insult one another by patronizing a stranger. In many cases, groups also provided physical spaces where members could meet or socialize, outside of work contexts, thereby strengthening ties and revealing further opportunities for collaboration.[47]

In many ways, such associations were an expanded model of the peer-to-peer and friendship ties that were essential for every merchant starting out in their career. Merchants commonly refer to their friends as an essential part of their business and reputation. *Amicitia* was by no means an exclusively elite construct but was utilized at every level of Roman society.[48] Merchants boasted of their kindness to their friends and offered each other help and support, while groups of merchants wove friendship and brotherhood into the very names of their associations. Being "friendly" and upholding obligations of friendship was seen as a mark of good character, and loyalty to friends was a strong indicator of the qualities that would make for a trustworthy and reputable businessman.

All these different kinds of connections were the best starting point for a merchant looking to build a reputation. Whether it came from their family, local community, or from a formal or informal network of peers, friends, or

---

45. As argued first, and most persuasively by van Nijf, *Civic World of Professional Associations*. There is now a growing consensus that voluntary associations served many, interconnected, social, economic, and religious roles in the lives of members.

46. Broekaert, "Partners in Business."

47. Donahue, *Roman Community at Table*, on the Roman context. More generally, see Putnam, *Bowling Alone*; and Robert D. Putnam, "Social Capital: Measurement and Consequences," *Isuma: Canadian Journal of Policy Research* 2 (2001) on the social capital and networks tied to community associations.

48. Thoroughly discussed in Verboven, *The Economy of Friends*, sec. III.3.

associates, merchants cultivated support from a variety of sources to help them get started. Rarely could any merchant begin in his trade all on his own—a majority leaned on others to help them build and then maintain their reputations over the course of a lifetime.

Living Reputation

Once a merchant was established in his or her profession and had the beginnings of a reputation, good or bad, the work of maintaining or improving a reputation began. As we discussed in the previous chapter, much of this work was actually passive, the background noise to merchants buying and making and serving and selling. The habits and behaviors that a merchant displayed in the casual moments of plying their trade—everyday conversations and practice—were generally understood to be the best means of judging, and therefore maintaining, a reputation. Predictability in business and character was a foundation upon which reputation could be built: the things that people saw a merchant do every day could be reasonably taken as an indicator of what a merchant would do tomorrow. Eventually, everyone could say they "knew" a merchant and "knew" his reputation.

Yet this slow and steady process was often supplemented by merchant efforts to improve their reputation with, at times, splashy displays of the character traits to which they aspired. They adopted strategies in the hope that this investment in their reputation would pay off in social capital and public recognition, which would lead to increased business and profits. These strategies often tread a fine line between advertising merchant businesses and advertising merchant personae, and it is often difficult to spot the point where reputation of the merchant, vendor, or craftsman transforms into the reputation of the store, stall, or workshop. In the face-to-face communities of the Roman world, merchants were the embodiment of their businesses, as such, businesses often metonymically represented the merchant. Reputation strategies targeted both together, aiming to improve the commonly held opinions about the individual, the work they did, and the spot where they did it by advertising the quality of the goods and the person who sold them.

This is not to say that these strategies were foolproof. As we have mentioned, reputation was a matter of reception, and an effort to improve one's reputation might easily backfire or come with unintended consequences. We have already seen the case of the moneylender Milo, who strove to present himself as modest, frugal, and cautious, but was seen by his neighbor, an innkeeper, as miserly, antisocial, and duplicitous.[49] Another merchant, Lucius Licinius Nepos, reported in his funerary monument that he was disappointed in his hopes to do well in business, in part because he had been abandoned by his friends, the same tool that so many merchants used to support their businesses and grow their reputations.[50] Each strategy presented an opportunity, as well as a risk, which led merchants, at times, to approach the same goal from a number of different angles.

Thus, while Mithres boasted about his courtesy toward his friends, and merchants joined associations and clubs to develop new and deeper social ties, others struggled to accept the idea of dependence, even mutual dependence, on their friends.[51] Paul, who so obviously utilized the support of Aquila and Priscilla in Corinth, professed his commitment to self-sufficiency in his writings. In his first letter to the Thessalonians, he said:

> παρακαλοῦμεν δὲ ὑμᾶς ἀδελφοί, περισσεύειν μᾶλλον, καὶ φιλοτιμεῖσθαι ἡσυχάζειν καὶ πράσσειν τὰ ἴδια καὶ ἐργάζεσθαι ταῖς χερσὶν ὑμῶν, καθῶς ὑμῖν παρηγγείλαμεν, ἵνα περιπατῆτε εὐσχημόνως πρὸς τοὺς ἔξω καὶ μηδενὸς χρείαν ἔχητε.
>
> But we urge you, brothers, to excel more and more, and to strive to live a quiet life and to attend to your private matters and to work with your hands, according to what we have told you, so that you live with decency in the eyes of those outside and so that you may not have need of anyone.[52]

Paul's motivation for such a statement of independence is partly a response to his unique circumstances as a Christian preacher. Pieter Botha has suggested that Paul came under attack as something of a parasite during the course of his travels, as he was commonly housed by wealthy Christian families who, at times, were later persecuted for their association with the apostle.[53] Paul's

49. Apul., *Met.* 1.21.

50. CIL 6.9659, Nepos describes only his hopes in trade, *negotiando*, but does not identify a specific profession. He reports, lines 7–8: *spe deceptus erat et a mult/is bene meritus amicis*. See the discussion below.

51. See chapter 2, CIL 9.4796.

52. 1 Thessalonians 4:10b–12.

53. Pieter J. J. Botha, "Paul and Gossip: A Social Mechanism in Early Christian Communities," *Neotestamentica* 32.2 (1998): 282. For the arrest of Paul's host, Jason: Acts 17:6–7. On the perception of labor, more generally in Jewish and Christian sources, see Göran Agrell, *Work, Toil and Sustenance: An Examination of the View of Work in the New Testament, Taking into Consideration Views Found in Old Testament, Intertestamental, and Early Rabbinic Writings* (Lund: Verbum-Håksn Ohlssons, 1976).

discussions of his profession in his writings address this accusation, demonstrating that he had paid his own way and expected nothing from his hosts.[54] It was vital to both his professional reputation, and the work of his ministry, that the help his hosts offered was seen to be a service to God, not to Paul as an individual.[55] We have no reason to suppose that Paul disowned or devalued the help that he received from others in his community, but it was rhetorically important that he adopt a stance of self-sufficiency, so that he was not seen as taking advantage of the kindness of others.

Moreover, self-sufficiency was an ideal that was held by many in the Roman world. Already we have seen this to an extent with the issue of debt: it was a merchant's dream to never be indebted, to never need to borrow from a moneylender. Beyond this, however, there was a common fantasy in Roman society of never needing to buy from others, but to be able to provide everything from one's own property. This fantasy was often a central part of anti-merchant rhetoric, laden with the implication that all merchants were actively trying to escape their profession, but that did not stop merchants themselves from dreaming of achieving the kind of prosperity that would make that possible.[56] It is represented in the fantastic wealth attributed to Trimalchio in the *Satyricon*, who is described as providing every element of his lavish feast from his own properties, somewhere in the world.[57] This kind of success was considered aspirational, even if it was typically depicted as, and was in nearly every case, an unattainable dream.

Paul takes up a small piece of this rhetoric but did not reject friendship or the idea of a mutually supportive community. Rather, his concern was that his Christian followers lead a moral life in the eyes of the non-Christian community, τοὺς ἔξω. His awareness of this audience, which judged Christians to be at least secretive, if not also deceitful and immoral, led him to approach dependency on others with caution. Paul and the other Apostles associate with many merchants and tradesmen, especially in Acts, where they commonly live at the houses of artisans, but they approached non-Christians with caution and, as

54. See also 1 Thessalonians 2:9: μνημονεύετε γάρ, ἀδελφοί, τὸν κόπον ἡμῶν καὶ τὸν μόχθον· νυκτὸς καὶ ἡμέρας ἐργαζόμενοι πρὸς τὸ μὴ ἐπιβαρῆσαί τινα ὑμῶν ἐκηρύξαμεν εἰς ὑμᾶς τὸ εὐαγγέλιον τοῦ Θεοῦ. Remember, brothers, our toil and our hardship. Working night and day not to be a burden to you, we announced to you the gospel of God.

55. For service to God over Paul, see e.g., 1 Corinthians 1:10–12.

56. Chris Wickham, *Framing the Early Middle Ages: Europe and the Mediterranean 400–800* (Oxford: Oxford University Press, 2007), 289, on self-sufficiency. See also: Luuk de Ligt, "Demand, Supply, Distribution: The Roman Peasantry between Town and Countryside; Rural Monetization and Peasant Demands," *Münstersche Beiträge zur antiken Handelsgeschichte* 9.2 (1990): 30–31, with explicit reference to the ideal autarkic peasant as compared to the greedy merchant, 32.

57. Petron., *Sat.* 38.

in Paul's case, often had to demonstrate their generosity and goodwill to avoid further damage to their reputations and that of their common religious cause.[58]

Both generosity and goodwill were necessary virtues for Roman merchants, regardless of their faith, and displaying them was a priority, especially for merchants whose success left them open to accusations of greed. Nevertheless, strategies for building a reputation for these traits were challenging. Though merchants could simply claim such characteristics, as some did in their funerary monuments, it was difficult to make such claims without offering proof. This, however, could be costly and many merchants struggled to afford the kind of display that could make generosity appear to be a consistent personality trait, rather than a mere token effort.

One tactic was to leave a permanent mark on the built environment. Merchants, especially in groups, often pooled resources to invest in a collective symbol of their dedication to their community. An especially fine, and expensive, example of these efforts is the so-called Arch of the Argentarii. The structure, a decorated *porta* defining one of the entrances to the Forum Boarium in Rome, was dedicated in 203/204 CE, by a coalition of bankers and cattle merchants in honor of the imperial family of Septimius Severus. The structure is a large and ornamental monument that advertises the work and loyalty of these merchants through its reliefs and inscription.

Though a complicated monument, and an incomplete one in its current state of preservation, the iconography of the Arch of the Argentarii highlights several features significant for these local merchants. Immediately apparent is the representation of cattle at the entrance to the cattle market. A frieze of a sacrificial procession lies at eye level on the right-hand side of passersby (Fig. 4). For cattle merchants, this would have been an obvious advertisement, and assertion of their role in the provision of sacred animals, as well as those that were needed for food in the city. In the context of the greater neighborhood, the arch stood on a major route, straddling the *vicus Jugarius*, an ancient and major commercial thoroughfare that connected the Forum Romanum, the Forum Holitorium, and the Forum Boarium. Aside from its commercial role, the road also connected major religious centers in the city, including the important Ara Maxima in the Forum Boarium, one of the city's oldest cult sites.[59]

58. Acts of the Apostles 10:6 Simon lodges with Simon the Tanner, 16:15 Paul stays with Lydia, a trader in purple dye, 18:3 Paul lives with the tentmakers, Aquila and Priscilla.

59. The Ara Maxima celebrated Hercules' victory seizing the cattle of Cacus. This altar to Hercules was important in the Severan period, as attested by an inscription erected by an urban prefect (CIL 6.312), and the affinity that the Severan dynasty had with Hercules (see Clare Rowan, *Under Divine Auspices: Divine Ideology and the Visualisation of Imperial Power in the Severan Period* [Cambridge: Cambridge University Press, 2012], esp. ch. 3), makes it likely that this arch, which

Figure 4. Frieze of sacrificial procession from the Arch of the Argentarii. Diletta Menghinello (CC BY-SA 4.0).

The arch was a commanding topographical statement that shaped the way that residents engaged with the Forum Boarium and the city beyond it. Whatever the state of the *vicus Jugarius* prior to the arch's construction, following its completion travelers, tradesmen, locals, and passersby were all forced to adjust their movements through the arch's central passageway to take advantage of the road's hard surface and avoid other potential obstacles. The arch constrained free travel, making it difficult, if not impossible, to walk around or off the edge of the roadway. It also would have structured the movement of carts and animals, as the width of the passage would have forced everyone to file through in a semiorderly fashion.[60]

While waiting to enter, or passing through the arch, travelers would be

refers extensively to the Severans and Hercules was likely aimed at both a local and an imperial audience.

60. Samuel Ball Platner, *A Topographical Dictionary of Ancient Rome* (Oxford: Oxford University Press, 1929), measures the passage at 3.30m, probably allowing two carts, or about four oxen, to pass at a time. However, Sandro de Maria, *Gli archi onorari di Roma e dell'Italia romana* (Rome: L'Erma di Bretschneider, 1988), 308, measured the passage at only 2.91m. This is still wide enough for traffic to pass but may have required wider carts to go one at a time.

encouraged to read the inscription on the lintel, which named the groups of merchants involved, as well as to view the reliefs of the imperial family and the smaller friezes. In the latter case, their own passage with animals for sacrifice or sale through the arch might have been pleasingly mirrored by that in the sacrificial procession. At times when traffic was slower, the arch would have provided a cover from rain, or shade from the sun. Furthermore, the arch constrained and directed the view of the forum as people entered, and of the road and city beyond as people exited.[61] The arch created a lens that revealed the space and gave the merchants involved in its commission some power over, and claim to, the forum itself.

This claim was a reputational strategy designed to leave a lasting mark on the landscape that would be forever associated with these merchants. The arch advertised their financial success, as well as their organization, cooperation, and generosity, in the form of an expensive dedication. Their inscription offers the monument to the divinity of the imperial family, signifying their loyalty and piety, and concludes with the following description of themselves:

> . . . ARGENTARI(i) • ET • NEGOTIANTES • BOARI(i) • HVIVS LOCI QVI INVEHENT DEVOTI . . .
>
> . . . The bankers and cattle merchants of this place, those who will bring in (goods), dedicated (this) . . .[62]

61. There has already been some work on these kinds of sight lines, based on the Arch of Constantine, Elizabeth Marlowe, "Framing the Sun: The Arch of Constantine and the Roman Cityscape," *Art Bulletin* 88.2 (2006). It is currently impossible to conduct a similar study on the Arch of the Argentarii because of the arch's inclusion in the church wall of San Giorgio al Velabro. In any event, the Arch of the Argentarii is north-south facing, which meant that light would pass across its south side, so it probably lacked the solar associations that seem to be essential to the Arch of Constantine.

62. CIL 4.1035, line 6. This line is slightly larger than the text before it and contains an emendation. The first five words are large and clear, as are the final three, but from *loci* through *invehent* the words are crammed together and are placed on top of one another, with two rows of text forming in the middle of the line. *Loci qui* rests atop *invehent*. It is possible that this was a simple error. The space is adequate to accommodate *loci*, which seems a logical choice for the passage, while *qui invehent*, as a subordinate clause, seems unnecessary for the content. It is likely to have been a later addition to the text, and the edit may have coincided with one of the instances of *damnatio memoriae* in which portions of the reliefs were erased. However, *invehent* requires some further explanation, as it is in the future tense, which has led to some consternation among commentators. Generally, a present tense, *invehunt*, is substituted, and the vowel change is attributed to a simple mix-up. See De Maria, *Gli archi onorari*, 185 n. 30; and Anne Daguet-Gagey, "L'arc des argentiers, à Rome: À propos de la dédicace du monument (CIL VI, 1035 = 31232 = ILS 426)," *Revue historique* 307.3 (2005), for a full discussion of the history of this verb; and Giardina, "The Merchant," 263, who believes, as I do, that the tense may be intentional. L. Richardson, *A New Topographical Dictionary of Ancient Rome* (Baltimore: Johns Hopkins University Press, 1992), believes that *boari* refers to the location, rather than to the group of people, and that it was the *argentarii* and *nego-*

This brief text reveals the identity of the merchants who were involved in the construction of the arch. Though it does not offer a list of named members, it significantly narrows down the number of potential contributors, first by their professions, then by their location, and finally by an aside about the services they offered: the importation of, presumably, cattle. This service was likely the one that brought the bankers and cattle merchants together, as both were needed to navigate the potentially complex financial and logistical processes of transporting livestock to the city. The inclusion of this detail seems calculated to set these merchants apart. Their description of *qui invehent*, implies that there were at least some traders, *qui non invehent*, who would not bring in their goods, and consequently that there was something special about those who did or would. This was a clever bit of advertising, which, in combination with the many virtues this monument displayed, created a material intersection of word, image, and structure that showed these merchants comprehensively and in the best possible light.

As a reputation strategy, the construction of a large monument was an effective and dramatic statement, as well as one that had the ability to ground merchants in a community in a physically obvious way. As we will discuss in the next chapter, many merchant groups were at risk for being seen as "foreign" or as "interlopers," both because of their mobility and because many were not landowners and consequently could not conform to that model of *Romanitas*. The Arch of the Argentarii combated these kinds of accusations by making a visible, expensive contribution to the forum, and by using the visual language of the imperial family for their own purposes. These merchants physically claimed a place by the construction of the arch and adopted a Roman visual language to express their allegiance to, and awareness of, the Roman state.[63]

Of course, not everyone was a member of such a wealthy coalition of merchants and some endeavored to go it alone, relying on informal networks of friends and peers for support and community. These merchants also found ways to proclaim the excellence of their reputation through visual means. Already we have seen the example of the wall painting on Verecundus' work-

---

tiantes who organized this monument. He believes that the *negotiantes* were wholesale traders, but does not hypothesize what wares they may have dealt in. I side with Michael MacKinnon, "Pack Animals, Pets, Pests, and Other Non-Human Beings," in *The Cambridge Companion to Ancient Rome*, ed. Paul Erdkamp (Cambridge: Cambridge University Press, 2013), 123, that these are cattle dealers, because of the iconographic emphasis on cattle and because *boari* as a location would make *huius loci* redundant, despite being part of the original inscription.

63. Similar strategies are at work in many cities in Roman Greece. Apameia, for example had a *plateia* built by a group of shoemakers; see Emanuel Mayer, *The Ancient Middle Classes: Urban Life and Aesthetics in the Roman Empire, 100 BCE–250 CE* (Cambridge, MA: Harvard University Press, 2012), 79.

Figure 5. Wall painting of the Procession of the Carpenters, Regio VI.7.8–9, now in the Museo Archeologico Nazionale di Napoli (MANN inv 8991). Carlo Raso (CC-PD).

shop, but his was hardly the sole example of a shop's physicality being pressed into the service of reputation.[64] Just down the street from Verecundus in Pompeii, a bar covered its façade with paintings of the gods, while across town a carpenter's workshop displayed its owner and his colleagues participating in a religious procession (Fig. 5).[65] This painting displays the virtue of piety in these merchants, who carried with them a large litter, known as a *ferculum*, which depicted their patron goddess Minerva, now reconstructed from her extant

64. Regio IX.7.6–7, as discussed in chapter 2.

65. Regio XI.7.1, *Taberna* of the four deities (Apollo, Jupiter, Mercury, and Diana). The Procession of Cybele is described in Clarke, *Art in the Lives of Ordinary Romans*, 87–94. The wall painting of the carpenters is now in Naples (MANN inv. 8991) and was originally painted on the pilaster between Regio VI.7.9, the House of Tullius, and Regio VI.7.8, Workshop. The dimensions for the workshop space are unavailable and it is unclear how many merchants worked in the space. On production spaces in Pompeii, more generally, see Flohr, "*Nec quicquam ingenuum*."

shield, as well as a mythological scene showing the master craftsman Daedalus, and a series of, presumably, mortal carpenters at work.

These scenes of labor, like the bankers' claims about importing, advertised the specialized techniques of these craftsmen. Their skills are displayed, like those of Evangelus, discussed in the previous chapter, to convey a commitment to hard work and quality.[66] Though the details would likely be, as they are to us, difficult to decipher in the context of a procession or as one passed by the workshop, the viewer might suspect that these were special skills that marked these artisans out as particularly capable.[67] Importantly, these skills were shown to be observed and approved of by Minerva, which conveyed to the viewer that the success of these merchants, their prosperity and skillful execution of their commissions, was the result of the goddess' will, not of merchant deception. Their piety is further accentuated in the imagined fabrication of the *ferculum* itself, which represented a pious investment in the procession as well as a display of the very woodworking skills they advertised.[68]

Charlotte Potts has argued that images of this kind of procession represent not only a claim to merchant piety, but also to the status of the merchants involved, as participation in these events was selective, and not open to all.[69] Walking in a procession represented a level of community acceptance and recognition, which this carpenter memorialized on the wall of his small workshop. Though the premises of this workshop were not grand and were located on a quieter street than that of Verecundus, this artisan increased the profile of his shop in a way that both broadcast his standing in the community and made claims about his skill as a craftsman.

Other merchants used their space differently, investing not in an array of images, but in means to display their goods. Across the Mediterranean, shops are commonly identified by their wider entrances, designed to welcome in customers, while in Dura Europos, excavations have revealed that shops were constructed with special windows and raised displays so that customers could see,

66. Though each likely addressed different audiences. The Arch stood in a prominent public place, visited by the peers and business partners of the commissioners as well as many wholly unrelated passersby, whereas Evangelus' funerary art would have reached a far more restricted group of viewers that was more than likely composed of close family and acquaintances. The *loculusplatte* could have been viewed by other mourners in the columbarium, though much would have depended on its positioning relative to eye-level.

67. For an excellent interpretation of the specifics of the work, see Roger B. Ulrich, *Roman Woodworking* (New Haven: Yale University Press, 2008), 44–45.

68. There is no direct evidence that the painting of the *ferculum* records a real-world event, but the *ferculum* is remarkably detailed and the creation of such an object is perfectly plausible. The wall painting would therefore represent a commemoration of the procession.

69. Charlotte R. Potts, "The Art of Piety and Profit at Pompeii: A New Interpretation of the Painted Shop Façade at IX.7.1–2," *Greece & Rome* 56.1 (2009).

even from outside, what a merchant had to offer.[70] Counters are common in both archaeological finds and in representations of shops, and in each case they offered a merchant an opportunity to present himself as well as the products for sale, as he presided over and organized sales. Quality was the main virtue on display here, as well as honesty and fairness. Graffiti from Pompeii and Dura attest that merchants sometimes did their accounting on the walls of their shop, which, if nothing else, left their correct or faulty arithmetic on display for some time.[71]

For the merchant without a physical space, this kind of reputation strategy was unavailable or at least more challenging. Yet neither reputation strategies nor reputation judgments were limited to the visual. Every commercial space in the ancient world was also filled with conversation and sound that could communicate much to the attentive listener. Seneca the Younger seems to have been particularly sensitive to this noise, as he complained in a letter that he was unable to find any quiet in his urban lodging due to the noise coming from merchants in the nearby baths:

> *Praeter istos, quorum, si nihil aliud, rectae voces sunt, alipilum cogita tenuem et stridulam vocem, quo sit notabilior subinde exprimentem nec umquam tacentem . . . iam biberari varias exclamationes et botularium et crustularium et omnes popinarum institores mercem sua quadam et insignita modulatione vendentis.*

> Beyond those whose voices, if nothing else, are acceptable, think on the barber continuously emitting his weak and grating voice, so that he may be more noticeable, and is never quiet. . . . Then the various shouts of the drink seller and the sausage seller and the cake seller and all the food vendors selling their goods, and each with his own distinct call.[72]

These merchants, whether fairly or unfairly portrayed in this sketch, clearly intended to be heard. Seneca stresses that they have an *insignita modulatio*, a distinctive call, and he seems to believe, even if it is only for literary effect, that he can recognize each in turn. Among tradesmen, sound was evidently a tool in

70. Jennifer A. Baird, "Shopping, Eating and Drinking at Dura Europos: Reconstructing Contexts," in *Objects in Context, Objects in Use: Material Spatiality in Late Antiquity*, ed. Luke Lavan, Ellen Swift, and Toon Putzeys (Leiden: Brill, 2007), 421.

71. E.g., CIL 4.5380, an accounting list from a *taberna*, Pompeii Regio IX.7.24.

72. Sen., *Ep.* 56.2, to Lucilius. Another loud merchant is a milk seller in Calp., *Ecl.* 4.25–26. For a discussion of a series of examples from Horace, see Charles Knapp, "Roman Business Life as Seen in Horace," *Classical Journal* 2.3 (1907): 116.

the arsenal, however irritating one's neighbors might find it, for gaining attention and broadcasting a reputation.[73]

Whether it was a pleasant sound or not, it must be assumed that in busy commercial districts these cries were an effective means of helping customers find the goods they wanted, or even of convincing them to buy things they did not need.[74] An effective seller might be both dealer and impresario, wooing his customers not only through tempting offers, but also through jokes or more personal conversation with familiar figures.[75] Seneca is clear: these cries were an effort to advertise, and to present oneself and one's goods as *notabilior*, more noticeable, than one's peers, once again demonstrating the comparative nature of reputation.

As Victoria Rimell has argued, being noticed is very much akin to fame and seeking a reputation.[76] Drawing attention involved not only the immediate possibility of a sale for merchants, but also made a claim to a space, one's position within it, and the right one had to sell there. That one could be noticed, but not driven off, signaled that one was behaving in a socially acceptable way and was therefore in the right place. In line with this, Seneca' account seems to stress the similarity of businesses in the district he describes. His account mentions primarily food-sellers, who must have been expected to ply their trades in this space. Their calls were part of the normal soundscape, aimed at both drowning out and drawing in more customers than their competitors.[77]

These merchants adopted a clear strategy to be seen or heard, and to promote their reputation as the best in their field, or at least the best choice for this buyer. Our evidence for what exactly they said or did to achieve these aims is fairly slim. A fable derived from Aesop reports that a cobbler feigned expertise

73. Claire Holleran, *Shopping in Ancient Rome: The Retail Trade in the Late Republic and the Principate* (Oxford: Oxford University Press, 2012), 202, discusses rhetorical sources that refer to the sounds made by street vendors, which were evidently well known enough to be a comprehensible reference.

74. A subject of interest to scholars of contemporary business, e.g., Pedro Bordalo, Nicola Gennaioli, and Andrei Shleifer, "Competition for Attention," *National Bureau of Economic Research*, Working Paper 19076 (2013); and Ken Sacharin, *Attention! How to Interrupt, Yell, Whisper, and Touch Consumers* (New York: John Wiley and Sons, 2004).

75. This is a central feature of what we know about popular culture in general. Humor and wittiness were tools for establishing membership in a community and for asserting status among and above others, see Jerry P. Toner, *Popular Culture in Ancient Rome* (Cambridge: Polity, 2009), esp. 95–102; also Martial, *Epigrams*, 10.3, on the insults at times used by sellers.

76. Victoria Rimell, *The Closure of Space in Roman Poetics: Empire's Inward Turn* (Cambridge: Cambridge University Press, 2015), 171.

77. Since there is no reason to believe that Seneca was living near the forum, this also fits more generally into an ongoing discussion about the omnipresence of commercial activity in Roman cities. See Mayer, *The Ancient Middle Classes*, 74–85, for a convincing treatment of the naturally bustling urban landscape, which would have been filled with many temporary stalls for food, as well as permanent shops and *tabernae*.

as a doctor and, *verbosis adquisivit sibi famam strophis*, acquired a reputation for himself with wordy trickery.[78] The exact words are not preserved, but we can imagine the sort of claims a quack doctor might make about his miracle cure, and the kinds of persuasion he might employ to stand out in a field that was notoriously unreliable.[79]

Reliefs offer different insights; an example from Narbonne depicting a walking merchant preserves not only an image of the seller (Fig. 6), who carried his wares in a basket around his neck, but also an inscription that seems to record his cry: MAḶA MYLIERE(s) MYLIERE(s) MEAE.[80] By these words, he hoped to endear himself to female customers, perhaps relying on charm to help his sales. However, more critically for reputation, this seller recognized, or perhaps hoped, that he would be remembered for his iconic cry. It was, to him, as essential a part of his character as his name and preserved something fundamental about his business: a mobile trade in what is probably apples that appealed to women and relied on a slogan to reach customers.

Whether they sold portable goods as they meandered the streets, set up a temporary stall on a street corner, or invested in a brick-and-mortar store, merchants of all kinds competed for attention and sales. Reliefs and wall paintings depict the next steps after a customer had been lured, including street vendors presenting their wares to customers.[81] The careful examination of goods shown in these scenes likely depicts a testing ground for reputation, where a customer could see for themselves whether a merchant's claims were borne out in the goods they sold. Thus, for all the strategies merchants adopted, reputation ultimately came down to the distance between the claims that merchants made

78. Phaedrus, *Fab.*14, *Ex sutore medicus*. These fables are complicated sources. Their frequent copying and reworking suggest their popularity in the Roman period, but the person of "Aesop" is extremely uncertain. The myth claims that he was a slave of Greek origin, perhaps from as early as the seventh century BCE, but the preserved Greek and Latin texts are from the first century CE. The attitudes preserved in the fables are, consequently, difficult to pin down, but we might assume that popular narratives that survived frequent revisions were stories that continued to appeal to contemporary audiences.

79. The quack doctor is a ubiquitous trope. See chapter 4 for further discussion.

80. CIL 12.4524, Paul Tournal, *Catalogue du musée de Narbonne* (Paris: Emmanuel Caillard, 1864), #451; Emilio Magaldi, *Il commercio ambulante a Pompei* (Naples: Tipografia Ospedale Psichiatrico Provinciale L. Bianchi, 1930), 15; Otto Schlippschuh, *Die Händler im römischen Kaiserreich Gallien, Germanien und den donauprovinzen Rätien, Noricum und Pannonien* (Amsterdam: Hakkert, 1987), #38. Holleran, *Shopping*, 207, 209, and 212, describes this relief as coming from a sarcophagus, but this is not argued elsewhere. The top right corner of the stone has been damaged, leading to competing reconstructions of MAIA and MALA. Tournal records a suggestion of pastries in the shape of young women, using MAIA, though this seems thin, given that MALA seems plausible and a more common product. Holleran notes that the *mala*-bad, *mala*-apples distinction is likely to be part of the joke here. Once again, humor is a useful tool in trade.

81. Holleran, *Shopping*, 203–4. Visually, this is accessible via the fresco (MANN inv. 9062) of the Pompeian forum from the atrium of the house of Julia Felix.

Figure 6. Funerary relief of an apple seller, Le Musée Archéologique de Narbonne inv. 837.1.5. Jane Sancinito.

and the reality of what they did and sold on a daily basis. Even large, dramatic efforts to shift reputation in a positive direction were only ever as convincing as the reality that lay behind them.

This did not convince merchants to stop trying, but there was a general awareness that it was wise to temper one's claims with a dose of reality. As the author of the *Disticha Catonis*, a collection of proverbs commonly dated to the third or fourth century CE, said, *Quod praestare potes, ne bis promiseris ulli, Ne sis ventosus, dum vis bonus esse videri*, as long as you would seem to be a good man, do not be vain or promise any more than what you are able to fulfill.[82] Bold claims may have flown about in the oral culture of merchants, but in our extant examples, merchants restrained themselves to claiming that they were good, honest men who sold fair measures of quality wares, at least during their lifetimes. After death, merchants expanded their repertoire of reputation strategies to shape their posthumous reputation for the rest of time.

Reputation of the Dead

Much of the most explicit evidence regarding merchant reputation strategies comes from funerary contexts. In death, merchants and their heirs found a motivation to sum up the work of a lifetime and make a final set of claims about who they had been. Posthumous reputation is not unfamiliar to the modern world, as the genres of obituary and eulogy continue to thrive as accepted parts of the grieving process, but in antiquity the cultivation of this kind of reputation took on a slightly different cast. Though grief and hopes for the afterlife are present in these materials, there was also a trend of drafting statements for this context well before the fact, while the subject was still living.

The goals of such efforts are somewhat unclear, as posthumous reputation is a rather neglected corner of the study of reputation.[83] In existential terms, it is believed that the desire to craft one's posthumous reputation is based on the desire to demonstrate that life had meaning and value. The fear that life might, ultimately, be an exercise in futility and absurdity is combated by efforts to shape how one will be remembered, and for how long, after death. Of course, the parameters for what constituted a meaningful life were socially constructed,

82. *Disticha Catonis*, 25. On this interesting source see Serena Connolly, "Disticha Catonis Uticensis," *Classical Philology* 107.2 (2012).

83. The best sources are Craik, *Reputation*, ch. 9; Scarre, "Caring about One's Posthumous Reputation"; and Luper, "Posthumous Harm." The brief comments of Bromley, *Reputation*, 48, effectively summarize the thinness of scholarship on this issue.

not to mention contested. As we will see in the next chapter, many who lived lives that, from elite Roman perspectives, would have been viewed as lowly or meaningless, nevertheless took great pride in their achievements. For merchants in the Roman world, funerary art and inscriptions offered an opportunity to make claims about the importance of work in their lives. Such assertions were both personal and social. Not only did the content of these kinds of memorials add to the body of data constituting one's personal reputation, but these objects also made a statement about the value of work to the community and the position that work should have in Roman society.[84]

More concretely, however, this evidence invites us to think about who benefited most from such memorials. There has been a strong scholarly impulse to assume that merchants hoped that their inscriptions or monuments would benefit the reputations of their heirs, but, while this would make sense, we often lack evidence to corroborate the assumption.[85] There is some data to support the idea that sons pursued the trades of their fathers, but we rarely, if ever, see a business clearly transmitted from one generation to the next.[86] Family businesses seem to have been common, with wives and children frequently assisting their husbands and fathers in work, but family names do not seem to have been used metonymically for a business, names do not seem to have been put to use by successive generations, nor do we have evidence of named businesses being purchased by new owners who hoped to capitalize on the reputation of the old.[87]

In cases where family, friends, or freedmen and women are responsible for the funerary image or inscription, it is tempting to assume that they did so, at least in part, to benefit themselves. While grief and emotional investment are present in many of these sources, we often struggle to tease out the feeling that lay behind the construction of a monument and to know how the experience

84. This impulse is, of course, not exclusive to merchants in the Roman world. Including elements of (auto)biography into funerary art or inscriptions was a habit that is found at all levels of Roman society. We are as likely to find politicians and priests recording their *res gestae* as we are to find shoemakers, though there is a wealth of evidence for the latter, see, e.g., Joshel, *Work, Identity, and Legal Status*, for a concentrated study.

85. Toner, *Popular Culture*, 15: "some of the poor may have aspired to longer-term dynastic ambitions, as is seen in some gravestones of freedmen marking their success for perpetuity."

86. On fathers passing their trade on, see the fishermen in Matthew 4:21–22, Mark 1:19–20; weavers in Julio-Claudian Egypt, in Liu, "Group Membership." There is also some evidence to suggest that fathers sometimes arranged for their sons to be trained in fields other than their own, normally for reasons of social advancement: see Hawkins, *Roman Artisans*, 200; Petron., *Sat.* 46; Luc., *Somn.* 2.

87. As with Verecundus (Regio IX.7.6–7) or as implied in the case of Crobyle and Corinna, Luc., *D. meretr.* 1.

of grieving inflected the decisions that were made.[88] Furthermore, the reputation of the commissioner is implicated in such an undertaking, as their choice of inscription or design must convey information about their own character. Setting up funerary markers on behalf of relations, friends, or former masters was a display of the commissioner's *pietas*, and it is often unclear to what extent comments about a merchant's business were meant to provide Roman readers with information about the living, rather than merely the dead.

Thus, it is unclear if or when the reputation of a merchant was expected to benefit those he or she had left behind. What is certain, however, is that reputation was explicitly on the minds of both merchants and their heirs during the process of commissioning and erecting these monuments, and that work played a central role in the personae that these images and texts projected. We have already seen Lucius Nerusius Mithres and his fictional counterpart Trimalchio composing their funerary inscriptions during their lifetimes, and other texts are elaborate enough to suggest a similar level of attention, regardless of the commissioner. A useful example is that of Lucius Praecilius Fortunatus, a North African *argentarius*:

> HIC EGO QVI TACEO, VERSIBVS MEA(m) VITA(m) DEMONSTRO.
> LVCEM CLARA(m) FRUITVS ET TEMPORA SVMMA
> PRAECILIVS CIRTENSI LARE ARGENTARIAM EX(h)IBVI ARTEM.
> FYDES IN ME MIRA FVIT SEMPER ET VERITAS OMNIS.
> OMNI<S>BUS COMMUNIS EGO CVI NON MISERTVS? VBIQVE
> RISVS, LVXVRIA(m) SEMPER FRUITVS CVN CARIS AMICIS.
> TALEM POST OBITVM DOMINAE VALERIAE NON INVENI PVDICAE;
> VITAM CVM POTVI GRATA(m) HABVI CVM CONIVGE SANCTA<m>.
> NATALES HONESTE MEOS CENTVM CELEBRAVI FELICES
> AT VENIT POSTREMA DIES, VT SPIRITVS INANIA MEMBRA RELI(N)QVAT.
> TITVLOS QVOS LEGIS, VIVVS ME(A)E MORTI PARAVI,
> VT VOLVIT FORTVNA, NVNQVAM ME DESERVIT IPSA.
> SEQVIMINI TALES, HIC VOS EX(S)PECTO, VENIT<A>E.[89]

88. Valerie M. Hope and Janet Huskinson, eds., *Memory and Mourning: Studies on Roman Death* (Oxford: Oxbow Books, 2011), introduction and ch. 10.

89. Text of Michel Griffe, Jean-Marie Lassère, and Jean Soubiran, "Épitaphe du banquier Praecilius (CIL VIII, 7156 = IL Alg. 2, 820 = CLE, 512)," *Vita Latina* 146 (1997). Note that, like Mithres, this merchant uses an acrostic to structure his inscription.

I, who am silent here, reveal my life in verse.

I, Praecilius of Cirta, enjoyed a shining reputation and the greatest times, I practiced the banker's art. My honesty was wonderful, and I always told the whole truth. I was courteous to all. To whom did I not show compassion? I was joyful everywhere, always enjoyed luxury together with my dear friends. Such a great (change came upon me) after the death of my lady Valeria. I could not find her equal in modesty. As long as I was able, I maintained a blessed and pleasing life with my wife. In virtue, I celebrated one hundred happy birthdays. Yet the final day has come, as the spirit leaves my empty limbs. The inscription that you read I prepared while living for my death, as Fortune willed it, she never deserted me. Follow me in this way, I await you here, come.

Fortunatus' inscription reintroduces numerous features that we have already encountered. From his emphasis on the *luxuriam*—here not meaning tasteless wealth but rather the benefits of a successful career that he was able to share with his friends—to his consistency and courtesy, Fortunatus' choice of words demonstrates that the reputational concerns of merchants remained largely similar across the ancient, at least western, Mediterranean. Prominent here is his desire to display his good reputation, which he identifies as his *lux*, light.[90]

The claims that Fortunatus makes are numerous, but may be grouped, with only slight overlap, into three categories: those that are meant as proof of his good character in general, those that proclaim his generosity in particular, and those that speak to his lifelong consistency. Each of these factors aimed to shape a different aspect of Fortunatus' posthumous reputation, and each finds parallel in the funerary monuments of other merchants. This is important, especially in the case of the first category of claims, as "goodness" is at its core a value-laden, socially contingent state of being. Fortunatus makes claims to trustworthiness, honesty, courtesy, and, above all, success, each a characteristic that was considered "good" among the Romans. Above all else, Fortunatus' inscription asserts that he was a good man, whose moral standing was unquestionable and whose model was one to be emulated. In a different society, he might have felt the need to stress other characteristics, but among his Roman compatriots, the traits he selects are those that were most desirable among tradesmen.

Fortunatus' claims were very much in line with the norms of his society. Other merchants, especially from the middle of the first century through

90. On *lux*, TLL Vol. 8.2, 1904, lin. 83, and 1917, lin. 82, *caput alterum* I.A.2.a.α.

the beginning of the third century CE, were not shy about proclaiming their achievements in funerary inscriptions and monuments, and their claims generally fall along similar lines.[91] Thus Fortunatus' emphasis on his *fydes mira*, wonderful trustworthiness or honesty, is found frequently among merchant inscriptions, suggesting a common preference for this virtue. *Fides* is particularly emphasized in the funerary marker of Lucius Statius Onesimus, which was set up by his wife Statia Crescentina. She writes:

D.M.
IN HOC TVMVLO IACET CORPVS EXANIMIS
CUIUS SPIRITVS INTER DEOS RECEPTVS EST.
SIC ENIM MERVIT, L. STATIVS ONESIMVS
VIAE APPIAE MULTORVM ANNORVM NEGOTIA(n)S,
HOMO SUPER OMNES FIDELISSIMVS,
CUIUS FAMA IN AETERNO NOTA EST,
QUI VIXIT SINE MACVLA AN(nos) P(lus) M(inusve) LXVIII
STATIA CRESCENTINA CO(n)I(n)XV
MARITO DIGNISSIMO ET MERITO
CUM QUO VIXIT CUM BONA CONCORDIA
SINE ALTERITRVM ANIMI LESIONEM
BENE MERENTI FECIT.

For the spirits.

In this tomb lies the body of the lifeless man, whose spirit has been welcomed among the gods. For thus he, Lucius Statius Onesimus, deserved. Selling for many years on the Appian Way, he was an exceptionally honest man beyond all others, whose reputation is known in perpetuity, who lived without a stain for roughly sixty-eight years. Statia Crescentina, his wife, made this for a most worthy and deserving man, and lived with him with good harmony without any exchanged hurt feelings, made this for him, for he was deserving.[92]

91. Funerary inscriptions from this period and among those at this social-economic level drew from what Mayer, *The Ancient Middle Classes*, 100, calls "a rich repertoire of widely available formulae." Obviously, some carved their own path with their funerary inscriptions, but most relied on combination and variation from a narrower set of themes and topics.

92. CIL 6.9663, Rome, undated but certainly imperial. As with many of these inscriptions, the text has some oddities of spelling, most notably *alteritrum*, which appears to be a rendering of *alterutrum*.

The inscription is briefer than that of Fortunatus or the goat-skin seller, Mithres, but Statia's choices nevertheless present her husband in a comparable light. Like Fortunatus, Statia is explicit about the importance of reputation, here rendered as Onesimus' *fama*, which is to be known *in aeterno*, forever. Again, being *notus*, and *notus* for the right reasons, is important. Whereas Mithres lingers over his numerous qualities, Onesimus is mainly defined by one, his exceptional honesty or trustworthiness. Onesimus was *fidelissimus*.

Trustworthiness was a critical quality for a merchant or craftsman. Whether it involved personal loans, waiting for contracts to be fulfilled, or merely having faith that a product would meet expectations, those who engaged with artisans or retailers in the ancient world were often asked to have a certain amount of *fides* in those from whom they bought. Yet, for all its necessity, our evidence suggests that trust was rarely felt to the kind of superlative degree that Statia believed Onesimus deserved. Distrust marred many interactions between customer and merchant in the Roman world, with every action of the merchant coming under scrutiny for cut corners, dishonest practices, and even outright lying and theft.

Thus, the claim of honesty, and particularly superlative or *mira* trustworthiness, is an ideal characteristic for the good merchant, but the claim may very well mask a certain amount of anxiety. Though we will address this matter fully in the next chapter, Onesimus' inscription offers us a glimpse into the kind of worry that many merchants felt. Statia, after claiming the eternal status of Onesimus' good name, strives to make it clear that he lived without stain, *sine macula*, a phrase that here means something like without shame or dishonor. Statia feels she must disown the possibility of a *macula*, the mark that might tarnish the good name of her most worthy, *dignissimus*, husband.

She was not alone in this fear. As we mentioned briefly in chapter 2, the formula of *sine* with some trait to be denied is a common one in merchant inscriptions. It is reported in a funerary marker of a brothel keeper from Rome—her business was run *sine fraude*, without deceit.[93] The same phrase is echoed by the so-called Mactar Harvester; his text uses the formula twice, also advising the reader to live life *sine crimine*, without wrongdoing.[94] These denials all suggest

93. CIL 9.2029, the situation of Vibia Calybenis is complicated by her role as a sex worker, which likely engendered a greater-than-average level of distrust. Strong, *Prostitutes and Matrons*, 2, summarizes the stereotype neatly: "greedy, selfish, promiscuous prostitutes focused on their own self-interests." This is a typical view of merchants more broadly, though, as Strong and others have noted, this is the view of an exclusively elite audience. Merchant opinions, while harder to access, were likely to have been more nuanced in their view of each other.

94. CIL 8.11824 cf. p. 2372 = CLE 1238 = ILS 07457 = ILTun 528; 28. Also visible in another inscription, *L'Année épigraphique* 1960: 116 (Mactaris), found in Mactar, of Pinarius Mustulus, who *quaestui fraude [sine ulla]*. See Brent D. Shaw, *Bringing in the Sheaves: Economy and Metaphor in*

that merchants carried deep anxieties, especially the fear that these negative traits were what people actually believed to be true about them, even after all their efforts to the contrary.

Given the common nature of this fear, and the equally common approach of denial to combat it, it is interesting then that Fortunatus does not share Statia's approach. Rather, like Mithres, Fortunatus offers his reader his accomplishments without self-consciousness or hesitation. He credits *Fortuna* for his success, but only after noting how his own good behavior supported his luck. Honesty, courtesy, compassion, and generosity are the building blocks of his reputation, values that responded to negative stereotypes and which were recognized as positive in Roman society. The community recognized and valued these traits, which meant that cultivating them was also a means of signaling that you belonged to the same community. As we will discuss, merchants were consistently pressed to the edges of Roman society, figuratively, but also at times literally, and their morals were constantly questioned. Merchants responded by displaying how well they conformed to social norms and how much they, too, valued Roman *mores*.

Rather than lean into specific examples, Fortunatus' list seems intended to prove the specifics through the aggregate. He hopes that the reader will recognize one of his claims as true and conclude that the others must be equally so. If the reader could believe that Fortunatus was compassionate, then he would agree that he was also courteous and honest. It is, in general, a weak argument, except for the most obvious of the claims that Fortunatus makes and the only one that he does not put into quite so many words: that he was successful.

Fortunatus tells his reader that *fortuna* never deserted him, *Fortuna nunquam me deseruit*, but what he means to convey is that his business thrived throughout his life. This is most obvious in his reference to the "luxury" that he shared with his dear friends, a comment directly referring to his generosity, but which is undergirded by the tacit assumption that Fortunatus' work provided him with surplus wealth. Generosity is a common theme throughout many merchant inscriptions, and was among the most important virtues for merchants, in general, plagued as they were with accusations of greed. Displays and statements of generosity flew in the face of such stereotypes, so merchants were eager to show the ways in which they shared their prosperity. Mithres and Evangelus, among many other cases, use the provision of burial places for their family and freedmen as a symbol of their own generosity, while Fortunatus remains vaguer about the help he actually offered.

the Roman World (Toronto: University of Toronto Press, 2015), 58 n. 42, for discussion and comparison with the Mactar Harvester.

Despite his lack of specificity, his ability to be generous is crucial, and may be juxtaposed with another, less fortunate merchant from roughly the same period:

L(ucius) • LICINIVS
M(arci) • F(ilius) • POL(lia) •NEPOS •
CVIVS • DE • VITA • MERITO
POTE • NEMO • QVERI •
QVI • NEGOTIANDO • LOCVPLETEM
SE • SPERAVIT • ESSE • FVTVRVM
SPE • DECEPTVS • ERAT • ET • A • MULT-
IS • BENE • MERITVS • AMICIS •
HANC • CASVLAM • IN • PARV-
O • FECIT • SVPREMI • TEMPORIS
SEDEM • MAIORI • CVRA
QVAM • INPENSA • POTVIT •
. . .

Lucius Licinius Nepos, son of Marcus, of the Pollia tribe, about whose life, rightly, no one can complain, who hoped to make himself wealthy by selling, he was deceived in that hope and by many friends, though he deserved well (from them), he made this hut in a small space, a seat at the end of life, which he was able to do with (great) expense . . . [95]

Like Fortunatus, Lucius Licinius Nepos erected a long inscription detailing his life's achievements. However, Nepos quickly admits that his hopes of financial success were dashed. While the existence of the inscription, and possibly of a portrait bust to accompany it, rather belies the abject poverty that Nepos goes on to opine, his inscription poses a rather dramatic contrast to that of the banker. Nepos blames his bad luck in trade on his friends, who, by his estimation, should have helped him through his struggles and on his way to wealth and security.

This implies a fascinating business model, one that explicitly depended on the community to work. In fact, it closely resembles the situation that most merchants were in as they started out, when the help of others was essential to their own hopes for success. Compared, for example, with Paul's professed model for Christian workers, Nepos' view is diametrically opposed to the trend

95. CIL 6.9659=CIL 6.33814, Rome, lines 1–12. The inscription is possibly Trajanic in date, to match the bust in the Getty Museum (85.AA.111) that is believed to be from the same monument.

of self-sufficiency and self-reliance in merchant representation, which was more fitting, perhaps, to those who were already established in their trade. In general, Roman merchants are quick to stress their own labor, and what they had been able to achieve through their own resources, but many still sought to minimize the assistance they had received from others.[96] Nepos is unusual in that he is this explicit about this kind of economic obligation among friends and it is strange to see this kind of expression at this point in a merchant's career, that is to say, in a funerary context.[97]

Fortunatus, by contrast, relegates his friends to being only the recipients of his generosity, rather than a network on which he relied. Nepos plays up their role in his business life, and lays blame at their feet for his inability to provide a more lavish burial for his parents, which he describes with some shame.[98] His struggle to provide for others is the strongest indicator of the failure of his business. It separates him from those who could be generous and places him among those that could only receive generosity. The latter were akin to the poor or were considered parasitical clients to those with greater means.

For men like Fortunatus, the aim was to be a benefactor, to make generosity one of the outstanding features of his career. Consistent generosity, founded upon the ability to be generous, served as powerful signals that a business was doing well and that success had not turned the merchant's character toward greed or selfishness. As a form of proof, individuals or groups of merchants might make benefactions to the community, or participate in public events, as we have seen. Critically, an artisan or trader could not rest their reputation on a single kind or generous act but needed to make frequent displays of their good character in order to support a good reputation.

Thus, in Fortunatus' *luxuria(m) semper fruitus cun caris amicis*, the key word is *semper*, always. This was a continuous state of generosity, or at least a regular occurrence, and should not be mistaken for simple hyperbole. Fortunatus wished to present a totalizing and comprehensive statement on his life in his funerary inscription, which means that words like *semper*, *ubique*, *omnis*, and *nunquam*, while not necessarily literal, nevertheless are serving a vital reputa-

96. An interesting midpoint on the spectrum between total dependence and total independence is *Disticha Catonis* 1.23: *Si tibi pro meritis nemo succurrit amicus, incusare deos noli, sed te ipse coerce.* "If none of your friends assist you as you deserve, don't blame the gods, but check yourself." The language of "deserving" is present in both texts, suggesting that help must be earned, but that it can nevertheless be expected.

97. An interesting counterpoint is CIL 14.1271, where Longinia Procla mentions women who abandoned her while she was alive. These women are presumably her freedwomen, and it is not clear to what extent this abandonment was economic, social, or some combination of the two.

98. CIL 6.9659, lines 9–12. The inscription is nearly forty lines long and includes further complaints about the harshness of life, the generosity of Nepos, and the greed of men.

tional purpose. They stress consistency, reliability, and an unstinting dedication to a lifetime of good conduct.

Onesimus' inscription cultivates a similar theme in the claim that he worked for many years on the Appian Way. Statia found this consistency so important that she never actually relates what it was that her husband sold. Rather, it was more critical to suggest that his business had survived turbulence and challenges and that he had made a steady living. His reputation was best served by informing the reader that he had done not only his best, but that he had also regularly made good choices that enabled him to develop a thriving business, to look after his wife, and to be presented as the best version of himself in a permanent and totalizing way.

Conclusion

The reputation that a merchant received was not always directly tied to the strategies that he or she had chosen in life or after death. At times, their efforts rang somewhat false. It was possible for the audience to know too much, or too little, to be able to agree with the claims that were made, and, in still other instances, merchants could invest too much in style over substance. The pitfalls of reputation were manifold, and it was easy for a merchant to be known as less honest, good, or honorable than he or she had claimed.

Yet despite these risks, merchants still invested in a range of reputation strategies, each intended to help them become known for personal goodness, for the quality of their services or products, or for personal and professional success. Their achievements were not always evenly distributed, so a merchant might gain a reputation for a good product, but also for driving a hard bargain or cheating a little on weights, but the strategies were consistent in their effort to present merchants in the best light. As a result, the claims merchants made attempt to express, literally or figuratively, the superlative excellence of the merchant's life and work.

These strategies changed over the course of a merchant's lifetime and career. The tactics of the young or newly liberated, who had a small reputation but perhaps a willingness to take risks, were distinct from those used by merchants in the middle of their careers, or the efforts of aging merchants to sum up and cap off a lifetime of reputation.[99] Different businesses also required different

99. Horden and Purcell, *The Corrupting Sea*, 178–82, rightly note that risk was a major factor in all economic decision-making in the Mediterranean, but we can see specific risks taken by merchants, e.g., Petron., *Sat.* 76, Trimalchio loses his first inheritance in a shipwreck. Shipping was a

approaches. Thus, the mobile apple seller in Narbonne and the carpenter's workshop in Pompeii are not only preserved for posterity through different media, but they also reached their contemporary audience through different means. The carpenter could not bring his workshop to the middle of the forum, he needed to draw business to him, while the apple seller could bring himself wherever he was most likely to make a sale but lacked a space where he could be reliably found. Both hoped their audience, whether the passerby or the chosen target, would respond positively to the merchant they encountered and the persona he had adopted.

Yet, as Lucius Licinius Nepos found to his regret, hopes could be dashed. An undercurrent of worry is found in most merchant statements concerning reputation, a worry that, despite this hard work and investment, the audience was and would always be hostile to the circumstances of a merchant. Many seem to fear that vice and even criminality would be associated with them, and, as we have seen, some took steps to confront and deny such attitudes directly in their reputation strategies.

Negative feelings about merchants were rampant throughout Roman culture, and it is against these stereotypes that we see good reputations being put into use as social capital that was spent in concrete and strategic ways. In the coming chapter, we will look more closely at merchant stereotypes and at how reputation was mobilized against those who would belittle or stigmatize the Roman retailer, artisan, or transporter.

notoriously risky profession, necessitating insurance and other protections against loss.

CHAPTER 4

Defying the Stereotype and Using Reputation

Toranius mango Antonio iam triumviro eximios forma pueros, alterum in Asia genitum, alterum trans Alpis, ut geminos vendidit: tanta unitas erat. postquam deinde sermone puerorum detecta fraude a furente increpitus Antonio est, inter alia magnitudinem preti conquerente (nam ducentis erat mercatus sestertiis), respondit versutus ingenii mango, id ipsum se tanti vendidisse, quoniam non esset mira similitudo in ullis eodem utero editis; diversarum quidem gentium natales tam concordi figura reperire super omnem esse taxationem; adeoque tempestivam admirationem intulit, ut ille proscriptor animus, modo et contumelia furens, non aliud in censu magis ex fortuna sua duceret.

Toranius, the slave-dealer, sold two remarkably beautiful boys, the one born in Asia, the other beyond the Alps, to the triumvir Antony on the pretext that they were twins: so great was their similarity. Soon after, the deception was discovered by the furious Antony because of the language of the boys. He shouted at the dealer, complaining, among other things, about the magnitude of the price he had paid (for he had paid two hundred thousand sesterces for them). The crafty slave-dealer answered that this was the very reason that he had sold them at such a high price; for there would have been nothing particularly striking in the resemblance of the boys, if they had been born of the same womb, but children found to be so exactly like each other, though born in different countries, should be considered beyond all price. His answer produced such appropriate admiration that the mind of the proscriber, which was just raging because of the insult, came to value no part of his property more.

—Pliny, *Naturalis Historia*, 7.10

Toranius was a slave dealer in the late Republic. Our limited record suggests that he was a man who leveraged both his wits and his personal connections—to potentially two members of the second triumvirate—into a thriving and prominent business. Yet, like many slave dealers, Toranius' reputation was decidedly mixed.[1] Though he was on social terms with men of prominence, by

1. On the profession, see John Bodel, "*Caveat Emptor*: Towards a Study of Roman Slave-Traders," *Journal of Roman Archaeology* 18 (2005).

the Flavian period, his success, combined with anecdotal information like that shared by Pliny, had transformed his name into a byword for deceit, craftiness, and exploitative behavior.[2] His reputation was not benefited by the fact that slave dealers were considered an especially untrustworthy lot, even compared to merchants in general. They were believed to conceal faults in the people they sold and to make extravagant claims to justify their inflated prices.[3]

Certainly, this seems to have been the game Toranius was playing with Antony, yet, in the moment Pliny conjures, Toranius has wit enough to evade Antony's anger and transform the true origin of these "twins" into an asset. Antony, we are told, leaves feeling that he has actually "won" this game of commerce and ended up with "goods" worth more than he paid. While the text does not preserve Toranius' real or imagined choice of words, we must assume that his argument relied not only on the idea of novelty and rarity, as suggested, but also on the relationship Toranius already had with the triumvir, to call upon feelings of trust and to distract from the financial investment at hand.

For better or worse, Toranius was the "slave dealer to the stars," and that reputation outlived him by many generations. How he built that reputation, rising from the ranks of lesser tradesmen to a position of intimacy with important clients, is unknown, but Toranius was right to anticipate that, despite the general prejudice and the numerous stereotypes against his profession, he could claim tangible benefits by improving his personal standing. While another slave dealer would have been unlikely to get away with such deception, Toranius' reputation, and silver tongue, not only rescued him from Antony's rage, but elevated him further in the mind of his customer.

Merchants, in general, were right to expect that their investment in their reputations would pay off. The benefits of reputation could come in a variety of forms, ranging from profit and prosperity to social standing and goodwill. Though merchants actively sought the former rewards, the benefits of the latter were equally important for running a business in the Roman world. Holding a respected place in society was vital to a business' survival, and a merchant who was respected by his community, or simply by the "right" people within it, often found his business was correspondingly prosperous. Just as business success often led to further profits, social prominence often led to further honors, support, and opportunities. A good reputation, unchallenged by scandal or

2. Macrob., *Sat.* 2.4.28, a late and dubious source, suggests Toranius had dinner with Augustus. Suet., *Aug.* 69, refers to Toranius, but as an axiomatic slave dealer, not as an acquaintance of the emperor. On "Toranius" as an insult, see J. Albert Harrill, "The Vice of Slave Dealers in Greco-Roman Society: The Use of a *Topos* in 1 Timothy 1:10," *Journal of Biblical Literature* 118.1 (1999): 106.

3. As in Hor., *Epist.* 2.2.

rumor, helped a merchant to become steadily more well-known and wealthier in a process that could, theoretically, raise a merchant indefinitely, to remarkable heights.

To a degree, we have already encountered this in our analysis of reputation strategies. We have seen how merchant efforts often served multiple purposes, such as strategies that emphasized not only good products or services, but also the merchant's honesty, work ethic, or generosity. While some efforts were designed for immediate benefits and others were intended to pay off in the long term, every attempt was intended to make a return on the investment of time and money they required, at least eventually.

In this chapter, we will be analyzing that return by looking at how merchants mobilized their reputations for their own gain and at how others responded to them. We will be examining reputation as it was translated into social capital, a tool that merchants could wield actively, or benefit from passively. A good reputation could generate trust and comfort among consumers, emotions that flew in the face of Roman stereotypes about people in trade. These prejudices will also be of paramount importance in this discussion as we consider how merchants leveraged their reputations against stereotypes, presenting themselves as exceptions to the rule and requesting, if not total acceptance, at least the benefit of the doubt, based on their reputations.

Stereotypes about merchants are well preserved and documented across all levels of Roman society, and their nature was such that merchants at once contended with a generalized distaste for commerce that long pre-dated the Roman period, as well as specific prejudices that related to individual professions. Stereotypes threatened merchant reputation, and the denials and anxieties examined in the previous chapter reflect the awareness merchants had about the circulating preconceptions that made it difficult for groups and individuals to trust them. In terms of NIE, stereotypes raised transaction costs. They made making deals more time-consuming and may have prevented some from taking place at all, as both customers and merchants struggled to find new ways to generate trust in their business deals. It required a strong, positive reputation to overcome these concerns, and this was one of the primary uses of reputation as an institution.

In terms of evidence, the utility of reputation is most visible in cases where a reputation was insufficient for the purpose that a merchant had hoped to put it to, or in moments when two reputations came into direct conflict. The presence of a sufficiently good reputation generally smoothed the way for merchants, leaving us with few records of its commonplace success, while its absence often meant not only the failure of a merchant's initial purpose, but also further social or economic consequences that were worthy of record. In instances of conflict, two reputations came head-to-head, and the act of comparison made it possible to see whose claim to a good place in society was the stronger.

Like Toranius, most merchants held a mixed reputation, regardless of their overwhelmingly positive self-representation. The comparative nature of reputation itself encouraged others to think of merchants in relation to their peers, and their reputations were always composed of numerous different factors, which might be positive in some ways, or in some contexts, and negative in others. Thus, the moneylender Milo's reputation was summed up as a combination of his business practices, his personal appearance, and the company that he did (or in his case, did not) keep.[4] Though Milo is presented as having a uniformly negative reputation, he stresses that associating with Lucius, the protagonist of the *Metamorphoses*, will be beneficial to that latter facet of his reputation, recognizing the many ways in which reputation might be influenced.[5] Merchants were aware of the interdependent components of their reputation, and it is possible to find records of merchants who were known, for example, for high quality goods, while they were disparaged for keeping poor company.[6]

A mixed reputation led, naturally, to some unpredictable circumstances when reputations came into conflict. Much depended on the goodwill and social capital that a merchant had amassed through their reputation and what, precisely, they hoped to achieve in the moment. Reputation was built up slowly and could be put to work in small moments when trust could be helpful or in instances where a whole community would need to rally behind a merchant in crisis. That our sources provide us with instances where it seems the community did just that demonstrates that, as powerful and pervasive as negative stereotypes about merchants were, reputation could help a merchant overcome even the most extreme obstacles.

Stereotyping the Roman Merchant

From an elite perspective, merchants were a dirty, disreputable lot. Whether they were being mocked in Roman comedy, discussed in philosophy, populating the plots of novels, or flitting around the edges of political histories, merchants

4. Apul., *Met.* 1.21.

5. Apul., *Met.* 1.23.

6. Leviticus Rabbah 12.1. The text is primarily concerned with drunkenness, especially as it pertains to original sin, positing the grape as the fruit of the Tree of Knowledge. Nevertheless, the text uses the example of a drunkard, who, intent on sinning further, pursues high quality wine. The wine merchant is known to him through the rumor mill among the other drinkers, a group that is presented as disreputable in the text.

were degraded, satirized, and slandered with an admirable level of consistency over the centuries. Cicero, in a famous passage, distinguished the forms of *labor* that were suitable for a gentleman from numerous other kinds of work, including manual and artisanal labor, retail trade, and various services.[7] Each profession, he noted, was objectionable in a different way, either for the baseness of its work or for the character flaws that the job itself required, but he unified his theory with the notion that it was the moral uprightness of the farmer that was to be the most admired, above even the most gentlemanly large-scale importer.[8] It was the farmer who embodied the simplicity, self-sufficiency, honesty, and work ethic of the Romans, the core values that had established, to Cicero's mind, the power and achievement of the state. Merchants might aspire to the farmer's goodness, but they could never reach that state without giving up the profession that held them back. Retail traders were disposed to dishonesty, as it was the only way they could make a profit.

Cicero's purpose was to identify which Romans were deserving of honor, and which shame, and he ultimately drew the same line that Philostratus' vinedresser would later adopt, with commerce on one side, and agriculture on the other.[9] Neither of these authors had much in the way of hard evidence to support their position. Even in his letters, where we might reasonably expect to see details about his personal economic activity, Cicero mostly buys and sells through proxies and friends, rather than directly experiencing the deceit of retailers or the dirtiness of artisans himself. Philostratus occasionally reveals some intimacy with merchants, as in the case of his former teacher, Proclus of Naucratis, but he maintains a healthy distance from any of the practicalities of business in his writings.[10] Nevertheless, Roman elites rarely needed even anecdotal evidence to "prove" that merchants were dishonest, greedy, and lowly: they had a stereotype that was pervasive in Roman society, and one that was as accepted among merchants themselves as it was among common people and elites of all kinds.[11] It was more than enough to make their point.

Stereotypes reflect a general feeling toward a group in the same way that reputation reflects a feeling toward an individual, yet a stereotype draws on a different set of "evidence" to sustain itself. While a reputation may be developed from a combination of factors, including stereotypes, it is most profoundly influenced by the specific words and actions of the reputed. By contrast, ste-

7. Cic., *Off.* 1.150–51. Giardina, "The Merchant," disputes whether the Romans considered what merchants did as labor at all.

8. Cic., *Off.* 1.149 and 151.

9. Philostr., *Her.* 1.3–1.7.

10. Philostr., *V. S.* 21.603; D'Arms, *Commerce and Social Standing*, 4.

11. *Pace* Mayer, "Money Making, 'Avarice,' and Elite Strategies of Distinction." See: Sancinito, "Rapacious and Chatty, Deceitful and Memorable" in response.

reotypes are often divorced from reality, as a collection of exaggerated beliefs associated with a given group of people, typically structured around one or more socially constructed categories. Moreover, stereotypes exist not only as a byproduct of a human need to categorize, but also as a means of justifying social, political, and economic actions toward a group. They are socially contingent and depend heavily on the culture that produced them. Accordingly, they often serve to replicate and support those same conditions.[12]

When considering Roman merchants, the stereotype initially seems to *be* their reputation. The group is "reputed," after all, to be greedy and deceitful, and Romans felt thoroughly justified to discriminate and even legislate against merchants on those grounds. Yet, as we have seen, individual merchants attempted and even succeeded in distancing themselves from the stereotype, carving out a personal reputation for honesty, quality, and fairness. This was possible because, even if they are influenced by stereotypes, reputations are primarily tied to the information available about the individual, not the group, which provides an opportunity for the singular merchant, or even groups of merchants within the whole, to "prove" their virtue or earn their position as an "exception to the rule."

A stereotype is a larger social structure than reputation. In many ways, stereotypes provide an additional lens through which reputation may be viewed, and, more than anything else, they influence what meanings an audience will be inclined to attribute to information about a person and his or her reputation. Overwhelmingly in the case of Roman merchants, the stereotype promoted negative readings of merchant behavior and encouraged vigilance on the part of Roman consumers. They were urged to be looking out for instances of merchants' innate bad character, and it is no surprise that it is the Latin *caveat emptor*, let the buyer beware, that has persisted even in the English lexicon of worry about trade.[13]

Confirmation bias, the tendency to accept and seek out information that supports one's preconceived notions, lies at the heart of these readings.[14] Truly bad conduct on the part of Roman merchants supported the validity of the stereotype, while good conduct was seen as an aberration that could be attrib-

---

12. Most modern definitions of stereotypes, including this one, draw their inspiration from Gordon W. Allport, *The Nature of Prejudice* (Reading: Basic Books, 1954), 191. Charles Stangor and Mark Schaller, "Stereotypes as Individual and Collective Representations," in *Stereotypes and Stereotyping*, ed. C. Neil MacRae, Charles Stangor, and Miles Hewstone (New York: Guilford Press, 1996), 22, argue that stereotypes are, themselves, invested in maintaining the status quo, and will act to defend their position through appeals to emotion, even when the evidence is not supportive of their case.

13. As in Sen., *Ep.* 80.9, who urges buyers to note every detail and uncover every flaw when buying horses or slaves. The phrase *caveat emptor* is discussed further below.

14. Karen S. Cook, Russell Hardin, and Margaret Levi, *Cooperation without Trust?* (New York: Russell Sage Foundation, 2005), 29–30; Craik, *Reputation*, 50.

uted either to a fluke or to an individual who was "not like the rest." This was a perception that merchants themselves often encouraged both to bolster their own reputations and demean their competition. Critically, the stereotype itself was not threatened by the existence of good merchants. They were not "proof" that the stereotype was wrong, as long as Romans continued to find (or create) narratives about bad merchants that bolstered their belief in the evil character of tradesmen.

Such narratives, of course, were readily available. Not only were elites continually finding opportunities to disparage those of lower classes with real or imagined scenarios, but the daily frustrations of the marketplace naturally lead to disputes and feelings of wrongdoing that could fan the flames of stereotypical stories. The legal stigma of *infamia* stood at one end of a spectrum of ill-will that was bookended by the avoidance and frustrations of common people.[15] The way Romans viewed commerce itself, as a competitive endeavor and zero-sum game, was indicative of a mentality that cast merchants as the enemy and inflected their behavior with negative meanings. Common people, those who did their own shopping and dealt with merchants and artisans regularly, were both the most likely group to have positive, personal relationships with these professionals as well as the most likely to have had first-hand experiences that supported the stereotype.

As a result, all levels of Roman society contributed to the chorus of voices shaming merchants. Pompeian graffiti offer concrete examples, including not only instances of specific tradesmen whose behavior was substandard, but also more generalized, or generalizable, complaints. Many of these have to do with bad service or rudeness, while others address false measures or cut corners. *Tabernae* were often the focal points of these disputes, as the walls of the buildings themselves became the canvas on which to display the latest reviews, including where to get a bite to eat, where the wine was bad, or which prostitutes to patronize.[16] The physical landscape of Roman towns were shaped by these statements, and the presence of many such reviews could not only shame an individual merchant, but also supported the stereotype that all merchants were disposed to such bad behavior. This was especially the case because positive reports were, on the whole, less likely to warrant record.[17]

15. Bond, *Trade and Taboo*, 7–8, discusses *infamia* and socially imposed stigma as a binary pair, though she rightly notes that it is possible to have cases where both social and legal stigma were in force.

16. CIL 4.8903: *Ga(ius) Sabinius Statio plurima(m) sal(utem) Viator Pompeis pane(m) gustas Nuceriae bibes*; CIL 4.3948: *talia te fallant, utinam, mendacia, copo. Tu ve(n)dis aquam, et bibes ipse merum*; CIL 4.1751: *si quis hic sederit, legat hoc ante omnia. si qui futuere volet, Atticen quaerat a(ssibus) XVI*. On *tabernae*, generally, Ellis, *The Roman Retail Revolution*.

17. Prostitutes seem to garner most of the praise here, e.g., CIL 4.1751, CIL 4.10675, but there are some food vendors who are positively recognized: CIL 4.10677.

Assessing the audience for these graffiti is a challenging but important element of understanding how reputational information about merchants spread. A vast majority of Roman graffiti, which come primarily from inscriptions in Pompeii and Herculaneum, are little more than simple tagging, recording a name alone.[18] Occasionally, a descriptor is included, thus we have the somewhat uncommon case of a tag like that of "Anthus the fuller," but most appear in public places with little additional information or context.[19] Reviews of the kind discussed above represent a small minority of these texts, but our evidence suggests that graffiti that extended beyond naming could generate substantial engagement from passersby and visitors to the same spaces. As a form, graffiti aspire to reach a broad audience, and though in the Roman world we do see writing appearing inside buildings, they remain public or semipublic spaces that would have been viewed by visitors. Other texts directly address or involve the reader, engaging them in a manner similar to funerary monuments.[20] Moreover, Rebecca Benefiel, in studying graffiti from the house of Maius Castricius, has argued that this kind of informal writing inspired substantial dialogue.[21]

A strong example of this is the lament of the weaver, Successus, whose comment on his failing courtship of a slave girl inspired a volley of graffiti between him and a rival:

Successus textor amat coponiaes ancilla(m) nomine Hiredem quae quidem iliumnon curat sed ille rogat ilia(m) com(m)iseretur	Successus the weaver loves the slave of the innkeeper, [her] name is Iris. She doesn't care about him at all, but he asks that she pity him.
Scribit rivalis vale	A rival is writing (now). Bye.
Invidiose quia rumperes se(ct)are noli formonsioremet qui est homo pravessimus et bellus	(Just) because you are bursting with jealousy, don't lash out at someone more handsome and who is a very tough and beautiful man.
Dixi scripsi amas Hiredem qua(e) [t]e non curat S[u]a Successo ut su[p]ra [-----]s[-----] Severus	I have spoken. I have written. You love Iris, who doesn't care for you. To Successus, as above (*lacuna*) Severus.[22]

18. On tagging, see Polly Lohmann, "Tagging in Antiquity: Pompeian Graffiti between Individuality and Convention," *SAUC—Street Art and Urban Creativity* 6.1 (2020).

19. CIL 4.8108.

20. E.g., CIL 4.1751 and 8903.

21. Rebecca R. Benefiel, "Dialogues of Ancient Graffiti in the House of Maius Castricius in Pompeii," *American Journal of Archaeology* 114.1 (2010).

22. The graffiti appear at Regio I 10, 2–3, now known as the Caupona of Iris, after her role in this narrative. There is some possible doubt over whether Severus is the name of the rival mentioned in the earlier text. Nothing in the hands, as preserved, provides much evidence either way.

Though only two contributors are seemingly involved in this dialogue, it is an exchange that in both its location, outside a *taberna*, and content, a spat between would-be lovers, would have appealed to readers seeking to keep abreast of the drama unfolding. Successus names himself as a weaver and subsequently describes himself as a tough and handsome man, which invokes both his personal and professional reputation in this moment. The initial graffito was a plea for his personal cause, but the subsequent exchanges make it a matter of honor to "win" the battle of wits and romance in front of this audience: the passersby and patrons of this establishment, who may have known one, the other, or all of the individuals involved. Certainly Iris, as an enslaved worker presumably of the *taberna*, would have been known by others in the area, even if they were unfamiliar with the rivals. Members of the audience may have been inclined, through personal experience, to choose one side or another or to ask Iris' opinion on the matter, either earnestly or in jest. For our purposes, the information that Successus initially provided about his profession potentially inflects everything that followed. To Successus, it likely was a statement of his identity and a note of his economic stability designed to win over the reluctant Iris, but to the rest of the community, it may have meant something very different, and his choice to identify by his work in this setting may have ultimately helped or hindered his business. Sadly, our knowledge of these rivals begins and ends here, so we cannot say if Successus' failure to woo Iris ultimately suggested to the community that he was a good, bad, or indifferent weaver.

In general, comments in graffiti were designed to refer to a specific tradesman, rather than to merchants as a group. Nevertheless, popular sources demonstrate that, even among those living and working beside merchants, there was a generalized belief in negative stereotypes about those involved in commerce. Aesop's *Fabulae* are full of tales that preserve aspects of stereotypes against merchants, often going trade by trade in their assessment of how the general faults of greed and deception played out in the case of a particular artisanal group. In one case, Zeus and Hermes distribute falsehood among the various trades, pouring the excess into cobblers, turning them into the greatest cheats of all.[23] This story was evidently so commonly told that variations in the narrative developed, leaving some stories with tanners, instead of cobblers, as

23. Aesop, *Fab.* Hermes and the Cobblers: Laura Gibbs, *Aesop's Fables* (Oxford: Oxford University Press, 2002), #519 = Ben Edwin Perry, ed. *Babrius and Phaedrus* (Cambridge, MA: Harvard University Press, 1965), #103.

the guiltiest party.[24] The form of the fable was such that this substitution was simple, and it likely shifted in the telling as a response to day-to-day events. The same effect is present in Roman aphorisms, which often lambast tradesmen and their faults, and are preserved in a variety of forms reflecting multiple branches of an oral tradition.[25]

While, as we will discuss, belief in these stereotypes did not prevent solidarity among nonelite groups, especially when their communities were accosted by more elite figures, our sources do show that merchants were still distrusted, and there were even suggestions at times that they were in league with the state to take advantage of the common people.[26] The stereotype, in all its variations, was a standard trope in popular forms of literature, graffiti, and, presumably, oral culture. Whether or not the stereotype was supported by reality, it influenced the interpretations of customers and peers as they made up their mind about the reputation of an individual merchant. Moreover, stereotypes supported the "othering" of merchants, something that is also common across our sources. Rather than being viewed as family or friends, neighbors or colleagues, merchants are commonly depicted as fundamentally different from other members of Roman society—a "them," rather than an "us"—and that distinction greatly damaged the chances that a merchant might be given the benefit of the doubt.

The Roman penchant for othering merchants is most obvious in cases of physical distance. Many traders, because their business required travel, were treated as outsiders, even in communities where they regularly lived and worked. "Foreign" merchants themselves became a standard trope in imperial and late antique texts, something that is especially visible in the case of so-called "Syrian" or "Phoenician" merchants appearing in the Western Mediterranean.[27] There is often little or no specific evidence for attaching a Syrian origin to such

24. Perry, *Babrius and Phaedrus*, #103 records the same story with tanners.

25. Syrus offers the best examples, in that his work was copied, adapted, and supplemented with new material, either lines attributed to "Pseudo-Syrus," or excerpts culled from other, real or spurious, authors. These were gathered in the medieval period into an anthology known as *De moribus*, which was commonly used in teaching from at least the ninth century, from the manuscript tradition, J. Wight Duff and Arnold M. Duff, *Minor Latin Poets*, vol. 1, *Publilius Syrus, Elegies on Maecenas, Grattius, Etc.* (Cambridge, MA: Harvard University Press, 1982), 7. The sayings of the *Disticha Catonis* share a similar history (see Connolly, "Disticha Catonis Uticensis") and generally focus more on moral issues associated with merchants, like greed and dishonesty (e.g., 1.29, 2.19, 4.4).

26. Petron., *Sat.* 44 *Aediles male eveniat, qui cum pistoribus colludunt 'Serva me, servabo te.'* May evil befall the aediles, who collude with the bakers, "Guard my interests, I will guard yours."

27. As in Salvian, *De gubern.* 4.14, where the merchants are not only Syrian, but also liars. While there was undoubtedly a tradition of trading activity originating in this region of the Mediterranean, not all of these individuals were visitors or immigrants, and not all were from Syria. Discussed in Mark Handley, *Dying on Foreign Shores: Travel and Mobility in the Late-Antique West* (Portsmouth: Journal of Roman Archaeology, 2011).

people, but an assigned "easternness" tapped into historical stereotypes about Phoenicians, trade, and usury that remained in force throughout the Roman period.[28]

This accusation of foreignness also served to isolate even those merchants whose work did not take them physically far from home. The stereotype determined that even normal merchants were "outsiders" in places where they would otherwise have been viewed as locals. Apuleius' moneylender, Milo, is on the receiving end of this treatment when he is described by his neighbor, an innkeeper, in terms that suggest his physical separation from the community. While Lucius describes Milo as prominent, *primoris*, the innkeeper immediately twists his word choice to demonstrate that Milo is aloof from the main population of Hypata:

> *"Nostine Milonem quendam e primoribus?" Arrisit, et "Vere" inquit "primus istic perhibetur Milo, qui extra pomerium et urbem totam colit." "Remoto" inquam "ioco, parens optima, dic oro et cuiatis sit et quibus deversetur aedibus." "Videsne" inquit "extremas fenestras, quae foris urbem prospiciunt, et altrinsecus fores proximum respicientes angiportum? Inibi iste Milo deversatur"*

> "Do you know a man named Milo, one of the prominent citizens?" She smiled and said, "Yes, that Milo is certainly regarded as foremost, since he lives over the border and outside the entire city." "Please, don't joke, good mother," I said, "I beg you to tell me what sort of man he is and what house he lives in." She replied, "Do you see those distant windows, which look out on the city, and, on the other side, the door looking back out on the alley nearby? There is where that man Milo lives."[29]

She describes him as living *extra pomerium*, outside the boundaries of the city, to emphasize that he is antisocial and "foreign." It may be that the passage is intended to be comical, as the innkeeper, from where she and Lucius stand, can point out Milo's house, which she describes as down an alley nearby. Not only is his home within a line of sight from her inn, but it is close enough to another structure to share a common passageway. Wherever the *pomerium* may have been, the innkeeper could only have just been within it herself, yet

28. Sid. Apoll., *Epist.* 1.8.2; Giardina, "The Merchant," 248, notes that in Byzantine records it was westerners who were considered greedy, so it is foreignness, rather than geography, that determines the direction of this stereotype.

29. Apul., *Met.* 1.21.

she felt able to represent Milo as distinct, separate, and far from the community where he lived and worked.

Of course, Milo was also depicted as socially and morally distant from his neighbors as he went about his business dressed like a beggar and holding his borrowers to outrageous standards. This reflects another common form of "othering," that, even if merchants were physically part of the community, they were so out of touch with traditional *mores* that they would consider, or even commit, acts that "normal" Romans would dismiss as unacceptable.[30] Accordingly, they would never respect the rules of society and would perpetually seek out profit at the expense of their customers, neighbors, and friends. They would not respect their contracts or keep their promises, if wealth was the alternative.

Philostratus' *Vita Apollonii* offers a case that depicts the supposed distance between "Roman" and "merchant" morality in an especially dramatic way. Apollonius, the sophist, in dialogue with an Indian sage, Iarchas, debates the nature of justice and honesty in a lengthy section, culminating in a story that Apollonius tells about his own conduct when he was working as a ship captain. In the narrative, having sworn an oath to a group of pirates that he would betray his ship, Apollonius ultimately chooses to flee with his cargo.[31] Apollonius is proud of himself, concluding that it took a truly just man, "to refuse . . . to betray the interests of merchants," when he himself was acting in that capacity. He admits to Iarchas that he encouraged the pirates to elaborate on their plans so that he could judge their offer, waiting to make his choice and weigh his options.[32] Iarchas, perhaps understandably, does not see this as an especially good example of just behavior, but in Philostratus' view the circumstances are emblematic of Apollonius' legendary greatness.[33] Because he was a "good" merchant, Philostratus carefully explains that Apollonius rightly wished to leave his profession, and implies that a lesser merchant would have accepted the offer of the pirates, not only as a means to acquiring financial security and respectability, but also because merchants are inherently inclined to cheat everyone, including each other.

In some cases, our sources are willing to accept that the merchant tendency to adopt stereotypical and disreputable behaviors was born from the fear and

30. Othering also often had a visual component, see Maria Pipili, "Wearing an Other Hat: Workmen in Town and Country," in *Not the Classical Ideal: Athens and the Construction of the Other in Greek Art*, ed. Beth Cohen (Leiden: Brill, 2000).

31. Philostr., *V. A.* 3.24.

32. Philostr., *V. A.* 3.24.3, μὴ ἀποδόσθαι . . . ἀπεμπολῆσαι τὰ τῶν ἐπόρων. ἀπεμπολάω literally translates to "sell" but in this context means something closer to the idiomatic "sell out," making "betray," as in F. C. Conybeare, *Philostratus: The Life of Apollonius of Tyana* (New York: Macmillian, 1912), the most accurate rendering of the phrase.

33. Iarchas responds that the absence of injustice is not justice, thus returning the narrative to its central philosophical purpose.

desperation that came with their unpredictable lives, as in the case of Lucian's Crobyle and Corinna, who slide, painfully, from their somewhat respectable positions as the wife and daughter of a merchant, respectively, into poverty and prostitution.[34] In other cases, our authors suggest that merchants, like brigands and pirates, had their own internal systems of honor and morality, just ones that were different from the Roman norm.[35] More often, however, Romans believed that merchants were simply "like that"—inclined by nature to be less moral than the average man. Ultimately, Crobyle and Corinna, rather than being motivated by a simple desire to survive, want luxuries and wealth, and Lucian's narrative is clear that they are naturally rapacious women. Believing this made it easier to accept that merchants deserved their treatment, and that more social and legal pressure, not less, was needed to keep this group from robbing everyone else blind, from falling prey to their innate urge to cheat and deceive.[36]

This is the heart of the matter. While stereotypes about merchants show some variety relating to specific professions, the core was that merchants were greedy and would do anything to make a profit. Greed, *avaritia* or φιλαργυρία, is seen as the cardinal sin of those in trade, and as the source of all their subsequent misdeeds.[37] Despite seeing merchants daily, Romans believed that merchants were without normal, moral limitations. No wrongdoing was beyond their imagination, and they could never be trusted to do the right thing, meaning that the onus always lay upon the customer, magistrate, or nonmerchant to hold a tradesman to their promises. The stereotype reached such an extreme that fictional and narrative sources regularly attribute crimes to merchants, ranging from simple lying to grave-robbing and murder.[38]

This kind of hyperbolic storytelling may well have been designed more to entertain than to reflect reality, but these stereotypes were in the air, and merchants were faced with the challenge of responding to them appropriately. As we have seen, merchants used a range of techniques for building their reputations, and each was engaged, in part, as a response to these pervasive beliefs.

34. Luc., *D. meretr.* 6.1. On relationships like theirs, see Anise K. Strong, "Daughter and Employee: Mother-Daughter Bonds among Prostitutes," in *Mothering and Motherhood in Ancient Greece and Rome*, ed. Lauren Hackworth Petersen and Patricia Salzman-Mitchell (Austin: University of Texas Press, 2012).

35. Cic., *Off.* 2.39.

36. Ulp., *Dig.* 4.9.1.1.

37. As in 1 Timothy 6:10, ῥίζα γὰρ πάντων τῶν κακῶν ἐστιν ἡ φιλαργυρία. For greed is the root of all evil things.

38. Lying: CIL 4.3948. Grave-robbing: Chariton, *Callirhoe* 12, the pirate Theron presents himself as a merchant upon his arrival in Miletus and no one can tell the difference, despite the fact that his goods are taken from Callirhoe's "tomb." Murder: Philostr., *V. A.* 4.32.2, Apollonius accuses ship captains of intentionally wrecking ships, and killing their crew in the process, to commit insurance fraud.

Some chose to ignore them entirely, sticking to their own virtues and allowing their behavior to speak for itself. For some, this may have been a sufficient means of distinguishing themselves from the group, but others struggled and clearly display their anxiety through attempts at denial or, even, in one notable case, apology:

VITALIS • C • LAVI • FAVSTI
SER(vus) • IDEM • F(ilius) • VERNA • DOMO
NATVS • HIC • SITVS • EST • VIXIT
ANNOS • XVI • INSTITOR • TABERNAS
APRIANAS • A POPULO • ACCEPTVS
IDEM AB • DIBUS • EREPTVS • ROGO
VOS • VIATORES • SI • QVID MINVS
DEDI • ME(n)SVRA • VT • PATRI • MEO • ADICERE
IGNOSCATIS • ROGO • PER • SVPEROS
ET • INFERNOS • VT • PATREM • ET MATRE(m)
COMMENDATOS • (h)ABEATIS
ET • VALE

Here lies Vitalis, slave of Gaius Lavus Faustus and son of the same man, born a slave to the house. He lived sixteen years, a manager of the Apriana Tavern, though accepted by the people, he was snatched away by the gods. I ask you, travelers, if I gave you some lesser measure so that I might enrich my father, forgive me. I ask those above and those below that you hold my father and mother in your favor. And so farewell.[39]

The case of Vitalis is unique in our corpus of merchant funerary inscriptions, as it presents not only some of the traditional virtues merchants commonly tried to highlight, but it also accepts, and attempts to justify, behavior that is seen as stereotypically bad. Vitalis was an *institor*, a business manager on behalf of, in this case, his master-father.[40] In and among the more common statements about Vitalis' age, family, and work, the inscription records that he may have cheated his customers out of some portion of the product(s)

39. ILS 7479, Macedonia. Given Vitalis' youth, this stone was likely raised by his mother or, more probably, father. The first-person voice is therefore putting words into the young man's mouth, rather than reflecting his own chosen funerary representation.

40. It was common for young people, even children, to work as *institores*. Aubert, *Business Managers*, 6–9 and 56 discusses these figures, who could be either enslaved or free, and that they could oversee a wide-ranging set of business ventures.

they were buying, giving them "some lesser measure." Other merchants took care to deny that they ever cheated their customers. They display their evenly balanced scales and utilized language of trust and honesty, but Vitalis' inscription instead asks for forgiveness while leaning on a crucial "if" to exculpate him.[41] It is a huge departure from other merchant inscriptions, perhaps even a gamble on the part of Vitalis' family that may or may not have paid off, but it does offer a clear case where stereotype and business practices overlapped. It is a case tailor-made to reaffirm the stereotype, to justify the distrust Romans felt toward greedy, deceitful traders who stole from their customers.[42]

Yet the inscription does not show Vitalis as a cheerful rogue, who enjoyed cheating buyers and reveled in the social stigma that hounded members of his and other professions. Rather, the text stresses that his cheating was the result of his loyalty and duty to his father, and it mentions that he was generally *acceptus*, accepted or perhaps welcomed, among his fellow men. The inscription therefore presents Vitalis as sociable and dutiful toward his family, virtues that are common throughout Roman inscriptions at large, not just among merchants. Even his false measures are justified as the result of his responsibilities to others, thereby recasting them as a reflection of his work ethic and family obligations, rather than as an extension of a greedy nature. After all, he was enslaved; he did not profit from the false measures himself.

Vitalis' case is neither a "gotcha," reflecting the truth behind the stereotype, nor an anecdote that can exonerate merchants and prove their universal goodwill and innocence. Merchant work did require that they seek profit, at times at the expense of others, but they were neither as callous and avaricious as the stereotype made them out to be, nor as innocent as their own self-representation claimed. In looking at stereotypes, the question is not one of fairness or accuracy, but of the impact these views had on the social and economic playing field. For merchants, the most common stereotypes created an uphill battle, one that required them to undertake substantial work if they wished to build basic levels of trust, and one where they were more likely to be caught and called out for any misdeeds or shortcuts.

41. Scales are extremely common in merchant reliefs. Already we have discussed the *Loculusplatte* of Evangelus, but there are also examples like the Relief of a Forge (MANN Inv. 6575), or the relief of a goldsmith in the Vatican attached to CIL 6.9210 who works beneath a massive scale.

42. As in Ov., *Fast.* 5.680–90, where, in a hymn in honor of Mercury, merchants pray that they will continue to be able to steal from their customers in the coming year.

Trust, Honesty, and New Institutional Economics

Stereotypes posed a serious obstacle for Roman merchants. Whether in the form of legislation that restricted merchant business or as ostracism and limited social mobility, merchants found themselves battling against the pervasive idea that their morals were *other* than those of their neighbors and customers. As a consequence, merchant transaction costs were higher than those of nonmerchants who engaged in similar economic activity. A senator selling the products of his villa or a farmer trading his agricultural surplus faced a fundamentally different set of challenges than the retailer in the forum. While the former could command a measure of trust by virtue of status or inherent respectability in Roman society, the latter could not assume that they would be considered trustworthy, unless they had developed a good reputation, especially for personal *fides* or other specific virtues. Without trust, merchants could expect their deals to be plagued by delays and disputes, each of which cost them time, effort, and profit.

Collectively, NIE terms these hindrances "transaction costs," the expenses associated with making sales, contracts, and deals, including decision-making, resolving disputes, and planning.[43] While no business can operate without some of these costs, the central theory of institutional economics is that these expenses can be reduced if institutions are allowed, through the participation of the majority of relevant actors, to structure economic activity. Institutions simultaneously incentivize behaviors and beliefs that reduce transaction costs while disincentivizing behaviors or beliefs that increase them. Institutions encourage patterns in economic activity, sequences of events and incentivized choices that have predictable outcomes. This predictability leads to quick and easy deal- and decision-making that discourages both customers and vendors from wasting time and resources double-checking and disputing common practices.[44]

Institutions are especially necessary in contexts where economic information is unevenly distributed, and risks are high. The Roman economic landscape was unpredictable. There was little transparency about economic conditions and merchants often made decisions based more on their best guess than solid information about prices, supply, or demand.[45] Institutions, and especially

43. North, "Transaction Costs," and Oliver E. Williamson and Scott E. Masten, *The Economics of Transaction Costs* (Northampton: Edward Elgar, 1999).

44. North, *Institutions*, 23–24, based on Ronald A. Heiner, "The Origin of Predictable Behavior," *American Economic Review* 73.4 (1983); see also North, *Institutions*, 12, "when it is costly to transact, institutions matter."

45. Bang, *The Roman Bazaar*, ch. 3.

social institutions, helped to level the playing field, at least for merchants who chose to operate their businesses within communities that they knew well. In those contexts, knowledge of local norms became an asset that helped merchants to predict the behavior of their peers and customers. Whatever imbalances or unpredictable risks that remained were shared by all.

NIE posits that once institutions are embraced by most people, transaction costs will be greatly reduced and there will be fewer instances of conflict. Though adherence to institutions reduces the total number of options a merchant will have, the paths that remain available will appear "natural" and "neutral," in that they will conform to the legal and moral standards shared by most people. Moreover, they will seem, to a degree at least, economically advantageous because they reduce costs, enabling a seller to move quickly onto the next deal or commission. While it might be possible to exceed the limitations imposed by institutions, to enrich oneself through cheating or dishonesty, for example, most will see this path as both socially and economically impractical, since they will be aware of the possible punishments that being caught as a free rider might incur.

Issues of punishment for free riders, including social and economic sanctions, will be discussed in the next chapter, but in the context of the institutional uses of reputation, and specifically in the context of overcoming negative stereotypes, it is the benefits of institutions that are the most relevant. While stereotypes dictated that merchants should be distrusted, avoided, and recognized as morally deviant, institutions bridged the gap between what Romans believed, in the abstract, about merchants, and what Romans believed, in the specific, that the merchants they knew and dealt with on a day-to-day basis would do in a given situation.

Stereotypes about greedy and dishonest merchants undermined the trust, *fides*, that Romans had in merchants and convinced them that the only means of securing the least-disadvantageous deal was to monitor merchants closely, to haggle over their proposed prices, and to dispute the quality and quantity of their wares. Interestingly, while Roman sources are clear that merchants are the ones morally in the wrong, they instruct customers to take this burden on themselves, perhaps because they viewed merchants as fundamentally incorrigible. The principle of *caveat emptor*, let the buyer beware, was in full force in both law and literature, pressuring customers to look out for their own best interest.[46] This was in line with the general feeling in Roman society that commerce was equivalent to conflict and that merchants, even if they were not actively engaging in deception, were nevertheless the enemy.

46. As in Seneca, *Ep.* 80.9. See also Bodel, "*Caveat Emptor*."

Had customers consistently applied this philosophy, commerce would have ground to a halt. Merchants would have been second guessed at every turn and transaction costs would have skyrocketed to insurmountable levels. Instead, customers accepted that while the general category of "merchant" might be greedy and dishonest, and it was wise to be on the lookout to protect oneself, it was possible to trust some merchants, specifically those who were worthy of *fides* because of their history of, and reputation for, good behavior.[47]

We have already discussed the importance of *fides* in merchant reputation strategies, and seen the examples of Fortunatus and Onesimus, whose funerary markers emphasized their trustworthiness in their presentation of their posthumous reputations.[48] *Fides* was a multivalent word among merchants, referring to the virtue of honesty practiced by merchants, the trust that others placed in them, as well as serving as a specialized term for credit in the context of moneylending. It was *fides* that merchants hoped to display, *fides* that motivated customers to patronize a business or make a deal, and *fides* that maintained the systems of friendship and collegiality through which merchants both borrowed and lent.[49]

While it was possible to establish legal *bona fides* for contracts, *fides* was also a behavior that was signaled through consistent social interactions. Elizabeth Meyer has recently noted the importance of *fides* as both a legally enforceable standard and as a performative act.[50] Officials and businessmen alike were legally required to act in good faith in their dealings and Meyer's study has shown that the tablets that were used to record contracts were constructed and sealed in such a way as to telegraph the *fides* that partners were expected to have in their contents and legitimacy.[51] The existence of archives of contracts are themselves a testament to *fides* in the long term; they record lifetimes of deals that, even when they went awry, were nevertheless founded upon legally correct and morally upright actions on the part of the merchant.[52] Archives

47. See Broekaert, "Partners in Business," 226–30, on trust among *collegia* members.

48. Griffe, Lassère, and Soubiran, "Épitaphe du banquier"; and CIL 6.9663.

49. Bang, *The Roman Bazaar*, 259–62. On friendship economics, see Verboven, *The Economy of Friends*; Kirschenbaum, *Sons, Slaves, and Freedmen*, 160–71; also, indirectly, Konstan, *Friendship*. *Fides* also had a special valence within early Christian communities, see Teresa Morgan, *Roman Faith and Christian Faith:* Pistis *and* Fides *in the Early Roman Empire and Early Churches* (Oxford: Oxford University Press, 2015).

50. Meyer, *Legitimacy and Law*, ch. 6, especially 148, 245. See also Terpstra, *Trading Communities*; and Wim Broekaert, "Vertical Integration in the Roman Economy: A Response to Morris Silver," *Ancient Society* 42 (2012).

51. Meyer, *Legitimacy and Law*, 125.

52. Wim Broekaert, "Conflicts, Contract Enforcement, and Business Communities in the Archive of the Sulpicii," in *The Economy of Pompeii*, ed. Miko Flohr and Andrew Wilson (Oxford: Oxford University Press, 2016), argues that trust and reputation undergird all these legal transac-

tracked past outcomes and precedents that could be relied upon and referred to in the future.

Romans often used physical means to display their *fides*, to prove that everything was above board. Seals, stamps, and other marks certifying quality and correctness were common throughout the Roman world, and were applied on numerous kinds of goods, ranging from foodstuffs to metal work. Each was designed to offer some implicit or explicit guarantee to the consumer or business partner of the quality, weight, or content of the goods.[53] While some kinds of marks may be attributed to legal standards, including religious laws, others are clearly the result of private merchants seeking to certify their product's authenticity and excellence.[54]

At times, it is clear that these marks were intended to work in concert with a merchant's reputation. Personal names and marks not only signal ownership but are also intended to communicate pride in a product's quality that should be associated with a specific producer. A well-documented example is that of Aulus Umbricius Scaurus, who was a prominent manufacturer and distributor of garum in Pompeii. His business is known from the collection of vessels that once held his fish sauce and from the mosaics that Scaurus commissioned for the atrium of his home that recreated those containers in two dimensions.[55] The vessels make up a substantial portion of the total extant garum containers and are identified by their painted markings, *tituli picti*, which present Scaurus'

---

tions, especially since extralegal resolutions, including arbitration, of disputes are evident in our extant archives (e.g., TSulp. 25, 34–39, 48, discussed in Bang, *The Roman Bazaar*, 266–67).

53. While an updated and comprehensive analysis of all these means of certification is greatly to be desired, there is piecemeal information available about many kinds of marker, including George Galavaris, *Bread and the Liturgy: The Symbolism of Early Christian and Byzantine Bread Stamps* (Madison: University of Wisconsin Press, 1970) on bread stamps; Virginia Grace, "Standard Pottery Containers of the Ancient Greek World," *Hesperia Supplements* 8 (1949); and Virginia Grace, "Stamped Wine Jar Fragments," *Hesperia Supplements* 10 (1956), on oil and wine marks; and regional studies, such as David Amit, "Jewish Bread Stamps and Wine and Oil Seals from the Late Second Temple, Mishnaic, and Talmudic Periods," in *"See, I Will Bring a Scroll Recounting What Befell Me" (PS 40:8): Epigraphy and Daily Life from the Bible to the Talmud*, ed. Esther Eshel and Yigal Levin (Göttingen: Vandenhoeck und Ruprecht, 2014) on these markers in Judaea.

54. Alexander J. Ramos, *Torah, Temple, and Transaction: Jewish Religious Institutions and Economic Behavior in Early Roman Galilee* (Lanham: Lexington Books, 2020) presents an example of religious and informal institutions operating in this way.

55. Scaurus' home in Pompeii, Regio VII.16.15/16, is north of the Porta Marina and has never been fully published. The best record is that of August Mau, *Pompeii: Its Life and Art* (New York: Macmillan, 1902), ch. 36. The site has been largely destroyed; a bomb hit the site on September 13, 1942, as part of the hostilities of World War II, as recorded in Amedeo Maiuri, "Pompei: Sterro dei cumuli e isolamento della cinta murale," *Bollettino d'arte* 45 (1960): 172. The mosaics, depicting *urcei*, complete with *tituli* and once arranged at the four corners of the atrium, are preserved individually today in the Museo Archeologico Nazionale di Napoli and were recovered after the bombing. Robert I. Curtis, "A Personalized Floor Mosaic from Pompeii," *American Journal of Archaeology* 88.4 (1984): 557–58, especially n. 5, describes the lack of accessible notes from this emergency excavation.

name alongside the type and, often, a description of the quality of the garum.[56]

The evidence of *tituli picti*, and especially those of Scaurus, shows that these labels were seen, at times, not only by workers along the chain of production and distribution, but also by the final consumers.[57] Consequently, they served not only as a shipping tag, but also as an advertisement of sorts: a form of branding that connected the merchant with the product and asserted that if one was of good quality, so, too, was the other. Even without a taste-test, this kind of labeling was a concrete strategy for encouraging *fides*. The mere fact that the merchant believed in a product and was willing to attach his personal reputation to it, that he trusted its quality in this way, was a tacit promise to the general population that a merchant would stand behind his wares and would be responsible for any possible deficiencies that were later discovered. Just as merchants used their places of business as a tool to build their reputations and advertise their connection to their communities, merchants who labeled their products by name used the goods as a statement of their accountability, honesty, and goodwill.

In Scaurus' case, these statements actually grew into chains of trust that included not only Scaurus' reputation, but also those of his freedmen-agents, and even, in one case, a seemingly independent retailer.[58] That others desired to connect themselves to this network of producers and distributors indicates that merchants also could seek out well-reputed and trusted sources of goods, the better to support their own economic and social standing, since no merchant could reasonably be expected to seek out companions whose work or reputation would impair their own status. Scaurus seems, therefore, to have been well-regarded, especially since his name never seems to have been defaced or removed, even as the vessels were subsequently reused.

56. Robert I. Curtis, *Garum and Salsamenta: Production and Commerce in Materia Medica* (Leiden: Brill, 1991), 91–92, describes a corpus of 140 marked vessels. Of these, Scaurus and Scaurus-associated vessels constitute 28 percent of the total. A near-complete list appears in Robert Étienne and F. Mayet, "Le Garum à la mode de Scaurus," *Gerión* 3 (1991). *Tituli picti* were also used on *amphorae* of olive oil and wine, though it is not always clear as a *titulus* is sometimes little more than a name. On *tituli picti*, see Piotr Berdowski, "*Tituli picti* und die antike Werbesprache für Fischprodukte," *Münstersche Beiträge zur antiken Handelsgeschichte* 22.2 (2003).

57. As in Wilhelmina F. Jashemski, "The Excavation of a Shop-House Garden at Pompeii (I. XX. 5)," *American Journal of Archaeology* 81.2 (1977): 227.

58. Martial, an innkeeper and imperial freedman, left his own *titulus* alongside that of Scaurus at CIL 4.9406. The role of Martial in this network is opaque but indicates a slightly more elaborate system of distribution and sale than a single, integrated chain of production, supply, and retail. Similarly complicated arrangements are visible in the case studies of Morris Silver, "Glimpses of Vertical Integration/Disintegration in Ancient Rome," *Ancient Society* 39 (2009). We lack an image of this vessel from which we might determine the number of hands present on the *urceus*, but Curtis, *Garum and Salsamenta*, 197–200 (appendix III) notes that *tituli picti* were commonly expanded upon by subsequent owners, with paint applied in different hands and colors.

Seals and labels were a quick and relatively inexpensive means of sending reputation information and, critically, for lowering transaction costs. Labeled goods, especially if they were associated with a recognized "brand," required less inspection or consideration than their unlabeled or unfamiliar counterparts.[59] There was trust, *fides*, inherent in the acceptance of these tags that made it possible to advance to the next stages of a deal without hesitation or additional costs, making them a profitable investment of merchant effort, one that paid back far more than merchants spent in terms of the time or cost of the writing.

Investing in reputation, more generally, worked in a similar fashion. The strategies that we examined in the previous chapter were also intended to provide a concrete return on investment in the form of lower transaction costs and, in general, greater predictability in marketplace interaction. While a case might be made for the generalized desire merchants may have had to be accepted in their communities, the framework of NIE clearly delineates that adherence to institutional limits and taking actions to perform and publicize that conformity was a practice that was driven by a desire for concrete benefits. There was a utility to pursuing a good reputation, in that seeking one was seen as an admirable trait by others and possessing one secured valuable advantages over those whose reputations were less good or less widely known.

Most essential among these advantages was an inherent claim to trustworthiness. Acquiring a reputation for *fides* was as an escape route for merchants from the negative stereotypes that pervaded Roman culture. While we will return to the costs and limitations that that acquisition entailed in the following chapter, the benefits are clear, as merchants were able, with a good reputation in hand, to stand up for themselves and smooth their path to success.

Social Capital and the Benefit of the Doubt

The advantages of a good reputation for merchants came in two forms: active and passive. In the former case, merchants could choose to lean on their reputations to achieve particular ends, such as securing a loan or the upper hand in a dispute, while in the latter, well-reputed merchants enjoyed a general air of goodwill, which manifested itself in fewer obstacles and the lower transaction

59. "Brand" is, naturally, an anachronistic term, though as Adrian Room, "The History of Branding," in *Brands: The New Wealth Creators*, ed. Susannah Hart and John Murphy (New York: New York University Press, 1998), 13–14, notes, there are elements of Greco-Roman merchant conduct that echo the mnemonic devices used by later individuals and companies.

costs we have discussed. In both cases, merchants drew upon a store of goodwill that they had accrued over time, and while they rarely made a dent in their balance through their passive, day-to-day enjoyment of their good reputation, they could potentially gamble with that resource when instances of conflict or special need arose.

Generally, this store of influence falls under the umbrella of "social capital," a theoretical concept that holds a variety of definitions among social scientists. The two perspectives of greatest relevance for the Roman world are those of Robert Putnam and Pierre Bourdieu, who, when combined, capture social capital as it was experienced by Roman merchants: as a resource that developed out of social relationships and connections and built itself around mutual obligations, cultural norms, and societal values.[60] Merchants acquired social capital alongside and directly from their reputations, and periodically had to choose to "spend" it on especially "expensive" scenarios when transaction costs grew beyond acceptable levels. As we will discuss, instances of conflict often required recourse to social capital, which could be made manifest through an appeal to one's social network for support. This support might be something as small as a statement of agreement with a merchant's side of an argument or as large as a loan or apprenticeship. Once this favor was requested, the social capital was "spent," and further bids for aid would be refused if a merchant asked for more than they could "afford" with their remaining capital. A merchant would have to build up the resource again through the doing of favors and social niceties before they would have access to the resource again.[61]

Importantly, those with a good reputation would replenish their supplies more quickly that those with a bad one, and the well-reputed often had more social capital to begin with. Additionally, our evidence suggests that they were more often assisted voluntarily, without having to explicitly request aid, than their peers with weaker social networks and less-robust reputations. An inter-

60. Putnam, *Bowling Alone*, places an emphasis on associations, which is not entirely apt for many Roman merchants, who could also acquire social capital through less formalized social networks. Bourdieu, "Le capital social"; and Bourdieu, "The Forms of Capital," argues for social capital as a weaponizable feature of class struggles and power dynamics in societies, which will be a relevant facet of some of the ancient cases we will examine but should not be interpreted as the conscious thought process of Roman merchants, whose interests are clearly focused upon their personal status within their communities and their economic success. As we have previously argued, merchants could only truly escape their status in the Roman world by abandoning their profession, which was not the goal of many of these figures. "Social capital" is also a commonly used concept among scholars of the Roman economy, as in Liu, "Group Membership."

61. For an early modern example, see Sebouh Aslanian, "Social Capital, 'Trust' and the Role of Networks in Julfan Trade: Informal and Semi-Formal Institutions at Work," *Journal of Global History* 1.3 (2006).

esting case is recorded by Dio of Prusa, whose efforts to construct a portico were met with, to his mind, sudden and outsized resistance by the populace on behalf of a local blacksmith.[62] Though he intended the structure to act as a symbol of his generosity and commitment to the city of Prusa, Dio recounts that "some people" were complaining about the destruction of τὸ χαλκεῖον τὸ τοῦ δεῖνος, the blacksmith shop of "So-and-so," an artisan who receives no further identification.[63]

As Dio relates the objections raised by the community, it becomes increasingly clear that his reputation had come into direct conflict with that of this blacksmith. Throughout the speech, he attempts to claim that the voices of dissent were few and insignificant, while his own actions were, or should have been, seen as above reproach. He provides a mocking parody of his detractors' objections, that the smithy had been a place of importance for the community, that it was the site of happy events that should have been preserved: εἰ μὴ μενεῖ ταῦτα τὰ ὑπομνήματα τῆς παλαιᾶς εὐδαιμονίας.[64] He claims that it was not as if he destroyed the Propylaea or the Parthenon of Athens—places, in his mind, that held true value—and refuses to acknowledge that a blacksmith's workshop might, for the right audience, hold the same or even greater significance. He cannot conceive, as a member of Rome's most elite, that, to some at least, So-and-so's reputation was more influential than his own.

To the blacksmith's community, he was evidently seen as deserving of whatever resistance they could muster. Even though the neighborhood seems to have been unable to defend the building, Dio clearly struggled with the consequences of having been so out of touch with these local feelings. His own reputation was materially damaged by his failure to grasp the reputation of others. Over time, by his own admission, he was termed, "a destroyer of cities and citadels," and seen as an interloper and an agent of gentrification, rather than of renewal.[65]

Dio's portico became a symbol of imposition and destruction, rather than

62. Dio Chrys., *Or.* 47.10–11, 17, 19–20.

63. Dio Chrys., *Or.* 47.11, the same smithy is mentioned at 40.8–9, suggesting that the matter was more important than Dio initially implied. Further, it is not clear if Dio actually knew this man's name or wanted to minimize his importance in his speech by repressing his identity. Either way, Dio's choice of words heightens the reader's feeling that Dio had wandered into a neighborhood where he did not understand the powerful personalities and meanings that defined the local community.

64. Dio Chrys., *Or.* 40.8.

65. Dio Chrys., *Or.* 47.10. A similar situation in North Africa is discussed in J. Andrew Dufton, "The Architectural and Social Dynamics of Gentrification in Roman North Africa," *American Journal of Archaeology* 123.2 (2019).

generosity and beautification. By contrast, this interaction built up the reputation of the blacksmith and his shop. The dispute caused the community to reconsider the significance of the man and his work and to consider the functions that his smithy had served in the community as a landmark and gathering place. Indeed, the place may only have achieved this level of significance in the moment it was threatened or destroyed, in the way that locals, even today, choose to give directions and discuss current events with references to where and how things "used to be."[66]

Dio's experience demonstrates how profoundly challenging it could be to "read the room" when it came to reputation, but in cases like this it was often the local and familiar that had an advantage over the outsider, or even over the elite. Reputation was more efficacious among those who knew the reputed well. In instances of conflict, a powerful reputation could be leveraged to bring matters to a head, and ultimately convey protection, secure profit, or forge new connections that would bring about new opportunities. In the Acts of the Apostles, a silversmith, Demetrius, uses his reputation and that of his fellow artisans in just this way to compete with the apostle Paul. Demetrius gathers his colleagues and says:

> Ἄνδρες, ἐπίστασθε ὅτι ἐκ ταύτης τῆς ἐργασίας ἡ εὐπορία ἡμῖν ἐστίν, καὶ θεωρεῖτε καὶ ἀκούετε ὅτι οὐ μόνον Ἐφέσου ἀλλὰ σχεδὸν πάσης τῆς Ἀσίας ὁ Παῦλος οὗτος πείσας μετέστησεν ἱκανὸν ὄχλον, λέγων ὅτι οὐκ εἰσὶν θεοὶ οἱ διὰ χειρῶν γινόμενοι. οὐ μόνον δὲ τοῦτο κινδυνεύει ἡμῖν τὸ μέρος εἰς ἀπελεγμὸν ἐλθεῖν, ἀλλὰ καὶ τὸ τῆς μεγάλης θεᾶς Ἀρτέμιδος ἱερὸν εἰς οὐθὲν λογισθῆναι, μέλλειν τε καὶ καθαιρεῖσθαι τῆς μεγαλειότητος αὐτῆς, ἣν ὅλη ἡ Ἀσία καὶ ἡ οἰκουμένη σέβεται.
>
> Gentlemen, you know that we are prosperous from this work, and you see and you hear that, not only in Ephesus, but practically in all Asia, this Paul has persuaded a large crowd to convert, saying that gods made by human hands are not gods. And not only is it a danger that our business will come into disrepute, but also that the temple of the great goddess Artemis will not be considered important, and the temple will be deprived of her divine majesty, which the whole of Asia and the world worships.[67]

66. The special relationship between locals and their knowledge of their space is discussed in De Certeau, *The Practice of Everyday Life*, and his notion of "local authority" dovetails with the kind of power that opposed Dio in this case.

67. Acts 19:25–27.

Following this speech, Demetrius leads a growing crowd through the streets of Ephesus, chanting in honor of Artemis, but the conflict, he is clear, is at least as much about reputation as religion. The good name of the goddess is on the line, of course, but so is the reputation of the artisans. Demetrius fears that his trade will "come into disrepute," and that he and his peers will lose their livelihood. Paul has evidently made some inroads and Demetrius means to lay his reputation and social capital on the line to settle the matter.

The author of Acts attempts to portray the event as the actions of a disorganized, unruly mob that failed to achieve anything, while the Christian mission attracted many new followers. It is hinted that many who took part in the demonstration did not know what was happening, but merely joined to make mischief or in the belief that it was a religious procession. While this implies that the crowd did not associate the march with Demetrius and the silversmiths, the text is clear that at least some did. When the city clerk orders the gathering to disperse, he is clear that the craftsmen need to take their concerns through the proper channels, which implies that they not only had sufficient clout to do so, but also that those assembled knew that it was these artisans who had led the charge to defend Artemis and her workers.[68]

Acts downplays the event, but Paul was evidently in some danger and left Ephesus shortly after this demonstration.[69] By any metric that mattered to them, Demetrius and his colleagues had been successful. They mobilized their reputation to protect their trade and to motivate the community to come to their defense, to the extent that they were able to make their perceived enemy, and another merchant, feel unwelcome. They were able to draw a crowd and sustain its energetic denouncement of their opponent and support for their goddess for several hours. It was a potentially dangerous ploy, as the crowd might well have turned violent or unruly, but it was a gamble that ultimately drew the attention of authorities and took advantage of the popularity and good reputation of these craftsmen in an effective manner.

It is in conflict that we see the power of reputation writ large, but in many other instances merchants were able to be less overtly contentious while still leveraging their social capital to reach their goals. Unfortunately, many of the successes of day-to-day recourse to social capital are now invisible to us. It is in these cases that reputation passively conveyed its benefits, but often the circumstances were so commonplace as to be fundamentally beneath the notice

68. Acts 19:32.
69. Acts 19:38.

of our sources. Nevertheless, it was in casual conversation and daily life that reputation was often at its most powerful in overcoming stereotypes. It was in these regular occurrences that customers perceived specific merchants as "different from the rest" and were willing to believe that they, too, had good days and bad, were, at least mostly, morally upright, and worthy of basic levels of respect and trust.

It is difficult to define the boundaries of this trust or to see exactly how far reputation could be pushed before an issue became a matter for explicit recourse to social capital, but there were clearly instances where the benefit of the doubt was extended to merchants. This was a great advantage to artisans and tradesmen who were plagued by the effects of negative stereotypes. The idea that every merchant was attempting to defraud every customer was so pervasive that even limited, conditional trust from customers—that this specific merchant, here, today, was probably not going to cheat this specific customer—was a valuable concession that, in itself, could lower transaction costs dramatically.

Most often the benefit of the doubt probably manifested itself simply in a customer choosing to patronize one merchant over another. If one deal went well, then it was likely the next would as well, and both customers and merchants enjoyed the benefit of lower transaction costs and minimal active decision-making. Becoming a regular customer relieved a buyer of the need to make a conscious choice, while having regular customers was a sign that the merchant's reputation and past conduct were predictors of similar good behavior in the future. Moreover, to the merchant, this kind of consumer confidence was indicative that a store of goodwill was already accruing in an abstract and incalculable way.

As in the more explicit cases discussed above, that cache of social capital could be actively spent, though it was less often a massive clash of personalities than it was a simple matter of asking a colleague or customer to try something new or to be patient. When something went wrong, as it did for Toranius, merchants were able to lean on their reputation, and the memory of all the times when everything went right, to help resolve a matter with minimal upset or long-term repercussions.

Reputation assisted Roman merchants in a myriad of ways, ranging from loans and disputes with magistrates to the daily routine of sales and commissioned work. Its greatest power was in helping merchants to break free of the cycle in which all merchants were painted with the same brush and characterized by the greed associated with their professions, rather than their own, personal conduct. Reputation could smooth the way to interpersonal trust, and that trust generated a setting in which stereotypes against merchants were weakened or neutralized, so that trade could proceed, and merchants could continue to make a living.

Conclusion

All Roman merchants struggled, to some extent, to preserve and develop a good reputation in the face of the prejudices that Roman society held against them. Even as they worked to present their good qualities, they were hounded by the stereotype of the greedy, deceitful, and nasty merchant. While some tradesmen may have been justly accused of cheating their customers and behaved in ways that validated the stereotype, many others were unjustly accused—honest professionals who were doing their best. Individual merchants worked to distance themselves from this model and strove to present themselves as "not like that." Doing so required that they display strong evidence of virtues that directly opposed stereotypes, finding others willing and able to vouch for their character, and holding a position of respect in the local community.

Despite the challenge, some merchants nevertheless developed good reputations and put them to use in their social and business lives. In general, moments of conflict, when a merchant's reputation or livelihood was challenged, reveal the shape and extent of a reputation, and allow us to see how a merchant could use reputation to preserve or even elevate their status in the community. Often these moments show us how reputation favored locals over outsiders, as reputational power came from familiarity and trust, which were more easily granted to those who were seen every day than to unfamiliar people who only appeared irregularly in a community and attempted to impose their will.

Trust was the basis of reputation as an institutional force. A reputation for *bona fides* could be used to ease concerns among customers and to motivate peers to accept risks they would otherwise avoid. Merchants took care to appear transparent in their sales and personal conduct, the better to receive commissions and develop stronger interpersonal ties. Merchants with a good reputation received the benefit of the doubt, and customers and peers alike engaged in economic business with well-reputed merchants because such people were understood to have bought into the institutional limitations that reputation required.

In the next chapter, we will look at this institutional system more closely, and argue for the power of reputation to limit merchant choices and punish deviation from its standards. Merchants structured their choices and approaches around their concern for their reputation. Both their desire for a good name and their fear of a bad one directed the paths that were available to them, and, as we will discuss, there were consequences and incentives that were highly effective at constraining merchants and forcing them into socially acceptable behaviors. Communities policed merchant conduct and merchants policed one another, driving out and punishing those who threatened to give others a bad name.

CHAPTER 5

Institutionalizing Reputation, or Information and What to Do with It

Δυσκόλου ταβλίζοντος, κατεπέτασσέ τις ἀργὸς καθήμενος. ὁ δὲ θυμούμενος ἠρώτησεν αὐτόν. "ποίας τέχνης; καὶ διὰ τί ἀργεῖς;" ἐκείνου δὲ εἰπόντος ὅτι "ῥάπτης μέν εἰμι, ἔργον δὲ οὐκ ἔχω." διαρρήξας τὸν ἑαυτοῦ χιτῶνα, καὶ ἐπιδούς, εἶπε· "λαβὼν ἐργάζου καὶ σιώπα!"

Once a cranky man was playing a game and an idle man sat down and started chatting. Growing irritated, he asked the man, "What do you do? Or rather, what don't you do?" The man replied that "I am a mender of clothing, but I have no work." Tearing his *chiton* and handing it over, the cranky man said: "Now that you have that, work and be silent!"
—*Philogelos*, 190

Merchants with a good reputation proceeded through their daily tasks with fewer obstacles than those with a bad reputation. They could choose moments to leverage their good name, to prove a point or defend their rights, or they might merely enjoy the privileges that it passively conveyed on them, such as social standing and economic stability. Yet, as we have seen, a good reputation was never a static thing. The casual and failed attempt of an idle clothing mender to make a new connection demonstrates that the work was never done; there were always social and business ties to be built or maintained, and unexpected bias to counter. The cranky men of the world had no desire to be charmed by merchants and, without an established relationship, it was unlikely that their connection would grow stronger. Without a reputation, men like the clothing mender could be reduced to an irritation, flies to be swatted or, at the very least, kept humorously busy.

In the previous chapter, the benefits that reputation conveyed were emphasized—the reduced transaction costs and the foundation of trust—but reputation could also be utilized to check merchants, to compel them to conform to the standards of Roman society, or just to go away. The joke preserved in the collection of the *Philogelos* ends with the clothing mender merely being thrown a garment and ordered to keep quiet, but Roman merchants who were out of line could be pressured to change their conduct in numerous ways, and they often conformed rather than risk damage to their reputation. This pressure was a central element of the institutional force of reputation, and, especially where institutions like the law might fail or be corrupted, reputation served as a stand-in, allowing communities to police themselves.

This policing is commonly termed "private-order enforcement," and generally refers to the extralegal systems that supported and enforced contracts.[1] Reputation was a preferred tool of private-order enforcement in the Roman world because, as we discussed in chapter 1, state systems were at times difficult to access, limiting opportunities to seek redress. In private suits, a defendant could not be compelled to appear in court, and even once found guilty, he or she was not forced by an agent of the state to make good on either the original dispute or the subsequent fines assessed. Going to the law publicly shamed a malefactor, but it was the local community that saw to it that punishments were enforced. Peers and acquaintances adjusted their behavior toward the guilty party, steadily transforming their disapproval into tangible consequences that the malefactor would feel. In this respect, reputation was more flexible than the law. It could be put into effect with greater nuance than a verdict of guilty or not guilty, and changes in reputation could continue to be felt long after a fine was paid and a matter legally settled.

Importantly, just as a good reputation came with active and passive benefits, so too did a bad reputation come with serious hindrances and minor inconveniences. In general, a bad reputation also intensified the distrust that most merchants experienced in some general way. These problems encouraged merchants to pursue some courses of action and avoid others, in a bid to have a good reputation and make their lives easier, rather than more difficult. In short, reputation worked as an institution, a structure in the social and economic world that restricted merchant choices, in that it made some courses of action cost prohibitive. The benefits of institutions were many, supporting, most essentially, the smooth and regular conduct of exchange by fostering trust. In essence, the strength of institutions was that they made trade more predictable and allowed customers and merchants alike to conduct their business with the assumption of shared norms and standards of behavior, while

1. As in Victor P. Goldberg, "The Enforcement of Contracts and Private Ordering," in *Handbook of New Institutional Economics*, ed. Claude Ménard and Mary M. Shirley (Berlin: Springer, 2008); and Avner Greif, *Institutions and the Path to the Modern Economy: Lessons from Medieval Trade* (Cambridge: Cambridge University Press, 2006), ch. 2.

ensuring that those who wished to cheat the system were dissuaded or met with fitting punishments.

Much of the system—both the spread and efficacy of reputation itself—depended upon information: who had it, what interpretation had they made of it, and what did they intend to do with it. Already we have discussed that reputation was constructed from signals, certain words, actions, or behaviors that were interpreted by audiences large and small, but the spread of information was not haphazard. At least at times, information was moved deliberately by members of its audience, and the active decision to share information heavily influenced both the quality and extent of reputation—the major factors in its impact as an institution.

Examining the institutional impact of reputation on Roman merchants requires a two-fold approach: a study of the mechanisms that spread reputational information, with an eye, especially, to how negative information circulated and why, on the one hand, and an examination of the methods of private-order enforcement that were available to ancient communities, on the other hand. For the former, the best-attested paths through which reputation was spread are letters of recommendation and talk, gossip, and oral communication, more generally. Together, these mechanisms enabled communities, both locally and at a distance, to share a common pool of information and prevent undetected free riding by merchants. For the latter, this information was transformed into action, and punishment came to those who had wrongfully claimed the benefits that the institution of reputation commonly provided. The forms that this private-order enforcement took are generally specific to the structures that a merchant was connected to, and thus look different in the context of merchant associations than they do in other settings, but they share a common trend of exclusion and avoidance that removed malefactors from both social and economic communities, leaving them isolated and without the support of a network of friends, peers, and customers.

Especially important is the regularity with which we see this network, and merchants in particular, policing their peers. Whether as part of groups or individually, our sources show that retailers, artisans, and transporters were all invested in ensuring that those around them, their colleagues and competitors, adhered to the same standards that they themselves maintained. This, too, is a result of the institutional power of reputation. Dedicating oneself to developing and maintaining a good reputation necessarily required that a merchant give up some profitable opportunities and spend time, effort, and money investing in displays of reputation, rather than simply enjoying leisure and profits. Any peer or competitor that ignored these burdens and decided not to pay attention to his reputation gained an advantage over everyone else. Unless there were clear and well-enforced consequences that made that tactic unappealing, free riders would not only get ahead but also proliferate, weakening the entire system. Merchants went out of their way, acted at their own expense or even to their own detriment, to ensure that free riders would be punished and made an example of.

That merchants bought into this system, and ultimately became some of its most determined enforcers, demonstrates the utility of the institution and offers us a means to gauge its power in social and economic settings. Rather than existing on the fringes of merchant lives, institutional reputation was a central concern and one that dictated not only their behavior with regard to their personal goals, but also the way that they viewed and responded to their peers. Sharing and acting upon reputational information strengthened the systemic power of reputation, allowing it to be an effective means of policing merchant behavior and adding structure and predictability to both social and economic activity in the Roman world.

The Spread of Reputation

As we discussed in chapter 2, it was a rare exchange or interaction with a merchant that could not, in theory, offer some evidence of his or her reputation. The corollary of that truth is that it was a rare piece of evidence for reputation that did not spread beyond its initial witnesses. We have already seen this in the form of the neighbors who learned of the duplicity of the salt merchant in the Midrash.[2] These figures were not directly involved in the events that had transpired but they became key figures in determining how far knowledge of the deceit of the merchant would spread. Reputation is akin to a community's common knowledge, and it was in the hands of specific people to ensure that information about reputation became "commonly" understood.[3]

Despite the necessity of individuals sharing information about reputation, it is rare to have an extant narrative that clearly articulates how information actually moved. Often, the details of an event or action have evidently traveled some distance from their point of origin, but the chain of interlocutors has been lost or deemed unimportant to the narrator who ultimately relates it. Revealing the sequence of conversations that transported knowledge from point a to point b

2. Midrash on Psalms 12:1, discussed in chapter 2.

3. Craik, *Reputation*, discusses reputation explicitly as a network with nodes who spread information. The idea is also to be found in Wickham, "Gossip and Resistance," discussed further below.

(or c or d) may have even been considered a bad idea, one that could make the information seem unreliable, as second- or third-hand knowledge was recognized as less trustworthy than autopsy in the Roman world.[4] Offering information without a clear provenance may have glazed over some of the points at which the reliability of the chain seemed dubious or had become unclear.

Whatever the exact sequence, much of our information about merchant reputation lacks a clear source and looks suspiciously like what we might call rumor rather than verifiable fact. As we will shortly discuss, "gossip" was likely the most common means by which reputation information reached new ears, as it was an informal practice that easily fit into the daily lives of people living in close-knit, face-to-face communities. Despite the ubiquity of this kind of talk, conversation often leaves little material evidence behind. Generally, our suspicion, drawn from other contexts and modern studies, suggests that gossip moved through populations in patterns that conform to our expectations regarding proximity and social closeness: we are more likely to gossip with those with whom we have some comfort as well as with those whom we see regularly.[5] Beyond this, gossip moves through populations via the "hubs" formed by knowledgeable or influential people. These individuals are not necessarily prototypical "gossips," but they are figures that could accumulate knowledge by virtue of access to multiple sources of information and holding a position of some social significance and trust in their community.[6] As recognized and recognizably important community members, they potentially had the power not only to receive information but also to reinflect it with new meaning, thereby shifting reputations by recontextualizing the information they heard and then passed on.[7]

These nodes in the information network are often lost to us in the historical record, but there is one form of evidence that consistently allows us to trace the path of information about reputation: letters of introduction and recommendation. A generous corpus of these documents persists, surviving among

4. Morgan, *Roman Faith and Christian Faith*, 39–45.

5. Chris Wickham, "*Fama* and the Law in Twelfth-Century Tuscany," in *Fama: The Politics of Talk and Reputation in Medieval Europe*, ed. Thelma S. Fenster and Daniel Lord Smail (Ithaca: Cornell University Press, 2003), 22; Wickham, "Gossip and Resistance," 23; and Virginia J. Hunter, "Gossip and the Politics of Reputation in Classical Athens," *Phoenix* 44.4 (1990): 300.

6. Wickham, "Gossip and Resistance," 14, terms at least some such people "megaphones," as they tend to amplify information when they receive it. On the potential impact of gossiping on their reputations, see Ralf D. Sommerfeld, Hans-Jurgen Krambeck, and Manfred Milinski, "Multiple Gossip Statements and Their Effect on Reputation and Trustworthiness," *Proceedings: Biological Sciences* 275.1650 (2008).

7. Bromley, *Reputation*, 15, "people who are part of our wider social network are likely to share the impressions formed by the people we regard as important and influential."

papyri as well as in epistolary collections and religious texts.[8] Their purpose was to give travelers access to a more established patron's or friend's network of acquaintances. In cases of business, these letters were often intended to create a relationship between a more senior merchant and a younger tradesman, or to utilize an established network of acquaintances on behalf of an established merchant who was traveling to a new place. The sender communicated to their recipient about the third person's reputation, his or her skills, temperament, background, and purpose or purposes of travel. Letters, as a result, offer us insight into how one person might discuss and shape the reputation of another with a specific and defined audience in mind, namely one that they wished to be of service to the third party.

Our extant examples of letters of these types show how the reputation and character of the recommended might be put into words by the author and how the framing might suggest readings and interpretations to the recipient, who otherwise would have little context with which to judge an unfamiliar person. While the letters themselves would rarely have been sufficient for the addressee to form a full opinion, these documents often provide a starting point for an acquaintance that would never have been available to travelers who lacked such an introduction.[9] When our evidence permits us to see it, it is clear that these letters, whether they traveled before a merchant or were carried by him, were supplemented with later conversations that verified the traveler's identity, conveyed more sensitive information that could not be consigned to paper, and laid the groundwork for the relationship that the recipient and the reputed could eventually have.

Letter writing, or, more accurately, letter sending, represented a substantial act of trust. Choosing a person to address indicated that that person was considered trustworthy and that his or her social standing was important and useful. As with choosing a master for an apprentice, letters of introduction were a sign that the recipient was, in some way, an expert or person of prominence. The choice often indicated closeness between the letter writer and his addressee. As we will see shortly, this could sometimes be wishful thinking, a desire for intimacy between an inferior and a superior, but the exchange of

8. Hannah Cotton, *Documentary Letters of Recommendation in Latin from the Roman Empire* (Konigstein: Anton Hain, 1981), notes that these letters were commonly used in military contexts, but there is ample evidence for their use among workers and those searching for work. Both groups would have had cause to travel and need the help of friends-of-friends (or partners-of-partners) to find their footing in a new place. As we will discuss, letters were often slightly coy about the precise favors or employment that was being sought, for a number of reasons.

9. Thus, we see the fear Encolpius experiences when he needs to settle a dispute about a stolen cloak in a new place, Petronius, *Sat.* 12–15, also discussed in Terpstra, *Trading Communities*, 9–10.

favors, and especially those involving a third party, was a common practice of Roman *amicitia* and it is often explicitly framed in that way.[10]

Even more than this kind of trust, the contents of letters, even at their most formulaic, were designed to communicate directly and, generally, exclusively with a single recipient, who was trusted to be careful with the information within. In many cases, secrecy was either implicitly or explicitly sought and a letter signaled the intimacy that the sender felt they had, even at a distance, with the recipient.[11] Despite the perils that potentially lay in wait for letters (which might be destroyed, lost, or intercepted) and letter carriers (who risked their own safety on the road), writers continued to assure their correspondents that they had tried to entrust their words to trustworthy messengers.[12] At times, those carriers were the recommended merchants themselves, at which point it became all the more important that the contents of a letter remained secret. An unbroken seal could convey that the bearer was ignorant of the contents, had not forged or edited the document in some way, and was who he or she claimed to be.[13] A broken seal implied the untrustworthiness of the messenger, who either did not adequately protect the letter or had nefariously opened it him- or herself.

Still, there was some information that was best kept out of writing entirely, something which we see in the third Epistle of John.[14] This is a strange and semi-public letter but alongside its theological statements, the text is both a letter of recommendation, praising and introducing a young man named Demetrius, and a response to other letters of recommendation. It is addressed to a man named

---

10. Thoroughly discussed in Verboven, *The Economy of Friends*, sec. III.3, though elements of this kind of favor exchange are also treated in Archibald, "Making the Most of One's Friends"; Richard White, "Friendship: Ancient and Modern," *International Philosophical Quarterly* 39.1.153 (1999); Kirschenbaum, *Sons, Slaves, and Freedmen*, 160–71 among others. In cases of social imbalances, it is also worth noting the phenomenon of the "Ben Franklin Effect" which posits that those who are asked for a favor become more inclined to grant further favors in the future, due, in large part, to the flattery inherent in being asked and therefore being acknowledged for their social superiority.

11. Janet Gurkin Altman, *Epistolarity: Approaches to a Form* (Columbus: Ohio State University Press, 1982), 47, 59ff.

12. Hence Cic., *Att.* 7.9.1, *"cotidiene" inquis "a te accipiendae litterae sunt?" si habebo cui dem, cotidie . . . L. Quinctius familiaris meus cum ferret ad bustum Basili vulneratus et despoliatus est."* "You ask, 'Are letters to be accepted from you daily?' If I can find someone to give them to, yes, daily. . . . Lucis Quinctius, my friend, was wounded and robbed near the tomb of Basilus while carrying a letter." See John Nicholson, "The Delivery and Confidentiality of Cicero's Letters," *Classical Journal* 90.1 (1994).

13. E.g., P.Oxy. 2.292, lines 1–7; Acts 15:27. Apuleius, *Met.* 1.26 is the best example for the identity of the messenger/traveler being questioned. This may be an attempt by Apuleius to stress Milo's suspicious nature, but he questions Lucius closely about their mutual friend.

14. The identity of John is a matter of debate, see David Rensberger, *The Epistles of John* (Louisville, KY: Westminster John Knox Press, 2001).

Gaius, who has evidently sent men, carrying letters, to John, who reports that he was pleased to meet these new Christian brothers. In his reply, John praises Gaius' generosity and kindness, stresses the importance of hospitality among Christians, and then describes an ongoing conflict that he was having with a man named Diotrephes, who seems to have been a rival in John's local church community. He writes that Diotrephes has slandered John and his friends, and that, beyond that crime, Diotrephes has not welcomed travelers, in direct contrast to both John and Gaius. After disparaging Diotrephes, John concludes:

> Πολλὰ εἶχον γράψαι σοι, ἀλλ᾽ οὐ θέλω διὰ μέλανος καὶ καλάμου σοι γράφειν· ἐλπίζω σὲ εὐθέως δὲ ἰδεῖν, καὶ στόμα πρὸς στόμα λαλήσομεν.
>
> I have many things to write to you, but I do not want to write to you with ink and pen. I hope to see you soon, and we will chat face to face.[15]

John evidently had some reservations about conversing openly through the medium of this letter. Despite his clear frustration with Diotrephes, it seems that John felt some things must be said in person, rather than trusting them to paper, which, in its more permanent form, might be passed on to those who should not see it. Given the ultimate publication of the letter, this was likely wise. John felt comfortable discussing the faults of, and referring to the dispute with, Diotrephes, but he still placed limits on what belonged in a letter. It is not clear how John might further have incriminated Diotrephes, or what else he might have needed to share with Gaius, but he wanted to avoid those words being intercepted in a letter and saved them for their next meeting.

John's letter demonstrates a wide diversity of purpose. It brings both praise and censure, thanks a friend and requests a favor, all in a single document, which is untypical of most letters of recommendation. Generally, these documents conform to a standard set of conventions, which, while they did not prevent creativity, nevertheless established guidelines that many chose to adhere to. Within the ancient world, these *formulae* were even publicly available in books on letter writing, which outlined how one ought to address, frame, and conclude letters of various types.[16] Letters of recommendation were understood to be a "commendatory" type of letter, which aimed, in the main, to praise its

15. 3 John 1:13–14.

16. Stanley K. Stowers, *Letter Writing in Greco-Roman Antiquity* (Louisville, KY: Westminster John Knox Press, 1986), 154–55; and Carole Poster and Linda C. Mitchell, eds., *Letter-Writing Manuals and Instruction from Antiquity to the Present: Historical and Bibliographic Studies* (Columbia: University of South Carolina Press, 2007), 22ff. The two extant examples are from Ps. Demetrius and Ps. Libanius.

subject to the recipient. They serve as an introduction, but are typically used in an exclusively positive sense, honoring the subject, rather than giving a comprehensive account of his or her full reputation.

Letter writers, recipients, and the praised were all well aware of these features of letters of introduction and recommendation. A second-century CE text from Alexandria records the experiences of a young man who seems to have been serving in a naval position in Egypt. After he recounts a list of what he has sent to and received from his father, who is the addressee of the letter, Claudius Terentianus states his intention to seek alternative employment in a cohort:

> . . . si deus
> volueret spero ṃe frugaliter
> [v]icịturum et in cohortem
> [tra]ṇsferri hic a[ut]ẹm sene aer[e]
> [ni]hil fiet neque epistulae com-
> ṃandaticiae nihil valunt nesi
> si qui sibi aiutaveret.

> . . . if god is willing, I hope that I will live frugally and be transferred to a cohort. But here nothing may be done without money, and letters of recommendation are worth nothing unless a man helps himself.[17]

Terentianus is well aware of the type of letter that was commonly used by ambitious individuals who hoped to leverage their social network for their personal and professional advancement. As Hannah Cotton has argued, letters of recommendation, Terentianus' *epistulae commendaticiae*, were especially important to the up-and-coming soldier, where promotion might depend more on who one knew than what one did.[18] Yet Terentianus seems to understand that there were finite limits to what a letter could do for one's reputation, and that, if a person wished to advance, he would have to "help himself," presumably by performing all the virtues that letters recorded, and additionally distinguishing himself in other ways.

17. P.Mich. 8.468, lines 35–41. Dated to the early second century CE in Michael Trapp, ed., *Greek and Latin Letters: An Anthology with Translation* (Cambridge: Cambridge University Press, 2003), #5; also discussed in R. W. Davies, "The Enlistment of Claudius Terentianus," *Bulletin of the American Society of Papyrologists* 10.1–4 (1973).

18. Cotton, *Documentary Letters*, 132. Other examples are known from Vindolanda and in Greek, as well. The need for promotion based on social ties may have intensified in the high Empire, as there were fewer chances for a soldier to demonstrate his bravery in direct conflict with Rome's enemies.

Perhaps in anticipation of this challenge, showing, not merely telling, is often a theme in these letters. Another letter offers a good example, as a *beneficiarius*, Aurelius Archelaus, writes to his military tribune, Julius Domitius, on behalf of a certain Theon.[19] The latter's profession is unclear, but he has, evidently, been in the employ of Archelaus performing some kind of service. He may have been a guard, as Archelaus professes that he feels safe because of Theon's actions, but the details are not preserved. In the letter, Archelaus stresses that Theon is the "sort of man" that he knows Domitius likes, which he knows to be true because of the *acta* he has seen Theon perform.[20] These deeds have included sacrifices on Archelaus' behalf, including leaving behind family, property, and some kind of personal business.

As a genre, letters are often frustratingly coy or unspecific about the work that the recommended might be seeking. Archelaus' letter, like many others, comes from a military context, but the minimal internal evidence suggests that Theon's work is somehow external to that system. Unfortunately for us, Archelaus does not provide further details. We cannot know what Theon's business was before he came into Archelaus' service, or what work he proposes to do now for Domitius. Many letters are vague in this way, which has made it difficult to assess the role that such documents played for and among economic actors in the Roman period.

The pattern that is visible suggests that this was a feature of the genre. Letters were designed to be unambiguously positive, but vague on particulars, perhaps to give both the recipient and the recommended freedom to work out the details themselves. A direct request would put the recipient on the spot, making a demand that they would seem to be ill-mannered to refuse, while it might also leave the recommended without flexibility, if the letter only mentioned housing, for example, but the traveler was actually in greater need of transportation or a loan. An open request for aid set everyone up to succeed or save face, and forestalled the need for multiple letters, which would be time-consuming and impractical. Moreover, letters regularly place more stress on the relationship between the sender and the recipient rather than on the character and capabilities of the bearer, clarifying that the favor that was being requested, as part of the relationship of *amicitia* between the two benefactors, was considered more important than the details of the recommended person's livelihood.[21] While the texts are not devoid of descriptors of the third party, that

19. P.Oxy. 1.32=CPL 249.

20. P.Oxy. 1.32 lines 15–17.

21. Discussed profitably in Cam Grey, "Letters of Recommendation and the Circulation of Rural Laborers in the Late Roman West," in *Travel, Communication and Geography in Late Antiquity: Sacred and Profane*, ed. Linda Ellis and Frank L. Kidner (Aldershot: Ashgate, 2004), esp. 29–32.

figure is often of secondary importance to the maintenance and enactment of the central friendship.

From Hellenistic Egypt, we have letters of recommendation that are slightly more explicit in their requests and clear in their economic purpose. The Zenon archive includes messages relating business deals and messengers whom the author encourages the recipient to look after and promote.[22] The short distances involved likely explain the difference, as it was easier to provide and request details when letters could reach their destination in a matter of days. Consequently, for the Roman period, we may be suffering from an absence of evidence, on top of a shift in the *formulae* that served as the building blocks of such letters. Literary references to letters, such as the one carried by Lucius in Book 1 of the *Metamorphoses*, provide us some additional reason to believe that these documents were more commonplace than our extant evidence would initially suggest.[23]

In the case of Archelaus, he expresses his hope that Domitius will help Theon and make use of his talents, but he ultimately only asks that the more powerful man grant Theon an audience so the two can become acquainted. Though this is likely only the tip of the iceberg of the benefits Archelaus hoped Theon would gain from a meeting, it is a humble request that suits a junior officer asking a favor of a superior. In actuality, Archelaus is politely groveling, as the letter admits that this is at least the second time that Archelaus has approached Domitius about this matter.[24]

Unlike many letter writers, Archelaus has little to offer Domitius in return for this favor and does not make any effort to promise anything more than the most abstract of benefits: Theon's good service. Typically, letters of introduction contain language indicating that the writer knows this kind of favor required repayment in kind, at the very least.[25] In contrast to Archelaus, Apollonius, writing in the early first century CE, tells Sarapion, a *strategos* and *gymnasiarch*, that he "will be indebted" to him for any help he offers to the third party, Isidorus. Apollonius is explicit that "whatever [Sarapion] wish[es] to signify, [Apollonius] will do without delay."[26] Instead of making a similar offer, Archelaus leans on a personal appeal, asking Domitius to imagine that the two stood face-to-face, rather than one addressing the other through the distancing medium of words on papyrus.[27]

---

22. E.g., P.Cair. Zen. 1.59016 or P.Cair. Zen. 1.59034.

23. Apul., *Met.* 1.22.

24. P.Oxy. 1.32 lines 4–6, *iam tibi et pristine commen/daueram Theonem amicum/ meum.* Already on a previous occasion I had commended my friend Theon to you.

25. Stowers, *Letter Writing*, 156–57.

26. P.Merton 2.62, lines 9–12, τọῦτο δẹ̀ πόηṣạṣ/ ἔση μοι κεχαṛ[ισ]μένος. κạὶ ṣὺ δὲ/ περὶ ὧν ἐάν αἴρῃ σήμανον, καὶ/ ἀνόκνως πόησωι.

27. P.Oxy. 1.32, lines 31–33, *hanc epistulam · ant[e] ocu/ḷos habeto domine puta[t]ọ / me tecum loqui.* Hold this letter before your eyes, sir, and imagine that I am speaking with you.

As in John's letter, it seems that some things were better dealt with in person, or some requests were more effective when made face-to-face. We will address oral communication in depth, but in this context, it is important to bear in mind that our letter reflects only a small portion of the total information about reputation that circulated in the Roman world, and that these letters generally reflected only the positive elements of their subject's character as a result of their purpose: to secure some kind of benefit. Though the content of these letters at times borders on exaggeration, such statements were fitting for a document that had to accomplish specific work. The consequence of a less-than-glowing letter was rejection, failure, as well as damage to both the writer and the subject's position in society; it was an expenditure of social capital that risked a loss of both revenue and face. For traveling merchants, a bad letter might lead to temporary homelessness or contracts left unfulfilled. A positive letter was essential, as was personal willingness to welcome travelers in return.

Already we have mentioned Heliodorus' *Aethiopica*, which stresses the importance of hospitality as a reciprocal process: merchants acted as hosts so they might be hosted in turn. In the passage in question, an old man describes the reason why his son has offered hospitality to Knemon, a young Athenian who has just arrived in Egypt:[28]

> Βίος γὰρ, ὦ παῖ, κἀκείνῳ πλάνος καὶ ἔμπορος καὶ πολλαὶ μὲν πόλεις, πολλῶν δ᾽ἀνθρώπων ἤθη τε καὶ νοῦς εἰς πεῖραν ἥκουσιν ὅθεν, ὡς τὸ εἰκός, ἄλλους τε κἀμὲ οὐ πρὸ πολλῶν τῶνδ᾽ ἡμερῶν ἀλύοντα καὶ πλανώμενον, ὁμορόφιον ἐποιήσατο.

> For he leads a wandering life, boy, and (works as) a merchant. Many cities and the customs and minds of many men have reached his experience. On account of this, as is reasonable, he shares his home with others and even me a few days ago when I was lost and grieving.[29]

For this merchant, opening his home was a natural extension of his work in trade. He needed to display generosity and serve as a good host, so that his own needs would be met when he traveled. Welcoming guests was a benefit to his reputation, just as Diotrephes' refusal to do so was a mark of his bad character. While we only have John's word about Diotrephes' motives, and he may have had justification for his refusal, John's efforts to spread Diotrephes' bad reputa-

28. J. R. Morgan, "The Story of Knemon in Heliodoros' Aithiopika," *Journal of Hellenic Studies* 109 (1989), includes a summary of the main events of Knemon's subplot.
29. Heliod., *Aeth.* 2.22.

tion for hospitality, and proclaim his own virtue in comparison, demonstrates how value-laden this behavior was in the Roman world.

Hospitality, akin to guest friendship, was a social norm with clear benefits to the host and clear consequences for the inhospitable. These rewards and punishments were axiomatic and foundational in Greco-Roman culture, and they weave themselves into all kinds of narratives and common sayings.[30] Often, as in the case of John's letter, hospitality was also seen as a reflection of piety, as providing housing for the traveling stranger was seen as a sacred duty across a variety of faiths.[31] Failure to offer housing was an affront to Zeus in the pagan conception of guest-host relations, and John similarly considered it a black mark against Diotrephes in a Christian context. In the later period, inns and hostels were often founded by prominent religious figures, and eventually some of these became housing that was exclusively available to religious pilgrims.[32]

Merchants offered hospitality, received it in their turn, and asked for it on behalf of their acquaintances. Paul, after his tent-making was established in Corinth, sends a note of recommendation on behalf of Phoebe, a member of the church at Cenchreae, as part of his letter to the Romans.[33] Phoebe intends to travel to Rome and may have been the messenger meant to deliver the letter in question. Paul asks the Romans to help Phoebe however they can, and mentions her in the context of his greetings to the tentmakers, Priscilla and Aquila, whom he calls his fellow-workers in Christ.[34] While we cannot extrapolate a mercantile purpose to Phoebe's travels from this scant evidence, a letter like Paul's would have served a traveling merchant well and the cultural expectation of hospitality among pagans and Christians alike would have been a valuable asset.

Still, not every merchant or traveler was fortunate enough to have a well-connected friend or patron who was willing and able to write a letter on his behalf and happened to have an acquaintance at his desired destination. Those that traveled without such documents found themselves at a disadvantage unless they were going somewhere where word of their business and character had proceeded them. Yet, as much as this would seem to be desirable, the reputation that was spread by word-of-mouth was often of a more mixed nature

30. E.g., Aesop, *Fab.* The Frog and the Mouse; The Eagle and the Beetle. Both stress improper hospitality and its consequences.

31. Olivia Remie Constable, *Housing the Stranger in the Mediterranean World: Lodging, Trade, and Travel in Late Antiquity and the Middle Ages* (Cambridge: Cambridge University Press, 2003), 48.

32. Constable, *Housing the Stranger*, 17–18.

33. Romans 16:1–2.

34. Romans 16:3.

than that of letters, and incorrect information could easily accompany accurate representations of a merchant's character.

Recent scholarship has worked to reclaim the term "gossip" as a way to refer to spreading information in this way, as both "conversation" and "talk" are too vague to encapsulate this specific kind of oral communication.[35] Gossip, of course, is hardly a neutral term in common English usage. It carries negative connotations that imply everything from pointlessness to malice, and it is often a term that conveys a gendered bias against female information-sharing.[36] Still, in a more technical sense, gossip is a label that can be applied to a kind of talk not specified by other terms. Chris Wickham has offered a useful definition that captures the neutrality of the activity: gossip is "talking about other people behind their backs."[37] By this definition, gossip is a commonplace action in every culture, and may convey both value-laden and value-neutral information through either intentional divulging or casual discussion. Small talk may be gossip, just as much as a salacious rumor, with the commonality being at least two people discussing something about a third who is not present.

Such a neutral definition, of course, disguises the judgment that most societies, Rome included, made of gossiping. It is part of gossip's contradictory nature that it can be seen in our sources as both an "idle" pastime, taken up by the merely bored, and a morally suspect activity advanced by the malicious and even criminal.[38] In either case, gossip was cast in a negative light, and it reflected badly on the participants. This is conspicuous in the ways that Romans define their own actions, which are generally "not gossip," while the talk of others was more likely to be so. Thus, "gossip" was generally in the eye of the beholder, which makes Wickham's neutral definition even more important, as it permits us to consider a speech-act as gossip, whether or not the speaker did.[39]

Despite the social stigma attached to both spreading and consuming gos-

---

35. Defense of gossip has picked up steam since the 1980s, though the origin of most of these efforts seems to lie in Max Gluckman, "Papers in Honor of Melville J. Herskovits: Gossip and Scandal," *Current Anthropology* 4.3 (1963), which posited the social utility of gossip and opened further investigation.

36. Wickham, "*Fama*," 15–16; Patricia Meyer Spacks, *Gossip* (New York: Alfred A. Knopf, 1985), 38–42.

37. Wickham, "Gossip and Resistance," 11.

38. Previous studies have attempted to create a "typology" of gossip that assessed levels of "seriousness" or "truthfulness." The former is a metric of Spacks, *Gossip*, 5ff., the latter is implied, at times, in Hans-Joachim Neubauer, *The Rumour: A Cultural History* (London: Free Association Books, 1999). No such effort will be made here.

39. Both John and Paul are guilty of written "gossip" about figures in their lives. John's accusations against Diotrephes and Paul's against Cephas in Galatians 2:11–14 are clearly gossip and share a common negative tendency as they disparage a figure who is not the intended recipient of the letter.

sip, oral communication of this kind was a tool that was commonly used by merchants, as well as by the wider community, to spread information about specific economic matters, or, more commonly, about the actions, character, or practices of individual economic agents. Reputation was spread and cemented by this means, which also permitted members of a community to determine among themselves what the common opinion about and judgment of an incident would be. Beyond this, gossip also provided merchants with information to which they may not otherwise have had access, transmitting details or even just vague impressions of events that few had witnessed first-hand. Accordingly, it was an activity that saved time and energy, sparing at least one person the effort of personal observation.[40]

Still, talk is "cheap," in that gossip is a relatively low-cost method of spreading and receiving information, and, as a result, it is not always accurate. Once again, Apuleius' *Metamorphoses* provides an instructive example.[41] When Lucius meets a cheesemonger, Aristomenes, on the road to Hypata, the man informs Lucius that he had been traveling because he had, "learned that . . . some fresh, tasty cheese was being sold at quite a good price."[42] When he arrived, he discovered that the cheese had already been sold to another merchant, Lupus. The exact means through which the cheesemonger learned about this bargain are not expanded upon, but he evidently did not arrive in time to see the cheese himself and was informed by someone locally of his wasted effort. News of the original price may have come via a colleague, some producer or wholesaler, and been transmitted to Aristomenes via letter or messenger. We have substantial evidence from Egypt of letters being sent, especially to agents operating remotely, with details about what to buy, when, and for what price.[43] While this is a possible source, it is equally plausible that Aristomenes learned about this deal through casual conversation with those not involved in the cheese trade. In either case, "Lupus has bought the cheese," constitutes gossip by our definition, as do the details that Aristomenes seems to know about the product's quality and price.

By his own admission, Aristomenes had worked in this area of Thessaly for some time. He bought and sold goods in the region and had an acquaintance nearby with whom he eventually spends the night in the narrative of Apuleius' *Metamorphoses*. Despite his familiarity with the area, Aristomenes suffered for

40. Noted by both Whitfield, *People Will Talk*, and Spacks, *Gossip*.

41. On this same episode as evidence for market volatility, see Bang, *The Roman Bazaar*, 137.

42. Apuleius, *Met.* 1.5 *comperto . . . caseum recens et sciti saporis admodum commodo pretio distrahi*.

43. Aubert, *Business Managers*, e.g., BGU 1049 (41 CE), P.Fay. 123 (100 CE), BGU 27 (second or third century CE).

being a relative outsider to the communities in which he worked. While he might have been known by many and known well enough to receive information about products that came on the market, he was not close enough, physically or socially, to the source of this information to reach the cheese in time. As we discussed in the previous chapter, local knowledge was important, and it is critical in the realm of gossip, which spreads news according to its own systems of logic, depending upon the sensitivity of the information and the proximity of those to whom it is of interest.

Among gossipers, Aristomenes' need to travel, and his lateness learning of this cheese, marks him as a merchant who was, to an extent, an outsider in this community. He was not on site to buy the cheese immediately and operated with this handicap. Even though he clearly bought and sold there with some regularity, he was not in the innermost circle of communication in this matter and was therefore at a disadvantage. Those who lived locally had better information and received it more quickly than those who came through only periodically. They were also better known by their potential interlocutors and may well have had a better reputation as a result of that social proximity. These were serious advantages, which may have translated into additional consideration and benefits. The cheesemaker might be persuaded to hold onto his cheese, keeping it off the market and in reserve, for a merchant with whom he was particularly close, but such advantages were more likely to be available to his closest friends and trading partners, not to a mobile merchant like Aristomenes.

As we saw with the merchants in chapter 4, Aristomenes' "foreignness" in Thessaly, not merely his physical distance, was likely a factor in his lack of access to the gossip network. Elements of trust are commonly at play in such cases, and the choice of whom to share information with was one that was made based on social closeness and real or reputed trustworthiness. Gossip could even be a tool to manufacture and support closeness. In Plutarch's *De garrulitate*, we see how friendship could be supported, though trust and secrecy could also be undermined, by gossip. Plutarch is strongly opposed to gossip, for moral reasons to which we will return shortly, and his discussion of how gossip spreads information demonstrates that friendship often determined the course of information even more than the relevance of the content.

> εἰ δ᾽ ἀφεὶς ἐκ σεαυτοῦ κατέχεις ἐν ἑτέρῳ τἀπόρρητον, εἰς ἀλλοτρίαν πίστιν καταπέφευγας τὴν σεαυτοῦ προέμενος. κἂν μὲν ἐκεῖνος ὅμοιός σοι γένηται, δικαίως ἀπόλωλας· ἂν δὲ βελτίων, σῴζῃ παραλόγως ἕτερον εὑρὼν ὑπὲρ σεαυτὸν πιστότερον. ἀλλὰ 'φίλος οὗτος ἐμοί.' τούτῳ δ᾽ ἕτερός τις, ᾧ πιστεύσει καὶ οὗτος ὡς ἐγὼ τούτῳ: κἀκεῖνος ἄλλῳ πάλιν·

> But if, having let the secret slip from yourself, you want to contain it in another, you have taken refuge in another person's trust after abandoning your own. And if that man turns out to be the same as you, you are justly ruined, but if he is better, you are unexpectedly saved, since you managed to find someone more trustworthy than yourself. But "this man is my friend." But this man has another friend, whom he will trust also, just as I trusted him, and that one will trust (yet) another again.[44]

Plutarch derides those who, though unable to keep a secret themselves, nevertheless will tell someone else a secret, expecting them to be trustworthy. He makes friendship the basis of this trust, presupposing that, among friends, there will be very few secrets. Simultaneously, he recognizes that these networks of trusted friends mean that nothing can be kept a secret for long. Everyone is equally incapable of keeping juicy news to themselves, and no one feels that they should exclude their friend from the social group created by gossiping. Plutarch hopes that everyone will eventually be "ruined" by their desire to gossip, since they are all "betraying" the trust implicit or explicit in the original secret.

His treatment of the matter is, typically, moralizing in tone, yet there is something fundamentally true about gossip revealed in this passage. Plutarch's friends tell each other things not only because they cannot help themselves and are unable to keep a secret, but because they also trust their friend. Telling a secret to a friend offers a demonstration of that trust and was an essential marker of the strength of the bond between the two people. As Nicholas Emler and Gianni Guastella have both put it, sharing reputational information helped members of social networks, friends, neighbors, or family, understand whom they ought to trust.[45] This is not only because the information may warn a person away from a potentially dangerous social or business partner, but because the very act of sharing the information demonstrates that there is trust between the two speaking. Particularly in the case of sensitive or particularly secret information, sharing creates an atmosphere of intimacy. The communicator tells his interlocutor that he is sharing this information specifically with him or her, and that it is not for general consumption.[46] As with the secret contents of a letter, the interlocutor in such a case is made to feel special, important, and trustworthy, even if they will be unable to keep the secret themselves.

Trust was difficult to manufacture in commercial settings, as we have seen,

---

44. Plut., *De garr.* 10.

45. Emler, "Social Psychology of Reputation," 182; Guastella, *Word of Mouth*; see also Gluckman, "Gossip and Scandal," 314.

46. Wickham, "Gossip and Resistance"; and Gluckman, "Gossip and Scandal."

due to the numerous stereotypes that painted merchants as dishonest and dishonorable. Gossip was merely one tool, and a potentially unreliable one at that, for developing trust. As Aristomenes learned, gossip did not have to be accurate, or could be accurate, but only under specific, time-sensitive, conditions. Guastella has already noted that a key issue with gossip, and its companion, rumor, is that its veracity depends on someone being willing to vouch for it, and for the speed with which it reaches a relevant ear.[47] Most gossip is, at best, second-hand knowledge, and it comes with provisos about when and where it was heard, rather than when and where it was witnessed. Thus, most gossipers are not able or willing to say if their gossip is true and will preface their statements in ways that automatically hedge and prevaricate. Furthermore, as with other kinds of information, old gossip is rarely useful, except in so far as it reveals something that is still true about the present.

Plutarch's treatise offers another useful case. He uses the example of the rumor of the Athenian defeat in Sicily, and the barber who was called to relate the story he had heard to the assembly:

> γενομένης δὲ ταραχῆς οἷον εἰκός, εἰς ἐκκλησίαν ἀθροισθεὶς ὁ δῆμος ἐπὶ τὴν ἀρχὴν ἐβάδιζε τῆς φήμης. ἤγετ᾽ οὖν ὁ κουρεὺς καὶ ἀνεκρίνετο, μηδὲ τοὔνομα τοῦ φράσαντος εἰδὼς ἀλλ᾽ εἰς ἀνώνυμον καὶ ἄγνωστον ἀναφέρων τὴν ἀρχὴν πρόσωπον. ὀργὴ δ᾽ οὖν καὶ βοὴ τοῦ θεάτρου: 'βασάνιζε καὶ στρέβλου τὸν ἀλάστορα· πέπλασται ταῦτα καὶ συντέθειται· τίς δ᾽ ἄλλος ἤκουσε; τίς δ᾽ἐπίστευσεν;' ἐκομίσθη τροχός, κατετάθη ὁ ἄνθρωπος.
>
> Since confusion arose, quite reasonably, the people who had gathered in the assembly went to the source of the rumor. Therefore, the barber was brought in and questioned, but he did not know the name of the one he had spoken to, instead summoning up a nameless and faceless beginning. Accordingly, there was anger and a shout from the crowd, "Torture and punish the wretched man. He made these things up and put it together himself. Who else heard it? Who believed it?" The torture wheel was brought, and the man was stretched.[48]

As a profession, barbers in the Greco-Roman world had a reputation for being apt to gossip.[49] It was a stereotype that seems to have been borne out in

47. Guastella, *Word of Mouth*, 135ff.; and Neubauer, *The Rumour*, 172.
48. Plut., *De garr.* 13.
49. This is an extensive trope. See Toner, "Barbers, Barbershops," for an analysis of the relevant evidence.

practice, as barbershops became places for people to gather and share information. The result, however, was that a barber might pick up a bit of news without being certain of its source, or aware of its original context. This barber was unable to name his informant when taken before the *ekklesia*, and was not only doubted, but also tortured, for having spread his true, but as-yet-unsubstantiated, news.

The case raises an interesting point about the intersection of gossip and truth, and, more crucially, the moral value placed on truth.[50] Quite rightly, Romans were slow to give gossip full credence. Aristomenes chalks his failure up to bad luck, and we might suppose that the slowness of land travel was a contributing factor, as well. Still, the *Metamorphoses* strongly implies that Aristomenes' rumor of cheese was not false, spread maliciously to waste his time, but simply too little information, coming too late to be useful. It is a case of accident, not intent, but as Plutarch rightly notes, gossip did not necessarily need to be true. There was potentially a great advantage in circulating a fabricated story. Wickham argues that doing so may have represented a substantial portion of the pleasure in gossiping, and that rumors thrive in society because their content, including embellishments added for narrative interest, encourages interlocutors to pass on the information.[51] Still, spreading rumors was considered morally reprehensible, and as we can see in the case of the barber, this behavior was believed to be worthy of severe punishment. It was imagined that the one who spread such information did so to seek some personal gain or to bring harm upon others.[52]

The forms that that gain might take were varied. While "being a gossip" was not a good thing, being knowledgeable or sociable was. Spreading information, even information that was incorrect, could be beneficial to one's social standing, and if unfounded rumors damaged the reputation of a rival, the gossiper was within their rights to claim any advantage they could get in the marketplace. Still, our sources show that Romans were naturally wary of gossip, and of the intentions that one might have for sharing it. Quintilian, arguing, at least in part, against the use of gossip in the courtroom, is clear that gossip was something:

---

50. A moral emphasis shared by early Christian sources, though gossip is by no means absent from the New Testament. See John W. Daniels, "Gossip in the New Testament," *Biblical Theology Bulletin* 42.4 (2012). It is also frequently gendered in those contexts, see Marianne Bjelland Kartzow, *Gossip and Gender: Othering of Speech in the Pastoral Epistles* (Berlin: Walter de Gruyter, 2009).

51. Wickham, "Gossip and Resistance," 12.

52. Theophrastus, *Char.* 3, "Idle Chatter" suggests that the major harm done is wasting the time of the unwilling listener, but also provides a window into what constituted this kind of conversation. An interesting piece is a comment on the price of wheat: ὡς ἄξιοι γεγόνασιν οἱ πυροὶ ἐν τῇ ἀγορᾷ, how fair the prices of wheat have been in the market.

> *quod nulli non etiam innocentissimo possit accidere fraude inimicorum falsa vulgantium.*
>
> which can even happen to anyone, even the most innocent person, through the deceit of enemies spreading rumors.[53]

Among merchants, this must have been a serious concern. While Aristomenes does not seem to have been led astray intentionally, it would have been an easy matter for one merchant to feed another outdated or even fabricated information, leading to the loss of time and money. The one who spread the rumor enjoyed the passive joy of watching a rival chase down the same false lead and the material advantage of putting their own time to good use. Salvian, in the fifth century CE, reports that lying, to each other, but especially to customers, was endemic among Syrian merchants.[54] While the lies he describes are not gossip in the strictest sense, it is clear that, at least from the outside, the oral culture of merchants was believed to be full of such examples of deceit, treachery, and backstabbing.

Of course, merchants must have, in the normal course of business, gossiped about many things, including topics that were as "innocent" as the price of cheese.[55] Still, there seems to have been a higher proportion of negative information spread via gossip than by other means of sharing reputation information, like the letters of recommendation examined above. As a mechanism for spreading negative information, true or otherwise, rumor and gossip posed a looming threat to merchants and the success of their business ventures. Publilius Syrus preserves the worry in its most essential form: *quem fama semel oppressit vix restituitur*, he whom gossip has once put down will be scarcely restored.[56]

The feared permanence of the damage done by gossip to reputation made it a prime tool for the kind of private-order enforcement that communities wished to use against those who flouted social norms. As a "cheap" form of information dispersal, it was commonly understood that bad behaviors could easily, and therefore quickly, become common knowledge, and that even the

53. Quintilian, *Inst.* 5.3.

54. Salvian, *De guber.* 4.14.69.

55. More than the content of such conversations, we are overwhelmingly provided with details about where they occurred. Shops are especially common locations for gossiping, see Toner, "Barbers, Barbershops"; Lewis, "Barbers' Shops and Perfume Shops."

56. Publilius Syrus, *Sent.* 572. *Fama* remains a complicated term in Latin, at once encompassing reputation, rumor, gossip, and some forms of common knowledge. Any of these translations might be valid in this aphorism.

honest and fair could be wrongly slandered if they did not make sufficient effort to keep their customers, peers, and general acquaintance appeased by their norm-abiding behavior.

The dissemination of information via gossip in the Roman world was by no means an idle exercise. Despite its connotations in English, gossip spread information purposefully: the better to share how well the personal and professional behavior of an individual conformed to the expectations and institutions of the community. As information spread, anomalous behavior was quickly identified and framed in terms of collective approval or disapproval, of honor or scandal, of "goodness" or "badness." Through these conversations, actions were either rapidly or gradually associated with moral standards, and each new conversation helped to solidify or refine what the community believed or thought about both the specific person and the kind of person, in the abstract, who would behave in this way. Gossip helped to deal with both the cases at hand and offer guidelines for how the collective would interpret and respond to similar situations in the future.

Beyond helping the community to reinforce and shape its own norms, gossip also assisted as the community decided what its next steps should be, to determine what it meant to do in order to encourage good behavior or to censure its opposite, both now and in the future. At times, little action was necessary, as the rumor mill itself held the power to influence reputation, while at other points the affront to community standards required specific responses or the escalation of a previous response for someone who had not amended their previously censured behavior.

At all times however, reputation was adjusted not only based on what an individual did or did not do, but also on the current position of the community in relation to those actions or inactions. As we discussed in chapter 2, behaviors which might seem perfectly neutral from the outside could carry a very different meaning for a community that was closely monitoring previous free riders and was expecting to find further reasons to distrust them. Similarly, the emulation of a known bad apple could associate even a perfectly innocent person with trouble, making something as simple as a kind of dress or approach to a problem into a cause for suspicion. Precedents carried heavy weight in the community, which meant that histories of social and economic interactions between neighbors and peers could influence events far in the future, based on what someone had once done, and how the community had responded then.

Above all, the responses of the community were the result of highly localized associations that did not necessarily appear elsewhere in the Mediterranean world or even in neighboring towns or different neighborhoods in the same city. Still, they were extremely powerful within their small worlds, and helped both locals and outsiders to make up their minds about how they would behave and respond, even if they had less information or personal experience. As a result, even a newcomer might quickly learn if there was a reason to be careful around some members of the community, even if their bad behavior, or the precedent by which that behavior was judged as "bad," had happened long before their arrival. These small communities had long memories and many incentives to share what they recalled.

Prevention, Policing, and Punishment

Still, the key to upholding the strength of social institutions, whether local or universal, was the prevention of outrages against the system.[57] Institutions flourished, in part, because of their seeming inevitability, and the invisibility of those who successfully evaded their restrictions. While gossip could throw light on those who had violated social norms, much of the work to preserve institutions had to be done long before that point was reached. The community worked hard to prevent anyone even attempting to game the system, not only as a means of protecting themselves from free riders or cheats, but also to present the system as inviolable. Doing so created an aura of inertia, so that it appeared, from the outside, to be too much bother, or too risky, to even attempt to go against the norm. When contravention could not be avoided, it was necessary to make malefactors appear abnormal or at the very least very rare.

In the latter goal, gossip was an essential tool for keeping community members in line. As others were verbally shamed behind their backs for certain kinds of conduct, it was made apparent to the whole audience that their behavior was remarkably and unusually bad. The subject of the gossip was painted as an outsider, or at least someone who had made an egregious mistake of some kind. More than this, the existence of gossip implied that all members of the community were being monitored and would be discussed in similar terms if their behavior was found wanting. These kinds of conversations, as well as their tone and content, went a long way in conveying to both experienced and new listeners where social boundaries lay, and revealed who was pushing against, or crossing, the lines drawn by society as a whole. Furthermore, while this kind of talk was undoubtedly enjoyable for the participants, it was known to be seriously damaging to the reputation of the discussed. Having participated in gossip, no one was in a hurry to be gossiped about themselves.

57. Toner, *Popular Culture*, 26–37; also Fuhrmann, *Policing the Roman Empire*.

Gossip, anecdotes, and even fiction helped to instruct the community about its standards of behavior and reconcile the needs of its individual members with the demands of living together in a society. As we will discuss shortly, this was clearly apparent in merchant associations, where these same issues were litigated through the process of developing charters and maintaining group order, but it was also a problem faced by society at large. As a result, we see numerous instances in Roman popular culture where issues of merchant morality were summed up in pithy statements, jokes, or parables that clarified the unenviable fate that awaited those who violated social norms and pointed out the benefits of compliance with moral standards.

These kinds of popular sources acted as a set of deterrents that reminded everyone that the community had the power to materially damage an individual's reputation, should he or she deviate from the community's prescribed norms, and that other punishments might be carried out against the particularly objectionable. These texts represent the kinds of narrative and witticism that could have easily circulated in the oral culture of Roman society, and their morals are echoed in texts like the graffiti of Pompeii, which double down on jokes and insults as a means to shame and publicly expose problematic behaviors.[58]

These sources also helped to inculcate the populace with proper social norms from an early age. Many were narratives that were accessible to children and, in the case of fables, they were made especially palatable through the metaphorical use of animals. Morals were easily conveyed in this way, and often conclude with a helpful summary:[59]

> Κρέας κύων ἔκλεψεν ἐκ μαγειρείου,
> καὶ δὴ παρῄει ποταμόν· ἐν δὲ τῷ ῥείθρῳ
> πολὺ τοῦ κρέως ἰδοῦσα τὴν σκιὴν μείζω,
> τὸ κρέας ἀφῆκε, τῇ σκιῇ δ' ἐφωρμήθη.
> αλλ' οὔτ' ἐκείνην εὗρεν οὔθ' ὃ βεβλήκει,
> πεινῶσα δ' ὀπίσω τὸν πόρον διεξῄει.
> [Βίος ἀβέβαιος παντὸς ἀνδρὸς ἀπλήστου
> ἐλπίσι ματαίαις πραγμάτων ἀναλοῦται.]

> A dog stole a piece of meat from a butcher's shop and went along the river. In the stream, when it saw the reflection of the meat, much larger

58. Noted by Fuhrmann, *Policing the Roman Empire*, 46.

59. It was likely that these were popular texts in Roman classrooms, as they remain today. See Stanley F. Bonner, *Education in Ancient Rome: From Cato the Elder to Pliny the Younger* (New York: Routledge, 1977), 178 and 254; and Christian C. Laes, "Children and Fables, Children in Fables in Hellenistic and Roman Antiquity," *Latomus* 65.4 (2006).

> than reality, the dog let go of the meat and dashed for the image. But he did not find that, nor what he had cast aside. Still hungry he crossed the ford. [The life of every greedy man is insecure, spent in vain hope of profits.][60]

Other texts deal more specifically with merchants, casting them as characters in lessons all their own, but texts such as this one target the moral failings which were often associated with the group. Without naming names, the fable encourages the reader (or listener) to consider their own tendencies toward greed and to see the consequences of the efforts of those around them who chose to seek profit above all else. The dog's failure here is a comfort to the person who has had an unpleasant encounter with a person who shared the dog's moral failing, and the comparison with an animal was, in this case, generally unflattering enough to suggest that it should be avoided, if possible.

The succinct moral of the story is not always preserved for us in the textual tradition, but it is easy to see how most of these texts represent narratives that confirmed and supported the moral standards of Roman society. That multiple versions survive of these stories, often with only slight variation, suggests their widespread telling and retelling as axiomatic touchstones of morality and advice. Merchants were undoubtedly as familiar with these tales as those of other walks of life and may have seen themselves or their competitors in narratives like the hen who lay golden eggs, the lying wolf and fox, or the ant and the fly.[61]

Though often in more complex ways than fables, comedy could also reveal norms through witticisms and inversion. In our earliest surviving book of jokes, we see numerous examples of incompetent, morally repellent, and irritating merchants being mocked for their behavior, while witty, morally upright community members succeed in shaming them. Two jokes stand out in particular. First:

> Εὐτράπελος φλυάρου κουρέως ἐρωτήσαντος "πῶς σε κείρω;" "σιωπῶν" ἔφη.

> When a talkative barber asked, "how should I cut your hair?" A witty man replied, "silently."[62]

60. Babrius, *Fab.* 79; also preserved in a variant form as Phaedrus, *Fab.* 1.4
61. Babrius, *Fab.* 123; Phaedrus, *Fab.* 1.10, 4.25.
62. *Philogelos* 148.

In this case, we see gossip identified as a potential problem, when placed into the hands of a merchant, rather than the community. Once again, the barber offers a useful stereotype to exploit: they were a talkative, gossipy bunch, known to be suspiciously well-informed through their constant access to people and their information networks.[63] Beyond the stereotype, however, Sian Lewis and Jerry Toner have both recently argued for the significance of barbershops as important places of local information sharing and for the distrust that elite people had of such places.[64] Just like Dio and the blacksmith's forge, the local importance of a merchant or tradesman's shop was not likely to register with wealthy men and women who did not patronize the business, and there is strong evidence to suggest that these sites of popular gathering and gossip were considered to be suspect by outsiders looking in on these complex networks of connection, interdependency, and information-sharing.[65]

In this joke, the barber is eager to chat with his customer, perhaps assuming that this person, like most, would treat this relationship as one of mutual exchange. Instead, he is rebuffed by the witty client who knows better than to trust the "idle chatter" of the barber. Both the stereotype and the pithy response help to emphasize the comic force of the joke, but we can imagine that the multiple versions of this apparently common and old witticism would have intentionally, or even inadvertently, shamed barbers for their inability to keep quiet or keep a secret.[66]

The second example targets not gossip, but incompetence, tinged with no small amount of greed, both common themes in the *Philogelos*:

> Σιδώνιος ἰατρὸς λεγάτον ἀπὸ ἀρρώστου αὐτοῦ χιλίας δραχμὰς μετὰ τὸ ἀποθανεῖν αὐτὸν κομισάμενος, ἐκφερομένου δὲ αὐτοῦ τῇ κηδείᾳ ἀκολουθῶν ἐνεκάλει ὡς ὀλίγον αὐτῷ λεγάτον κατέλιπεν. ἐπεὶ οὖν καὶ ὁ υἱὸς τοῦ τελευτήσαντος νόσῳ ἐμπαρεὶς παρεκάλει αὐτὸν ἐπισκεπτόμενον ἀνταγωνίσασθαι τῇ νόσῳ, ὁ ἰατρὸς ἔθη· "ἐὰν πεντακισχιλίας δραχμὰς εἰς λεγάτον καταλείψῃς, ἐγώ σε ἰατρεύσω ὡς τὸν πατέρα σου."

63. Plut., *De garr.* 13, ἐπιεικῶς δὲ λάλον ἐστὶ τὸ τῶν κουρέων γένος οἱ γὰρ ἀδολεσχότατοι προσρέουσι καὶ προσκαθίζουσιν, ὥστ᾽ αὐτοὺς ἀναπίμπλασθαι τῆς συνηθείας. It follows that barbers are chatty, for the idlest gossipers come in and sit before them, so that they are filled with the habit.

64. Toner, "Barbers, Barbershops"; Lewis, "Barbers' Shops and Perfume Shops."

65. Dio Chrys., *Or.* 47.11.

66. *Philogelos* 148. Several versions of this joke survive. One (Plut., *Regum* 25) attributes it to Archelaus I of Macedon, which suggests that it was already believed to be old in the imperial period.

> A Sidonian doctor received a legacy of a thousand drachmas after the death of a sick man who had been his patient. At the procession and funeral, he complained that he had been left such a small legacy. Later, when the son of the dead man had fallen ill in his turn and he was called in to treat him, the doctor said, "If you leave me five thousand drachmas in a legacy, I will heal you as I did your father."[67]

Sidonians are stereotypically stupid in the *Philogelos*, so the humor is in part derived from the fact that this doctor does not see how unethical his behavior is. His lack of self-awareness is comic, but his greed and incompetence are equally at play. The doctor has not saved his first patient and plans to extort a legacy from the next generation by threatening to withhold his comically bad care. There are numerous jokes that play on the lack of skill of physicians, but this joke also plays up the commonly held belief that workers of all kinds only labored for the love of profit.[68]

Greed is treated as a central motive for merchants of all kinds, but it was particularly distasteful in a profession upon which lives depended. Greed, in this case, is funny because it is familiar to the community, but it is also recognized as a serious moral vice, one that needs to be exposed. This doctor is comically upfront about his desire for a legacy, but it is likely that many doctors were suspected of having similar motives, especially if the practice of posthumously rewarding one's doctor was common in the Greco-Roman world. The anxiety that such rewards might make doctors less committed to their healing arts likely made this joke sit somewhat uncomfortably with some in its audience.

In both cases, these jokes are intended to shame the shameless about behaviors that ran counter to society's norms but were stereotypically associated with these trades. On the one hand, merchants and service providers might have been the recipients of a great deal of information, but it was unacceptable for them to be indiscreet about it after the fact, violating an implied confidence and the secrecy that was evidently critical to the relationship between a man and his barber. If such a man could not be trusted, then it was at least comically wise to share nothing with such a man—if not actually morally praiseworthy to reject and distrust whatever information he might wish to share with you. On the other hand, charlatans and cheats were ridiculed and publicly shamed in the imagined world of jokes. As we will discuss, this was not always the preferred approach in reality, yet, within this setting it was best not only to prove

67. *Philogelos* 139.

68. Other doctor jokes: *Philogelos* 174–77, 182–86, 189, 253. Thematically, doctors are primarily incompetent and bad tempered.

such people wrong, but also to make their bad behavior common knowledge through public shaming that included the mockery of the whole community.

Of course, not everyone had the perfect punchline to put a merchant in his place when the moment called for it, but the ubiquity of these kinds of joke suggests that Roman society was not only entertained by, but also fantasized about, putting a bad actor in his or her place. Shaming such a person was a pleasant notion, one bandied about casually as "just a joke," though the threat of such embarrassment may have acted as a form of deterrent to those who might have considered such behaviors or a form of shame for those who recognized themselves in the character, however obliquely.[69]

It is difficult to track the efficacy of such prevention strategies, as members of the same trade remained the target of the same or similar jokes over an extended period of time, but there were other methods of shaming that targeted particular individuals, in an effort to get them to change their ways. Graffiti are often particularly instructive in this light, as they have no qualms about naming names when merchants did not behave as they should:

> DVO SODALES HIC FVERVNT ET CUM DIV MALVM
> MINISTRVM IN OMNIA HABERENT
> NOMINE EPAPHRODITVM VIX TARDE
> EVM FORAS EXIGERVNT
> COMSVMPSERVNT PERSVAVISSIME CUM FU`TV´ERE ((sestertii))
> CVS

> Two friends were here, and then they had all kinds of bad service from a waiter named Epaphroditus, soon after, they threw him out. Then they spent one hundred and five and a half sestertii very pleasantly with prostitutes.[70]

It is unclear what service Epaphroditus was meant to have provided, or whether he was a freed or enslaved person attached to any particular one of the services available at this complex, which included baths, a bar or inn, and, apparently, a small-scale brothel.[71] The graffito leaves a mixed "review" of sorts but takes the time to shame one particular person for poor service in a semiper-

69. As the comical aedile Pythias in Apul., *Met.* 1.24–25 claimed to do to the old fishmonger.

70. CIL 4.10675, Herculaneum, outside bar/inn joined to the maritime baths.

71. It was relatively common for *tabernae* to provide this trifecta of services, but it is rarely certain which, if any, was considered to have been the primary purpose of the business. The provision of alcohol, with multipurpose rooms above or behind the front room, seems to have been the layout of many spaces near the bay of Naples.

manent fashion. Others choose to be more specific about their dissatisfaction, while still others used this same medium for praise.[72] Regardless of the level of pleasure or displeasure on display, graffiti offered customers and competitors alike the time to draft up the perfect, pithy line that would express how they felt, and convey the information they believed others should know.

We generally lack responses to these street-side taunts and accusations, but it is clear that fear of damage to one's good reputation did keep some from wandering too far from the straight and narrow. Already we have seen the case of Apollonius, who did not wish to turn to piracy because he was just getting a good name as an honest ship captain.[73] His fear, in that case, was not that he would be punished by law, but that he believed the turn to piracy was an irrevocable step after which he could not return to legitimate forms of trade.

Interestingly, Apollonius' black-and-white vision of the situation may not have been accurate. Both historically and in Roman fiction, bandits and pirates commonly seem to have maintained legitimate day jobs, turning to crime only as it suited them or their commanders.[74] These men could move and work in society and even be respected, trusted, and supported under the right circumstances, all while performing clearly illegal actions like robbery and kidnapping. In fiction, pirates are sometimes depicted as holding down normal positions working in harbors or aboard ships, the better to spy out opportunities for theft, but we may also assume that some just needed a steady job between their bouts of piracy and took work that complemented their skills.[75]

It is clear from both historical and fictional sources that piracy was culturally frowned upon and that the legal prohibitions against piracy and theft wielded serious punishments. Still, the survival of pirates throughout the Roman period suggests that those who took up this work still found outlets for their ill-gotten gains, as this kind of fencing required community support.[76] While it is tempting, in line with Roman prejudices, to assume that this was merely the handiwork of criminals being aided by dishonest merchants, our evidence suggests that some people, and even some people not involved in

72. CIL 4.4957, Pompeii, Inn of the Muledrivers: *Miximus in lecto fateor peccavimus hospes. Si dices quare nulla matella fuit.* CIL 4.10677, Herculaneum: *Pranderunt hic iucundissime et futuere simul.*

73. Philostr., *V. A.* 3.24, discussed in chapter 4.

74. Knapp, *Invisible Romans*, 295–97.

75. Pirates might also hold positions of legitimate employment, as slave dealers (or as suppliers for slave dealers), as merchant shippers, or even as mercenary soldiers. Chariton, *Callirhoe*, 1.7; Ach. Tat. 2.17. See Philip de Souza, *Piracy in the Graeco-Roman World* (Cambridge: Cambridge University Press, 1999), 43–48, 63–65.

76. Regardless of Pompey's efficacy and the "Pax Romana," at least some pirates remain visible at every point in Roman history, see De Souza, *Piracy*, esp. ch. 6.

trade, may have received personal benefits from these illegal activities, making the lines much blurrier and raising the issue of what, exactly, was unacceptable about these behaviors.[77]

Much seems to have depended upon who was preyed upon and who benefited, but, interestingly, the illegality of piracy and banditry does not seem to have ranked highly in these considerations. In general, novels cast these figures as antagonists when they make the mistake of kidnapping the protagonists, who are generally elite, wellborn, and attractive young people, but make little fuss over other instances where they enslave and sell other people, fencing their victims with legitimate slave dealers or at auctions in foreign ports.[78] As a result, complaints about pirates, and efforts to shame those who turned to, or considered, piracy focus on a set of issues similar to those that apply to merchants in general: deceit, dishonesty, and greed, rather than explicitly targeting predation, illegality, or criminality.[79]

In practice, this was likely due to the relative "expense" of dealing with malefactors, piratical and otherwise, through the law. As a deterrent, the penalties of the law were serious threats, but they were ones that were substantially more difficult to enforce than the punishments that were readily available to small communities. It was slightly easier to set up and enforce local regulations, which many communities did, but a host of sources lament the challenges of accessing and getting responses from regional and imperial powers.[80]

The general population, whether from the belief that magistrates were in league with merchants or simply because they were ineffective, most often found other institutions that could step into policing roles. Christopher Fuhrmann, in his landmark study of this matter, notes that religious institutions often bore a substantial portion of this burden, which we see reflected in the numerous religious texts that emphasize the immorality of cheating, lying, and greed.[81] As with the jokes and fables discussed above, religious beliefs helped to prevent behaviors that threatened community standards, while religious leaders proclaimed the specific punishments that would befall those who transgressed the laws of the gods or broke oaths made by or in their presence.

Social and economic organizations also did a great deal of policing work,

77. Apuleius, *Met.* 4.1, bandits arrive at a village and give gifts to the locals from their plunder. In Eutrop., *Brev.* 9.21, Carausius, who usurped imperial power in Britain and Gaul in the late third century, was suspected of allowing piratical raids to occur, so that he could seize at least some of their plunder for himself.

78. E.g., Xen. *Ephes.* 1.14; Chariton, *Callirhoe*, 1.7–14, 2.12; Heliod., *Aeth.* 5.22–30.

79. The case of Theron (Chariton, *Callirhoe*, 1.7–14) is the most instructive. Greed is Theron's primary motive and all his criminal activity stems from his desire to enrich himself.

80. An articulate complaint is made in SB 20.14401.

81. Fuhrmann, *Policing the Roman Empire*, 46–48.

the better to protect their reputation as a group. Members, often all merchants of one sort or another, observed and regulated each other, navigating the complicated needs of groups that were made up of individuals who each held personal ambitions along with their loyalties to their peers. Associations offered a variety of rewards for good conduct, including positions of honor, titles, and support, while they simultaneously presented clear standards for how merchants should treat each other and the community as a whole.

Charters preserved from Roman Egypt show groups that were explicit about what they expected of their members, and they list the punishments that would be levied in response to potential crimes. Already we have seen the case of the sheep and cattle herders in chapter 2, where the focus of the charter was firmly placed on punishment, rather than on the structure of the group, its leadership, or even the advantages that the group could offer to its members.[82] In their inverse, these lists of crimes generally create a set of behavioral standards, ranging from attendance policies to social conduct. The charters also record how associations involved themselves in the milestones of their members personal lives, thereby claiming a position in the lives of merchants that echoed the watchful eye and close involvement of the community at large.[83]

All these restrictions, to some degree or other, would have been necessary to maintain order within the group, but some clearly extend beyond the narrow confines of a peaceful meeting of the organization. While a serious matter that likely reflected underlying conflicts within the group, the pushing and shoving that the cattle herders condemn in their meetings would have little immediate impact outside of a group meeting. The punishment of a simple fine seems to reflect the relatively commonplace nature of such social friction, but the fact that fines were to be assessed by the group on a case-to-case basis suggests that the group wanted to judge each conflict individually to determine which were accidents or misunderstandings and which were symptoms of greater problems.

As we discussed in chapter 1, merchant groups often strove to keep conflicts out of the public eye through their charters, as their regulations provided a standardized means of punishing members and judging specific matters.[84] The initial prohibition against misconduct in the case of the cattle herders leaves the

82. P.Mich. 5.243, lines 3–4, 6–8, see discussion in chapter 2. See Venticinque, *Honor among Thieves*, 7–14, on the context of these charters. See also P.Lond. 7.2193, lines 13–17, for similar restrictions for a religious group.

83. Groups asked members for contributions on the birth of children, marriages, and the purchase of property, e.g., P.Mich. 5.243, 5–6; and IG 2^2.1368, 125–35.

84. In P.Mich. 5.245, the group reserves the right to arrest members who fail to meet their group (and state) obligations.

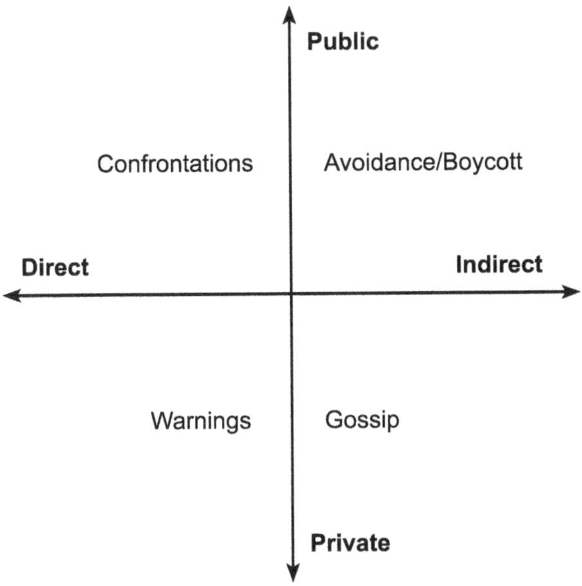

Figure 7. Spectra of social punishment: direct-indirect and public-private. Jane Sancinito.

group with substantial leeway in how it might respond to a given case. Alongside fines, many groups reserved the right to expel members as a means of protecting their own reputations and depriving the malefactor of the resources that they enjoyed as a group member.[85]

Despite the clarity we have in our sources about group strategies for sanctioning and fining members, private individuals were not without their own, albeit less visible, means of exacting punishment. Among this population, there was a spectrum of damage that could done, depending on the severity of the offense, ranging from mild reprimands and reminders of the rules to permanent setbacks to reputation and social standing, but generally, we may assess the types of punishments that were inflicted based on two axes: direct-indirect and public-private (Fig. 7). Examples of punishment exist along both these axes and demonstrate the variety of options community members had for expressing displeasure and bringing harm on those who had wronged them.

Direct and public action, we must assume, most often happened in the heat of the moment, when cheating or some other form of disreputable conduct was detected and immediately addressed. This was a confrontation that occurred with witnesses, who served as audience as the matter at hand was litigated

85. Venticinque, *Honor among Thieves*, 55–62, discusses how groups controlled member behavior and ultimately determined if a member should be expelled or retained.

between the accuser and the accused. In general terms, this was the kind of situation that pitted one reputation against another and allowed the populace to pass judgment on who was in the right and who was in the wrong.

Apuleius' *Metamorphoses* provides an instructive, and comic, example in the form of a conflict between Pythias, the aedile of Hypata, and a local fishmonger.[86] Though the scene leans heavily on comedic tropes, it displays how reputation, both its presence and its absence, might direct the way in which a petty dispute in the marketplace played out. In the episode, Lucius approaches a fishmonger, and haggles with him over the cost of the fish. After his purchase, he encounters an old acquaintance, Pythias, who is now serving as the aedile of Hypata.[87] Upon learning of Lucius' purchase, Pythias is enraged that his friend has been cheated and scolds the fishmonger—publicly shaming him by destroying the fish in front of him. After this display, Pythias concludes, "'it is enough for me, Lucius,' he said, 'to have given the little old man this great insult.'"[88]

Pythias goes away, leaving Lucius bewildered, without either his money or his fish, but the interaction of Pythias and the fishmonger, if set in a real, rather than fictional Greece, was one that would have had real implications in the realm of reputation. Pythias was a new market official; the fishmonger, though only described in a limited sense, is an old man and may have been the more established of the two within the community. Their respective reputations were potentially on the line in this conflict, as Pythias attempted to prove himself to be a serious and diligent official and the fishmonger maintained that he had not cheated a customer.[89] The audience of Hypata's market surrounded them and would litigate the issue both in real time and in the days and weeks that followed in order to determine who had been the victor. Importantly, there was no need for one side to be unequivocally correct. A direct and public attempt to punish a merchant put both parties in the spotlight and had equal potential to go badly for the accuser as for the accused. Pythias might be branded an officious and bullying magistrate, just as easily as the fishmonger could be viewed as a cheat.

86. Danuta R. Shanzer, "'Piscatum opiparem . . . praestinavi': Apuleius, *Met.* 1, 24–25," *Rivista di Filologia e di Istruzione Classica* 124 (1996), argues convincingly for a connection to Plautine comedy, though others have seen the matter as satirical; notes 1–5 provide a full bibliography.

87. Given that the events take place in Thessaly, Pythias is more accurately an *agoranomos*, but Apuleius utilizes the Latinized term throughout.

88. Apuleius, *Met.* 1.25, "*Sufficit mihi, o Luci,*" *inquit* "*seniculi tanta haec contumelia.*"

89. There is no evidence in the scene that the fishmonger behaved improperly. Lucius' claim that he had been "twisted" *extorsimus* to get his deal is probably hyperbolic and intended to make Lucius look like a good haggler, rather than make the fishmonger look like a crook. Again, Lucius has been "victorious" in the "battle" of the marketplace and had earned (or perhaps received) a small discount from the fishmonger. Rather than feeling hard-done-by Lucius may complain as a means of communicating his skill in negotiation without resorting to bragging.

While both "direct" and "public" lie on a spectrum, greater publicity implicated reputations, and risked them, to a greater degree than direct action taken in private. We can see two possibilities in this kind of approach to punishment. One the one hand, privacy invited the opportunity for cooler heads to prevail: a disgruntled customer or peer might take a merchant aside and offer them a warning, one which did not threaten the reputation of either party and might, in some circumstances, allow both sides to move beyond a conflict with their dignity intact. It is not necessarily "punishment," as such, except in so far as it was a means of correcting improper conduct and to address individuals who had knowingly or unknowingly transgressed social or economic norms. This kind of polite, measured approach to conflict was the model that was desired by merchant associations in cases of internal dispute. Groups hoped to arbitrate matters and allow both parties to leave the grievance behind them, without further escalation.

On the other hand, private but direct punishment could also take on a more physical or even a brutal cast. The presence of an audience prevented certain extremes of behavior as the accuser was concerned for their own reputation and standing in the community. In private, however, threats and violence were viable means of forcing merchants and customers alike to honor their promises and adjust their behavior. The records of Egypt, and especially those compiled by Ari Bryen, are littered with evidence for conflicts that led to violence, several of which may be traced to some kind of economic dispute, ranging from property rights to loans to unfulfilled contracts.[90] Rather than reputation, or even right or wrong, physical power and the ability to follow through on threats were the main issues at stake in this kind of punishment, and it was a method of correction that was more readily available to the physically fit or well-connected than to the weak or socially isolated.

For such people, it was often preferable to avoid direct forms of punishment, where the risk was high without a necessarily equivalent reward. Like its direct counterpart, indirect punishment could be demonstrated publicly as well as privately, though they are more closely intertwined than their direct counterparts. Public acts of indirect punishment generally include forms of boycott or social shunning and are most effective if one or both parties have a long-standing, publicly recognized relationship that underwent a dramatic change.[91] A casual buyer, for example, who only occasionally patronized a busi-

90. Bryen, *Violence*, appendix B provides a list of examples. Many have some underlying economic dispute, e.g., #1 BGU 4.1105; #3 SB 18.13087; #6 P.Louvre 1.1; and others.

91. Nicolas Tran, "Les procédures d'exclusion des collèges professionnels et funéraires sous le Haut-Empire: Pratiques épigraphiques, normes collectives et non-dits," in *Les exclus dans*

ness, would hold less clout in a boycott than one who had been a frequent and loyal patron in the past. Reputation, too, is heavily implicated in such an action. A popular business, patronized by many people, one with a good reputation, would not be obviously hindered by the absence of one customer, however loyal they had previously been. The social status and reputation of the customer was equally important, not only because of their real or imagined buying power, but because of the influence they would have over the practices of others. A patron with many clients could inspire, even without asking, a widespread exodus from a business, if he made plain his own desire to cut ties.

Similarly, if a matter were resolved and peaceful relations were restored, an influential person could undo much of the damage that their avoidance had created, but much relied on the accuser's ability to convey their return to civility in a public fashion. The reconciliation would have to be even more public than the dispute, and it required an extremely influential person to wholly remove the mark against a merchant's reputation after they had been singled out in this way.

This form of indirect punishment made clear that there was a dispute, but could do nothing to explain its origin, which naturally inspired the kind of indirect, private punishment that we have discussed throughout this chapter: gossip. Shunning or ostracism, if properly carried out, encouraged the community to seek out why one person was avoiding another and doing so meant acquiring information. While this could, potentially, be gained by speaking to the shunner or to the shunned, these were issues that were generally discussed in private, rather than laid out for public consumption. Once some detail was available, the information retained an air of secrecy, and it circulated as gossip, rather than being subjected to public reporting. Even after a reconciliation, the rumor mill might keep the details of the dispute in circulation, implicating the reputation of one or more of the people involved, making the whole affair a matter of "common knowledge" even if it was not "public knowledge."

Institutionally speaking, the threat of any of these tactics clarified for merchants what their true options were. While it might still be worth it, in some circumstances, to run the risk of the community's disapproval, the knowledge that being outed as a free rider would and could incur serious sanctions clarified the paths that offered the best balance of risk and reward. To an extent, that balance was a personal calculation, regularly undertaken by merchants both consciously and subconsciously, but merchant concerns for their reputation also served as a shortcut to this mental math. A bad reputation was a very real

l'Antiquité: Actes du colloque organisé par l'université Lyon III les 23 et 24 septembre 2004, ed. Catherine Wolff (Paris: De Boccard, 2007) covers the processes of exclusion of members from associations in the late Empire.

threat, as these sanctions could be compounded over time, until transaction costs became insurmountably high, leading to the end of a merchant's career.

Each of these forms of punishments had some ability to linger as marks against the reputation of a merchant. Some punishments, and especially those that were carried out directly, might blow over shortly after they were applied, only to reemerge later in some escalated form, as in the cases of violence reported in the papyri.[92] Others, dealt with privately, might put a temporary strain on an interpersonal relationship, but eventually be forgiven, if not forgotten. Indirect punishments might linger far longer. A boycott could conceivably last a lifetime, if not across generations. We know that this was a tactic that could be undertaken even by large groups, such as the Jewish population of Jerusalem in the first century CE, when Roman red-slipped pottery was boycotted as a means of expressing displeasure at Roman rule.[93] Our evidence for boycotts in the Roman period among individuals is fairly slim, but the early medieval period offers some useful comparisons.[94] Groups and individuals alike held grudges and avoided both individuals and their businesses long after an initial wrong had been committed.

But the consequences of this are much broader—they are social and structural. Many of these forms of punishment required some form of self-restraint or even self-punishment in order to be effective. To punish a merchant, a customer often broke or materially damaged the social relationship they had with the merchant and often the ultimate result was that a customer "could not," literally or figuratively, patronize that business anymore. In urban settings, like we have seen in Pompeii among cloth makers and cleaners, there were undoubtedly other choices available to the average consumer, if their relationship with one purveyor should sour, but in more rural communities, a damaged relationship might well mean going without some kind of good or service, or having to inconvenience oneself to secure the same goods at a greater distance or higher price. Accepting this kind of hindrance into one's daily life suggests the seriousness with which community members approached the punishment of merchants. Most succinctly: it was worth some, or even a great deal of inconvenience, if it meant seeing someone who had outraged social or economic norm punished.

92. As in the case of the dispute between Ptolemaios, son of Diodorus, and Ptolemaios, the son of Pappos, PSI 13.1323 and SB 20.14401.

93. Andrea M. Berlin, "Romanization and anti-Romanization in pre-Revolt Galilee," in *The First Jewish Revolt: Archaeology, History, and Ideology*, ed. Andrea M. Berlin and J. Andrew Overman (New York: Routledge, 2002), 67–69, makes this case based on the sudden disappearance of Roman pottery from ethnically Jewish sites in this period. While "boycott" may be too strong an appellation of this action, there does seem to have been an active and deliberate avoidance of red slip at sites that have been reliably identified as Jewish.

94. Broekaert, "Partners in Business," offers a useful collection of the evidence.

Institutionally, this kind of punishment, the variety that harmed the punisher as much as the intended target, is commonly referred to as "altruistic punishment" as it offers a benefit to the whole community while an individual is left to bear most of the burden personally.[95] Any correction to the malefactor's behavior, in such cases, would be generally enjoyed by others, while the original complainant might receive little or no personal benefit. They would only be vindicated by their protection of community standards and the possibility that they would gain a reputation for their public-mindedness that would benefit them in other ways.

Merchants bought into this system, and at times accepted that the only way to structure their trading world, lower transaction costs, and generate trust was to bear some of the costs personally. Not only did they agree to adhere to social norms themselves to build up a good reputation, but they also acted as enforcers of those norms, expending time and energy, certainly, and possibly money as well, to see to it that no peer or competitor enjoyed an unfair advantage. They did so individually but also as members of associations, where they not only bought in to a system that secured them benefits, but also held some assurance that their competitors would be punished if they erred. Merchants expected that everyone around them would be as concerned with maintaining a good name as they were, and that they would behave accordingly. When everything ran as expected, as social norms dictated, the playing field was fundamentally even. Merchants could function on the assumption that most of their peers would act as they did, would judge as they judged, and disapprove as they disapproved. The status quo was maintained through these means, and the knowledge that many were equally willing to sacrifice to see to it that the institution survived offered everyone comfort and confidence.

Through punishment, policing, and, of course, prevention, institutions were upheld, and reputation was consistently implicated throughout these efforts to maintain the social and economic system. The texts we have regarding these issues do not always lean on reputation as their primary rationale for the benefit of adopting socially approved behaviors. Rather, as the allusion to religious texts and the use of fables above implies, their tone and language focus on the moral implications of certain kinds of merchant behavior, something which merchants themselves bought into, not only presenting their own moral worth,

95. On the economics of altruistic punishment and the maintenance of cooperation, Martijn Egas and Arno M. Riedl, "The Economics of Altruistic Punishment and the Demise of Cooperation," *Proceedings of the Royal Society Biological Sciences* 275 (2008). See also Ernst Fehr and Simon Gächter, "Fairness and Retaliation: The Economics of Reciprocity," *Journal of Economic Perspectives* 14.3 (2000); and Gürerk, Irlenbuschand, and Rockenbach, "The Competitive Advantage of Sanctioning Institutions."

but accepting it as a reasonable standard by which they and others might be adequately judged. Reputation is subtextual, but it nevertheless functioned as a guide for both business and personal decision-making.

Conclusion

Strong institutions, especially those of a social nature, have an air of inevitability around them. They are natural and seemingly inviolable, until, sometimes, they suddenly aren't. Reputation, as an institution, was an instinctual concern of merchants, one that they naturally gravitated toward because it was already part of their information-gathering and information-sharing practices as well as the naturalized norms of their community. Merchants, like other Romans, were steeped in the background noise of Roman *mores* and sought to develop and project a version of themselves that conformed with what they believed their neighbors, peers, acquaintances, and family expected, not only of them specifically, but of someone in their position more generally.

As they gained and shared information, by talking and writing, as well as by implying and inferring and witnessing, merchants monitored their own behavior in light of the behavior of their peers and the reception it received among diverse audiences. In light of that information, they were in a position to decide what they would do in response to that person and their actions. In some cases, emulation was desirable, while in others it was best to distance oneself from a person of disrepute. Merchants could decide to take risks, making dramatic displays of their own character, or simply plod along the course of society's expectations. While the former was dangerous, it was also potentially rewarding, as a means of gaining a good reputation, at either a higher or lower cost than usual.

Yet those who chose to ignore reputation took on an even greater risk, as deviation from community standards, once discovered, was strongly criticized by the community, and was punished accordingly. The community made its disapproval of such people widely known and made efforts to make punishments visible and long-lasting. Customers, peers, and acquaintances had access to similar information networks as merchants and had a range of means to disincentivize conduct of which they disapproved: preemptively making their feelings known, publicly monitoring the social and business operations of merchants, or variously shaming or punishing bad behavior after the fact.

Merchant fear of a bad reputation suggests both the success of the community in these efforts and the buy-in of merchants into the system. Had merchants cared less about the way that they were perceived, perhaps by leaning on the effective monopoly that many merchants held over certain types of goods in certain markets, it might have been possible to spare themselves the expense of reputation strategies all together, but our evidence does not provide cases of dramatic resistance.

Reputation remained a powerful institution, largely because merchants themselves continually subscribed to the common belief that adhering to the limits imposed by reputation was valuable, and that the potential benefits outweighed the restrictions. While the natural and predictable conflicts of daily life made the development and maintenance of reputation a constant process in which each action was weighed and measured to judge its relative conformity to expectations, the security and predictability provided by possessing a good reputation, and by dealing with those who also had a good reputation, was known to be worth the effort.

In markets that lacked strong imperial or governmental structures, reputation dynamics served as a, if not the, dominant form of institutional structure. Merchants moderated their behavior, not out of concern that misconduct like a broken contract or cheating on their measures would lead to immediate and severe legal consequences, but because of their fear that their behavior would become commonly known and be detrimental to their reputation, and through it, their prospects. The damage to their reputation would make it more challenging for them to do business in the future and their public or private shaming would make clear to others that adhering to normative behavior, whether or not it aligned with Roman law, was an important part of running a business.

Conclusion

It would not necessarily be inaccurate to answer the question of how merchants ran successful businesses in the Roman world with "not alone," though such a response borders on glibness. As an answer, it certainly neglects the nuance that we have seen in the efforts of merchants to present themselves and their businesses in the best possible light. Still, "not alone" does capture some of the essential outcomes of this study of the social and economic strategies of this group. The challenges of informational imbalances, price fluctuation, and irregular, unreliable protection and structure from formal, state institutions were not ones that a single, small-scale actor could overcome by themselves. Rather, it was vitally important to have those challenges, those transaction costs, mitigated by obedience to shared norms that provided structure and increased predictability. Merchants relied on others—their peers and even their competitors—to promote and adhere to these standards so that some amount of trust could thrive, even under the adverse conditions of ancient commerce.

The challenge, of course, is that such norms do not appear fully formed, *ex nihilo*, simply because they are needed, nor do they survive just because a segment of the population continues to find them useful. Norms require a consistent buy-in, the participation and the consensus of a community, in order to function, and institutions, both social and legal, grow weak in the face of too many people choosing to disregard them. Both norms and institutions must be made to seem inevitable, a process that is only possible if they convey concrete and desirable benefits or if their absence leads to real and serious dangers. While it has been commonplace to make the case that laws, contracts, and market regulations offered both a carrot and a stick to merchants and artisans in the Roman world, less work has been done as yet on how social structures offered similar incentives and disincentives for merchant behavior.

In this study, reputation has been considered as a social institution of particular importance to Roman merchants, on the grounds that we can plainly see merchants buying into its institutional system, reaping its rewards, and accepting its limitations. Merchants recognized reputation as a means of improving or maintaining their social standing in their communities and, indeed, of framing their personal identity for their local audience(s). The language of reputation is found throughout Roman literary and epigraphic culture, but its presence in merchant sources, when it is combined with language relating to work or that identifies a profession, suggests that reputation was not a general, or even a culturally specific, abstraction, but a concrete element of merchant conceptions of their personal and professional identities. The use of reputational language in this context also allows us to dismiss the idea that merchants, especially in their art and funerary inscriptions, were simply mimicking an upper-class preoccupation with reputation. Merchants consistently link their *fama* or δόξα to their successful and ethical completion of their work, which flies in the face of any notion that they were, or felt they should be, embarrassed by their profession.

The success of a merchant, then, was not measured against the extent to which their lives conformed to the lifestyles that were aspired to and maintained by elites. This directly contradicts the way that many elite authors wrote about people in trade, as well as the often tacit assumption that the goal of all tradesmen was to become successful enough to leave commercial affairs behind them, as the fictional Trimalchio and Apollonius both eventually did. Rather than buying into this rhetoric, which was designed to keep merchants "in their place," this reading of our sources opens the window into a community that believed it was possible to have a good reputation *as* a merchant, not just *despite* being one.

Nevertheless, this is a complicated claim. Merchants were evidently proud of their professional achievements, recording and broadcasting them in a variety of media. Furthermore, merchants readily believed that they themselves held a good reputation, or that they could acquire one in the future, if they adopted the right strategies. Despite this confidence, merchants also adjusted their behavior in direct correlation to the expectations of society. Thus, we see merchants attempting to advertise virtues that run counter to the pervasive negative stereotypes that circulated about them, rather than highlighting unrelated, personal strengths of character or conduct. While merchants do not generally display any shame related to their work, they remain highly aware of the perceptions, not only of their immediate community but also of the Roman world at large. This awareness borders on an anxiety, which, if it does not undercut the determination of people in trade to connect their identity to their profession, did fundamentally color the choices such people made in their self-presentation.

As discussed in chapter 2, this is because reputation as a social norm and institution is dependent on its audience, which changed depending on a merchant's context. As the previous chapters have demonstrated, Roman merchants rarely had a sympathetic audience and were aware of the bias that robbed them of goodwill, trust, and the all-important benefit of the doubt. Merchant reputation, as a result, was structured by the expectations of the communities in which they lived and worked. While merchants were, themselves, part of the communities that shaped the terms of reputation, audiences of merchants and nonmerchants alike consistently judged people in trade based on stereotypical, popular beliefs about how retailers, artisans, and transporters were likely to behave. Thus, merchants stressed that their reputations were firmly divorced from stereotypical traits and framed themselves as the positive antithesis of the greedy, dishonest, and antisocial caricature against which they were consistently measured.

These efforts were expensive, both in terms of time and funds. Striving to portray themselves as virtuous and community-minded was costly to merchants, as building interpersonal relationships took time and the displays that many merchants used, preserved for us in monuments, workspaces, and art, required a financial outlay. This expenditure limited merchant access to other avenues of investing in their business and cut back on immediate profits, but it was routinely understood as an investment that would pay off down the line. Publilius Syrus, ever ready with a cutting summary, framed it this way: *cui omnes bene dicunt possidet populi bona*, the man of whom all speak well will receive the favors of the people.[1]

Developing a reputation was further understood to be a necessary element of building and maintaining any business, even if the process of making a good name for oneself claimed resources that could be spent in other ways, such as buying more stock, hiring (or buying) new staff, or simply saving for the future. Further, the process of building a good name required merchants to rely on others, whether family and friends or peers and colleagues. Merchants started out by borrowing, effectively, the good name of others, people who would vouch for them until their work and personality could speak for itself. This interdependence was not always publicly recognized, because there was a strong bias in Roman society in favor of both self-sufficiency and narratives that presented merchant work as the result of a "boot-straps" mentality, but merchants starting out attached themselves to communities and associations where they would have the most support and where they could lean on the goodwill of others.

On top of these practical costs, reputation also served as a restriction,

1. Publilius Syrus, *Sent.* 126.

one that made some business practices unattractive, despite their short- or long-term profitability. Appropriate or "good" merchant behavior was circumscribed by reputation, and merchant practices conformed with its terms or found themselves experiencing the consequences that were brought about by a bad reputation.

Despite these disadvantages, building a good reputation and participating in this system was considered a worthwhile endeavor. Possessing a good name was believed to be a vital tool for achieving economic success. Merchants saw the reward in attempting to represent themselves in certain ways and allowed their options to be limited in order to secure those rewards. Merchants with a good reputation found that their transaction costs were reduced, that they needed to spend less time proving their honesty and quality, and that conflicts were more often settled in their favor. Some were able to avoid disputes entirely, simply because they were known to be good, reliable, or trustworthy. Reputation also helped merchants to establish rankings among themselves, to see when a comparison with their peers would be favorable and when it would not. Often, the same strategies that promoted a good reputation could additionally serve to advertise a merchant's business and represent it as somehow special or important.

Given the pervasiveness of reputation as a social institution, the strategies for performing and advertising one's good reputation were varied, but each came with benefits that could lead to profit, even if it was less immediate than the gains a merchant could enjoy by cheating a customer or hoarding their wealth. In the long term, reputation strategies paid out in regular customers, word of mouth advertisement, and common knowledge that a certain merchant should be preferred over his peers, because he was trustworthy, reliable, and maintained high standards of quality. A good reputation also cut back on petty annoyances and advanced a merchant's public standing, to the point, as we saw with Dio of Prusa and the blacksmith, that an artisan could be more highly regarded than a city benefactor, at least among certain audiences.[2]

Even in light of this kind of recompense, reputation maintenance was not cast as a mercenary activity. Rather, as our sources present it, caring for one's reputation was perceived to be a positive sign that a person cared the appropriate amount for their position in society and had prioritized behaviors that conformed with community norms. Even if there were concerns that flashy displays of generosity and virtue were performative, rather than sincere, it was the absence of any such behavior that provoked the most concern, as in the

2. Dio Chrys., *Or.* 47.10–11.

case of Milo the moneylender, especially since so often it was friendliness and sociability that were emphasized in a merchant's projection of his reputation.

Reputation was grounded in the community and establishing one's place within it, and as a result seeking a good reputation was not seen as a self-interested practice. Instead, it was seen as part of the dues one paid to live in Roman society and hold a place of significance in the community, whether that be a town, neighborhood, or association. These dues were not assessed in any kind of formal way, even in the case of groups in which membership came with a fee, but were based on how well a merchant was perceived to look after others. Thus, demonstrations of consistent service and generosity to others are most often stressed in merchant efforts to advertise their reputations. Whether these virtues came in the form of public benefactions or private ties of *amicitia*, merchant bragging about these specific kinds of good conduct was not a shameful undertaking, and, for our purposes, it reinforces our conception of the Roman trading world as a fundamentally interdependent sphere.

More than this, the virtues that merchants took care to display—generosity, friendship, honesty, and so forth—served as signals to the community that a merchant was not a free rider, but rather another supporter and enforcer of the norms the community shared. In advertising their own "goodness," merchants claimed that they would not only avoid misconduct themselves but would make efforts to police and punish those who shirked their responsibilities. At times these claims seem somewhat performative, as in the case of John's complaints about Diotrephes, but in other cases it seems that merchants were serious, and would use their own energy and resources to see to it that norms were enforced.[3] Rather than immediately turning to the state to see to it that cheaters and free riders were punished, merchants, like customers and community members, used private information networks and strategies to reveal, shame, and even ostracize those who failed to keep up a good reputation and treated social norms as optional, rather than essential, structures.

These efforts are regularly couched in language that binds reputation to moral values in our sources. People who broke with social conventions were labeled "bad" or "nasty," echoing the stereotypes that labeled merchants as "greedy" or "liars." It is here that the institutional force of reputation becomes apparent, and it is also the point at which it differs most from an institution like law. While a person who broke the law has committed a crime and will be expected to atone in a manner assessed by a judge, his or her status as "a criminal" is, for the kind of market infractions that typically affected merchants,

3. 3 John 1.

temporary and all but erased upon payment of the fine or completion of the contract. In the case of reputation, the impact of an infraction, be it commercial or social, lingered and was called upon frequently as a kind of social criminal-record. Being "a bad person" was a stain that was much more challenging to remove than a simple fine.

While legal stigma, and especially that which constrained merchants and tradesmen, might linger over a merchant's lifetime in the form of concrete prohibitions that limited upward mobility, social stigma pervaded the lives of tradesmen, even when they did not seek to move beyond or out of their profession.[4] A bad reputation could restrict a merchant's options for credit, reduce the amount of business they received, make prospective partners more wary and confrontational, and, most problematically, a bad reputation could create a vicious cycle in which a merchant could not afford the kind of reputation strategies that might help them salvage their good name. "Badness" in this case lingered and was reinforced by the long memories of close-knit communities that were vigilantly on guard against those who contravened local norms.

Yet, despite the very real risk that they themselves might one day be saddled with a bad reputation, as a result of malicious gossip or simple misinformation, merchants were still the ones who adopted a language of "goodness" when it came to their reputation. Merchants strove to be and appear "good," and couched their efforts to foster a good reputation as reflections, not of their good practices, but of their good nature. Thus, the Mithreses of the Roman world emphasized their kindness to their friends and generosity to the less fortunate, rather than their skill in sourcing the highest quality goat skins. While quality does appear as a concern among merchants, it is always secondary to their character. Thus, it was possible for Onesimus' business to not even be identified, while his wife carefully advertised and preserved the memory of his extreme honesty.[5] These character traits are near-universal and could easily be applied to members of many professions or even to elite men of leisure. *Fides*, especially, was a virtue that transcended the realm of trade, which makes it all the more interesting that merchants chose this as their supreme virtue, rather than hard work or high quality. These were important, to be sure, but secondary to moral concerns.

For the Roman merchant, then, appearing approachable, sociable, and hon-

---

4. Bond, *Trade and Taboo*; Lennon, *Dirt and Denigration*, cf. Flohr, *The World of the* Fullo. Importantly for our purposes, stigma is not coterminous with a bad reputation: Yuri Mishina and Cynthia E. Devers, "On Being Bad: Why Stigma Is Not the Same as a Bad Reputation," in *The Oxford Handbook of Corporate Reputation*, ed. Michael L. Barnett and Timothy G. Pollack (Oxford: Oxford University Press, 2012).

5. CIL 6.9663, see chapter 3.

est was more clearly the aim of reputation strategies than advertising that one was good at one's job. Perhaps, all things considered, most merchants felt that they were their peers' equal in terms of their skills—able to mend a shoe, bake a loaf of bread, sell a bolt of cloth, or transport produce with moderate facility—but it was in matters of customer service and interpersonal relationships that one could more successfully distinguish oneself. Plutarch scorns the mediocre innkeeper who hopes to draw in repeat customers by offering them effusive welcomes, but such an action seems wholly consistent with what a "good" merchant should be doing to stand out, advertise his business, and secure a reputation as a frontrunner in his field.[6] Friendliness, social literacy, and conformity with community standards more closely align with "goodness" than talent, skill, and quality.

Though the adoption of this language by merchants was intended to make their professions more approachable and likable, this framework nevertheless formed the foundation of the way that outsiders spoke about those in trade. The rhetoric of "goodness," helped nonmerchants to justify the institutional checks that were used to restrain merchants both socially and economically. A "bad merchant" was easily elided with a "bad person," and "bad people" in the Roman world deserved the treatment they received, including legal stigma and social marginality, even in the field of commerce, where merchants were undeniably necessary. We have already noted that stereotypes justify the status quo, but in the Roman world this same justification was additionally framed as maintaining the *mores* that both merchants and the wider community recognized as inviolable. A good merchant was one that understood, conformed to, and enforced these norms, and merchants, on the whole, did nothing to upset or restructure current thinking on issues of morality. Rather, they policed each other just as much as they allowed themselves to be policed.

Importantly, this kind of moralizing was not merely performative, but rather was an integral part of how merchants viewed themselves and the choices they made. The prominence of *fama* and δόξα in merchant funerary monuments and inscriptions demonstrates how intimately connected reputation was to a merchant's sense of self. One's reputation was the identity that one wore on a day-to-day basis and it was critical to preserve it for posterity. Merchants perhaps carried an exaggerated sense of their own ability to influence and encapsulate their reputation, but they considered their reputations to be the result of a lifetime of good behaviors, consistent practices, and personal virtues that were recognized and understood by everyone around them. It was through this com-

6. Plut., *De vitioso* 8.

mon knowledge that they defined themselves, just as they used similar means to define and categorize everyone around them.

The Roman world, and especially that world as experienced by small-scale merchants, traders, and artisans, was a close-knit, face-to-face place where customers and sellers battled out their social standing alongside their negotiations over prices. Reputation was the result of a history of meetings and connections and incidents that lent structure to the meetings and connections and incidents that would come in the future. Merchants and customers alike used it to make business decisions, to decide whom to trust, whom to avoid, and how to respond when challenges arose. In general, however, reputation was a passive partner to trade, the sort of institution that merchants only brought to the level of their conscious thought when it came time to reflect on their lives, or when they needed to leverage their social capital. Unconsciously, it was their regular companion, guiding their choices and making it easier for them to predict the choices of others.

As the strength of Roman legal and governmental institutions waxed and waned over time and varied across the swath of the Mediterranean territory the Romans controlled, it was local and especially social institutions that held firm, keeping the market in relative check and structuring the behavior of merchants. Merchant reputation, both their concern for it and the actions of others to police it, helped to define what conduct was acceptable and what was to be avoided. As merchants strove to be moral and respectable members of their communities, whether the state could or would intervene to uphold the law of the land became a secondary concern, because merchants could be expected to police themselves and each other, thereby supporting a system where responsibility to each other kept the economy running.

We have come a long way from Philostratus' merchant, trying to navigate a difficult conversation with a biased vinedresser, yet his experience and decision-making is fundamentally more intelligible when situated in a world that we know valued social relationships and social standing as much as profits.[7] In fact, the social network that the merchant was, fictionally, a part of contextualized his financial successes, clarifying which profits reflected "good" praxis on his part and which did not. Bearing reputation in mind helps us to see real figures like Mithres, Sotas, and even the apostle Paul as part of complex systems of interdependency, mutual awareness, and competition that were not allowed to run wild, but had their own structure and logic that protected the economy from self-destruction. More than this, when we consider that each merchant's

7. Philostr., *Her.* 1.3–1.7.

choices were analyzed by his contemporaries in light of his reputation, we can see how appearances and social connections inevitably influenced the decisions any merchant made and felt he could make.

Physical issues of supply, seasonality, and prices have thus far been the concern of scholars of the Roman economy, even those who have adopted an institutional, or new institutional, approach. While the lives of Roman merchants offer plentiful fodder for such investigations, this work cannot, on its own, provide a means of understanding why merchants acted as they did. When we see a merchant changing the type of product he transported, economic rationalism says that we must attribute this to the goods that were available to him and to his inherent desire for profit. New institutional theory, at least as applied by Roman economists, suggests that, if a merchant did not pursue profit, it was because he abided by the legal standards established by the state, in order to have recourse to those same standards should others break their contracts or otherwise violate the law. While there is truth behind such reasoning, this perspective limits our possible conclusions, somewhat conforms to Roman stereotypes about the greed of those in commerce, and places all agency in the hands of traditional sources of authority. When merchants are situated in a community, and when their concern for their reputations comes into play, we can deduce that the personalities of producers and retailers, customs officials and service providers were all influences upon the economic choices that were made, and we must accept that those choices were no less rational for being motivated by social, as well as economic, considerations.

Ultimately, it is the interconnectedness of these factors, the social and the economic, that motivated, limited, and rewarded Roman merchants. There has, rightly, been pushback against the application of New Institutional Economic theory to the ancient economy, but there remains room, within its structures, to consider the institutional power of society to regulate itself. Doing so returns agency to merchants, artisans, and transporters as well as to the small worlds they inhabited. It ultimately clarifies how a merchant could, and how merchants did, get by and ahead despite the irregularity and unpredictability of the Roman world.

Bibliography

Abrahams, Roger D. "A Performance-Centred Approach to Gossip." *Man* 5.5 (1970): 290–301.

Adams, Colin E. P., and Nikolaos Gonis. "Two Customs-House Receipts from the Bodleian Library." *Zeitschrift für Papyrologie und Epigraphik* 126 (1999): 213–18.

Agrell, Göran. *Work, Toil and Sustenance: An Examination of the View of Work in the New Testament, Taking into Consideration Views Found in Old Testament, Intertestamental, and Early Rabbinic Writings*. Translated by Stephen Westerholm. Lund: Verbum-Håksn Ohlssons, 1976.

Aguilar, John L. "Trust and Exchange: Expressive and Instrumental Dimensions of Reciprocity in a Peasant Community." *Ethos: American Anthropological Association* 12.1 (1984): 3–29.

Allen, Robert C. "How Prosperous Were the Romans? Evidence from Diocletian's Price Edict (301 AD)." In *Quantifying the Roman Economy*, edited by Alan Bowman and Andrew Wilson, 327–45. Oxford: Oxford University Press, 2009.

Allport, Gordon W. *The Nature of Prejudice*. Reading: Basic Books, 1954.

Almeida, E. Rodríguez. *Los tituli picti de las ánforas olearias de la Bética I*. Madrid: Editorial de la Universidad Complutense, 1989.

Altman, Janet Gurkin. *Epistolarity: Approaches to a Form*. Columbus: Ohio State University Press, 1982.

Amit, David. "Jewish Bread Stamps and Wine and Oil Seals from the Late Second Temple, Mishnaic, and Talmudic Periods." In *"See, I Will Bring a Scroll Recounting What Befell Me" (PS 40:8): Epigraphy and Daily Life from the Bible to the Talmud*, edited by Esther Eshel and Yigal Levin, 159–74. Göttingen: Vandenhoeck und Ruprecht, 2014.

Ando, Clifford. *Imperial Ideology and Provincial Loyalty in the Roman Empire*. Berkeley: University of California Press, 2013.

Ando, Clifford. "Legal Pluralism in Practice." In *The Oxford Handbook of Roman Law and Society*, edited by Paul du Plessis, Clifford Ando, and Kaius Tuori, 283–93. Oxford: Oxford University Press, 2016.

Andrade, Nathanael J. *Syrian Identity in the Greco-Roman World*. Cambridge: Cambridge University Press, 2013.

Andreau, Jean. *Banking and Business in the Roman World*. Cambridge: Cambridge University Press, 1999.

Andreau, Jean. *Patrimoines, échanges et prêts d'argent: L'économie romaine*. Rome: L'Erma di Bretschneider, 1997.

Andreau, Jean. "Sull'economia di Pompei." In *Pompei*, edited by P. G. Guzzo, 109–10. Milan: Mondadori Electa, 2001.

Aoyagi, Masanori, and Umberto Pappalardo. *Pompei: Regiones VI–VII; Insula Occidentalis.* Vol. 1. Naples: Arbor Sapientiae, 2006.

Appadurai, Arjun, ed. *The Social Life of Things: Commodities in Cultural Perspective.* Cambridge: Cambridge University Press, 1988.

Archibald, Zofia H. "Making the Most of One's Friends: Western Asia Minor in the Early Hellenistic Age." In *Hellenistic Economies*, edited by Zofia H. Archibald, John Davies, Vincent Gabrielsen, and G. J. Oliver. New York: Routledge, 2001.

Arnaud, Pascal. "Cities and Maritime Trade under the Roman Empire." In *Connecting the Ancient World: Mediterranean Shipping, Maritime Networks and Their Impact*, edited by Christoph Schafer, 1–30. Rahden: Marie Leidorf, 2016.

Ascough, Richard S. "The Thessalonian Christian Community as a Professional Voluntary Association." *Journal of Biblical Literature* 119.2 (2000): 311–28.

Ascough, Richard S., Philip A. Harland, and John S. Kloppenborg. *Associations in the Greco-Roman World: A Sourcebook.* Waco: Baylor University Press, 2012.

Aslanian, Sebouh. "Social Capital, 'Trust' and the Role of Networks in Julfan Trade: Informal and Semi-Formal Institutions at Work." *Journal of Global History* 1.3 (2006): 383–402.

Atkins, Margaret, and Robin Osborne. *Poverty in the Roman World.* Cambridge: Cambridge University Press, 2006.

Aubert, Jean-Jacques. *Business Managers in Ancient Rome: A Social and Economic Study of* Institores, *200 B.C.–A.D. 250.* Leiden: Brill, 1994.

Aula, Pekka, and Saku Mantere. *Strategic Reputation Management: Towards a Company of Good.* New York: Routledge, 2008.

Badian, Ernst. *Publicans and Sinners: Private Enterprise in the Service of the Roman Republic.* Ithaca: Cornell University Press, 1972.

Bailey, F. G. *Gifts and Poison: The Politics of Reputation.* New York: Schocken Books, 1971.

Baird, Jennifer A. "Shopping, Eating and Drinking at Dura Europos: Reconstructing Contexts." In *Objects in Context, Objects in Use: Material Spatiality in Late Antiquity*, edited by Luke Lavan, Ellen Swift, and Toon Putzeys, 413–38. Leiden: Brill, 2007.

Baird, Jennifer A., and Claire Taylor. *Ancient Graffiti in Context.* New York: Routledge, 2012.

Baldacci, Paolo. "Commercio e stato nell'età dei Severi." *Rendiconti dell'Istituto Lombardo di Scienza e Lettere* 101 (1967): 729–47.

Banaji, Jairus. *Exploring the Economy of Late Antiquity: Selected Essays.* Cambridge: Cambridge University Press, 2016.

Banfield, Edward C. *The Moral Basis of a Backward Society.* New York: Free Press, 1958.

Bang, Peter F. "Imperial Bazaar: Towards a Comparative Understanding of Markets in the Roman Empire." In *Ancient Economies, Modern Methodologies: Archaeology, Comparative History, Models and Institutions*, edited by Peter F. Bang, Mamoru Ikeguchi, and Hartmut G. Ziche, 51–88. Bari: Edipuglia, 2006.

Bang, Peter F. *The Roman Bazaar: A Comparative Study of Trade and Markets in a Tributary Empire.* Cambridge: Cambridge University Press, 2011.

Bang, Peter F., Mamoru Ikeguchi, and Hartmut G. Ziche. *Ancient Economies, Modern Methodologies: Archaeology, Comparative History, Models and Institutions*. Bari: Edipuglia, 2006.

Banner, Michael. *The Ethics of Everyday Life: Moral Theology, Social Anthropology, and the Imagination of the Human*. Oxford: Oxford University Press, 2014.

Bar-Isaac, Heski, and Steven Tadelis. "Seller Reputation." *Foundations and Trends in Microeconomics* 4.4 (2008): 273–351.

Barot, A. "Les naviculaires d'Arles a Beyrouth." *Revue archéologique* 4.5 (1905): 262–72.

Bendlin, Andreas. "Associations, Funerals, Sociality, and Roman Law: The *Collegium* of Diana and Antinous in Lanuvium (CIL 14.2112) Reconsidered." In *Aposteldekret und antikes Verinswesen: Gemeinschaft und ihre Ordnung*, edited by Markus Öhler, 207–96. Tübingen: Mohr Siebeck Verlag, 2011.

Benefiel, Rebecca R. "Dialogues of Ancient Graffiti in the House of Maius Castricius in Pompeii." *American Journal of Archaeology* 114.1 (2010): 59–101.

Berdowski, Piotr. "Roman Businesswomen I: The Case of the Producers and Distributors of Garum in Pompeii." *Analecta Archaeologica Ressoviensia* 3 (2008): 251–71.

Berdowski, Piotr. "*Tituli picti* und die antike Werbesprache für Fischprodukte." *Münstersche Beiträge zur antiken Handelsgeschichte* 22.2 (2003): 18–54.

Bergmann, Jörg. *Discreet Indiscretions: The Social Organization of Gossip*. Translated by John Bednarz Jr. Berlin: Walter de Gruyter, 1994.

Berlin, Andrea M. "Romanization and anti-Romanization in pre-Revolt Galilee." In *The First Jewish Revolt: Archaeology, History, and Ideology*, edited by Andrea M. Berlin and J. Andrew Overman, 57–71. New York: Routledge, 2002.

Bernal-Casasola, Dario, and Daniela Cottica. "Produzione e vendita di pesce sotto sale e suoi derivati a Pompei nel 79 d.C.: Le evidenze dalla cosiddetta Bottega di garum (I, 12, 8)." In *L'exploitation des ressources maritimes de l'Antiquité: Activités productives et organisation des territoires, actes des rencontres, 11–13 octobre 2016*, edited by Ricardo González Villaescusa, Katia Schörle, Frédéric Gayet, and François Rechin, 235–52. Antibes: Éditions APDCA, 2017.

Bintliff, J. L. "Going to Market in Antiquity." In *Zu Wasser und zu Land, stuttgarter Kolloquium* 7, edited by S. H. Olshausen, 209–50. Stuttgart: Franz Steiner Verlag, 2002.

Birley, Anthony R. *Garrison Life at Vindolanda: A Band of Brothers*. Stroud: Tempus, 2002.

Birley, Anthony R. *The People of Roman Britain*. Berkeley: University of California Press, 1980.

Birnbaum, Michael H. "Morality Judgment: Test of an Averaging Model with Differential Weights." *Journal of Experimental Psychology* 99.3 (1973): 395–99.

Biscotti, Barbara. "Il mercante e il contadino." *Labeo: Rassegna di diritto romano* 45.3 (1999): 368–91.

Blanton, Thomas R., and Raymond Pickett. *Paul and Economics: A Handbook*. Minneapolis: Fortress Press, 2017.

Boak, A. E. R. "The Organization of Gilds in Greco-Roman Egypt." *Transactions and Proceedings of the American Philological Association* 68 (1937): 212–20.

Boak, A. E. R., and H. C. Youtie, eds. *The Archive of Aurelius Isidorus in the Egyptian Museum Cairo and the University of Michigan*. Ann Arbor: University of Michigan Press, 1960.

Boatwright, Mary T. *Hadrian and the Cities of the Roman Empire*. Princeton: Princeton University Press, 2002.

Bodel, John. "*Caveat Emptor*: Towards a Study of Roman Slave-Traders." *Journal of Roman Archaeology* 18 (2005): 181–95.

Boldizzoni, Francesco. *The Poverty of Clio: Resurrecting Economic History*. Princeton: Princeton University Press, 2011.

Bolton, Gary E., Elena Katok, and Axel Ockenfels. "Cooperation among Strangers with Limited Information about Reputation." *Journal of Public Economics* 9.8 (2005): 1457–68.

Bond, Sarah E. "Altering Infamy: Status, Violence, and Civic Exclusion in Late Antiquity." *Classical Antiquity* 33.1 (2014): 1–30.

Bond, Sarah E. *Trade and Taboo: Disreputable Professions in the Roman Mediterranean*. Ann Arbor: University of Michigan Press, 2016.

Bonner, Stanley F. *Education in Ancient Rome: From Cato the Elder to Pliny the Younger*. New York: Routledge, 1977.

Bordalo, Pedro, Nicola Gennaioli, and Andrei Shleifer. "Competition for Attention." National Bureau of Economic Research. Working Paper 19076 (2013).

Botha, Pieter J. J. "Paul and Gossip: A Social Mechanism in Early Christian Communities." *Neotestamentica* 32.2 (1998): 267–88.

Bourdieu, Pierre. "The Forms of Capital." In *Handbook of Theory and Research for the Sociology of Education*, edited by J. G. Richardson, 241–58. New York: Greenwood Press, 1986.

Bourdieu, Pierre. "Le capital social." *Actes de la recherche en sciences sociales* 31 (1980): 2–3.

Bowersock, Glanwell W. "The *Aethiopica* of Heliodorus and the *Historia Augusta*." *Historiae Augustae Colloquium Genevese* 2 (1994): 42–52.

Bowes, Kim. "When Kuznets Went to Rome: Roman Economic Well-Being and the Reframing of Roman History." *Capitalism: A Journal of History and Economics* 2.1 (2021): 7–40.

Bowman, Alan K. "Documentary Papyrology and Ancient History." In *Atti del XXII Congresso internazionale di papirologia, Firenze, 23–29 agosto 1998*, edited by Isabella Andorlini, Guido Bastianini, Manfredo Manfredi, and Giovanna Menci, 137–45. Florence: Istituto Papirologico G. Vitelli, 2001.

Bowman, Alan K., and Andrew Wilson, eds. *Quantifying the Roman Economy: Methods and Problems*. Oxford: Oxford University Press, 2013.

Bradley, Keith R. "Child Labour in the Roman World." *Historical Reflections* 12.2 (1985): 311–30.

Bradley, Keith R. *Slavery and Society at Rome*. Cambridge: Cambridge University Press, 1994.

Bresson, Alain. "Économie et institution: Bilan critique des thèses polanyiennes et propositions nouvelles." In *Autour de Polanyi: Vocabulaires, théories et modalités des échanges, Nanterre, 12–14 juin 2004*, edited by Philippe Clancier, Francis Joannes, Pierre Rouillard, and Aline Tenu, 97–111. Paris: De Boccard, 2005.

Bresson, Alain. *The Making of the Ancient Greek Economy: Institutions, Markets, and Growth in the City-States*. Princeton: Princeton University Press, 2015.

Brewster, Ethel Hampson. *Roman Craftsmen and Tradesmen of the Early Roman Empire.* Menasha: Collegiate Press, 1917.

Broekaert, Wim. "Conflicts, Contract Enforcement, and Business Communities in the Archive of the Sulpicii." In *The Economy of Pompeii*, edited by Miko Flohr and Andrew Wilson, 387–414. Oxford: Oxford University Press, 2016.

Broekaert, Wim. "Creatio ex nihilo? The Origin of the Corpora Nauiculariorum Reconsidered." *Latomus* 67.3 (2008): 692–706.

Broekaert, Wim. *Navicularii et negotiantes: A Prosopographical Study of Roman Merchants and Shippers.* Rahden: Marie Leidorf, 2013.

Broekaert, Wim. "Partners in Business: Roman Merchants and the Potential Advantages of Being a *Collegiatus*." *Ancient Society* 41 (2011): 221–56.

Broekaert, Wim. "Tied Down, Wings Cut? The Relation between the State and the Navicularii during the Later Roman Empire." In *Transforming Historical Landscapes in the Ancient Empires*, edited by Borja Antela Bernárdez and Toni Ñaco del Hoyo, 169–73. Oxford: B.A.R., 1986.

Broekaert, Wim. "Vertical Integration in the Roman Economy: A Response to Morris Silver." *Ancient Society* 42 (2012): 109–25.

Broekaert, Wim, and Wouter Vanacker. "Raiders to Traders? Economics of Integration among Nomadic Communities in North Africa." In *Rome and the Worlds beyond Its Frontiers*, edited by Daniëlle Slootjes and Michael Peachin, 96–122. Leiden: Brill, 2016.

Bromley, D. B. *Reputation, Image and Impression Management*. New York: John Wiley and Sons, 1993.

Brughmans, Tom, and Jeroen Poblome. "Roman Bazaar or Market Economy? An Agent-Based Network Model of Tableware Trade and Distribution in the Roman East." *Antiquity* 90 (2016): 393–408.

Bruschi, Christian. "Les munera publica: L'état et la cité au début du Bas Empire." In *Sodalitas: Scritti in Onore di Antonio Guarino*. Vol. 3, edited by Vincenzo Giuffrè, 1311–31. Naples: Jovene, 1984.

Bryen, Ari Z. "Law in Many Pieces." *Classical Philology* 109.4 (2014): 346–65.

Bryen, Ari Z. *Violence in Roman Egypt: A Study in Legal Interpretation*. Philadelphia: University of Pennsylvania Press, 2013.

Buecheler, Franz, Alexander Riese, and Ernst Lommatzsch. *Anthologia latina sive poesis latinae supplementum*. Edited by Franciscus Buecheler and Alexander Riese. Leipzig: Teubner, 1895.

Buonopane, Alfredo, and Carla Corti. "T. Aelius Evangelus: Due inscrizioni, una compagna, una figlia naturale, una moglie e un *lanificium*." *Sylloge Epigraphica Barcinonensis* 16 (2018): 123–38.

Burford, Alison. *Craftsmen in Greek and Roman Society*. Aspects of Greek and Roman Life. Ithaca: Cornell University Press, 1972.

Calpino, Teresa J. *Women, Work and Leadership in Acts*. Tübingen: Mohr Siebeck, 2014.

Campbell, John Kennedy. *Honour, Family and Patronage: A Study of Institutions and Moral Values in a Greek Mountain Community*. Oxford: Oxford University Press, 1964.

Campbell, Virginia L. "The Epitaph of Aulus Umbricius Scaurus (CIL X 1024): A Reconsideration." *Zeitschrift für Papyrologie und Epigraphik* 174 (2010): 229–36.

Carrié, Jean-Michel. "L'economia e le finanze." In *Storia di Roma*. Vol. 3, *L'Età Tardoantica*. I, *Crisi e Trasformazioni*, edited by Andrea Carandini, 751–87. Turin: Giulio Einaudi editore, 1993.

Carrié, Jean-Michel. "Les associations professionnelles à l'époque tardive: Entre munus et convivialité." In *"Humana sapit": Études d'antiquité tardive offertes à Lellia Cracco Ruggini*, edited by Jean-Michel Carrié and Rita Lizzi Testa, 309–32. BAT 3. Turnhout: Bropols, 2002.

Carroll, Maureen. *Spirits of the Dead: Roman Funerary Commemoration in Western Europe*. Oxford: Oxford University Press, 2006.

Carroll, Maureen. "Vox tua nempe mea est: Dialogues with the Dead in Roman Funerary Commemoration." *Accordia Research Papers* 11 (2007/2008): 37–80.

Carter, Michael. "Gladiatorial Ranking and the '*SC de Pretiis Gladiatorum Minuendis*' (CIL II 6278 = ILS 5163)." *Phoenix* 57.1/2 (2003): 83–114.

Champlin, Edward. "The Testament of the Piglet." *Phoenix* 41.2 (1987):174–83.

Charlesworth, Martin Percival. "Providentia and Aeternitas." *Harvard Theological Review* 29.2 (1936): 107–32.

Cherry, David. *Frontier and Society in Roman North Africa*. Oxford: Clarendon Press, 1998.

Chio, Filippo Boscolo. "Carpentarii a Patavium." In *Epigrafia 2006*, edited by M. L. Caldelli, G. L. Gregori, and S. Orlandi, 811–20. Rome: Edizioni Quasar, 2008..

Christensen, Arne Søby. *Lactantius the Historian: An Analysis of the De mortibus persecutorum*. Copenhagen: Museum Tusculanum Press, 1980.

Christol, Michel. "Les naviculaires d'Arles et les structures du grand commerce maritime sous l'Empire romain." *Provence historique* 32.127 (1982): 5–14.

Christol, Michel. "Remarques sur les naviculaires d'Arles." *Latomus* 30 (1971): 645–63.

Clarke, John R. *Art in the Lives of Ordinary Romans: Visual Representation and Non-Elite Viewers in Italy, 100 B.C.–A.D. 315*. Berkeley: University of California Press, 2003.

Cleary, Simon Esmonde. *The Roman West, AD 200–500: An Archaeological Study*. Cambridge: Cambridge University Press, 2013.

Clemente, Guido. "Il patronato nei collegia dell'impero romano." *Studi Classici ed Orientali* 21 (1972): 142–229.

Coase, Ronald H. "The Nature of the Firm." *Economica* 4.16 (1937): 386–405.

Coase, Ronald H. "The New Institutional Economics." *Zeitschrift für die gesamte Staatswissenschaft / Journal of Institutional and Theoretical Economics* 140.1 (1984): 229–31.

Coase, Ronald H. "The Problem of Social Cost." *Journal of Law and Economics* 3 (1960): 1–44.

Coleman, James S. *Foundations of Social Theory*. Cambridge, MA: Belknap Press, 1990.

Concannon, Cavan W. *Assembling Early Christianity: Trade, Networks, and the Letters of Dionysios of Corinth*. Cambridge: Cambridge University Press, 2017.

Connolly, Joy. *The State of Speech: Rhetoric and Political Thought in Ancient Rome*. Princeton: Princeton University Press, 2007.

Connolly, Serena. "Disticha Catonis Uticensis." *Classical Philology* 107.2 (2012): 119–30.

Connolly, Serena. *Lives behind the Laws: The World of the Codex Hermogenianus*. Bloomington: Indiana University Press, 2010.

Constable, Olivia Remie. *Housing the Stranger in the Mediterranean World: Lodging, Trade, and Travel in Late Antiquity and the Middle Ages*. Cambridge: Cambridge University Press, 2003.

Conybeare, F. C. *Philostratus: The Life of Apollonius of Tyana*. 2 vols. New York: Macmillan, 1912.

Cook, Karen S., Russell Hardin, and Margaret Levi. *Cooperation without Trust?* New York: Russell Sage Foundation, 2005.

Corcoran, Simon. "The Codex of Justinian: The Life of a Text through 1,500 Years." In *The Codex of Justinian: A New Annotated Translation, with Parallel Latin and Greek Text*, edited by Bruce Frier, xcvii–clxiv. Cambridge: Cambridge University Press, 2016.

Corcoran, Simon. *The Empire of the Tetrarchs: Imperial Pronouncements and Government AD 284–324*. Oxford: Clarendon Press, 2000.

Corcoran, Thomas H. "Roman Fishermen." *Classical World* 56.4 (1963): 97–100, 102.

Corti, Carla. "Pesi e misure nei commerci, arti, mestieri e professioni." In *Pondera: Pesi e Misure nell'antichita*, edited by Carla Corti and Nicoletta Giordani, 143–66. Campogalliano: Museo della Bilancia, 2001.

Cottier, Michel. "The Customs Districts of Roman Egypt." In *Proceedings of the Twenty-Fifth International Congress of Papyrology, Ann Arbor 2007, American Studies in Papyrology*, edited by Traianos Gagos, 141–48. Ann Arbor: University of Michigan Press, 2010.

Cotton, Hannah. *Documentary Letters of Recommendation in Latin from the Roman Empire*. Konigstein: Anton Hain, 1981.

Courtney, E. "Greek and Latin Acrostics." *Philologus* 134 (1990): 1–13.

Coutsoumpos, Panayotis. *Paul, Corinth, and the Roman Empire*. Eugene: Wipf and Stock, 2015.

Cracco-Ruggini, Lellia. "Collegium e corpus: La politica economica nella legislazione e nella prassi." In *Istituzioni Giuridiche e Realtà Politiche nel Tardo Impero (III–V Sec. D. C.)*, edited by G. G. Archi, 63–94. Milan: A. Giuffre, 1976.

Cracco-Ruggini, Lellia. "Esperienze economiche e sociali nel mondo romano." In *Nuove Questioni di Storia Antica*, edited by G. Giannelli, Adriana Soffredi, Gabriella Guidi, Luisa Bongrani Fanfoni, Marta Sordi, and Marcello Fortina, 685–813. Milan: Marzorati, 1968.

Craik, Kenneth H. *Reputation: A Network Interpretation*. Oxford: Oxford University Press, 2009.

Crawford, Michael H. "Discovery, Autopsy and Progress: Diocletian's Jigsaw Puzzles." In *Classics in Progress: Essays on Ancient Greece and Rome*, edited by T. P. Wiseman, 145–65. Oxford: Oxford University Press, 2006.

Crawford, Michael H., and Joyce Reynolds. "The Aezani Copy of the Prices Edict." *Zeitschrift für Papyrologie und Epigraphik* 26 (1977): 125–51.

Crawford, Michael H., and Joyce Reynolds. "The Publication of the Prices Edict: A New Inscription from Aezani." *Journal of Roman Studies* 65 (1975): 160–63.

Creed, J. L., ed. *Lactantius: De mortibus persecutorum*. Oxford: Clarendon Press, 1984.

Crogiez-Pétrequin, Sylvie, and Pierre Jaillette, eds. *Société, économie, administration dans le "Code Théodosien."* Villeneuve d'Ascq: Presses Universitaires de Septentrion, 2012.

Curtis, Robert I. "A. Umbricius Scarus of Pompeii." In *Studia Pompeiana et Classica in Honor of Wilhelmina F. Jashemski*, edited by Robert I. Curtis, 19–50. New York: Caratzas, 1988.

Curtis, Robert I. *Garum and Salsamenta: Production and Commerce in Materia Medica.* Leiden: Brill, 1991.Curtis, Robert I. "A Personalized Floor Mosaic from Pompeii." *American Journal of Archaeology* 88.4 (1984): 557–66.

Curtis, Robert I. "Product Identification and Advertising on Roman Commercial Amphorae." *Ancient Society* 15/17 (1984): 209–28.

Curtis, Robert I. "The Salted Fish Industry of Pompeii." *Archaeology* 37.6 (1984): 58–75.

Czajkowski, Kimberley, and Benedikt Eckhardt. "Law, Status and Agency in the Roman Provinces." *Past and Present* 241.1 (2018): 3–31.

Daguet-Gagey, Anne. "L'arc des argentiers, à Rome: À propos de la dédicace du monument (CIL VI, 1035 = 31232 = ILS 426)." *Revue historique* 307.3 (2005): 499–519.

Damon, Cynthia. *The Mask of the Parasite: A Pathology of Roman Patronage.* Ann Arbor: University of Michigan Press, 1997.

Daniels, John W. "Gossip in the New Testament." *Biblical Theology Bulletin* 42.4 (2012): 204–13.

Dari-Mattiacci, Giuseppe, and Dennis P. Kehoe, eds. *Roman Law and Economics.* 2 vols. Oxford: Oxford University Press, 2020.

D'Arms, John H. *Commerce and Social Standing in Ancient Rome.* Cambridge, MA: Harvard University Press, 1981.

D'Arms, John H. "M. I. Rostovtzeff and M. I. Finley: The Status of Traders in the Roman World." In *Ancient and Modern: Essays in Honor of Gerald F. Else*, edited by John W. Eadie, 159–79. Ann Arbor: University of Michigan Press, 1977.

Davidson, James. *Courtesans and Fishcakes: The Consuming Passions of Classical Athens.* New York: St. Martin's Press, 1997.

Davies, R. W. "The Enlistment of Claudius Terentianus." *Bulletin of the American Society of Papyrologists* 10.1–4 (1973): 21–25.

de Blois, Lukas, ed. *Administration, Prosopography and Appointment Policies in the Roman Empire.* Leiden: Brill, 2001.

de Blois, Lukas. *Image and Reality of Roman Imperial Power in the Third Century AD: The Impact of War.* New York: Routledge, 2018.

de Certeau, Michel. *The Practice of Everyday Life.* Berkeley: University of California Press, 2011.

de Hoz, Javier. "The Greek Man in the Iberian Street: Non-Colonial Greek Identity in Spain and Southern France." In *Greek Identity in the Western Mediterranean: Papers in Honour of Brian Shefton*, edited by Kathryn Lomas, 411–27. Leiden: Brill, 2004.

de Laet, Siegfried J. *Portorium: Étude sur l'organisation douanière chez les Romains, surtout à l'époque du Haut-Empire.* New York: Arno Press, 1975.

de Ligt, Luuk. "Demand, Supply, Distribution: The Roman Peasantry between Town and Countryside; Rural Monetization and Peasant Demands." *Münstersche Beiträge zur antiken Handelsgeschichte* 9.2 (1990): 24–56.

de Ligt, Luuk. *Fairs and Markets in the Roman Empire: Economic and Social Aspects of Periodic Trade in a Pre-Industrial Society.* Leiden: Brill, 1993.

de Ligt, Luuk. "The Nunidinae of L. Bellicius Sollers." In *De Agricultura: In Memoriam*

Pieter-Willem de Neeve, edited by Heleen Sancisi-Weerdenburg, 238–62. Amsterdam: J. C. Gieben, 1993.

de Ligt, Luuk. "Restraining the Rich, Protecting the Poor: Symbolic Aspects of Roman Legislation." In *After the Past: Essays in Ancient History in Honour of H. W. Pleket*, edited by Willem Jongman and Marc Kleijwegt, 1–46. Mnemosyne Supplements 233. Leiden: Brill, 2002.

de Ligt, Luuk. "Roman Law and the Roman Economy: Three Case Studies." *Latomus* 66.1 (2007): 10–25.

de Ligt, Luuk. "The Roman Peasantry: Demand, Supply, Distribution between Town and Countryside II; Supply, Distribution and a Comparative Perspective." *Münstersche Beiträge zur antiken Handelsgeschichte* 10.1 (1991): 33–77.

de Ligt, Luuk, and P. W. de Neeve. *Ancient Periodic Markets: Festivals and Fairs*. Pavia: Amministrazione di Athenaeum, Università di Pavia, 1988.

della Corte, Matteo. *Case ed abitanti di Pompei*. Naples: Fausto Fiorentino, 1965.

de Marchi, Neil, and Mary S. Morgan, eds. *Higgling: Transactors and Their Markets in the History of Economics*. Durham: Duke University Press, 1994.

de Maria, Sandro. *Gli archi onorari di Roma e dell'Italia romana*. Rome: L'Erma di Bretschneider, 1988.

de Munck, Bert, Steven L. Kaplan, and Hugo Soly, eds. *Learning on the Shop Floor: Historical Perspectives on Apprenticeship*. New York: Berghahn Books, 2007.

de Robertis, Francesco Maria. "Il corpus naviculariorum nella stratificazione sociale del Basso Impero." *Rivista del Diritto della Navigazione* 3 (1937): 189–215.

de Robertis, Francesco Maria. *Lavoro e lavoratori nel mondo romano*. New York: Arno Press, 1979.

de Robertis, Francesco Maria. *Storia delle corporazioni e del regime associativo nel mondo romano*. Bari: Adriatica, 1971.

de Ruggiero, Ettore. *Dizionario epigrafico di antichità romane*. Rome: Istituto Italiano per la Storia antica, 1895.

de Salvo, Lietta. *Economia privata e pubblici servizi nell'impero romano: I corpora naviculariorum*. Messina: Samperi, 1992.

de Salvo, Lietta. "Nuove testimonianze (e riletture) di testi epigrafici relativi a navicularii e battellieri." In *Orbis Antiquus: Studia in Honorem Ioannis Pisonis*, edited by Ligia Ruscu, Carmen Ciongradi, Rady Ardevan, Cristian Roman, and Cristian Gădzac, 120–24. Cluj-Napoca: Nereamia Napocae Press, 2004.

de Souza, Philip. *Piracy in the Graeco-Roman World*. Cambridge: Cambridge University Press, 1999.

Dickmann, Jens-Arne. "A 'Private' Felter's Workshop in the Casa dei Postumii at Pompeii." In *Making Textiles in Pre-Roman and Roman Times: People, Places, Identities*, edited by Margaria Gleba and Judit Pásztókai-Szeöke, 208–28. Oxford: Oxbow Books, 2013.

Diehl, Ernst. *Vulgärlateinische Inschriften*. Berlin: Walter de Gruyter, 1910.

Dohrmann, Natalie B. "Law and Imperial Idioms: Rabbinic Legalism in a Roman World." In *Jews, Christians, and the Roman Empire: Poetics of Power in Late Antiquity*, edited by Natalie B. Dohrmann and Annette Yoshiko Reed, 63–78. Philadelphia: University of Pennsylvania Press, 2013.

Donahue, John F. *The Roman Community at Table during the Principate*. Ann Arbor: University of Michigan Press, 2004.

Donahue, John F. "Toward a Typology of Roman Public Feasting." *American Journal of Philology* 124.3 (2003): 423–41.

Drake, H. A., ed. *Violence in Late Antiquity: Perceptions and Practices*. Burlington: Ashgate, 2006.

Drexhage, Hans-Joachim, Heinrich Konen, and Kai Ruffing. *Die Wirtschaft des römischen Reiches (1.-3. Jahrhundert): Eine Einführung*. Berlin: Walter de Gruyter, 2002.

Duff, J. Wight, and Arnold M. Duff. *Minor Latin Poets*. Vol. 1, *Publilius Syrus, Elegies on Maecenas, Grattius, Etc*. Cambridge, MA: Harvard University Press, 1982.

Dufton, J. Andrew. "The Architectural and Social Dynamics of Gentrification in Roman North Africa." *American Journal of Archaeology* 123.2 (2019): 263–90.

Dugger, William M. "Douglass C. North's New Institutionalism." *Journal of Economic Issues* 29.2 (1995): 453–58.

Duncan-Jones, Richard P. *The Economy of the Roman Empire: Quantitative Studies*. Cambridge: Cambridge University Press, 1982.

Duncan-Jones, Richard P. *Money and Government in the Roman Empire*. Cambridge: Cambridge University Press, 1994.

Duncan-Jones, Richard P. "Roman Customs Dues: A Comparative View." *Latomus* 65.1 (2006): 3–16.

Duncan-Jones, Richard P. "Scaurus at the House of Trimalchio." *Latomus* 32.2 (1973): 364–67.

Duncan-Jones, Richard P. *Structure and Scale in the Roman Economy*. Cambridge: Cambridge University Press, 1990.

Dyck, Andrew R. "Dressing to Kill: Attire as a Proof and Means of Characterization in Cicero's Speeches." *Arethusa* 34.1 (2001): 119–30.

Dyer, Christopher. *Making a Living in the Middle Ages: The People of Britain, 850–1520*. New Haven: Yale University Press, 2002.

Ebel, Charles. "Southern Gaul in the Triumviral Period: A Critical Stage of Romanization." *American Journal of Philology* 109.4 (1988): 572–90.

Egas, Martijn, and Arno M. Riedl. "The Economics of Altruistic Punishment and the Demise of Cooperation." *Proceedings of the Royal Society Biological Sciences* 275 (2008): 871–78.

Ellart, Carlos Sánchez-Moreno. "About the Meaning of '*Colens in Asse*' in CIL VI 33840." *Zeitschrift der Savigny-Stiftung für Rechtsgeschichte* 128 (2011): 388–405.

Ellis, Steven J. R. "The Rise and Re-Organization of the Pompeian Salted Fish Industry." In *The Making of Pompeii: Studies in the History and Urban Development of an Ancient Town*, edited by Steven J. R. Ellis, 59–88. Portsmouth: Journal of Roman Archaeology, 2011.

Ellis, Steven J. R. *The Roman Retail Revolution: The Socio-Economic World of the* Taberna. Oxford: Oxford University Press, 2018.

Elsner, Jas. "Sacrifice and Narrative on the Arch of the Argentarii at Rome." *Journal of Roman Archaeology* 18 (2005): 83–98.

Emler, Nicholas. "Gossip, Reputation, and Social Adaptation." In *Good Gossip*, edited by Robert F. Goodman and Aaron Ben-Ze'ev, 117–38. Lawrence: University Press of Kansas, 1994.

Emler, Nicholas. "A Social Psychology of Reputation." *European Review of Social Psychology* 1.1 (1990): 171–93.
Emler, Nicholas. "The Truth about Gossip." *Social Psychology Section Newsletter* 27 (1992): 23–37.
Epstein, Joseph. *Gossip: The Untrivial Pursuit*. Boston: Mariner Books, 2012.
Erdkamp, Paul. "Grain Funds and Market Intervention in the Roman World." In *Feeding the Ancient Greek City*, edited by Richard Alston and Onno M. van Nijf, 109–25. Leuven: Peeters, 2008.
Erdkamp, Paul. *The Grain Market in the Roman Empire: A Social, Political and Economic Study*. Cambridge: Cambridge University Press, 2005.
Erdkamp, Paul. "'A Starving Mob Has No Respect': Urban Markets and Food Riots in the Roman World, 100 BC–AD 400." In *The Transformation of Economic Life under the Roman Empire: Proceedings of the Second Workshop of the International Network Impact of Empire (Roman Empire, c. 200 B.C.–A.D. 476), Nottingham, July 4–7, 2001*, edited by Lukas de Blois and John Rich, 93–115. Leiden: Brill, 2002.
Ermatinger, James W. *The Economic Reforms of Diocletian*. St. Katharinen: Scripta Mercaturae, 1996.
Étienne, Robert. "Le garum a Pompéi: Production et commerce." *Revue des Études Anciennes* 100 (1998): 199–215.
Étienne, Robert, and F. Mayet. "Le garum à la mode de Scaurus." *Gerión* 3 (1991): 187–94.
Fehr, Ernst, and Urs Fischbacher. "The Economics of Strong Reciprocity." In *Moral Sentiments and Material Interests: The Foundations of Cooperation in Economic Life*, edited by Herbert Gintis, Samuel Bowes, Robert Boyd, and Ernst Fehr, 151–92. Cambridge, MA: MIT Press, 2005.
Fehr, Ernst, and Simon Gächter. "Fairness and Retaliation: The Economics of Reciprocity." *Journal of Economic Perspectives* 14.3 (2000): 159–81.
Fenster, Thelma S., and Daniel Lord Smail. *Fama: The Politics of Talk and Reputation in Medieval Europe*. Ithaca: Cornell University Press, 2003.
Finley, Moses. *The Ancient Economy*. Berkeley: University of California Press, 1973.
Fiske, Susan T., Amy J. C. Cuddy, Peter Glick, and Jun Xu. "A Model of (Often Mixed) Stereotype Content: Competence and Warmth Respectively Follow from Perceived Status and Competition." *Journal of Personality and Social Psychology* 82.6 (2002): 878–902.
Fitzgerald, John T., ed. *Greco-Roman Perspectives on Friendship*. Atlanta: Scholars Press, 1997.
Fitzsimmons, Anthony, and Derek Atkins. *Rethinking Reputational Risk: How to Manage the Risks That Can Ruin Your Business, Your Reputation and You*. London: Kogan Page, 2017.
Fletcher, William, ed. *Lactantius: On the Deaths of the Persecutors*. Armidale: Northern Antiquities Press, 1867.
Flohr, Miko. "*Nec quicquam ingenuum habere potest officina*? Spatial Contexts of Urban Production at Pompeii, AD 79." *Babesch* 82.1 (2007): 139–58.
Flohr, Miko. *The World of the* Fullo: *Work, Economy, and Society in Roman Italy*. Oxford: Oxford University Press, 2013.

Flohr, Miko, and Nicolas Monteix, eds. *Shops, Workshops and Urban Economic History in the Roman World.* Heidelberg: Propylaeum, 2020.

Flohr, Miko, and Andrew Wilson, eds. *The Economy of Pompeii.* Oxford: Oxford University Press, 2017.

Forbes, Clarence A. "The Education and Training of Slaves in Antiquity." *Transactions and Proceedings of the American Philological Association* 86 (1955): 321–60.

Foss, Pedar, and John J. Dobbins, eds. *The World of Pompeii.* London: Routledge, 2007.

Foster, Benjamin R. "*Agoranomos* and *Muhtasib*." *Journal of the Economic and Social History of the Orient* 13.2 (1970): 128–44.

Frakes, Robert M., Elizabeth DePalma Digeser, and Justin Stephens, eds. *The Rhetoric of Power in Late Antiquity: Religion and Politics in Byzantium, Europe and the Early Islamic World.* London: I.B. Tauris, 2010.

Frayn, Joan M. *Markets and Fairs in Roman Italy: Their Importance from the Second Century BC to the Third Century.* Oxford: Clarendon Press, 1993.

Freu, Christel. "*Disciplina, patrocinium, nomen*: The Benefits of Apprenticeship in the Roman World." In *Urban Craftsmen and Tradesmen in the Roman World,* edited by Andrew Wilson and Miko Flohr, 183–99. Oxford: Oxford University Press, 2016.

Frézouls, Edmond. "Prix, salaires et niveaux de vie: Quelques enseignements de l'*Édit du Maximum* (I)." *Ktèma: Civilisations de l'Orient, de la Grèce et de Rome antiques* 2 (1977): 253–68.

Frézouls, Edmond. "Prix, salaires et niveaux de vie: Quelques enseignements de l'*Édit du Maximum* (II)." *Ktèma: Civilisations de l'Orient, de la Grèce et de Rome antiques* 3 (1978): 289–300.

Frier, Bruce, ed. *The Codex of Justinian: A New Annotated Translation, with Parallel Latin and Greek Text.* Cambridge: Cambridge University Press, 2016.

Frier, Bruce W., and Dennis P. Kehoe. "Law and Economic Institutions." In *The Cambridge Economic History of the Greco-Roman World,* edited by Walter Scheidel, Ian Morris, and Richard P. Saller, 113–43. Cambridge: Cambridge University Press, 2007.

Fuhrmann, Christopher J. *Policing the Roman Empire: Soldiers, Administration, and Public Order.* Oxford: Oxford University Press, 2012.

Fülle, Gunnar. "The Internal Organization of the Arretine *Terra Sigillata* Industry: Problems of Evidence and Interpretation." *Journal of Roman Studies* 87 (1997): 111–55.

Gagos, Traianos, and Peter van Minnen. *Settling a Dispute: Toward a Legal Anthropology of Late Antique Egypt.* Ann Arbor: University of Michigan Press, 1994.

Galavaris, George. *Bread and the Liturgy: The Symbolism of Early Christian and Byzantine Bread Stamps.* Madison: University of Wisconsin Press, 1970.

Gardner, Jane F. "Proofs of Status in the Roman World." *Bulletin of the Institute of Classical Studies* 33.1 (2010): 1–14.

Gardner, Jane F. "Women in Business Life: Some Evidence from Puteoli." In *Female Networks and the Public Sphere in Roman Society,* edited by Päivi Setälä and Liisa Savunen, 11–27. Rome: Institutum Romanum Finlandiae, 1999.

Garnsey, Peter. *Famine and Food Supply in the Graeco-Roman World: Responses to Risk and Crisis.* Cambridge: Cambridge University Press, 1989.

Garnsey, Peter. "Non-Slave Labour in the Roman World." In *Non-Slave Labour in the*

Greco-Roman World, edited by Peter Garnsey, 34–47. Cambridge: Cambridge Philological Society, 1980.

Garnsey, Peter. *Social Status and Legal Privilege in the Roman Empire*. Oxford: Clarendon, 1970.

Garnsey, Peter, Keith Hopkins, and C. R. Whittaker, eds. *Trade in the Ancient Economy*. Berkeley: University of California Press, 1983.

Garnsey, Peter, and Onno van Nijf. "Contrôle des prix du grain à Rome et dans les cités de l'Empire." In *La mémoire perdue: Recherches sur l'administration romaine*, edited by Claude Moatti, 303–15. Rome: École française de Rome, 1998.

Garraffoni, Renata Senna. "Robbers and Soldiers: Criminality and Roman Army in Apuleius' *Metamorphoses*." *Gerión: Revista de Historia Antigua* 22.1 (2005): 367–77.

Gayraud, Michel. *Narbonne anitque des origines à la fin du IIIe siècle*. Paris: Boccard, 1981.

Gerhard, Elmer Schultz. "Barter through the Ages." *Classical Journal* 32.8 (1937): 493–94.

Giacchero, Marta. *Edictum Diocletiani et collegarum de pretiis rerum venalium in integrum fere restitutum e latinis graecisque fragmentis*. 2 vols. Genoa: Istituto di storia antica e scienze ausilirie, 1974.

Giacchero, Marta. "Il mondo della produzione e del lavoro nell' 'Edictum de Pretiis.'" *Studi in onore di Arnaldo Biscardi* 6 (1987): 121–32.

Giacchero, Marta. "L'illusoria imposizione del giusto prezzo nell'editto-calmiere di Diocleziano." *Rendiconti lincei: Scienze morali, storiche e filologiche* 19 (1964): 95–109.

Giardina, Andrea. "The Merchant." In *The Romans*, edited by Andrea Giardina, 245–71. Chicago: University of Chicago Press, 1993.

Giardina, Andrea, ed. *The Romans*. Translated by Lydia G. Cochrane. Chicago: University of Chicago Press, 1993.

Giardina, Andrea, and A. J. Gurevič. *Il mercante dall'antichità al medioevo*. Roma: Editori Laterza, 1994.

Gibbs, Laura. *Aesop's Fables*. Oxford: Oxford University Press, 2002.

Gilmore, David G., ed. *Honor and Shame and the Unity of the Mediterranean*. Washington, DC: American Anthropological Association, 1987.

Gleba, Margarita, and Judit Pásztókai-Szeőke. *Making Textiles in Pre-Roman and Roman Times: People, Places, Identities*. Vol. 13, *Ancient Textiles*. Oxford: Oxbow Books, 2013.

Gluckman, Max. "Papers in Honor of Melville J. Herskovits: Gossip and Scandal." *Current Anthropology* 4.3 (1963): 307–16.

Goffman, Erving. *Behavior in Public Places*. Oxford: Blackwell, 1963.

Goffman, Erving. *Frame Analysis: An Essay on the Organization of Experience*. Cambridge, MA: Harvard University Press, 1974.

Goffman, Erving. *The Presentation of the Self in Everyday Life*. New York: Doubleday, 1959.

Goldberg, Jessica L. *Trade and Institutions in the Medieval Mediterranean: The Geniza Merchants and Their Business World*. Cambridge: Cambridge University Press, 2012.

Goldberg, Victor P. "The Enforcement of Contracts and Private Ordering." In *Handbook of New Institutional Economics*, edited by Claude Ménard and Mary M. Shirley, 491–511. Berlin: Springer, 2008.

Goldin, Barbara Diamond. *The Family Book of Midrash: 52 Jewish Stories from the Sages*. Lanham: Rowman and Littlefield, 2006.

Goodman, Robert F., and Aaron Ben-Ze'ev, eds. *Good Gossip*. Lawrence: University Press of Kansas, 1994.

Grace, Virginia. "Stamped Wine Jar Fragments." In *Small Objects from the Pnyx II*, by Lucy Talcott, Barbara Philippaki, G. Roger Edwards, and Virginia R. Grace. Hesperia Supplements 10, pages 113, 115, 117–89, 242–270. Athens: American School of Classical Studies at Athens, 1956.

Grace, Virginia. "Standard Pottery Containers of the Ancient Greek World." In *Commemorative Studies in Honor of Theodore Leslie Shear*. Hesperia Supplements 8, 175–89, 455–56. Athens: American School of Classical Studies at Athens, 1949.

Granovetter, Mark. "Coase Revisited: Business Groups in the Modern Economy." *Industrial and Corporate Change* 4.1 (1995): 93–130.

Granovetter, Mark. "Economic Institutions as Social Constructions: A Framework for Analysis." *Acta Sociologica* 35.1 (1992): 3–11.

Graverini, Luca. "The Robbers and the Old Woman (*Metamorphoses* Books 3.28–7.12)." In *Characterisation in Apuleius'* Metamorphoses: *Nine Studies*, edited by Stephen J. Harrison, 89–104. Newcastle upon Tyne: Cambridge Scholars Publishing, 2015.

Greenwood, John D. "Social Facts, Social Groups and Social Explanation." *Noûs* 37.1 (2003): 93–112.

Greif, Avner. *Institutions and the Path to the Modern Economy: Lessons from Medieval Trade*. Cambridge: Cambridge University Press, 2006.

Greif, Avner. "The Organization of Long-Distance Trade: Reputation and Coalitions in the Geniza Documents and Genoa during the Eleventh and Twelfth Centuries." *Journal of Economic History* 51 (1991): 459–62.

Greif, Avner. "Reputation and Coalitions in Medieval Trade: Evidence on the Maghribi Traders." *Journal of Economic History* 49.4 (1989): 857–82.

Grey, Cam. *Constructing Communities in the Late Roman Countryside*. Cambridge: Cambridge University Press, 2011.

Grey, Cam. "Contextualizing *Colonatus*: The *Origo* of the Late Roman Empire." *Journal of Roman Studies* 97 (2007): 155–75.

Grey, Cam. "Letters of Recommendation and the Circulation of Rural Laborers in the Late Roman West." In *Travel, Communication and Geography in Late Antiquity: Sacred and Profane*, edited by Linda Ellis and Frank L. Kidner, 25–40. Aldershot: Ashgate, 2004.

Griffe, Michel, Jean-Marie Lassère, and Jean Soubiran. "Épitaphe du banquier Praecilius (CIL VIII, 7156 = IL Alg. 2, 820 = CLE, 512)." *Vita Latina* 146 (1997): 15–25.

Grig, Lucy. *Popular Culture in the Ancient World*. Cambridge: Cambridge University Press, 2016.

Groag, Edmund. "Collegien und Zwangsgenossenschaften im dritten Jahrhundert." *Vierteljahrschrift für Sozial- und Wirtschaftsgeschichte* 2 (1904): 481–510.

Groen-Vallinga, Miriam J. "Desperate Housewives? The Adaptive Family Economy and Female Participation in the Roman Urban Labour Market." In *Women and the Roman City in the Latin West*, edited by Emily Hemelrijk and Greg Woolf, 295–312. Leiden: Brill, 2013.

Grüll, Tibor. "*Expositio totius mundi et gentium*: A Peculiar Work on the Commerce of Roman Empire from the Mid-Fourth Century—Compiled by a Syrian Textile Dealer?" In *Studies in Economic and Social History of the Ancient Near East in Memory of Péter Vargyas*, edited by Zoltán Csabai, 629–42. Ancient Near Eastern and Mediterranean Studies 2. Budapest: l'Harmattan, 2014.

Grunewald, Thomas. *Bandits in the Roman Empire: Myth and Reality*. Translated by John Drinkwater. London: Routledge, 2004.

Guastella, Gianni. *Word of Mouth:* Fama *and Its Personifications in Art and Literature from Ancient Rome to the Middle Ages*. Oxford: Oxford University Press, 2017.

Gürerk, Özgür, Bernd Irlenbuschand, and Bettina Rockenbach. "The Competitive Advantage of Sanctioning Institutions." *Science* 312.5770 (2006): 108–11.

Handley, Mark. *Dying on Foreign Shores: Travel and Mobility in the Late-Antique West*. JRA Supplementary 86. Portsmouth: Journal of Roman Archaeology, 2011.

Hardie, Philip. *Rumour and Renown: Representations of* Fama *in Western Literature*. Cambridge: Cambridge University Press, 2012.

Harland, Philip A. *Associations, Synagogues, and Congregations: Claiming a Place in Ancient Mediterranean Society*. Minneapolis: Fortress Press, 2003.

Harland, Philip A. *Dynamics of Identity in the World of the Early Christians*. London: Continuum Press, 2009.

Harland, Philip A. "Familial Dimensions of Group Identity: 'Brothers' (ΑΔΕΛΦΟΙ) in Associations of the Greek East." *Journal of Biblical Literature* 124.3 (2005): 491–513.

Harland, Philip A. *Graeco-Roman Associations: Texts, Translations and Commentary II; North Coast of the Black Sea, Asia Minor*. Beihefte zur Zeitschift für die neutestamentliche Wissenschaft 201. Berlin: Walter de Gruyter, 2014.

Harper, Kyle. *Slavery in the Late Roman World, AD 275–425*. Cambridge: Cambridge University Press, 2011.

Harries, Jill. "Creating Legal Space: Settling Disputes in the Roman Empire." In *Rabbinic Law in Its Roman and Near Eastern Context*, edited by Catherine Hezser, 63–82. Tübingen: Mohr Siebeck, 2003.

Harries, Jill. *Imperial Rome AD 284–363: The New Empire*. Edinburgh: Edinburgh University Press, 2012.

Harries, Jill. "Violence, Victims, and the Legal Tradition in Late Antiquity." In *Violence in Late Antiquity: Perceptions and Practices*, edited by Harold Drake, 85–102. Aldershot: Ashgate, 2006.

Harries, Jill, and Ian Wood, eds. *The Theodosian Code*. Ithaca: Cornell University Press, 1993.

Harrill, J. Albert. "The Vice of Slave Dealers in Greco-Roman Society: The Use of a *Topos* in 1 Timothy 1:10." *Journal of Biblical Literature* 118.1 (1999): 97–122.

Hartnett, Jeremy. *The Roman Street: Urban Life and Society in Pompeii, Herculaneum, and Rome*. Cambridge: Cambridge University Press, 2017.

Hasaki, Eleni. "Craft Apprenticeship in Ancient Greece: Reaching beyond the Masters." In *Archaeology and Apprenticeship: Acquiring Body Knowledge in the Ancient World*, edited by Willeke Wendrich, 171–202. Tucson: University of Arizona Press, 2013.

Hawkins, Cameron. *Roman Artisans and the Urban Economy*. Cambridge: Cambridge University Press, 2016.

Haynes, Denys Eyre Lancaster, and P. E. D. Hirst. *Porta Argentariorum*. London: Macmillan, 1940.

Heers, Jacques. "Types de navires et specialisation des trafics en Méditerranée à la fin du Moyen Age." In *Le Navire et l'économie maritime du Moyen-Age au XVIIIe siècle principalement en Méditerranée*, edited by Michel Mollat, 107–18. Paris: S.E.V.P.E.N., 1958.

Heiner, Ronald A. "The Origin of Predictable Behavior." *American Economic Review* 73.4 (1983): 560–95.

Hekster, Olivier, Gerda de Kleijn, and Daniëlle Slootjes, eds. *Crises and the Roman Empire: Proceedings of the Seventh Workshop of the International Network Impact of Empire, Nijmegen, June 20–24, 2006*. Leiden: Brill, 2007.

Henderson, M. I. "The Process '*De repetundis*.'" *Journal of Roman Studies* 41.1/2 (1951): 71–88.

Heres, Thea L."Rustpauze onderweg: Herbergen en wisselstations." *Hermeneus* 73.2 (2001): 87–101.

Herzfeld, Michael. "Honour and Shame: Problems in the Comparative Analysis of Moral Systems." *Man* 15.2 (1980): 339–51.

Hesseling, D. C. "On Waxen Tablets with Fables of Babrius (*Tabulae Ceratae Assendelftianae*)." *Journal of Hellenic Studies* 13 (1892–1893), 293–314.

Heurgon, Jacques. "L'arc des changeurs, à Rome." *Revue archéologique* 28 (1947): 52–58.

Hezser, Catherine. "From Oral Conversations to Written Texts: Randomness in the Transmission of Rabbinic Traditions." In *The Interface of Orality and Writing: Speaking, Seeing, Writing in the Shaping of New Genres*, edited by Annette Weissenrieder and Robert B. Coote, 36–51. Tübingen: Mohr Siebeck, 2015.

Hezser, Catherine. *Jewish Travel in Antiquity*. Tübingen: Mohr Siebeck, 2011.

Hirschfeld, O. "Die Getreideverwaltung in der rom. Kaiserzeit, Annona." *Philologus* 29 (1970): 1–96.

Höbenreich, Evelyn. *Annona: Juristische Aspekte der stadtrömischen Lebensmittelversorgung im Prinzipat*. Graz: Leykam Verlag, 1997.

Hock, Ronald F. "Paul's Tentmaking and the Problem of His Social Class." *Journal of Biblical Literature* 97.4 (1978): 555–64.

Hock, Ronald F. *The Social Context of Paul's Ministry: Tentmaking and Apostleship*. Minneapolis: Fortress Press, 1980.

Hock, Ronald F. "The Workshop as a Social Setting for Paul's Missionary Preaching." *Catholic Biblical Quarterly* 41.3 (1979): 438–50.

Hollander, David B., Thomas R. Blanton IV, and John T. Fitzgerald, eds. *The Extramercantile Economies of Greek and Roman Cities: New Perspectives on the Economic History of Classical Antiquity*. New York: Routledge, 2019.

Holleran, Claire. *Shopping in Ancient Rome: The Retail Trade in the Late Republic and the Principate*. Oxford: Oxford University Press, 2012.

Holliday, Peter J. "The Sarcophagus of Titus Aelius Evangelus and Gaudenia Nicene." *J. Paul Getty Museum Journal* 21 (1993): 85–100.

Honoré, Tony. "The Making of the Theodosian Code." *Zeitschrift der Savigny-Stiftung für Rechtsgeschichte* 10 (1986): 133–222.

Hooper, Finley P., and Matthew Schwartz. *Roman Letters: History from a Personal Point of View*. Detroit, MI: Wayne State University Press, 1991.

Hope, Valerie M., and Janet Huskinson, eds. *Memory and Mourning: Studies on Roman Death*. Oxford: Oxbow Books, 2011.

Hopkins, Keith. "Models, Ships and Staples." In *Trade and Famine in Classical Antiquity*, edited by Peter Garnsey and C. R. Whittaker, 84–109. Cambridge: Cambridge Philological Society, 1983.

Hopkins, Keith. "Taxes and Trade in the Roman Empire (200 B.C.–A.D. 400)." *Journal of Roman Studies* 70 (1980): 101–25.

Hopkins, Keith. *A World Full of Gods: The Strange Triumph of Christianity*. New York: Free Press, 2000.

Horden, Peregrine, and Nicholas Purcell. *The Corrupting Sea: A Study of Mediterranean History*. Oxford: Wiley-Blackwell, 2000.

Horstkotte, Hermann-Josef. *Die "Steuerhaftung" im spätrömischen "Zwangsstaat."* Frankfurt: Athenäum, 1988.

Houston, George W. "The Administration of Italian Seaports during the First Three Centuries of the Roman Empire." *Memoirs of the American Academy in Rome* 36 (1980): 157–71.

Huck, Olivier. "Les compilateurs au travail: Dessein et méthode de la codification théodosienne." In *Société, économie, administration dans le Code Théodosien*, edited by Sylvie Crogiez-Pétrequin and Pierre Jaillette, 79–127. Villeneuve d'Ascq: Presses Universitaires de Septentrion, 2012.

Humfress, Caroline. "Thinking through Legal Pluralism: 'Forum Shopping' in the Later Roman Empire." In *Law and Empire: Ideas, Practices, Actors*, edited by Jeroen Duindam, Jill Harries, Caroline Humfress, and Nimrod Hurvitz, 225–50. Leiden: Brill, 2013.

Hunter, Virginia J. "Gossip and the Politics of Reputation in Classical Athens." *Phoenix* 44.4 (1990): 299–325.

Hunter, Virginia J. *Policing Athens: Social Control in the Attic Lawsuits, 420–320 B.C.* Princeton: Princeton University Press, 1994.

Ingold, Tim. *Being Alive: Essays on Movement, Knowledge and Description*. London: Routledge, 2011.

Ingold, Tim. *The Perception of the Environment: Essays on Livelihood, Dwelling and Skill*. New York: Routledge, 2000.

Inzlicht, Michael, and Toni Schmader, eds. *Stereotype Threat: Theory, Process, and Application*. Oxford: Oxford University Press, 2012.

James, William. *The Principles of Psychology*. Vol. 1. London: Macmillan, 1890.

Jashemski, Wilhelmina F. "The Excavation of a Shop-House Garden at Pompeii (I. XX. 5)." *American Journal of Archaeology* 81.2 (1977): 217–27.

Johnstone, Steven. *A History of Trust in Ancient Greece*. Chicago: University of Chicago Press, 2011.

Jones, A. H. M. "The Caste System in the Later Roman Empire." *Eirene* 8 (1970): 79–96.

Jones, A. H. M. "Inflation under the Roman Empire." *Economic History Review* 5.3 (1953): 293–318.

Jones, A. H. M. *The Later Roman Empire, 284–602: A Social, Economic, and Administrative Survey.* Baltimore: Johns Hopkins University Press, 1986.

Jones, A. H. M. *The Roman Economy: Studies in Ancient Economic and Administrative History*. Totowa: Rowman and Littlefield, 1974.

Jones, Christopher P. "Philostratus' Heroikos and Its Setting in Reality." *Journal of Hellenic Studies* 121 (2001): 141–49.

Jones, Christopher P. "A Syrian in Lyon." *American Journal of Philology* 99.3 (Autumn, 1978): 336–53.

Joshel, Sandra R. *Slavery in the Roman World.* Cambridge: Cambridge University Press, 2010.

Joshel, Sandra R. *Work, Identity, and Legal Status at Rome: A Study of the Occupational Inscriptions.* Norman: University of Oklahoma Press, 1992.

Joshel, Sandra R., and Lauren Hackworth Petersen, eds. *The Material Life of Roman Slaves.* Cambridge: Cambridge University Press, 2014.

Kacprzak, Agnieszka. "Rhetoric and Roman Law." In *The Oxford Handbook of Roman Law and Society*, edited by Paul J. du Plessis, Clifford Ando, and Kaius Tuori, 200–218. Oxford: Oxford University Press, 2016.

Kampen, Natalie Boymel. "Biographical Narration and Roman Funerary Art." *American Journal of Archaeology* 85.1 (1981): 47–58.

Kampen, Natalie Boymel. *Image and Status: Roman Working Women in Ostia.* Berlin: Gebrüder Mann Verlag, 1981.

Kartzow, Marianne Bjelland. *Gossip and Gender: Othering of Speech in the Pastoral Epistles.* Berlin: Walter de Gruyter, 2009.

Keegan, Peter. *Graffiti in Antiquity.* New York: Routledge, 2014.

Kehoe, Dennis P. *Law and the Rural Economy in the Roman Empire.* Ann Arbor: University of Michigan Press, 2007.

Kehoe, Dennis P. "Legal Institutions and the Bargaining Power of the Tenant in Roman Egypt." *Archiv für Papyrusforschung* 41.2 (1995): 232–62.

Kehoe, Dennis P., David M. Ratzan, and Uri Yiftach, eds. *Law and Transaction Costs in the Ancient Economy.* Ann Arbor: University of Michigan Press, 2015.

Kim, Chan-Hie. *Form and Structure of the Familiar Greek Letter of Recommendation.* Missoula: Society of Biblical Literature, 1984.

Kirby, A. E., and A. M. Kent. "Architecture as Brand: Store Design and Brand Identity." *Journal of Product & Brand Management* 19.6 (2010): 432–39.

Kirschenbaum, Aaron. *Sons, Slaves, and Freedmen in Roman Commerce.* Washington, DC: Catholic University of America Press, 1987.

Klauck, Hans-Josef. *Ancient Letters and the New Testament: A Guide to Context and Exegesis.* Waco: Baylor University Press, 2006.

Kleinhans, Martha-Marie, and Roderick A. Macdonald. "What Is a *Critical* Legal Pluralism?" *Canadian Journal of Law and Society/La Revue Canadienne Droit et Société* 12.2 (1997): 25–46.

Kloft, Hans. "Trimalchio als Ökonom: Bemerkungen zur Rolle der Wirtschaft in Petrons *Satyricon.*" In *E fontibus haurire: Beiträge zur römischen Geschichte und zu ihren Hilfswissenschaften (Festschrift H. Chantraine)*, edited by Rosmarie Gunther and Stefan Rebenich, 117–31. Paderborn: Ferdinand Schöningh, 1994.

Kloppenborg, John S., and Richard S. Ascough. *Greco-Roman Associations: Texts, Translations and Commentary.* Vol. 1, *Attica, Central Greece, Macedonia, Thrace.* Beihefte zur Zeitschift für die neutestamentliche Wissenschaft 181. Berlin: Walter de Gruyter, 2010.

Kloppenborg, John S., and Stephan G. Wilson, eds. *Voluntary Associations in the Graeco-Roman World.* New York: Routledge, 2011.

Knapp, Charles. "Roman Business Life as Seen in Horace." *Classical Journal* 2.3 (1907): 111–22.

Knapp, Robert. *Invisible Romans*. Cambridge, MA: Harvard University Press, 2011.

Koenen, Ludwig. "Datierung einer Berliner Torzollquittung." *Zeitschrift für Papyrologie und Epigraphik* 8 (1971): 234.

Koenig, Fredrick. *Rumor in the Marketplace: The Social Psychology of Commercial Hearsay*. Dover: Auburn House, 1985.

Konstan, David. *Friendship in the Classical World*. Cambridge: Cambridge University Press, 1996.

Kraybill, J. Nelson. *Imperial Cult and Commerce in John's Apocalypse*. Journal for the Study of the New Testament Supplement Series 132. Sheffield: Sheffield Academic Press, 1996.

Kurke, Leslie. "Kaphleia and Deceit: Theognis 59–60." *American Journal of Philology* 110.4 (1989): 535–44.

Laes, Christian C. "Children and Fables, Children in Fables in Hellenistic and Roman Antiquity." *Latomus* 65.4 (2006): 898–914.

Laes, Christian C. "Child Slaves at Work in Roman Antiquity." *Ancient Society* 38 (2008): 235–83.

Langellotti, Michaela. "A World Full of Associations: Rules and Community Values in Early Roman Egypt." In *Private Associations in the Ancient Greek World: Regulations and the Creation of Group Identity*, edited by Vincent Gabrielsen and Mario C. D. Paganini, 179–95. Cambridge: Cambridge University Press, 2021.

Larran, Francis. *Le bruit qui vole: Histoire de la rumeur et de la renommée en Grèce ancienne*. Toulouse: Presses universitaires du Mirail, 2011.

Lassard, Yves. "Epistula Hadriani ad Athenienses (IG II-III, 1103)." *The Roman Law Library*, 2013, https://droitromain.univ-grenoble-alpes.fr/.

Lassard, Yves. "Lex Portus Tariff of Zraia." *The Roman Law Library*, 2014.

Launaro, Alessandro. "Finley and the Ancient Economy." In *M. I. Finley: An Ancient Historian and His Impact*, edited by Daniel Jew, Robin Osborne, and Michael Scott, 227–49. Cambridge: Cambridge University Press, 2016.

Lavan, Luke. *Local Economies? Production and Exchange of Inland Regions in Late Antiquity*. Leiden: Brill, 2015.

Lavan, Luke, Ellen Swift, and Toon Putzeys, eds. *Objects in Context, Objects in Use: Material Spatiality in Late Antiquity*. Leiden: Brill, 2007.

Lawler, Lillian B. "Some Lesser Lights." *Classical Journal* 30.2 (1934): 67–77.

Leach, Eleanor Winsor. *The Social Life of Painting in Ancient Rome and on the Bay of the Naples*. Cambridge: Cambridge University Press, 2004.

Lee, James. "*Confusio*: Reference to Roman Law in the House of Lords and the Development of English Private Law." *Roman Legal Tradition* 5.1 (2009): 24–66.

Lefebvre, Henri. *The Production of Space*. New York: Wiley, 1992.

Leković, Vlastimir. "Interaction of Formal and Informal Institutions: Impact on Economic Success." *Facta Universitatis: Economics and Organization* 8.4 (2011): 357–70.

Lendon, J. E. *Empire of Honour: The Art of Government in the Roman World*. Oxford: Clarendon Press, 1997.

Lennon, Jack. L. *Dirt and Denigration: Stigma and Marginalisation in Ancient Rome*. Tübingen: Mohr Siebeck, 2022.

Leon, H. J. "Sulphur for Broken Glass (Martial 1.41.3–5)." *Transactions and Proceedings of the American Philological Association* 72 (1941): 233–36.

Leppin, Hartmut. "Between Marginality and Celebrity: Entertainers and Entertainments in Roman Society." In *The Oxford Handbook of Social Relations in the Roman World*, edited by Michael Peachin, 660–78. Oxford: Oxford University Press, 2011.

Leppin, Hartmut. *Histrionen: Untersuchungen zur sozialen Stellung von Bühnenkünstler im Westen des römischen Reiches zur Zeit der Republik und des Principats*. Bonn: Habelt, 1992.

Letki, Piotr. "The State Factories (*Fabricae*) during the Time of Tetrarchy." *Classical Studies* 5 (2009): 63–78.

Levrero, Roberta. *Mercanti, prezzi e legislazione: Il commercio internazionale dei Romani*. Arti e mestieri nel mondo romano antico 8. Rome: Edizioni Quasar, 2014.

Lewis, Naphtali. "The Governor's Edict at Aizanoi." *Hellenika* 42 (1991): 15–20.

Lewis, Naphtali. *Life in Egypt under Roman Rule*. Oxford: Clarendon Press, 1985.Lewis, Sian. "Barbers' Shops and Perfume Shops: Symposia without Wine." In *The Greek World*, edited by Anton Powell, 432–41. London: Routledge, 1995.

Lis, Catharina, and Hugo Soly. *Worthy Efforts: Attitudes to Work and Workers in Pre-Industrial Europe*. Leiden: Brill, 2012.

Liu, Jinyu. *Collegia Centonariorum: The Guilds of Textile Dealers in the Roman West*. Leiden: Brill, 2009.

Liu, Jinyu. "The Economy of Endowments: The Case of Roman Associations." *Studia Hellenistica* 44 (2008): 231–56.

Liu, Jinyu. "Group Membership, Trust Networks, and Social Capital: A Critical Analysis." In *Work, Labour, and Professions in the Roman World*, edited by Koenraad Verboven and Christian Laes, 203–26. Leiden: Brill, 2016.

Lo Cascio, Elio, ed. *Credito e moneta nel mondo romano. Atti degli Incontri capresi di storia dell'economia antica; Capri, 12–14 ottobre 2000*. Bari: Edipuglia, 2003.

Lo Cascio, Elio. *Crescità e declino: Studi di storia dell'economia romana*. Rome: L'Erma di Bretschneider, 2009.

Lo Cascio, Elio. "The Early Roman Empire: The State and the Economy." In *The Cambridge Economic History of the Greco-Roman World*, edited Walter Scheidel, Ian Morris, and Richard P. Saller, 592–618. Cambridge: Cambridge University Press, 2007.

Lo Cascio, Elio. *Mercati permanenti e mercati periodici nel mondo romano. Atti degli Incontri capresi di storia dell'economia antica*. Bari: Edipuglia, 2000.

Lo Cascio, Elio. "Mercato libero e 'commercio amministrato' in età tardoantica." In *Mercanti e politica nel mondo antico*, edited by Carlo Zaccagnini, 307–25. Rome: L'Erma di Bretschneider, 2003.

Lo Cascio, Elio. "Prezzi in oro e prezzi in unità di conto tra il III e il IV sec. d.C." In *Économie antique: Prix et formation des prix dans les économies antiques*, edited by Jean Andreau, Pierre Briant, and Raymond Descat, 161–82. Saint Bertrand de Comminges: Musée archéologique départemental, 1997.

Lo Cascio, Elio. "The Role of the State in the Roman Economy: Making Use of the New Institutional Economics." In *Ancient Economies, Modern Methodologies: Archaeology, Comparative History, Models and Institutions*, edited by Peter F. Bang, Mamoru Ikeguchi, and Harmut Ziche, 215–34. Bari: Edipuglia, 2006.

Lo Cascio, Elio. "Setting the Rules of the Game: The Market and Its Working in the Roman Empire." In *Roman Law and Economics*. Vol. 1, edited by Giuseppe Dari-Mattiacci and Dennis P. Kehoe, 111–36. Oxford: Oxford University Press, 2020.

Lohmann, Polly. "Tagging in Antiquity: Pompeian Graffiti between Individuality and Convention." *SAUC—Street Art and Urban Creativity* 6.1 (2020): 6–12.

López Barja de Quiroga, Pedro. "Freedmen Social Mobility in Roman Italy." *Historia: Zeitschrift für Alte Geschichte* 44, H. 3 (1995): 326–48.

Lovén, Lena Larsson. "Female Work and Identity in Roman Textile Production and Trade: A Methodological Discussion." In *Making Textiles in Pre-Roman and Roman Times: People, Places, Identities*, edited by Margarita Gleba and Judit Pásztókai-Szeoke, 109–25. Oxford: Oxbow Books, 2013.

Lovén, Lena Larsson. "*Lanam fecit*: Woolworking and Female Virtue." In *Aspects of Women in Antiquity*, edited by Lena Larsson Lovén and Agneta Strömberg, 85–95. Jonsend: Paul Astroms Verlag, 1998.

Lovén, Lena Larsson. "Women, Trade, and Production in Urban Centres of Roman Italy." In *Urban Traders and Craftsmen in the Roman World*, edited by Andrew Wilson and Miko Flohr, 200–221. Oxford: Oxford University Press, 2016.

Lovén, Lena Larsson. "Wool Work as a Gender Symbol in Ancient Rome: Roman Textiles and Ancient Sources." In *Ancient Textiles: Production, Craft, and Society*, edited by Carole Gillis and Marie-Louise Nosch, 229–36. Oxford: Oxbow Books, 2007.

Luper, Steven. "Posthumous Harm." *American Philosophical Quarterly* 41.1 (2004): 63–72.

Lupfer, Michael B., Matthew Weeks, and Susan Dupuis. "How Pervasive Is the Negativity Bias in Judgments Based upon Character Appraisals?" *Personality and Social Psychology Bulletin* 26.11 (2000): 1353–66.

Lytle, Ephraim, ed. *A Cultural History of Work in Antiquity*. London: Bloomsbury Academic Press, 2019.

MacKinnon, Michael. "Pack Animals, Pets, Pests, and Other Non-Human Beings." In *The Cambridge Companion to Ancient Rome*, edited by Paul Erdkamp, 110–28. Cambridge: Cambridge University Press, 2013.

MacLean, Rose. *Freed Slaves and Roman Imperial Culture: Social Integration and the Transformation of Values*. Cambridge: Cambridge University Press, 2018.

MacMullen, Ramsay. "Judicial Savagery." *Chiron: Mitteilungen der Kommission für alte Geschichte und Epigraphik des Deutschen Archäologischen Instituts* 16 (1986): 147–66.

MacMullen, Ramsay. *Roman Government's Response to Crisis, A.D. 235–337*. New Haven: Yale University Press, 1976.

MacMullen, Ramsay. *Roman Social Relations: 50 B.C. to A.D. 284*. New Haven: Yale University Press, 1974.

MacMullen, Ramsay. "Women in Public in the Roman Empire." *Historia: Zeitschrift für Alte Geschichte* 29 (1980): 208–18.

Magaldi, Emilio. *Il commercio ambulante a Pompei*. Naples: Tipografia Ospedale Psichiatrico Provinciale L. Bianchi, 1930.

Maier, Paul L. "The Fate of Pontius Pilate." *Hermes* 99.3 (1971): 362–71.

Maiuri, Amedeo. "Pompei: Sterro dei cumuli e isolamento della cinta murale." *Bollettino d'arte* 45 (1960): 166–79.

Maloney, Robert P. "Usury in Greek, Roman and Rabbinic Thought." *Traditio* 27 (1971): 79–109.

Manning, J. G., and Ian Morris, eds. *The Ancient Economy: Evidence and Models*. Social Science History. Stanford: Stanford University Press, 2005.

Marlowe, Elizabeth. "Framing the Sun: The Arch of Constantine and the Roman Cityscape." *Art Bulletin* 88.2 (2006): 223–42.

Matthews, John. *The Journey of Theophanes: Travel, Business, and Daily Life in the Roman East*. New Haven: Yale University Press, 2006.

Matthews, John. *Laying Down the Law: A Study of the Theodosian Code*. New Haven: Yale University Press, 2000.

Matthews, John. "The Making of the Text." In *The Theodosian Code: Studies in the Imperial Law of Late Antiquity*, edited by Jill Harries and Ian Wood, 19–44. London: Bristol Classical Press, 1993.

Mattingly, Harold. "Jovius and Herculius." *Harvard Theological Review* 45.2 (1952): 131–34.

Mau, August. *Pompeii: Its Life and Art*. New York: Macmillan, 1902.

Mayer, Emanuel. *The Ancient Middle Classes: Urban Life and Aesthetics in the Roman Empire, 100 BCE–250 CE*. Cambridge, MA: Harvard University Press, 2012.

Mayer, Emanuel. "Money Making, 'Avarice', and Elite Strategies of Distinction in the Roman World." In *Skilled Labour and Professionalism in Ancient Greece and Rome*, edited by Edmund Stewart, Edward Harris, and David Lewis, 94–126. Cambridge: Cambridge University Press, 2020.

McGinn, Thomas A. J. *The Economy of Prostitution in the Roman World: A Study of Social History and the Brothel*. Ann Arbor: University of Michigan Press, 2004.

McGuire, Martin R. P. "Epigraphical Evidence for Social Charity in the Roman West C.I.L., I2, 1212; VIII, 7858; IX, 4796." *American Journal of Philology* 67.2 (1946): 129–50.

McLaughlin, Raoul. *Rome and the Distant East: Trade Routes to the Ancient Lands of Arabia, India and China*. London: A and C Black, 2010.

Meeks, Wayne A. *The First Urban Christians: The Social World of the Apostle Paul*. New Haven: Yale University Press, 1983.

Meißner, Burkhard. "Über Zweck und Anlaß von Diokletians Preisedikt." *Historia: Zeitschrift für Alte Geschichte* 49.1 (2000): 79–100.

Menard, Claude. "Methodological Issues in New Institutional Economics." *Journal of Economic Methodology* 8.1 (2001): 85–92.

Meramveliotakis, Giorgos. "New Institutional Economics: A Critique of Fundamentals and Broad Strokes towards an Alternative Theoretical Framework for the Analysis of Institutions." *Asian Journal of Social Science Studies* 3.2 (2018): 50–64.

Merola, Giovanna D. *Autonomia locale, governo imperiale: Fiscalità e amministrazione nelle province asiane*. Bari: Edipuglia, 2001.

Meyer, Elizabeth A. "Explaining the Epigraphic Habit in the Roman Empire: The Evidence of Epitaphs." *Journal of Roman Studies* 80 (1990): 74–96.

Meyer, Elizabeth A. *Legitimacy and Law in the Roman World*. Cambridge: Cambridge University Press, 2004.

Michell, H. "The Edict of Diocletian: A Study of Price Fixing in the Roman Empire." *Canadian Journal of Economics and Political Science* 13.1 (1947): 1–12.

Middleton, Neil. "Early Medieval Port Customs, Tolls and Controls on Foreign Trade." *Early Medieval Europe* 13.4 (2005): 313–58.

Millar, Fergus. *The Emperor in the Roman World, 31 BC–AD 337*. Ithaca: Cornell University Press, 1977.

Millar, Fergus. "The World of the Golden Ass." *Journal of Roman Studies* 71 (1981): 63–75.

Mishina, Yuri, and Cynthia E. Devers. "On Being Bad: Why Stigma Is Not the Same as a Bad Reputation." In *The Oxford Handbook of Corporate Reputation*, edited by Michael L. Barnett and Timothy G. Pollack, 201–20. Oxford: Oxford University Press, 2012.

Mitthof, Fritz. "Betrügerische Zollbeamte und der Procurator Usiacus: Bemerkungen zu P. Amh. II 77." *Zeitschrift für Papyrologie und Epigraphik* 159 (2007): 256–60.

Moeller, Walter O. "The Felt Shops of Pompeii." *American Journal of Archaeology* 75 (1971): 188–89.

Moeller, Walter O. *The Wool Trade of Ancient Pompeii*. Leiden: Brill, 1976.

Mommsen, Theodor. *De collegiis et sodaliciis romanorum*. Kiliae: Libraria Schwersiana, 1843.

Mommsen, Theodor, and Paul M. Meyer, eds. *Codex Theodosianus*. Berlin: Weidmann, 1905.

Montefiore, Claude Goldsmid, and Herbert M. J. Loewe, eds. *A Rabbinic Anthology*. Cambridge: Cambridge University Press, 1938.

Monteix, Nicolas. "'Caius Lucretius . . . , marchand de coleurs de la rue des fabricants de courroies': Réflexions critiques sur les concentrations de métiers à Rome." In *"Quartiers" artisanaux en Grèce ancienne: Une perspective méditerranéenne*, edited by Arianna Esposito and Giorgos M. Sanidas, 333–52. Villeneuve d'Ascq: Presses Universitaires du Septentrion, 2012.

Morel, Jean-Paul. "The Craftsman." In *The Romans*, edited by Andrea Giardina, 214–44. Chicago: University of Chicago Press, 1993.

Morello, Ruth, and A. D. Morrison, eds. *Ancient Letters: Classical and Late Antique Epistolography*. Oxford: Oxford University Press, 2007.

Moreno, Jacob Levy. *Who Shall Survive? Foundations of Sociometry, Group Psychotherapy, and Sociodrama*. Washington, DC: Nervous and Mental Disease Publishing, 1934.

Morgan, J. R. "The Story of Knemon in Heliodoros' Aithiopika." *Journal of Hellenic Studies* 109 (1989): 99–113.

Morgan, Teresa. *Roman Faith and Christian Faith:* Pistis *and* Fides *in the Early Roman Empire and Early Churches*. Oxford: Oxford University Press, 2015.

Morley, Neville. "The Poor in the City of Rome." In *Poverty in the Roman World*, edited by Margaret Atkins and Robin Osborne, 21–39. Cambridge: Cambridge University Press, 2006.

Morris, Ian. Foreword to *The Ancient Economy*, by M. I. Finley. 3rd ed., ix–xxxvi. Sather Classical Lectures 43. Berkeley: University of California Press, 1999.

Morris, Ian, Richard P. Saller, and Walter Scheidel. "Introduction." In *The Cambridge Economic History of the Greco-Roman World*, edited by Ian Morris, Richard P. Saller, and Walter Scheidel, 1–12. Cambridge: Cambridge University Press, 2007.

Mouritsen, Henrik. *The Freedman in the Roman World*. Cambridge: Cambridge University Press, 2011.

Mueller, Ilse. "Single Women in the Roman Funerary Inscriptions." *Zeitschrift für Papyrologie und Epigraphik* 175 (2010): 295–303.

Naumann, Rudolf, and Friederike Naumann. *Der Rundbau in Aezani: Mit dem Preisedikt des Diokletian und das Gebäude mit dem Edikt in Stratonikeia*. Istanbuler Mitteilungen 10. Tübingen: Wasmuth, 1973.

Nemoy, Leon, Saul Lieberman, and Harry A. Wolfson, eds. *The Midrash on Psalms*. Vol. 13. Translated by William G. Braude. New Haven: Yale University Press, 1959.

Nenci, G. "Ab asse quaesitum." *Rivista di Filologia e di Istruzione Classica* 11.9 (1964): 331–32.

Néraudau, Jean-Pierre. "La 'fama' dans la Rome antique." *Médiévales* 24 (1993): 27–34.

Neubauer, Hans-Joachim. *The Rumour: A Cultural History*. London: Free Association Books, 1999.

Nicholson, John. "The Delivery and Confidentiality of Cicero's Letters." *Classical Journal* 90.1 (1994): 33–63.

Noe, Thomas. "A Survey of the Economic Theory of Reputation: Its Logic and Limits." In *The Oxford Handbook of Corporate Reputation*, edited by Michael L. Barnett and Timothy G. Pollock, 114–39. Oxford: Oxford University Press, 2012.

North, Douglass C. *Institutions, Institutional Change and Economic Performance*. Cambridge: Cambridge University Press, 1990.

North, Douglass C. "Institutions." *Journal of Economic Perspectives* 5.1 (1991): 97–112.

North, Douglass C. "The New Institutional Economics." *Journal of Institutional and Theoretical Economics/Zeitschrift für die gesamte Staatswissenschaft* 142.1 (1986): 230–37.

North, Douglass C. "Transaction Costs, Institutions, and Economic History." *Zeitschrift für die gesamte Staatswissenschaft* 140.1 (1984): 7–17.

North, Douglass C. *Understanding the Process of Economic Change*. Oxford: Oxford University Press, 2005.

Noyes, Dorothy. "Group." *Journal of American Folklore* 108.430 (1995): 449–78.

Oliver, James H. "The Governor's Edict at Aezani after the Edict of Prices." *American Journal of Philology* 97.2 (1976): 174–75.

Oliver, James H. *Greek Constitutions of Early Roman Emperors from Inscriptions and Papyri*. Philadelphia: American Philosophical Society, 1989.

Olmsted, Donald Warren. *Social Groups, Roles, and Leadership: An Introduction to the Concepts*. East Lansing, MI: Institute for Community Development and Services, 1961.

Olmsted, Michael S. *The Small Group*. New York: Random House, 1959.

Origgi, Gloria. *Reputation: What It Is and Why It Matters*. Translated by Stephen Holmes and Noga Arikha. Princeton: Princeton University Press, 2018.

Pallottino, Massimo. *L'Arco degli argentari*. Rome: Danesi, 1946.

Panciera, Silvio. "Il ritratto e l'iscrizione di L. Licinius Nepos." *Rendiconti: Atti della Pontificia Accademia Romana di Archeologia* 61 (1988): 357–84.

Parada, Jairo. "Original Institutional Economics and New Institutional Economics: Revisiting the Bridges (or the Divide)." *Revista de Economia Institucional* 5 (2005): 43–61.

Peachin, Michael. *The Oxford Handbook of Social Relations in the Roman World.* Oxford: Oxford University Press, 2011.

Peña, J. Theodore. *Roman Pottery in the Archaeological Record.* Cambridge: Cambridge University Press, 2007.

Pentland, Alex, and Tracy Heibeck. *Honest Signals.* Cambridge, MA: MIT Press, 2008.

Pérez González, Jordi. "How Roman Sumptuary Specialists Called Themselves: A Corpus-Based Study." *Latomus* 78.4 (2019): 996–1037.

Peristiany, Jean G., ed. *Honour and Shame: The Values of Mediterranean Society.* Chicago: University of Chicago Press, 1966.

Perry, Ben Edwin, ed. *Babrius and Phaedrus.* Cambridge, MA: Harvard University Press, 1965.

Petersen, Lauren Hackworth. "The Baker, His Tomb, His Wife, and Her Breadbasket: The Monument of Eurysaces in Rome." *Art Bulletin* 85.2 (2003): 230–57.

Petersen, Lauren Hackworth. *The Freedman in Roman Art and Art History.* Cambridge: Cambridge University Press, 2006.

Petty, Ross D. "A History of Brand Identity Protection and Brand Marketing." In *The Routledge Companion to Marketing History*, edited by D. G. Brian Jones and Mark Tadajewshki, 97–114. New York: Routledge, 2016.

Pharr, Clyde. *The Theodosian Code and Novels, and the Sirmondian Constitutions.* Princeton: Princeton University Press, 1952.

Pickering, Michael. *Stereotyping: The Politics of Representation.* New York: Palgrave, 2001.

Pigeonneau, Henri. "L'annone romaine et les corps de naviculaires particulièrement en Afrique." *Revue de l'Afrique française et des antiquités africaines* 4 (1886): 220–37.

Pipili, Maria. "Wearing an Other Hat: Workmen in Town and Country." In *Not the Classical Ideal: Athens and the Construction of the Other in Greek Art*, edited by Beth Cohen, 150–79. Leiden: Brill, 2000.

Pitt-Rivers, Julian. "Honour and Social Status." In *Honour and Shame: The Values of Mediterranean Society*, edited by Jean G. Peristiany, 19–77. Chicago: University of Chicago Press, 1966.

Platner, Samuel Ball. *A Topographical Dictionary of Ancient Rome.* Oxford: Oxford University Press, 1929.

Polanyi, Karl. *The Great Transformation: The Political and Economic Origins of Our Time.* Boston: Beacon Press, 1944.

Polanyi, Karl. *The Livelihood of Man.* New York: Academic Press, 1977.

Pollack, Timothy G., and Michael L. Barnett, eds. *The Oxford Handbook of Corporate Reputation.* Oxford: Oxford University Press, 2012.

Pomeroy, Sarah B. *Goddesses, Whores, Wives, and Slaves: Women in Classical Antiquity.* New York: Schocken Books, 1995.

Posner, Eric A. *Law and Social Norms.* Cambridge, MA: Harvard University Press, 2009.

Poster, Carole, and Linda C. Mitchell, eds. *Letter-Writing Manuals and Instruction from Antiquity to the Present: Historical and Bibliographic Studies.* Columbia: University of South Carolina Press, 2007.

Potts, Charlotte R. "The Art of Piety and Profit at Pompeii: A New Interpretation of the Painted Shop Façade at IX.7.1–2." *Greece & Rome* 56.1 (2009): 55–70.

Putnam, Robert D. *Bowling Alone: The Collapse and Revival of American Community.* London: Simon and Schuster, 2000.

Putnam, Robert D. "Social Capital: Measurement and Consequences." *Isuma: Canadian Journal of Policy Research* 2 (2001): 41–51.

Rahyab, Susan. "The Rise and Development of the Office of *Agoranomos* in Greco-Roman Egypt." *New England Classical Journal* 46.1 (2019): 37–61.

Ramos, Alexander J. *Torah, Temple, and Transaction: Jewish Religious Institutions and Economic Behavior in Early Roman Galilee.* Lanham: Lexington Books, 2020.

Ramsöy, Odd. *Social Groups as System and Subsystem.* New York: Macmillan, 1962.

Rathbone, Dominic W. *Economic Rationalism and Rural Society in Third-Century A.D. Egypt: The Heroninos Archive and the Appianus Estate.* Cambridge: Cambridge University Press, 2012.

Rauh, Nicolas K. *The Sacred Bonds of Commerce: Religion, Economy, and Trade Society at Hellenistic Roman Delos, 166–87 B.C.* Leiden: Brill, 1994.

Ray, Nick M. "Consumer Behaviour in Pompeii: Theory and Evidence." In *The Economy of Pompeii*, edited by Miko Flohr and Andrew Wilson, 87–109. Oxford: Oxford University Press, 2017.

Rebillard, Éric, and Jörg Rüpke. *Group Identity and Religious Individuality in Late Antiquity.* Washington, DC: Catholic University of America Press, 2015.

Reents, Arthur Hermann. "Prosecutions *de repetundis* under the Roman Republic." Master's thesis, University of Nebraska, 1936.

Rees, Roger. "Letters of Recommendation and the Rhetoric of Praise." In *Ancient Letters: Classical and Late Antique Epistolography*, edited by Ruth Morello and A. D. Morrison, 149–68. Oxford: Oxford University Press, 2007.

Renfrew, Colin. "Trade as Action at a Distance: Questions of Integration and Communication." In *Ancient Civilization and Trade*, edited by Jeremy A. Sabloff and C. C. Lamberg-Karlovsky, 3–59. School of American Research. Albuquerque: University of New Mexico Press, 1975.

Rensberger, David. *The Epistles of John.* Louisville, KY: Westminster John Knox Press, 2001.

Rey-Coquais, Jean-Paul. "Sur l'inscription des naviculaires d'Arles à Beyrouth." *Syria* 70 (1993): 69–80.

Richardson, L. *A New Topographical Dictionary of Ancient Rome.* Baltimore: Johns Hopkins University Press, 1992.

Richter, Daniel S. "Lucian of Samosata." In *The Oxford Handbook of the Second Sophistic*, edited by Daniel S. Richter and William A. Johnson, 327–44. Oxford: Oxford University Press, 2017.

Richter, Rudolf. "The New Institutional Economics: Its Start, Its Meaning, Its Prospects." *European Business Organization Law Review* 6.2 (2005): 161–200.

Rickman, Geoffrey E. *The Corn Supply of Ancient Rome.* Oxford: Clarendon Press, 1980.

Rickman, Geoffrey E. "The Grain Trade under the Roman Empire." *Memoirs of the American Academy in Rome* 36 (1980): 261–75.

Riess, Werner, and Garrett G. Fagan. *The Topography of Violence in the Greco-Roman World.* Ann Arbor: University of Michigan Press, 2016.

Riggsby, Andrew M. *Mosaics of Knowledge: Representing Information in the Roman World.* Oxford: Oxford University Press, 2019.

Rimell, Victoria. *The Closure of Space in Roman Poetics: Empire's Inward Turn*. Cambridge: Cambridge University Press, 2015.

Roebuck, Derek. *Ancient Greek Arbitration*. Oxford: Holo Books, 2001.

Roebuck, Derek, and Bruno de Loynes de Fumichon. *Roman Arbitration*. Oxford: Holo Books, 2004.

Room, Adrian. "The History of Branding." In *Brands: The New Wealth Creators*, edited by Susannah Hart and John Murphy, 13–23. New York: New York University Press, 1998.

Rostovtzeff, Mikhail Ivanovich. *The Social and Economic History of the Roman Empire*. Translated by P. M Fraser. Oxford: Clarendon Press, 1957.

Rowan, Clare. *Under Divine Auspices: Divine Ideology and the Visualisation of Imperial Power in the Severan Period*. Cambridge: Cambridge University Press, 2012.

Rozenfeld, Ben Tsyion, and Joseph Menirav. *Markets and Marketing in Roman Palestine*. Leiden: Brill, 2005.

Runge, Carlisle Ford. "Institutions and the Free Rider: The Assurance Problem in Collective Action." *Journal of Politics* 46.1 (1984): 154–81.

Sabini, John, and Maury Silver. *Moralities of Everyday Life*. Oxford: Oxford University Press, 1982.

Sacharin, Ken. *Attention! How to Interrupt, Yell, Whisper, and Touch Consumers*. New York: John Wiley and Sons, 2004.

Safrai, Ze'ev. *The Economy of Roman Palestine*. New York: Routledge, 2003.

Saller, Richard P. "Framing the Debate over Growth in the Ancient Economy." In *The Ancient Economy: Evidence and Models*, edited by J. G. Manning and Ian Morris, 223–38. Stanford: Stanford University Press, 2005.

Salway, Benet. "The Publication and Application of the Theodosian Code: NTh1, the *Gesta Senatus*, and the *Constitutionarii*." *Mélanges de l'École française de Rome, Codifications et réformes dans l'Empire tardif et les royaumes barbares* 125.2 (2013): 2–32.

Samuels, Warren J., ed. *The Founding of Institutional Economics*. New York: Routledge, 1998.

Sancinito, Jane. "Cross-Cultural Confusion: The Messenger Turbo and the Innkeepers of the *Acta Archelai*." *Journal of Late Antiquity* 12.2 (2019): 466–87.

Sancinito, Jane. "Rapacious and Chatty, Deceitful and Memorable: Finding Non-Elite Stereotypes of Roman Merchants." In *Working Lives in Ancient Rome*, edited by Jordan Rogers and Del A. Maticic. London: Palgrave Macmillan, forthcoming.

Sanford, Eva Matthews. "Political Campaigns in Roman Municipalities." *Classical Journal* 25.6 (1930): 453–63.

Scarre, Geoffrey. "On Caring about One's Posthumous Reputation." *American Philosophical Quarterly* 38.2 (2001): 209–19.

Scheidel, Walter. *The Cambridge Companion to the Roman Economy*. Cambridge: Cambridge University Press, 2012.

Scheidel, Walter, Ian Morris, and Richard P. Saller, eds. *The Cambridge Economic History of the Greco-Roman World*. Cambridge: Cambridge University Press, 2007.

Scheidel, Walter, and Sitta von Reden, eds. *The Ancient Economy*. Edinburgh: Edinburgh University Press, 2002.

Schlippschuh, Otto. *Die Händler im römischen Kaiserreich Gallien, Germanien und den donauprovinzen Rätien, Noricum und Pannonien*. Amsterdam: Hakkert, 1987.

Schnur, Harry C. "The Economic Background of the *Satyricon*." *Latomus* 18 (1959): 790–99.

Schotter, Andrew. *The Economic Theory of Social Institutions*. Cambridge: Cambridge University Press, 1981.

Scott, James C. *Seeing Like a State: How Certain Schemes to Improve the Human Condition Have Failed*. New Haven: Yale University Press, 2008.

Scott, James C. *Weapons of the Weak: Everyday Forms of Peasant Resistance*. New Haven: Yale University Press, 1987.

Shanzer, Danuta R. "'Piscatum opiparem . . . praestinavi': Apuleius, *Met.* 1, 24–25." *Rivista di Filologia e di Istruzione Classica* 124 (1996): 445–54.

Shapiro, Carl. "Consumer Information, Product Quality, and Seller Reputation." *Bell Journal of Economics* 13.1 (1982): 20–35.

Sharman, J. C. "Rationalist and Constructivist Perspectives on Reputation." *Political Studies* 55 (2007): 20–37.

Shaw, Brent D. "Bad Boys: Circumcellions and Fictive Violence." In *Violence in Late Antiquity: Perceptions and Practices*, edited by Harold Drake, 179–96. Aldershot: Ashgate, 2006.

Shaw, Brent D. *Bringing in the Sheaves: Economy and Metaphor in the Roman World*. Toronto: University of Toronto Press, 2015.

Sheehy, Paul. *The Reality of Social Groups*. New York: Routledge, 2016.

Siegel, Neil S. "Free Riding on Benevolence: Collective Action Federalism and the Minimum Coverage Provision." *Law and Contemporary Problems* 75.3 (2012): 29–74.

Siisiäinen, Martti. "Two Concepts of Social Capital: Bourdieu vs. Putnam." *International Journal of Contemporary Sociology* 40.2 (2003): 183–204.

Sijpesteijn, Pieter Johannes. *Customs Duties in Graeco-Roman Egypt*. Zutphen: Terra Publishing, 1987.

Sijpesteijn, Pieter Johannes. "Eine weitere Torzollquittung aus der Amsterdamer Papyrussammlung." *Zeitschrift für Papyrologie und Epigraphik* 7 (1971): 45–46.

Silver, Morris. "Glimpses of Vertical Integration/Disintegration in Ancient Rome." *Ancient Society* 39 (2009): 171–84.

Silver, Morris. "In Dubious Battle: An Economic Analysis of Emperor Hadrian's Fish and Olive Oil Laws." *Roman Legal Tradition* 7 (2011): 1–15.

Sirks, A. J. Boudewijn. "The Colonate in Justinian's Reign." *Journal of Roman Studies* 98 (2008): 120–43.

Sirks, A. J. Boudewijn. "Did the Late Roman Government Try to Tie People to Their Profession or Status?" *Tyche: Beiträge zur Alten Geschichte, Papyrologie und Epigraphik* 8 (1993): 159–75.

Sirks, A. J. Boudewijn. *Food for Rome: The Legal Structure of the Transportation and Processing of Supplies for the Imperial Distributions in Rome and Constantinople*. Amsterdam: J.C. Gieben, 1991.

Sirks, A. J. Boudewijn. "Late Roman Law: The Case of Dotis Nomen and the Praedia Pistoria." *Zeitschrift der Savigny-Stiftung für Rechtsgeschichte: Romanistische Abteilung* 108.1 (1991): 187–212.

Sirks, A. J. Boudewijn. "The Sources of the Code." In *The Theodosian Code: Studies in the Imperial Law of Late Antiquity*, edited by Jill Harries and Ian Wood, 45–67. London: Bristol Classical Press, 1993.

Sirks, A. J. Boudewijn. "Where Did the Theodosian Compilers Take Their Texts From?" In *Société, économie, administration dans le Code Théodosien*, edited by Sylvie Crogiez-Pétrequin, and Pierre Jaillette, 154–63. Villeneuve d'Ascq: Presses Universitaires du Septentrion, 2012.

Skowronski, John J., and Donal E. Carlston. "Caught in the Act: When Impressions Based on Highly Diagnostic Behaviours Are Resistant to Contradiction." *European Journal of Social Psychology* 22.5 (1992): 435–52.

Skowronski, John J., and Donal E. Carlston. "Negativity and Extremity Biases in Impression Formation: A Review of Explanations." *Psychology Bulletin* 105 (1989): 131–42.

Smith, David, and Harry Kenward. "Roman Grain Pests in Britain: Implications for Grain Supply and Agricultural Production." *Britannia* 42 (2011): 243–62.

Smith, Eric Alden, and Rebecca Bliege Bird. "Costly Signaling and Cooperative Behavior." In *Moral Sentiments and Material Interests: The Foundations of Cooperation in Economic Life*, edited by Herbert Gintis, Samuel Bowles, Robert Boyd, and Ernst Fehr, 115–48. Cambridge, MA: MIT Press, 2005.

Soldevila, Rosario Moreno, Alberto Marino Castillo, and Juan Fernández Valverde. *A Prosopography to Martial's Epigrams*. Berlin: De Gruyter, 2019.

Sommerfeld, Ralf D., Hans-Jurgen Krambeck, and Manfred Milinski. "Multiple Gossip Statements and Their Effect on Reputation and Trustworthiness." *Proceedings: Biological Sciences* 275.1650 (2008): 2529–36.

Spacks, Patricia Meyer. *Gossip*. New York: Alfred A. Knopf, 1985.

Speidel, Michael A. "Wirtschaft und Moral im Urteil Diokletians. Zu Den Kaiserlichen Argumenten Für Höchstpreise." *Historia: Zeitschrift für alte Geschichte* 58.4 (2009): 486-505.

Sperber, Daniel. *The City in Roman Palestine*. Oxford: Oxford University Press, 1998.

Sperber, Daniel. "On Pubs and Policemen in Roman Palestine." *Zeitschrift der Deutschen Morgenländischen Gesellschaft* 120.2 (1970): 257–63.

Stangor, Charles, and Mark Schaller. "Stereotypes as Individual and Collective Representations." In *Stereotypes and Stereotyping*, edited by C. Neil MacRae, Charles Stangor, and Miles Hewstone, 3–40. New York: Guilford Press, 1996.

Stewart, Frank Henderson. *Honor*. Chicago: University of Chicago Press, 1994.

Stewart, Pamela J., and Andrew Strathern. *Witchcraft, Sorcery, Rumors and Gossip*. Cambridge: Cambridge University Press, 2004.

Still, Todd D. "Did Paul Loathe Manual Labor? Revisiting the Work of Ronald F. Hock on the Apostle's Tentmaking and Social Class." *Journal of Biblical Literature* 125.4 (2006): 781–95.

Stowers, Stanley K. *Letter Writing in Greco-Roman Antiquity*. Louisville, KY: Westminster John Knox Press, 1986.

Strong, Anise K. "Daughter and Employee: Mother-Daughter Bonds among Prostitutes." In *Mothering and Motherhood in Ancient Greece and Rome*, edited by Lauren Hackworth Petersen and Patricia Salzman-Mitchell, 121–39. Austin: University of Texas Press, 2012.

Strong, Anise K. *Prostitutes and Matrons in the Roman World*. Cambridge: Cambridge University Press, 2016.

Stroup, Richard L. "Free Riders and Collective Action Revisited." *Independent Review* 4.4 (2000): 485–500.

Sykuta, Michael E., and Michael L. Cook. "A New Institutional Economics Approach to Contracts and Cooperatives." *American Journal of Agricultural Economics* 83.5 (2001): 1273–79.

Tanzer, Helen Henrietta. *The Common People of Pompeii: A Study of the Graffiti.* Baltimore: Johns Hopkins Press, 1939.

Tchernia, André. *The Romans and Trade.* Oxford: Oxford University Press, 2016.

Teja, Ramón. "Las corporaciones romanas municipales en el Bajo Imperio: Alcance y naturaleza." *Hispania Antiqua* 3 (1973): 153–77.

Temin, Peter. *The Roman Market Economy.* Princeton: Princeton University Press, 2013.

Tengström, Emin. *Bread for the People: Studies of the Corn-Supply of Rome during the Late Empire.* Stockholm: P. Åströms Förlag, 1974.

Terpstra, Taco. *Trade in the Ancient Mediterranean: Private Order and Public Institutions.* Princeton: Princeton University Press, 2019.

Terpstra, Taco. *Trading Communities in the Roman World: A Micro-Economic and Institutional Prospective.* Leiden: Brill, 2013.

Thompson, Kori. "Bene Merenti: An Epigraphic Display of Social Identity and Expectational Difference between Roman Freeborn and Freed Women." Master's thesis, Northern Arizona University, 2011.

Tilley, Christopher. *A Phenomenology of Landscape: Places, Paths, and Monuments.* Oxford: Berg, 1994.

Toner, Jerry P. "Barbers, Barbershops and Searching for Roman Popular Culture." *Papers of the British School at Rome* 83 (2015): 91–109.

Toner, Jerry P. *Leisure and Ancient Rome.* Hoboken, NJ: Wiley Press, 1995.

Toner, Jerry P. *Popular Culture in Ancient Rome.* Cambridge: Polity, 2009.

Tournal, Paul. *Catalogue du musée de Narbonne.* Paris: Emmanuel Caillard, 1864.

Toynbee, J. M. C. *Death and Burial in the Roman World.* Baltimore: Johns Hopkins University Press, 1971.

Tran, Nicolas. *Les membres des associations romaines: Le rang social des collegiati en Italie et en Gaules, sous le Haut-Empire.* Rome: Publications de l'École française de Rome, 2006.

Tran, Nicolas. "Les procédures d'exclusion des collèges professionnels et funéraires sous le Haut-Empire: Pratiques épigraphiques, normes collectives et non-dits." In *Les exclus dans l'Antiquité: Actes du colloque organisé par l'université Lyon III les 23 et 24 septembre 2004*, edited by Catherine Wolff, 119–38. Paris: De Boccard, 2007.

Tran, Nicolas. "*Ordo corporatorum*: The Rules of Roman Associations and the *collegia* at Ostia in the Second and Third Centuries AD." In *Private Associations in the Ancient Greek World: Regulations and the Creation of Group Identity*, edited by Vincent Gabrielsen and Mario C. D. Paganini, 196–213. Cambridge: Cambridge University Press, 2021.

Trapp, Michael, ed. *Greek and Latin Letters: An Anthology with Translation.* Cambridge: Cambridge University Press, 2003.

Treggiari, Susan. "Lower Class Women in the Roman Economy." *Florilegium* 1 (1979): 65–86.

Treggiari, Susan. *Roman Freedmen during the Late Republic.* Oxford: Oxford University Press, 1969.

Tuan, Yi-Fu. *Space and Place: The Perspective of Experience*. Minneapolis: University of Minnesota Press, 1977.

Tuddenham, Read D. "Studies in Reputation. I: Sex and Grade Differences in School Children's Evaluations of Their Peers. II: The Diagnosis of Social Adjustment." *Psychological Monographs: General and Applied* 66.1 (1952): 1–58.

Tuddenham, Read D. "Studies in Reputation. III: Correlates of Popularity among Elementary-School Children." *Journal of Educational Psychology* 42.5 (1951): 257–76.

Turpin, William. "The Purpose of the Roman Law Codes." *Zeitschrift der Savigny-Stiftung für Rechtsgeschichte* 104 (1987): 620–30.

Twede, Diana. "Commercial Amphoras: The Earliest Consumer Packages?" *Journal of Macromarketing* 22.1 (2002): 98–108.

Ulrich, Roger B. *Roman Woodworking*. New Haven: Yale University Press, 2008.

Vanacker, Wouter. "Differentiated Integration Trajectories of the Nomadic Population in Roman North Africa." In *Integration in Rome and in the Roman World*, edited by Gerda de Kleijn and Stéphane Benoist, 197–216. Leiden: Brill, 2014.

van Minnen, Peter. "Did Ancient Women Learn a Trade outside the Home? A Note on SB XVIII 13305." *Zeitschrift für Papyrologie und Epigraphik* 123 (1998): 201–3.

van Niekerk, Gardiol J. "Orality in the Law of Contract: Manifestation and Proof of Intent in Ancient African and Roman Societies." *De Jure* 22 (2011): 364–80.

van Nijf, Onno. *The Civic World of Professional Associations in the Roman East*. Leiden: Brill, 1997.

Varone, Antonio. *Erotica Pompeiana: Love Inscriptions on the Walls of Pompeii*. Rome: L'Erma di Bretschneider, 2002.

Venticinque, Philip. "Family Affairs: Guild Regulations and Family Relationships in Roman Egypt." *Greek, Roman, and Byzantine Studies* 50.2 (2010): 273–94.

Venticinque, Philip. *Honor among Thieves: Craftsmen, Merchants, and Associations in Roman and Late Roman Egypt*. Ann Arbor: University of Michigan Press, 2016.

Verboven, Koenraad. "City and Reciprocity: The Role of Cultural Beliefs in the Roman Economy." Translated by Rodney Coward. *Annales: Histoire, Sciences Sociales* 67 (2012): 597–627.

Verboven, Koenraad. "Currency and Credit in the Bay of Naples in the First Century AD." In *The Economy of Pompeii*, edited by Miko Flohr and Andrew Wilson, 363–86. Oxford: Oxford University Press, 2017.

Verboven, Koenraad. *The Economy of Friends: Economic Aspects of Amicitia and Patronage in the Late Republic*. Brussels: Latomus, 2002.

Verboven, Koenraad. "*Faenatores, negotiatores* and Financial Intermediation in the Roman World (Late Republic and Early Empire)." In *Pistoi dia ten technen: Bankers, Loans and Archives in the Ancient World; Studies in Honour of Raymond Bogaert*, edited by Véronique Chankowski, Katelijn Vandorpe, and Koenraad Verboven, 211–29. Studia Hellenistica 44. Leuven: Peeters, 2008.

Verboven, Koenraad. "Friendship among the Romans." In *The Oxford Handbook of Social Relations in the Roman World*, edited by Michael Peachin, 404–21. Oxford: Oxford University Press, 2011.

Verboven, Koenraad. "A Funny Thing Happened on My Way to the Market: Reading

Petronius to Write Economic History." In *Petronius: A Handbook*, edited by Jonathan Prag and Ian Repath, 125–39. Oxford: Wiley-Blackwell, 2009.

Verboven, Koenraad. "Guilds and the Organisation of Urban Populations during the Principate." In *Work, Labour, and Professions in the Roman World*, edited by Koenraad Verboven and Christian Laes, 173–202. Leiden: Brill, 2016.

Verboven, Koenraad. "The Knights Who Say NIE: Can Neo-Institutional Economics Live Up to Its Expectation in Ancient History Research?" In *Structure and Performance in the Roman Economy: Models, Methods and Case Studies*, edited by Paul Erdkamp and Koenraad Verboven, 33–57. Collection Latomus 350. Brussels: Latomus, 2015.

Verboven, Koenraad. "Mentalite et commerce: Le cas des '*negotiatores*' et de ceux '*qui negotia habent*.'" In *Mentalités et choix économiques des Romaines*, edited by Jean Andreau, Jérôme France, and Sylvie Pittia, 179–97. Scripta Antiqua 7. Paris: De Boccard, 2004.

Verboven, Koenraad. "Professional *Collegia*: Guilds or Social Clubs?" *Ancient Society* 41 (2011): 187–95.

Verboven, Koenraad. "Resident Aliens and Translocal Merchant Organisations." In *Frontiers in the Roman World*, edited by Olivier Hekster and Ted Kaizer, 335–48. Leiden: Brill, 2011.

Verboven, Koenraad, and Christian Laes, eds. *Work, Labour, and Professions in the Roman World*. Leiden: Brill, 2016.

Vergunst, Jo Lee, and Tim Ingold. *Ways of Walking: Ethnography and Practice on Foot*. London: Routledge, 2016.

Veyne, Paul. "Vie de Trimalcion." *Annales: Histoire, Sciences Sociales* 16.2 (1961): 213–47.

Veyne, Paul, and Osywn Murray. *Bread and Circuses: Historical Sociology and Political Pluralism*. Translated by Brian Pearce. London: Penguin, 1992.

von Freyberg, Hans-Ulrich. *Kapitalverkehr und Handel im römischen Kaiserreich (27 v. Chr.–235 n. Chr.)*. Freiburg im Breisgau: Rudolf Haufe Verlag, 1988.

Waltzing, Jean-Pierre. *Étude historique sur les corporations professionelles chez les Romains depuis les origines jusqu'à la chute de l'Empire d'occident*. Louvain: Charles Peeters, 1895.

Weber, Max. *Economy and Society: An Outline of Interpretive Sociology*. Edited by Guenther Roth and Claus Wittich. Berkeley: University of California Press, 1978.

Weber, Max. *The Theory of Social and Economic Organization*. Translated by Talcott Parsons and A. M. Henderson. Oxford: Oxford University Press, 1947.

Westermann, W. L. "Apprentice Contracts and the Apprentice System in Roman Egypt." *Classical Philology* 9.3 (1914): 295–315.

Westermann, W. L. "Vocational Training in Antiquity." *School Review* 22.9 (1914): 601–10.

White, John Lee. *Light from Ancient Letters*. Minneapolis: Fortress Press, 1986.

White, Richard. "Friendship: Ancient and Modern." *International Philosophical Quarterly* 39.1.153 (1999): 19–34.

Whitfield, John. *People Will Talk: The Surprising Science of Reputation*. Hoboken, NJ: Wiley Press, 2012.

Whittaker, C. R. "The Poor." In *The Romans*, edited by Andrea Giardina, 272–99. Chicago: Chicago University Press, 1993.

Wickham, Chris. "*Fama* and the Law in Twelfth-Century Tuscany." In *Fama: The Politics of Talk and Reputation in Medieval Europe*, edited by Thelma S. Fenster and Daniel Lord Smail, 15–26. Ithaca: Cornell University Press, 2003.

Wickham, Chris. *Framing the Early Middle Ages: Europe and the Mediterranean 400–800*. Oxford: Oxford University Press, 2007.

Wickham, Chris. "Gossip and Resistance among the Medieval Peasantry." *Past and Present* 160 (1998): 3–24.

Wickham, Chris. "Marx, Sherlock Holmes, and Late Roman Commerce." *Journal of Roman Studies* 78 (1988): 183–93.

Williams, C. A. *Reading Roman Friendship*. Cambridge: Cambridge University Press, 2012.

Williamson, Oliver E. *Markets and Hierarchies: Analysis and Antitrust Implications; A Study in the Economics of Internal Organization*. New York: Free Press, 1975.

Williamson, Oliver E. "The New Institutional Economics: Taking Stock, Looking Ahead." *Journal of Economic Literature* 38.3 (2000): 595–613.

Williamson, Oliver E., ed. *The Transaction Cost Economics Project: The Theory and Practice of the Governance of Contractual Relations*. Northampton: Edward Elgar, 2013.

Williamson, Oliver E., and Scott E. Masten. *The Economics of Transaction Costs*. Northampton: Edward Elgar, 1999.

Wilson, Andrew, and Alan Bowman, eds. *Trade, Commerce, and the State in the Roman World*. Oxford Studies on the Roman Economy. Oxford: Oxford University Press, 2018.

Wilson, Andrew, and Miko Flohr, eds. *Urban Craftsmen and Traders in the Roman World*. Oxford Studies on the Roman Economy. Oxford: Oxford University Press, 2016.

Wilson, Harry Langford. "Latin Inscriptions at the Johns Hopkins University III." *American Journal of Philology* 30 (1909): 153–70.

Winter, John Garrett. *Life and Letters in the Papyri*. Ann Arbor: University of Michigan Press, 1933.

Wong, Sze-Sze, and Wai Fong Boh. "Leveraging the Ties of Others to Build a Reputation for Trustworthiness among Peers." *Academy of Management Journal* 53.1 (2010): 129–48.

Yoon, David I. "Ancient Letters of Recommendation and 2 Corinthians 3:1–3: A Literary Analysis." *Journal of Greco-Roman Christianity and Judaism* 12 (2016): 45–72.

Youtie, Louise C. "Papyri from Soknopaiou Nesos." *Zeitschrift für Papyrologie und Epigraphik* 37 (1980): 201–10.

Zaccagnini, Carlo, ed. *Mercanti e politica nel mondo antico*. Rome: L'Erma di Bretschneider, 2003.

Ziche, Hartmut. "Making Late Roman Taxpayers Pay: Imperial Government Strategies and Practice." In *Violence in Late Antiquity: Perceptions and Practice*, edited by Harold Drake, 127–36. Aldershot: Ashgate, 2006.

Zinovieff, Sofka. "Inside Out and Outside In: Gossip, Hospitality and the Greek Character." *Journal of Mediterranean Studies* 1.1 (1991): 120–34.

Index